ETHNICITY AND HOUSING

For Victor Blease
Former Chief Executive of the Northern Ireland Housing Executive
and
For Michael and Catherine
Working where 'housing' meets people

DAMES

Dansk Center for Migration
og Etniske Studier

**EUROPEAN RESEARCH CENTRE
ON MIGRATION & ETHNIC RELATIONS**

Ethnicity and Housing

Accommodating differences

Edited by
FREDERICK W. BOAL
School of Geography
The Queen's University of Belfast

Routledge
Taylor & Francis Group

LONDON AND NEW YORK

First published 2000 by Ashgate Publishing

Reissued 2018 by Routledge
2 Park Square, Milton Park, Abingdon, Oxon OX14 4RN
711 Third Avenue, New York, NY 10017, USA

Routledge is an imprint of the Taylor & Francis Group, an informa business

Publisher's Note
The publisher has gone to great lengths to ensure the quality of this reprint but points out that some imperfections in the original copies may be apparent.

Disclaimer
The publisher has made every effort to trace copyright holders and welcomes correspondence from those they have been unable to contact.

A Library of Congress record exists under LC control number: 99075557

ISBN 13: 978-1-138-63416-9 (hbk)
ISBN 13: 978-0-415-79199-1 (pbk)
ISBN 13: 978-1-315-21128-2 (ebk)

Contents

Part Four: the United States: principles and practice

Part Five: Israel: seeking the 'New Jerusalem'

Part Six: the United Kingdom: immigrants and natives

Figures and tables

Contributors

Arlidge, Simon, University of the West of England, Bristol, England, UK.

Asmal, Kader, Minister of Water and Forests, Government of South Africa, Cape Town and Pretoria, South Africa.

Boal, Frederick, Queen's University of Belfast, Belfast, Northern Ireland, UK.

Bowes, Alison, University of Stirling, Stirling, Scotland, UK.

Buchman, Adam, Association of Contractors and Builders in Israel, Tel Aviv, Israel.

Byrne, Liam, Dun Laoghaire-Rathdown County Council, Dublin, Ireland.

Churchman, Arza, Technion — Israel Institute of Technology, Haifa, Israel.

Dar, Naira, University of Stirling, Stirling, Scotland, UK.

Doherty, Paul, University of Ulster at Jordanstown, Newtownabbey, Northern Ireland, UK.

Efrat, Elisha, Jerusalem, Israel.

Falah, Ghazi, University of Toronto, Toronto, Ontario, Canada.

Fisk, Malcolm, Liverpool John Moores University, Liverpool, England, UK.

Gallibour, Eric, Université de Bordeaux II, Bordeaux, France.

Goering, John, United States Department of Housing and Urban Development, Washington DC, USA.

Goldberg, Abigail, Oxford Brooks University, Oxford, England, UK.

González, Sergio-Albio, Former Chief Designer, Jwaneng, Botswana.

Hachmann, Claus, GdW, Köln, Germany.

Herbert, Gilbert, Technion — Israel Institute of Technology, Haifa, Israel.

Maly, Michael, Roosevelt University, Chicago, Illinois, USA.

Maples, Rebeka, Ohio State University, Columbus, Ohio, USA.

McPeake, John, Northern Ireland Housing Executive, Belfast, Northern Ireland, UK.

Muller, John, University of the Witswatersrand, Johannesburg, South Africa.

Murtagh, Brendan, University of Ulster, Magee College, Londonderry, Northern Ireland, UK.

Nieuwenhuis, Wicher, Stadsdeel Zuidoost, Gemeente Amsterdam, Amsterdam Zuidoost, Netherlands.

Nyden, Philip, Loyola University, Chicago, Illinois, USA.

Peach, Ceri, University of Oxford, Oxford, England, UK.

Poole, Michael, University of Ulster at Coleraine, Coleraine, Northern Ireland, UK.

Priemus, Hugo, Delft University of Technology, Delft, Netherlands.

Sim, Duncan, University of Stirling, Stirling, Scotland, UK.

Somerville, Peter, University of Lincolnshire and Humberside, Lincoln, England, UK.

Tomlins, Richard, De Montfort University, Leicester, England, UK.

Upton, James, Ohio State University, Columbus, Ohio, USA.

Willemsen, Glenn, Stadsdeel Zuidoost, Gemeente Amsterdam, Amsterdam Zuidoost, Netherlands.

Preface

The purpose of this volume is to open up a discussion on the desirability and methodology of accommodating, both literally and metaphorically, the many ethnic differences that increasingly characterise cities. Ethnic difference has been brought into sharp focus by the massive migration flows that have helped define the twentieth century — a period designated the 'Age of Migration' by Stephen Castles and Mark Miller in their recent book of that title (Castles and Miller, 1993). However the juxtaposition of ethnic difference is also found in many locations to be of even longer standing than this, as illustrated in several of the case studies in the present volume.

Whatever the roots of the contrasting ethnicities, the provision of adequate and appropriate housing in secure environments has presented itself as a major and by no means easy task. In this project academics, housing practitioners and urban planners have parts to play. It is my hope that the analyses and experiences reported in *Ethnicity and Housing* will make a useful contribution to both practice and theory in this field.

An edited volume such as this one owes much to many people. Firstly I would like to acknowledge the support and encouragement given by Victor Blease, former Chief Executive of Northern Ireland's public housing authority, the Housing Executive. I would also particularly like to thank Gill Alexander of the Cartographic Unit in the School of Geography at the Queen's University of Belfast for preparing all the drawings deployed in this book. The quality of her work speaks for itself.

All the contributors to *Ethnicity and Housing* deserve my warmest thanks for making their writings available for publication. They are also to be commended for their forbearance and patience — they must have concluded occasionally that their work would never see the light of day. Also to be acknowledged here are Anne Keirby and the editorial and production staff at Avebury. Anne has helped greatly to keep me focused through a long drawn out process of editing and camera ready production.

Perhaps Bill Gates and his hordes at Microsoft also deserve a mention — for creating the amazing abilities of 'Word' and, equally, for introducing new versions of the software that from time to time seemed to be aimed at testing my limited word processing skills to near breaking point.

Finally, I wish to thank my wife, Sallie, for much support and for tolerating, most of the time, my long absences in front of the Apple Mac.

Part One
Introduction

1 Introduction

Frederick Boal

This volume has its origins in the 1995 Congress of the International Federation for Housing and Planning. This Congress was held in Belfast, in September of that year. The decision taken in the early 1990s to invite IFHP to Belfast was a bold step, given a context of continued ethnic conflict in Northern Ireland, punctuated as it was by occasional outbursts of violence. However this context was radically transformed when, in the later summer and early autumn of 1994, first the Irish Republican Army (IRA) and then the loyalist paramilitaries declared cease fires. In consequence it was possible for the final stages of organising the Congress to be undertaken with a greater degree of confidence than had earlier seemed possible.

As things turned out more than 800 delegates from 32 different countries attended. They found a city basking in the unaccustomed relaxation of a peaceful environment. Unfortunately this peace did not long survive, as less than five months after the Congress the IRA ended its cease-fire by exploding a massive bomb in London's Docklands. Nonetheless the time of the Congress itself was one conducive to new thinking, to an opening up of perspectives on the future that offered hope. This applied not only to delegates from Northern Ireland, but also to many of the Congress participants from much further afield.

The theme of the Congress was 'Accommodating Differences'. Such a designation was highly appropriate, issuing as it did an invitation that would both encourage the promotion of societies of tolerance and that would also stimulate consideration as to how best provide appropriate housing for diverse populations. 'Differences' were defined in broad terms. As the Congress's Registration Brochure and Call for Papers put it 'academics and practitioners from around the world will be invited to exchange views as to how to promote partnership and investment in communities affected by ethnic and social differences, economic peripherality and political upheaval'. The Brochure also noted that 1995 had been designated by UNESCO as the 'International Year Against Intolerance'. Moreover the Brochure stressed that the Congress wished to support this theme and in particular to highlight awareness of the social needs of minority groups such as the elderly and people with disabilities.

Thus 'difference' was a very broad church. However, given my own interest in ethnic relations, and enthusiastically encouraged by Victor Blease, then Chief Executive of the Northern Ireland Housing Executive, the body which was hosting the IFHP Congress, I decided to invite a number of Congress participants to make available their papers for inclusion in a book of essays that I planned to edit. The chapters that follow are those papers, together with a few specially commissioned additions.

Clearing the ground

The title of this volume, *Accommodating Differences: Ethnicity and Housing,* encapsulates all the many themes found therein. However, before allowing the individual author's contributions to speak for themselves, it will be useful to examine a number of matters.

Ethnicity

Recently Stephen Cornell and Douglas Hartmann have noted that 'terms such as ethnic, ethnic group and ethnicity are ... slippery and difficult to define' (Cornell and Hartmann, 1998, p. 16). They are not alone in expressing this sentiment. Twenty years earlier Thomas F. Petticrew wrote that:

> Ethnicity as a concept reminds one of St. Augustine's anguish over the concept of time: 'For so it is, O Lord My God, I measure it, but what it is that I measure I do not know'. Indeed we are in an even more unenviable position than Augustine, for we are not certain even how to measure ethnicity, nor can we rescue it fully from heated ideological usage. Yet like time, we are agreed upon its importance (Petticrew, 1978, p. 25).

One of the contributors to the present volume, Ceri Peach has elsewhere trawled the literature on ethnicity and has produced a list of 14 characteristics that have been associated with the term 'ethnic group' (Peach 1983, p. 103) (Table 1.1).

Table 1.1
Characteristics of ethnic groups

Common geographic origin
Migratory status
Race
Language or dialect
Religious faith
Ties that transcend kinship, neighbourhood and community boundaries
Shared traditions, values and symbols
Literature, folklore and music
Food preferences
Settlement and employment patterns
Special interests in regard to politics in the homeland and in the country
    of settlement
Institutions that specifically serve and maintain the group
An internal sense of distinctiveness
An external sense of distinctiveness

We can perhaps boil this list down to six attributes of an ethnic group — members will share certain basic cultural values; they will have a common origin or myth of origin and a sense of a shared past; they will be biologically self-reproducing; they will be socially self-reproducing; they will make up a network of contact among themselves; and finally, ethnic groups are categories of ascription by others and of self-identification by the members themselves.

The American social scientist Richard A. Schermerhorn makes, in one sentence, a brave and useful attempt to encapsulate the core attributes that characterise an ethnic group — 'a collectivity within a larger society having real or putative common ancestry, memories of a shared historical past, and a cultural focus on one or more symbolic elements as the epitome of their peoplehood' (Schermerhorn, 1978, p. 12). Cornell and Hartmann (1998, p. 19) add a rider to this (also noted by Schermerhorn) that ethnic groups are self-conscious populations; they see themselves as distinct.

The notion of distinctiveness carries the obvious corollary that 'others' must be present to be distinct from — there must be insiders and outsiders, 'us' and 'them'. As expressed by Cornell and Hartmann:

> Ethnicity is a matter of contrast — to claim an ethnic identity is to distinguish ourselves from others; it is to draw a boundary between 'us' and 'them' on the basis of the claims we make about ourselves and them .... An ethnic group cannot exist in isolation (1998, p. 20).

This is a key underlying theme in all the chapters in *Accommodating Differences*. The ethnic groups examined find themselves engaged in negotiating their position in society, and, more specifically their position in the housing market in a context characterised by the presence of 'others', who may be less or more advantageously placed than themselves, or who may find themselves on an equal footing.

Race

'Race' is another slippery concept. Pierre L. van den Berghe provides a definition:

> A race can mean a group of people who are socially defined in a given society as belonging together because of physical markers such as skin pigmentation, hair texture, facial features, stature and the like (van den Berghe, 1984, p. 217).

Thus racial groups are distinguished by socially selected physical traits while ethnic groups are distinguished by socially selected cultural traits. Ethnicity and race are not the same. However they are not mutually exclusive either. The differences between ethnic groups and races are usefully summarised by Cornell and Hartmann, as are the possible combinations of the two sets of variables, where certain collections of people are both ethnic groups *and* races at one and the same time (Table 1.2).

5

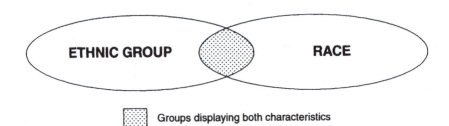

Table 1.2
'Ethnic group' and 'race': dimensions of identity

☒ Groups displaying both characteristics

Identity is based on putative common descent, claims of shared history and symbols of peoplehood	Identity is based on perceived physical differences
Identity may originate in either assignment by others or assertion by selves	Identity typically originates in assignment by others
Identity may or may not reflect power relations	Identity typically reflects power relations
Identity may or may not imply differences inherent differences of worth	Identity implies inherent of worth
Identity usually constructed by both selves and others group	Identity is constructed by others (at point of self-construction. becomes ethnic group as well as race)

Source: after Cornell and Hartmann (1998), p. 35

Many groups examined in this book are unambiguously ethnic, others less so, and some may be viewed as 'races'. However I would argue that what may be seen as racial categories are also ethnic groups. Thus, as Cornell and Hartmann claim, African Americans can be viewed in both racial and ethnic terms:

> They are held by others and often by themselves to be members of a distinct race, identified primarily by skin color and other bodily features. At the same time they also have become an ethnic group, a self-conscious population that defines itself in part in terms of common descent (Africa as homeland), a distinctive history (slavery in particular), and a broad set of cultural symbols (from language to expressive culture) that are held to capture much of the essence of their peoplehood. When they lay claim to an identity of their own making and meaning, and when they act on the basis of that identity, they are acting as an ethnic group (Cornell and Hartmann, 1998, p. 33).

Ethnicity and nationalism are frequently hand-in-glove. Stanley Lieberson defined nationalism as essentially an ethnic movement in which the distinctive characteristics of a 'people' are emphasised and praised and where the true and full expression of their unique qualities requires that a separate [state] exists (Lieberson, 1992, p. 202). The same perspective is provided by Cornell and Hartmann when they state that 'what most clearly distinguishes nationalism from ethnicity is its political agenda. Ethnicity may become nationalist, and nationalism typically is based on real or assumed ethnic ties. It is the goal of sovereignty and self-determination that sets nationalism apart (Cornell and Hartmann, 1998, p. 37).

Thus, in certain circumstances, ethnic relations are worked out (or worked on) within an agreed, consensual constitutional framework. In other circumstances there is a lack of consensus on the very existence of the state itself. In these circumstances the negative dimensions of ethnic relations are exacerbated, thereby complicating further the processes of conflict resolution. The chapters in this volume that deal with Jerusalem and Belfast particularly speak to this issue.

It would not be helpful, however, to too closely link nationalism and ethnicity in a one to one relationship. Where such a relationship does exist it has been designated 'ethnic nationalism'; an individual's deepest attachments are inherited, not chosen. What gives unity to the nation in this instance is 'not the cold contrivance of shared rights, but the people's pre-existing ethnic characteristics: their language, religion, customs and traditions (Ignatieff, 1993, p. 4). On the other hand 'civic nationalism' holds that a nation should be composed of all those — regardless of race, colour, religion, gender, language or ethnicity — who subscribe to the nation's political creed. The nation, in this case, is a community of equal, rights-bearing citizens, united in patriotic attachment to a shared set of political practices and ideals. (Ignatieff, 1993, pp. 3-4). It will be evident that an environment imbued with a civic nationalist ethos will be more broadly accommodating than one functioning on the basis of ethnic nationalism.

Contact

As noted earlier, ethnic groups exist in the company of others — contact is of the essence. Ethnic contact, however, occurs under a wide range of conditions with a concomitant wide series of outcomes. One of the most useful formulations here is that offered by Brewton Berry and Henry Tischler in their text *Race and Ethnic Relations* (1978). They note that some degree of conflict is likely to occur when racial and ethnic groups come into contact. Such conflict can produce a range of social situations (adjustments/accommodations). Berry and Tischler indicate five basic outcomes — annihilation or expulsion, assimilation and/or amalgamation, stratification, pluralism and segregation. (Berry and Tischler, 1978, p. 91).

Annihilation or expulsion can hardly be thought of in terms of accommodation, but they are possible outcomes of ethnic contact. Annihilation suggests genocide, while expulsion reminds us of the all-too-present reality of ethnic cleansing. Assimilation, on the other hand, leads to the absorption of one group

7

by another (most likely an immigrant group by a host society), though we need to heed Milton Gordon's strictures that assimilation is not a simple phenomenon, but is multi-dimensional. Thus assimilation can take place at different speeds in different aspects of society — cultural or behavioural, structural, marital, identificational, attitude receptional, behaviour receptional, civic (Gordon, 1964, p. 71). Amalgamation is less uni-directional and suggests a general melting of two or more groups, with change occurring for all. Of course assimilation may be resisted by a particular ethnic group, and it may be blocked by the 'host' or receiving society. The outcome of assimilation/amalgamation will be the disappearance of the ethnic groups involved, though this process may well extend over several generations.

Pluralism represents a pattern of social relations in which ethnic groups maintain much of their distinctiveness, but where there is also a common societal underpinning of shared culture and institutions. As Cashmore defines pluralism:

> Each group retains its own ethnic origins by perpetuating specific cultures (or 'subcultures') in the form of churches, businesses, clubs and media. It also encloses itself within its own set of primary group relations such as friendship networks, families and intra-group marriages. Yet all these groups participate collectively in some spheres, and collectively make up a plural society (Cashmore, 1984, p. 195).

Stratification is the division of society into ranks, grades or positions and involves an unequal distribution of privileges, material rewards, opportunities prestige and influence (Berry and Tischler, 1978, p. 195). Groups — in our case ethnic groups — are arranged on horizontal levels, characterised by relative advantage and disadvantage. The contrast between groups can be extreme and rigid, or it may be mild and fluid, or somewhere in between. In these circumstances ethnic groups are likely to remain distinctive, but unlike the attractions of equalitarian pluralism, the situation will inevitably be oppressive for the group or groups at the 'bottom of the heap'.

The final situation of group contact formulated by Berry and Tischler is that of segregation. Here the two authors provide the following definition:

> Segregation means the act, process or state of being separate or set apart. It is a form of isolation that places limits or restrictions on contact, communication and social relations. Usually it involves unequal treatment and it is commonly a condition forced on one group by another. There are, however, many instances where it is voluntary. It is essentially a pattern of accommodation which assumes a wide variety of forms and is the product of many complex motives (Berry and Tischler, 1978, p. 336).

Basically segregation means spatial separation between groups that in some sense still share a common society. It is a way of organising inter-ethnic relationships while, at the same time, it is also a factor contributory to the shaping and maintenance of those very relationships. Spatial separation (to varying degrees) presents itself as one of Berry and Tischler's five ethnic contact outcomes. However it is also likely to be present in several of the others

8

— in stratification, in the earlier stages of assimilation and in pluralism and, of course, at the extreme, in expulsion.

Ethnicity and housing: accommodating the differences

The situations examined by the contributors to this volume touch, to varying degrees, on four of Berry and Tischler's contact situations. Only annihilation/expulsion is absent from the case studies, but it is still useful to bear it in mind as an all-too-real possibility lurking in the background.

The contributors to *Ethnicity and Housing* not only focus on existing circumstances — they are also significantly motivated by desired objectives. It is clear that pluralistic accommodation is a predominant (if mainly unstated) ideology, with the door to assimilation being left open where that is a desired outcome. Some degree of segregation is not ruled out, though this can only be of a voluntary nature.

As noted at the beginning of this chapter, the essays offered here were, in the main, prepared initially for presentation at the 1995 IFHP Congress. Consequently I was not in a position to provide any guidelines for the authors. Nonetheless I believe that the collection has a coherence of its own, a coherence supplied by a common adherence to the objective of accommodating differences.

The chapters could have been presented in a variety of sequences and groupings. Here the principal organisational structure I have used is that of geographical area — South Africa, Israel, the United States, the United Kingdom, the Netherlands and Germany, with a couple of contributions from the less developed world (Botswana and French Guyana). The basic reason for this grouping is a concern that the case studies should be grouped where they were likely to share common institutional contexts.

Outside of these case study clusters lies Ceri Peach's chapter on segregation, a topic I consider foundational. Several additional topics have been included at the end of the volume. These broaden the discussion beyond those normally associated with housing, but their relevance will, nonetheless, be evident. I conclude with a short overview of the previous 26 chapters, seeking therein to draw out any commonalities and contrasts that are evident.

2 The consequences of segregation

Ceri Peach

Introduction

It is appropriate that a book on accommodating ethnic differences should be produced in Belfast, a city in which social cleavages are embedded in its geography, history and institutions, but which currently offers the prospect for social change. One of the happy by products of an unhappy situation is that the recent troubles have advanced our understanding of the dynamics of segregation. Just as the Belfast Royal Victoria Hospital has become one of the leading centres for the surgery of bullet wounds and kneecap injuries, the Geography Department of the University, particularly in the work directed by Fred Boal, has become one of the international centres for research on the causes and consequences of segregation. In a series of papers that have become classics in the literature, Fred Boal and his colleagues have demonstrated the social behavioural Himalaya that separates groups that live within a few metres of each other (Boal, 1969; 1970).

Is segregation a 'bad thing'?

Harlem in New York, Brixton in London, Kreuzberg in Berlin, the Goutte d'Or in Paris, the Shankill and the Falls in Belfast are well known examples of ethnic concentrations. They have an unfavourable public perception; ethnic segregation is often taken to be 'a bad thing'. It is seen as divisive, as preventing understanding, as reducing social interaction between groups and individuals and as leading to mistrust. There is a great deal of evidence for all of these assertions and some of it will be cited in the course of this chapter.

However, segregation is not all bad. Segregation, is in fact, one of the key methods of accommodating difference. There are positive as well as negative reasons for segregation. A great deal of the difficulty with policy comes from failing to distinguish between the positive and the negative and mistakenly trying to apply interpretations that relate to one to the other. One of the errors in the literature is attempting to see discrimination in what is voluntary segregation;

another is trying to find positive explanations for what is, in fact, enforced segregation.

The three generational model

Segregation is often thought of as an inevitable first stage of accommodation of ethnic minorities migrating to a foreign country. Immigrants enter the country and settle in the inner cities, in the zones in transition where they are highly segregated. The second generation moves out a little from the centre and disperses somewhat. The third generation completes this centrifugal movement. It moves to the suburbs. This progressive dispersal has been tracked by Cressey (1938) and Ford (1950) and can be demonstrated graphically.

Parallel to this process of geographic dispersal is the assumed model of assimilation. The first generation is socially unassimilated; the second partly assimilated/partly not and the third generation totally assimilated.

Spatial pattern and social process

It has therefore been a straightforward step to see a link between the spatial pattern and social process. It is clear that the pattern of segregation and the process of assimilation are linked and that there is not only a high degree of correlation between spatial pattern and social behaviour, but also an interaction between the two. There is, in the literature, a direct equation of spatial and social patterning. Segregated groups are unassimilated; spatially dispersed groups, that have the same distribution as the majority population are assimilated. The argument developed that what was true for a given group over time, was also true for all groups at any one time. Over time, a given group would start unassimilated in a highly segregated inner city area and, over generations, disperse and assimilate; at any given time more recent groups would be more segregated and less assimilated and older groups would be dispersed and assimilated. Thus there has evolved a kind of three stage model of immigrant ethnic minority assimilation, based largely on the US experience, a model which assumed an inevitability of progression.

A popular measure of dispersal and intermixture has been the index of dissimilarity (Peach, 1975). This has a range from 0 (no segregation) to 100 (total segregation) (see Figure 2.1). Having established these measures, it was possible to locate different ethnic and racial groups on this linear scale. If we look at American cities, for example, where most of this early work was carried out, it was shown that there was a kind of hierarchy of acceptance of the different national groups of immigrants. The 'old' groups, those from north west Europe — from Britain, Ireland, Germany and Scandinavia — showed little segregation from native born American Whites. They typically had indexes in the 20s or 30s on this scale from 0 to 100. Those from eastern and southern Europe — the Poles and Italians, for example — were more segregated, with indexes in the 40s 50s and 60s. The Hispanic or Latino populations showed higher indexes, this time in the 60s 70s and 80s while African Americans showed the highest levels of segregation of all, typically in the 80s and 90s. (see Figure 2.1) Comparison with London data from 1991 shows that the Bangladeshi population manifested scores in the high seventies (77). Roman

11

INDEX OF DISSIMILARITY

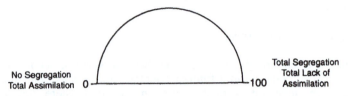

RELATIVE SEGREGATION ON INDEX OF DISSIMILARITY

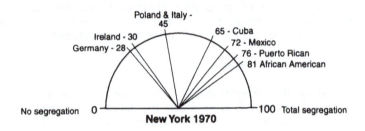

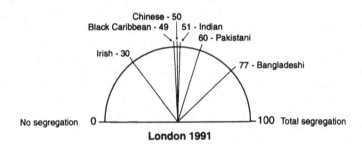

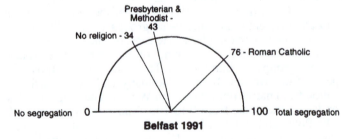

Figure 2.1   **Relative segregation measured on the index of dissimilarity**

Catholics in Belfast were at the same level (78). In other words, Belfast Roman Catholics and London Bangladeshis were at the same level as New York Puerto Ricans and slightly below New York black levels.

Not only did the US indexes differ in a consistent way between groups, but there was some indication for most groups of decreases over time. Groups would generally start with a higher level of segregation at the beginning of their periods of settlement, say at the beginning of the century than they showed at the end (Lieberson, 1963). There were, however, some notable exceptions to this such as the African American population which became more segregated over time and which seems to have arrived at a saturated level of hyper segregation (Massey and Denton, 1993). It is possible that Belfast has been moving in this direction.

Weakness of the three generational model

It is at this point, however, that the weaknesses of this three generational model of segregation begin to become apparent. Although the North West Europeans and the Southern and Eastern Europeans are more or less where they would be predicted to be in terms of the timing of their major migrations to the US, the Latino populations are less segregated than the African Americans. Indeed, black Americans have been in the US longer than most groups, but are by far the most segregated.

Not only is this the case, but African American segregation is different in kind from that experienced by other ethnic groups in the US. The point is well made by Philpott in an analysis of Chicago in the 1930s (Philpott, 1978). He demonstrated that the African American population inhabited the only true ghetto in Chicago. It was commonly stated that there were Irish, Italian or Polish ghettos in the city, but Philpott showed that only three per cent of the Irish population lived in Irish areas and that they formed only one third of the population of such areas. Only the Poles formed a majority in Polish areas and just about half of Poles and Italians lived in the areas that were supposed to be their exclusive turfs. However, for the black population, the situation was different in kind. Over 90 per cent of the African American population lived in black areas and over 80 per cent of the population of the black areas was black.

In addition the level of African American segregation, instead of decreasing, as is predicted in the three generational model, seems to have arrived at a saturated level of hyper segregation (Massey and Denton, 1993). The classic study of black segregation in the United States in the 1960s by the Taeubers (Taeuber and Taeuber, 1965) showed that irrespective of whether it was northern, southern, eastern or western cities, whether they were large or small, whether the black minority was large or small, whether they formed a high or low percentage, black levels of segregation were high. Although there have been some improvements since that time, the same general picture still held true in the mid-1990s.

There is a fundamental difference between two models of segregation in the USA. On the one hand, there is the European model, which is essentially voluntaristic and protective; on the other is the African American model of segregation, which is negative and imposed. The voluntaristic model is dilute and transient; the negative model is enforced, concentrated and dynamic.

In fact, if one were taking a Marxist view of the American black ghetto, one could argue that the ghetto is not a problem for capitalist society so much as a solution. If one views ethnic minorities as forming the reserve army of labour, representing a threat to the employment of established workers if they were to unionise and force a redistribution of surplus value, then the ghetto reinforces the visual threat of this group. Further, it allows easier policing of the perimeter by leaving the ghetto to look after itself. If it riots, it burns down only its own facilities. Race and the ghetto, in these terms, becomes the solution rather than the problem.

Behavioural effects of segregation

We turn now to explore firstly the reasons why spatial patterning should have effects on social process and secondly to what extent levels of segregation, both positive and negative, can be controlled by social engineering. The fundamental point about segregation is that it strongly influences whom you interact with. I would like to demonstrate this in four areas: language, friendship, marriage and violence.

Language

If you take a basic element of ethnicity, like language, it is clear that it is absorbed environmentally. I was not born with English-speaking genes nor with my particular accent. I absorbed it from my surroundings. If you were a group like the Amish (who featured in the Harrison Ford film Witness) who wished to maintain their identity in the United States, the key factor would be to maximise your interaction with your own group and to minimise the degree of interaction with outside groups or those whose belief system could act as an alternative model. The main point about ethnic identity is to instil into its members that their assumptions and beliefs and ways of doing things and view of history are the norm and all else is deviation. Their values must be the taken-for-granted elements of their life world. The best method of achieving this is by rural self-sufficiency and isolation. This is indeed the way in which the Amish have preserved their dress, language and way of speech.

It is possible to demonstrate in the American context of the 1930s, for example, that the more segregated the group in a city, the smaller the proportion of that group that was able to speak English. Correspondingly, the more dispersed the group, the higher the proportion able to speak the language (Duncan and Lieberson, 1959).

Not only did segregation affect the ability to speak English for non-English speakers, but it appears to have created the conditions for a distinct Black

English vernacular to come about (Labov, 1972). Work by Labov shows how very distinctive forms of Black English evolved in the African American ghettos and how belonging to gangs left permanent linguistic markers on members, to the extent that it was possible to identify from speech patterns who were central members and who were peripheral members of Harlem gangs, for example.

Friendship

Work by Festinger, Schachter and Back (1950) on new graduate student housing at MIT [Massachussetts Institute of Technology] demonstrated that there was a much higher probability of selecting friends from those living within a few feet of one's apartment door than from those living further away and that the intervention of a staircase produced a noticeable fall-off in the number of friends for the same distance on the same floor.

Marriage

The same mechanism operates at a larger scale, that of the city, in marriage. Cupid has arrows, but it turns out that he does not fire them very far for the most part. There is a very strong distance-decay effect in marriage (Bossard, 1932; Catton and Smircich, 1964; Kennedy, 1943; Ramsøy, 1966; Peach, 1974). These studies show that in any given city in the western world (excluding spouses who are already co-habiting), the largest number of marriages take place between brides and grooms living in close proximity and that as distance increases, the numbers fall (see Figure 2.2). The statistical

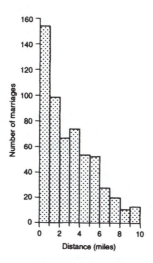

Figure 2.2   Marriage distance in San Francisco, 1980

probabilities, however, operate in exactly the opposite direction: at increasing distances from an individual there are progressively larger numbers of potential spouses. Thus not only do individuals choose those who are close at hand, but they dramatically overselect the proximate in relation to their mathematical chances.

It can also be demonstrated that the more segregated the group, the less likely it was to marry out into the host population. Put the other way, the more segregated the group, the more likely it was to marry into itself. Not only is this the case, but it is possible to demonstrate that the rates of marriages between different ethnic groups correlate strongly with the degree of residential segregation between those groups (Peach, 1980).

This was an important discovery because it demolished one of the myths about American patterns of assimilation. The first view of American assimilation was that the country was a melting pot into which all individual groups would disappear. This was replaced by the idea of a Triple Melting Pot (Kennedy, 1944; 1952) in which the Protestant north west Europeans (the British, the Germans and the Scandinavians) would lose their national identity in marrying each other but retain their Protestantism; the Catholic Irish, Italians and Poles would lose their national identities in marrying each other but retain their Catholicism and eastern and western European Jewry would lose their national origins in a single Jewish pool. The difficulty with this theory from the point of view of residential patterns was this. The Irish were Catholic, but residentially mixed with the British, Germans and Scandinavians. They were relatively segregated from the Italians and Poles. If the segregation hypothesis held, they would be expected to have high rates of intermarriage with the supposedly Protestant British Germans and Scandinavians and relatively less with the Italians and Poles. This was indeed the case. Not only was this so, but the Italians and Poles, who were relatively highly segregated from each other as well as from the British Germans and Scandinavians had relatively high rates of in-marriage (Italian:Italian and Polish:Polish) and rather low rates of marriage to their co-religionists. What this boils down to is that the degree of segregation between groups was a good predictor of rates of intermarriage.

Violence

What is true of positive interaction in the form of marriage is also true of violent interaction in the form of gang warfare. David Ley's work in Philadelphia (Ley, 1974) shows that the largest number of rumbles took place between gangs occupying adjacent turfs.

Segregation and concentration fulfils a protective role, like that of a herd of buffalo, holding off wolves. However, as with herds, it is easiest to pick off those on the edge or those in smaller rather than larger groups. The map of doorstep murders in Belfast, drawn from the work of Murray and Boal (1979), illustrates the principle. Each solid circle represents a Roman Catholic victim and each open circle a Protestant victim of those murders in which the only aim was sectarian revenge on a community' rather than on the individual. There are several patterns, although they are alike in allowing the killers to get into and out of an area of sectarian concentration quickly. One is for the selection of victims on the edge of the large concentrated distributions, like the Falls or Shankill

Roads. Another, more prominent in this map, is to pick victims in the small, detached clusters, like the Ardoyne, which are less defensible (see Figure 2.3).

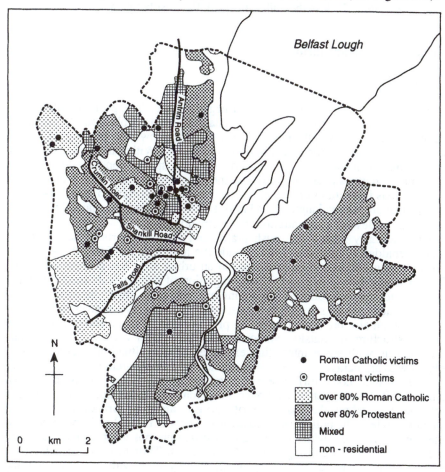

Figure 2.3   **Doorstep murders in Belfast, 1969-1977**
Source: redrawn after Murray and Boal (1979)

Demarcation of areas by means of graffiti and emblems is another way of defending and imposing territoriality on place. Belfast is one of the world leaders in this respect. We can also see some of the same defensive strategy in the way that gangs defend their turfs. For instance, in Philadelphia gangs spray can their tags on the walls to mark out territory. Where their territory abuts that of a rival gang, the rivals deface the originals with obscenities. The density of these obscenities increases in the areas of disputed territory so that the density of obscenities effectively demarcates the gang turf boundaries (Ley, 1974).

To summarise the story so far, we can see that social groups in cities are not distributed in a random way. Some are segregated to a greater extent than others. The levels of residential separation which they manifest correlates with important behavioural variables. The more segregated, the more in-married; the more segregated, the less the ability to speak the host language.

Reasons for segregation

Positive reasons for segregation

Segregation has both a positive and a negative side. The positive side is that concentration allows the group to maintain its social cohesion. It maintains cultural values, it strengthens social networks, it allows the passing of critical thresholds for the support of institutions and shops. Within the urban sphere, it is possible to maintain group cohesion through spatial concentration. Urban concentration allows the groups to pass the threshold size at which ethnic shops and religious institutions can be maintained and the proximity to members of the groups that allows the language and norms of the groups to be maintained.

In areas of Jewish concentration, the formation of *eruvs* — areas where it is possible to carry money and push prams and to do all sorts of activities that were forbidden to orthodox Jews outside the home on the Sabbath — can be allowed. Segregation, in other words, in an urban area, has positive elements. Not all segregation is negative. Chain migration of new arrivals from the home country to the established communities, thickens their densities. Such concentrations can be seen as existential rather than positive or negative.

Segregation also provides a defensive protection from attack and it reverses the power structure of outside authority. Michael Keith's work on riots has provided us with some interesting examples of this situation. Young British blacks who are harassed by the police outside their home areas can cock a snook at them on their home turf. The trigger events of most of the riots in English cities in 1981 were perceived police intrusion into these home turfs. Police reluctance to admit the existence of 'no-go' areas in British cities led to situations where the police patrolled areas of known criminal activity, in order to maintain a presence, while under strict instructions not to apprehend any law breakers, for fear of causing a riot (Keith, 1993). Thus in many British cities, the medieval concept of 'sanctuary' is alive, only now with the contemporary term of 'front line' or 'safe haven'.

Other ways in which the reversal of power relations can be produced in space is by carnivals. The Notting Hill Carnival which has taken place in London in late August each year since 1966 is a good example. However, processions and marches fill a similar role (Rogers, 1995; Smith, 1993). Finally, the separation of territory by (Peace) Walls, as in Belfast, represents the ultimate in defence and protection.

Negative factors in segregation

The negative side of segregation represents the attempts to keep underprivileged ethnic populations out of the residential areas of the dominant group. The most blatant examples of this were to be found in Apartheid South Africa, where the prohibition was legislated and legally enforced (see Figure 2.4; Lemon, 1991).

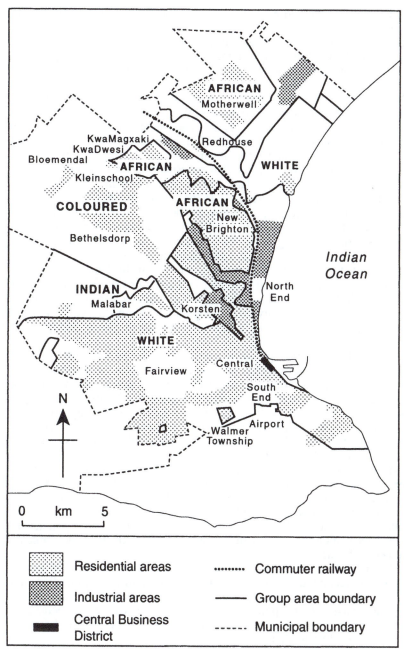

AFRICAN
Motherwell

KwaMagxaki
KwaDwesi
Bloemendal
AFRICAN
Kleinschool

WHITE

Redhouse

COLOURED

AFRICAN
New
Brighton

Bethelsdorp

Indian
Ocean

INDIAN
Malabar

Korsten

North
End

WHITE

Fairview

Central

South
End

Airport

Walmer
Township

N

0   km   5

Residential areas	Commuter railway
Industrial areas	Group area boundary
Central Business District	Municipal boundary

Figure 2.4   Ethnic zoning in Port Elizabeth
Source: redrawn after Christopher in Lemon (1991)

Cities were zoned for race and ethnicity and physical features like rivers, roads and railways were chosen to demarcate the territories.

In extreme cases, such as Johannesburg, the black south western township SOWETO was built 20 kilometres from the centre of the city so that its presence would not inhibit white urban development in the south-western sector of the city itself.

In the United States, negative forces of segregation were just as effective but applied through restrictive property covenants. When these were declared illegal they remained effective though less overt. The Realtor's Code of practice forbade the promotion of change of ethnicity in a neighbourhood. The Federal Housing Agency, which guaranteed the Savings and Loan companies which lent mortgage moneys, did so on condition that the Realtor's Code of Practice was observed in such undertakings. The Federal Government, in this way, underwrote discrimination and segregation in the housing market.

In Britain in the post war period, there has also been massive discrimination in housing. Openly discriminatory notices in private lettings ('No Coloureds') were pervasive until the passing of the Race Relations Act of 1965 (Peach et al., 1988, p. 569). The Caribbean and South Asian immigrant populations were effectively excluded from public housing until the end of the 1960s. Given that this housing accounted for between a quarter and a third of the British housing stock at this period and that it was designed essentially for working class families, the exclusion of minority ethnic populations from this key sector of housing dramatically restricted the residential spread of those groups and promoted segregation.

However, once the barriers in public housing were breached and the minority ethnic populations were able to gain access, a combination of discriminatory allocation and the weak position of members of those groups in negotiating types of property, led to a high concentration in the less desirable house types and areas. The areas tended to be inner rather than outer city and high rise flats rather than houses. Indeed, the higher up the high rise blocks one went in certain inner city areas, the blacker and more female-single-mother became the populations (Peach and Byron, 1993).

Where groups have moved into white defended space, incidents of racial harassment have been common and often families have been forced to flee.

In Belfast, as sectarian violence flared, public housing became even more segregated than the population as a whole. Housing estates became the objects of paramilitary struggles and ethnic cleansing and scorched earth policies to prevent the occupation of abandoned space by the 'other' side became commonplace in the city.

Effectively in Northern Ireland, there are two allocative systems of public housing : the official and the unofficial. Nobody is going to ask for an allocation of housing in the 'wrong' area. In any case, the politics of separation are effectively internalised in the population. Nobody will ask for a sectarianly inappropriate allocation. Segregation is in the minds as well as on the map. Confidence is a very fragile plant.

To summarise, ethnic segregation is a marked feature of western cities, although the reasons for segregation in some cases are strongly positive, in some cases strongly negative and in some, an opaque interaction between the two. However, when the situation of those groups experiencing high levels of segregation is examined, it is not clear that all of those that experience high levels of segregation are experiencing it for negative reasons.

We may take, for example, Bangladeshis in Britain, who manifest the highest levels of segregation of any ethnic minority group in the country. The general interpretation of their position is in relation to British racism. Studies by Deborah Phillips (1986) and by the CRE (1989) on housing allocation in the London Borough of Tower Hamlets shows clear evidence of council policies of channelling Bangladeshis onto particular council estates. Thus, at the micro scale, it is clear that discriminatory practices are contributory factors for the segregation pattern that exists.

However, what is a contributory factor at the micro scale may not be the determining factor at the macro scale. Tower Hamlets housing policy does not explain why nearly one quarter of the whole Bangladeshi population of Britain has chosen to live in a single London Borough. In other words, although the local authority might be controlling the distribution of Bangladeshis inside the Borough, there is no local authority directing Bangladeshis to Tower Hamlets in the first place. Bangladeshi choice seems to be a much more potent force than local authority prescription.

It is also clear that Bangladeshis are highly segregated in all British cities and that they are segregated from other ethnic minority groups, including the Pakistanis with whom they once shared a common nationality and who are also Muslims — not just from the white population (Peach, 1996).

The conclusion to be drawn from this is that although negative discriminatory forces are at work, constraining Bangladeshi distributions within cities, these may not be the key factors. It may be that the positive desire to maintain their community, to maintain village and kin ties, to preserve purdah and even the pure inertia of the original chain migration process have a higher explanatory power.

Cases of positive factors being mistaken for negative: false negatives

Taking this argument a stage further, it appears that Rex and Moore's argument about housing classes may also have been mistaken. Rex and Moore (1967) argued, in their classic study of immigrant housing in Birmingham in the early 1960s, that there were five housing classes and that immigrants were forced into the lowest of these, by white discriminatory behaviour. These classes were owner occupier without mortgage, owner occupier with mortgage, council tenant, landlord of a house with tenants, tenant in a multi-occupied house.

Now, while it was true that there was massive discrimination in the housing market against immigrants, it also appears true that this was not necessarily the reason for the concentration of Asian immigrants into the multi-occupied sector. Work by Dahya (1974) in the same Sparkbrook area of Birmingham suggested that multi-occupation was a rational, preferred solution for Pakistanis at this stage of the migration process. They were interested in maximising their savings and remittances to Pakistan; they were often kin of other lodgers or from the same village; they shared a common religion with its dietary and prayer requirements, they spoke little English and were often employed as a household gang. Under these circumstances, council housing or owner occupation was not particularly attractive.

However, once family reunification began, Pakistani and Indian settlers changed from renting accommodation to owner occupation. Currently about 80 per cent of Indian and Pakistani headed households are in owner occupied property.

At this stage it would appear that Indians and Pakistanis had moved to the top of the housing class ladder. However, Rex shifted the goal posts at this stage in order to demonstrate that discrimination was keeping them at the bottom (Rex and Tomlinson, 1979, p. 132). In the revised housing class formulation, it turned out that owner occupation was no longer the key attribute; it was owner occupation of semi detached or detached housing in the suburbs. Owner occupation of inner city terraced property dropped to the bottom of the housing class hierarchy.

The point is that although there was massive discrimination against Indian and Pakistani settlers in Britain, the housing choices that they made were dictated far more by Indian and Pakistani preference than by outside discrimination. The properties to which their access was barred, were properties in which they were not interested. According to the Rex thesis, they should have been asking for working class council house accommodation. However, the ethos of the group was essentially for property ownership. It was only the most disadvantaged of the South Asian ethnic minority populations, the Bangladeshis, who had to settle for council housing. In fact, of the very small numbers of Indians and Pakistanis who went into council housing, a very high proportion bought under the 'right to buy' legislation.

Cases of negative factors being mistaken for positive (structuration): false positives

However, if there are cases of positive choice being mistaken for negative discrimination in housing patterns, there are also cases of apparently positive choice, which are, in effect, negatively constrained. This discussion relates to structuration theory particularly as developed by Sarre, Phillips and Skellington (1989) in their study of ethnic minority group housing in Bedford. What they showed was that Caribbean council tenants tended to opt for old, inner urban terraced housing. What they were also able to demonstrate was that the proportion of Caribbean households opting for such property was much greater if the choice had been made after rather than before the visit of the housing officers. In other words there was strong evidence that the apparently free choice of housing was made with a strong steer from the allocating officers. Caribbean clients were internalising the expectations of those in authority.

Another example of negative issues being mistaken for positive comes in the argument that black segregation in the United States was the product of black poverty rather than white racism. Optimists have argued that African American segregation was due to poverty rather than race. Put bluntly, African Americans were thought to be segregated from whites because they were poor rather than because they were black. To establish whether this was the case, Taeuber and Taeuber (1964) produced an indirect standardisation method. Essentially, this produced the distribution of black population in Chicago that would have been expected if income alone had controlled their distribution, and compared the resulting level of segregation with that actually observed. For example, if the black population formed one per cent of the population of Chicago with an income of over $100,000 pa, it would be assumed in this model, that they would form one per cent of the population earning over $100,000 in each area containing such population, and so on for each income group. They concluded that wealth differences explained only 12 per cent of the observed levels of segregation.

Conclusion

Ethnic segregation comes about in urban areas for understandable reasons of social adjustment by newcomers to established society. Segregation has profound effects in social interaction and behaviour, from the language that you speak, the accent with which you speak it, the friendships that you make and the partners that you marry.

However, there are critical differences between segregation which comes about on a voluntaristic or existential way — Irish, Italian or Mexican areas in US cities, for example, or living within the Jewish *eruv* in Golders Green, London — and those brought about by negative discriminatory forces such as South African Apartheid or Black segregation in the United States.

In Belfast, Catholic segregation has a strongly defensive air about it, but Bangladeshis in Tower Hamlets, who have a similarly high level of segregation as Catholics in Belfast, seem to present a much more voluntaristic and existential pattern. While ghettos should be unacceptable to planners, it seems to me that we should be much more tolerant of ethnic areas. Encouraging ethnic areas without creating ghettos is the challenge of the 1990s and will continue to be a challenge into the twenty first century, but we need to know more about the dynamics of choice, the dynamics of interaction and the consequences of social engineering. We need experimental as well as observational analysis. In this chapter I have given a brief historical sketch of the extent and consequences of segregation in some western urban situations. The rest of *Accommodating Differences* gives a detailed insight on the state of the art.

Part Two
South Africa

3   Dealing with differences: the South African experience

Kader Asmal

(note: This is the transcript of a speech read on Dr. Asmal's behalf, at the International Federation of Housing and Planning Conference, Belfast, September 1995)

At the outset let me congratulate you all on arranging such a multi-faceted study of the issues, as reflected in your agenda. You are coming to grips with many matters that are central to modern-day humanity, and I wish you well in your deliberations. You will excuse me if I range somewhat wider over the spectrum of the South African experience than housing, as I seek to draw some of the threads together in what I have to say about conditions in my remarkable country.

The legacy of apartheid

Perhaps the most notable feature about South Africa is that it is, for the first time in its history, coming to grips with its past, including the forced cleavages caused by a Government that so relentlessly pursued apartheid. If ever there was a country that was artificially divided, it was South Africa. Its white rulers over many decades perfected a system based exclusively on separating people from one another. In every sphere of life apartheid required that people should live their lives apart from their fellows. The grim, well-known story need not be retold. Suffice it to say that apartheid played on, and grotesquely distorted the differences that naturally occur among people, and fashioned them into a system of racial oppression.

    We are left in South Africa with a geography which is still largely racial. Large sections of the country, used as dumping grounds for people classed as 'surplus' are impoverished and almost without hope. (I know since I regularly visit them in my capacity of Minister of Water Affairs and Forestry), while other parts — the lairs of the well-off — are on a par with California in terms of affluence. The rural poor find themselves largely without ready access to clean, safe water — while brimming dams serving privileged farmers sometimes exist close by. Apartheid left us skewed architecture and skewed geography — a plethora of entrances, formerly for black and for white; it left us duplicated toilets, bars, hotels, for black and for white; it left us towns that were cheek by jowl but worlds apart: the black town and the white town. The ugly tentacles of apartheid are still seen everywhere. It will take a long time to move away from the stultification bequeathed us by the past era — not to mention the other legacies in terms of human suffering, bitterness, dispossession.

The iron law of the central mechanism of residential segregation, the Group Areas Act, under which countless South Africans were evicted by officialdom from their homes and moved to where it would be racially tidy, has left an almost indelible mark on the physical landscape: rabbit-warrens of housing separated on a racial basis, distorted development in urban and rural areas to suit the social engineers of apartheid, inner cities virtually destroyed, not only by the flight of whites to more wealthy suburbs, but by the forced eviction of people of colour who could have otherwise offered a city like Cape Town life, *busyness* and safety.

And, above all else, we are left with the deepest sense of bitterness among those who were forced to move, and in the process did not even receive fair compensation — and who now look with understandable envy at the chic commercial and residential developments that were plonked over their erstwhile homes. All the problems of new towns, which are well-known world-wide, were compounded by apartheid. For instance, apartheid dumped people of widely differing standards of living but classified in similar race groups in far-off, dusty townships where there was no soul or community spirit, and where access to their places of work became a costly nightmare each day on expensive, but crowded trains, buses or taxis.

The way forward

Now that a democratic system is in place, it is necessary to take stock of the position and to chart a way forward. The watchword in all this is the Interim Constitution which, in the bill of fundamental rights, states that: 'Every person shall have the right freely to choose his or her place of residence anywhere in the national territory'. This guarantee must be seen against the backdrop of the guarantee of equality before the law and a prohibition on unfair discrimination on grounds of race, gender, sex, ethnic or social origin, colour, sexual orientation, age, disability, religion, conscience, belief, culture or language.

We must deal with our past in a comprehensive way, so that we may, as a new nation, mend both body and soul for the challenging times ahead. Those who were wronged must receive due compensation. This applies with equal force to the victims and families of official death squads as it applies to people dispossessed of their rightful land and housing. Before the splendid new democracy that has been fashioned can be deepened, it is necessary for the nation to be healed. Coming to terms with the past is a difficult and, for some, a painful matter. We shall soon have to close the book on the past, but before we begin to do it, we must not suppress it. There are good reasons why the book must remain open for a time, for instance:

1   There has to be a recognition of the illegitimacy of the system which operated previously.

2   The newly-acquired veneer of democracy by the previous upholders of apartheid enables political conservatives and neo-racists to anchor their undemocratic ideologies in white-washed national precedent, a past

mysteriously purged of apartheid. This sanitised version of history does not even expect forgiveness because the necessity for exculpation never arises. It must be laid bare.

3   The neglect of history will kindle resentment and may induce a chauvinist response. We cannot afford to deny the effects of the old order. Old antagonisms may fester, whether over land rights or other rights denied. The generosity of the majority must not be interpreted as allowing the minority to believe in their collective innocence.

4   It is essential that we confront the roots of violence and repression in our country if we are ever to eradicate their effects.

5   Another reason for accounting with the past is the necessity to avoid the revenge factor. In other so-called advanced countries, there have been traumatising acts of individual and collective revenge, often aimed at people at the margins of society and power, while the real culprits escaped. We should not fall into the trap of making a whole community into a scapegoat for the policies of the past. We must bring a measure of rationality into our response to the past.

6   There is also the catharsis argument which calls for an outlet of emotion, and, through an act of purgation, allows for change without violent disruption.

7   There is the truth and justice argument. We must get to the fullest possible truth, lay it bare and only then can we move on in our national life.

8   Then there is the crucial question of property. It was Machiavelli, I think, who warned that people will forgive almost any injustice, but not the alienation of their property. When one surveys the racist Land Acts of the past, the Group Areas legislation and restrictions on black entrepreneurs designed to impede and retard black progress, in favour of whites, it is obvious that there must be full inquiry and redress. I quote from an academic colleague who put it this way:

    It is a fact that no settlement will hold, no peace will be sustained, no treaty will work, no interregnum will be stable and no agreement will be valid which does not include some form of redressing of the ill-gotten gains of apartheid.

A Truth and Reconciliation Commission is being formed [September 1995] leading the way in the massive task of unearthing the fullest picture of the wrongs done to South Africans by South Africans.

Land reform

But what has to be done about the past beyond that? Our Interim Constitution provides for the restitution of land rights, which expressly means relief for

29

people dispossessed for racial reasons. This goes back to the infamous Land Act of 1913 which sought to give 13 per cent of the land to three-quarters of the people who were black. Some other countries, such as New Zealand in relation to the Treaty of Waitangi, have gone even further back in history, to the mid-19th century.

A Commission on the restitution of land rights has been set up, and I am told that there is already a brisk rate of inquiries. This Commission investigates people's claims to land in cases where they were dispossessed in terms of a law which would offend the equality and non-discrimination clauses of the new Constitution. People may approach this Commission to ask that they be given their land back, or other relief.

The actual form of relief is left in the hands of the Land Claims Court, with four members headed by a former Robben Island political prisoner who is a respected lawyer. This court is about to begin operating. It has wide discretion to decide on handing land back, setting fair compensation or ordering any other form of relief, e.g. giving successful applicants priority in state-assisted schemes whereby they may obtain alternative land. A Bill was published recently called the Land Reform Bill under which labour tenants who have been on farms can be given title to the land they occupy and farm. The significance of such a move should not be underestimated. In addition, the government is pursuing a land reform policy whereby redistribution of agricultural land will be considered.

Housing

On the housing front the Government, with the co-operation of the private sector, is moving with resolution to provide low-cost housing that is desperately necessary. There are difficulties, for instance the nervousness amongst financial institutions when it comes to lending money because of past defaulting over mortgages and rentals, but the Government and Provincial authorities are determined to get to grips with this vast problem.

In the previous dispensation, a comprehensive policy for housing the nation did not exist. Government-assisted housing projects for Africans in urban areas had been all but non-existent since the late 1960s, in line with apartheid's channelling of resources to the so-called Bantustans (rural reserves where Africans, particularly women and children, were increasingly concentrated). Housing assistance had been heavily slanted for political reasons, for instance used to woo support among the Coloured and Asiatic minorities for the sham legislative structures set up for these people in a 'tricameral' system of parliament. Following negative experiences during the disturbances in black townships in the 1980s, the banks had withdrawn from the low end of the housing market.

Hence the scale of the problem inherited by the Mandela Government can be appreciated.

A conservative estimate of the housing backlog, made in 1992, showed a requirement of one and a half million housing units. This figure was set to grow by at least 200,000 per year, as new households entered the market. At the same time, a number of factors mitigated against large-scale delivery of housing —

including the loss of capacity by the construction industry due to a severe recession which marked the final years of the previous administration.

When the Mandela Government was elected to power in 1994 it was therefore necessary to put in place a comprehensive housing policy in line with enlightened constitutional requirements, and one able to sustain housing development in the long term.

The White Paper on Housing adopted by the Cabinet on 7 December 1994 was the culmination of this policy-formulation process. The White Paper is set to become the blueprint for housing in South Africa which — as the document makes clear — is a task for generations. The White Paper provides the basis for a fundamental reorientation of housing policy and housing efforts in the country. To have proceeded with construction prior to its finalisation would have meant repeating the mistakes of the past: throwing money at parts of the problem without a coherent plan.

In addition to the White Paper, it became clear in the second half of 1994 that a broad consensus around housing was needed. This was achieved in October 1994 at a significant place, Botshabelo, a blighted town where apartheid dumped 350,000 black people some miles away from the Free State provincial capital of Bloemfontein. Botshabelo saw the adoption of the historic Housing Accord — a singular achievement for the late Mr. Joe Slovo, then Housing Minister and a person demonised all his life by the Nationalist South African Government because of his attachment to the Communist Party. This document contains the pledges of all important sectors involved in the housing process, from the banks via developers, government at all levels, and civil society to the homeless, to work towards the common goal of housing the nation. The document is significant because of its very public nature, and because of the commitment given by every sector.

Development Facilitation legislation passed by parliament, while very technical, will allow much more rapid release of buildable land than in the past. It is set to become a major counter to land invasions by releasing the pressure on communities in search of developable land.

I might mention that the problem of land invasion is enjoying the highest attention. It is regrettable but perhaps understandable that communities denied housing and land for years, will seize almost any opportunity to move on to land for settlement purposes which they view as their right in the new, democratic order. But sound planning, equity and a respect for peace and order require that this illegal activity cannot be countenanced. Stern warnings, including from President Mandela himself, have had to be issued against such activities. A problem is that local authorities in large parts of the country are weak or non-existent — once again a legacy of the past. It is thus of crucial importance that the local elections scheduled for 1 November do, in fact, take place so that legitimate and effective local government can be put in place to grapple with such problems — with the full support of Provincial and National Government. It is also self-evident that programmes for housing squatter and other communities must be speeded up radically to deal with the rising expectations of the masses.

A major breakthrough was the record of understanding with the Association of Mortgage Lenders (AML). In it, the banks pledge to return to the low end of the housing market. This will give countless poor families access to credit, allowing them a first-time opportunity to become owners of formal housing. This agreement also envisages a Builders Warranty Scheme, a major piece of consumer protection against shoddy workmanship and fly-by-night contractors.

The agreement with the banks aids only those in income brackets regarded as credit worthy, and it has been necessary to find mechanisms to support those subsidy recipients who will not qualify for bank loans. An important step in this regard was a visit by a delegation from the Housing and Urban Development Corporation of India (HUDCO). The Indians have long-standing and highly relevant experience in the creation of building support centres at which poor people can find reasonably priced building materials, simple tools and technical advice. The idea is to establish several of these as pilot projects in an effort to help people help themselves — and to create jobs, because most materials are made on site (building blocks, roof tiles, door frames, etc.) using local emerging entrepreneurs and labour.

As to types of houses recommended, there are different views on this. The national ministry does not favour one housing type over another. The feeling is that people must have maximum freedom of choice. What can be provided through the subsidy system is a *housing opportunity* — helping people to help themselves with housing. Building conditions differ in different parts of the country, so it would be difficult to lay down one standard house type. This seems the best and most pragmatic approach.

The considerably increased National Budget for housing for 1995/1996 represents a major step in the right direction for housing. It demonstrates the government's commitment to the targets set for housing within the country's Reconstruction and Development Programme. The announcement of an effective 80 percent increase in state allocations to housing sends a highly positive signal to the private sector, to communities, and to individual South Africans seeking access to housing.

It is worth noting a comment by the Minister of Housing, Ms Sankie Mthembi-Nkondo, who stresses that it would be a grave error if we in South Africa allowed quantity to dominate over quality. She has said:

> If we are to build a million housing units in the five years of South Africa's Government of National Unity — and I am absolutely convinced that we will reach our target — then we must constantly beware of the dangers of putting quantity before quality of life. The examples round the world are legion — of well intentioned, massive housing programmes gone wrong....

She spoke of the 'inability or the unwillingness of the planners and politicians to respond to the needs and desires of the people, to respond in a manner which allows their houses to become homes within communities which are economically and socially viable'.

Final comments

Before I close, may I be permitted a brief word about the special challenge that is presented by factors such as ethnic, cultural and political diversity in my country? I should like to venture the view that, whatever is happening elsewhere in the world, the major dynamic of a democratic South Africa will be the politics of oneness. We have been through our era of division. We have all manner of cultures and creeds in what has rightly been called the Rainbow Nation. But we shall never return to the point where differences, which are rightly cultural, are elevated to matters for the law and for the State. Our diversity makes up a rich mosaic of cultural significance. But our statehood will be colour blind. We shall remain non-racial, while recognising the cultural diversity that makes our country what it is. If other parts of the world spin inexorably off in the direction of fragmentation, if towns or cities elsewhere see merit in differentiating among various classes of residents, if some theatres of the world take the detour from rationality that is 'ethnic cleansing', South Africa will stay attached to a spirit of close unity among all its people. We can speak with hindsight and experience. Attempts to divide us were a costly, ghastly failure. Never again! And, as one sees a whole nation uniting behind the leadership of Mr Nelson Mandela, so one sees a remarkable consensus developing behind the Reconstruction.

4   Voices across the divide: undoing racial segregation in South Africa

Abigail Goldberg

The divide

Apartheid's rhetoric would have us believe that racial segregation in South Africa was spontaneous. Nel (1962, p. 207), among others (for example Davies, 1971, p. 227) suggested

> ... that the races in South Africa's urban areas have traditionally segregated themselves, and [apartheid] was adopted rather to consolidate the existing traditional patterns of racial separation, and to ensure that it be maintained in future, than to enforce something new.

Yet formidable military and police activity, an entrenched bureaucracy, imposing 'legal web' (Simon, 1989, p. 190) and highly engineered urban environment — locus of this paper — were required to both implement and maintain apartheid. These characteristics, it is argued here, are indicative not only of unwelcome minority rule, but another reality: racial mixing occurred frequently, persistently, and without incident.

Dynamic and successful mixed environments in fact denied the racial conflict which apartheid's promoters were convinced integration would ignite:

> We believe, and believe strongly, that points of contact — all unnecessary points of contact — between the races must be avoided. If you reduce the number of points of contact to the minimum, you reduce the possibility of friction .... The result of putting people of different races together is to cause racial trouble.
> (Minister of the Interior, 1950 in Western, 1981, p. 85)

On this basis, the minority leadership set out to create the *de jure* Apartheid City — a simplified urban structure of racially discrete residential segments which favoured whites with space, services and facilities (Figure 4.1). En route to the ideal, vibrant mixed, and accordingly contradictory, areas were to be erased. The process is described as 'the most extraordinary, ambitious and pernicious exercise in social and physical reconstruction ever conceived

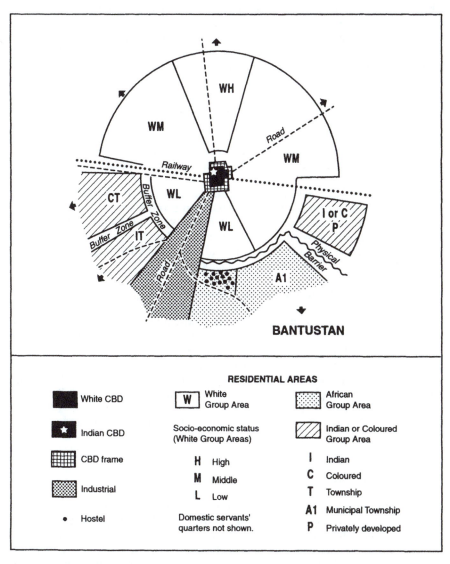

Figure 4.1   The ideal apartheid city
Source: redrawn after Simon (1989)

(Smit, 1992, p. 2). Where it met with resistance, and the stubborn refusal of residents to accept segregation, forced removals and the demolition of homes were favoured tools for ensuring its advancement.

Epitomising this process, Pageview/Vrededorp in Johannesburg 'microscopically contains the reality of a distinctly South African experience' (Carrim, 1990, p. 4) where shared living had resulted in a close-knit community, and where its environment was subsequently destroyed. Almost thirty years afterwards the area remains largely wasteland. As a first step towards rebuilding it in the post-apartheid spirit of reconciliation, the history and memory of Pageview/Vrededorp is reconstructed below. This history illustrates the ruthless power of apartheid, while defying its rationale for segregation.

Nature of the research: a qualitative approach

While quantitative methods in research, including such tools as questionnaires, offer a structured approach to which measurable responses are possible, it is argued that such an approach would be inappropriate to a study such as this:

> The facts are always less than what really happens .... If you get a law, like group areas, under which various population groups are ... uprooted from their homes and so on, well, somebody may give you the figures, how many people are moved, how many jobs were lost. But, to me it doesn't tell you nearly as much as the story of one individual who lived through that.
> (Nadine Gordimer, The Listener, 21 October 1976)

Moreover, Rogerson and Beavon (in Eyles, 1988) suggest that the emphasis on research in South Africa was for too long and to its own detriment 'dominated or, perhaps more correctly, obsessed by the thinking and predominant models of ... the Anglo-American ... quantitative tide' (1988, p. 84). This, they imply, encouraged 'a general legitimisation of the political *status quo* in South Africa; in other words, an uncritical acceptance of apartheid' (1988, p. 84). A qualitative approach was thus favoured for being more responsive. Emphasis has been placed on the stories people tell — and the researcher 'listening, for a change', (Slim and Thompson, 1993) to interviews with past and present residents, popular literature and archival documents.

Voices across the divide

Johannesburg was founded in 1886 following the accidental discovery of gold. The rough mining camp which sprang up overnight became permanent almost as quickly; and while maps of 1886 show a small grid layout settlement on a triangle of *uitvalgrond* (leftover land) between farms, by 1897 the settlement had grown more than sixfold (Figure 4.2). This map also indicates that segregated residential areas or 'locations', typical of colonial towns in Southern, Central and East Africa, had been designated. A 'Kafir' and a 'Coolie' location are apparent, as well as an unusually non-specific 'Location'. Records suggest that this 'Location' was later renamed Vrededorp, or 'Free Town', and granted to indigent whites with the exception of a southern portion set aside as the Malay Location after Islamic leaders petitioned President Paul Kruger for a place to develop 'away from the pig-eaters and liquid-drinker brothels and shebeens' (in Bird, 1989, p. 1). Vrededorp is easily recognised by its distinctive long, narrow blocks which remain today. Legend ascribes this morphology to President Kruger who, presented with a standard layout of

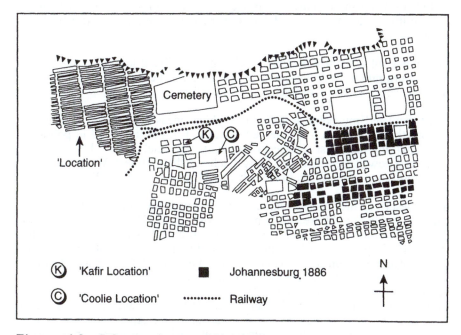

Figure 4.2   Johannesburg,   1886-1897
Source: redrawn after Frescure and Radford (1982)

plots 50 by 100 feet, remarked '*Ek sal hulle nie plase gee nie, maar net sitplekke*'('I will not give them farms, only places to sit') and firmly drew subdivisions across them (Johannesburg City Council, 1967).

Although even the 'white' portion of Vrededorp 'greyed' over time, the Malay Location appears to have been mixed from the outset. The first available records date from 1904 when an outbreak of bubonic plague saw the area evacuated and burnt. Archival documents list the evacuees as 1,612 'Asiatics', 1,420 'Africans' and 146 'Cape Coloureds' (Johannesburg City Council, 1967); and note that in July of the same year most people moved back. Ironically then, the next source of information is the autobiography of a white, despite there being no official recognition that whites were living in the 'Location'. Bernard Sachs describes how as a child he arrived around 1908 from Lithuania:

We were leaving behind Kamaai with its squalor for the land where, we were told, the streets were paved with gold and we would live in marble halls.... The cab pulled up, and we found ourselves before a three-storeyed tenement in the centre of one of Johannesburg's slums known as the Malay Camp. Our home consisted of three undersized rooms. There was also a kitchen but no bathroom, and no electric light .... The furnishings of our home were of the barest — a table to eat on, chairs on which to sit, and beds to sleep in. [We] looked out on a yard where 20 Africans, Coloureds and Indians lived in shabbily constructed rooms from where they conducted their illicit sales of liquor and dagga [vernaular for marijuana] (Sachs 1973, pp. 41-72)

The author subsequently became a well-regarded liberal journalist, his brother Solly a prominent trade unionist. It was in integrated Vrededorp that Solly Sachs developed his commitment to non-racialism:

I formulated my political and philosophical ideas at the age of sixteen or something and my job is to serve humanity. I'm not interested in politics or in anything else, just service to humanity. In racial hatred, I hope I shall never know it. (evidence of Solly Sachs at the Garment Workers' Union Commission of Enquiry, in Holscher and Emmett, 1990, p. 4)

Sachs describes life in the location as pulsing with both the din of the stamp batteries crushing gold ore and human activity. In the 1920s he left, returning only on occasion to visit the 'unique and colourful, garish all-night cafes' (Sachs 1973, p. 82) at which time he also became aware that the area 'had deteriorated even from its previous lowly state. The window panes from the tenements gaped at me, where they were not covered over with sugar bags still bearing the trademark' (1973, p. 77).

Promulgation of the Native Urban Areas Act in 1927 and the Slums Act in 1934 laid the legal groundwork for the creation of the Apartheid City, and the legal support for the first, forced, removals of blacks from Vrededorp to distant Soweto, the infamous black township on the outskirts of Johannesburg. The removals occurred swiftly and viciously, frequently dividing families and leaving little opportunity for on-the-ground defiance. Deeper resistance is however apparent in the adoption of the colloquial name 'Fietas' for Vrededorp:

Fietas, the name Fietas came about when the apartheid movement began to get stronger and stronger here. Then they moved people out, so these people used to meet in the jails, and they used to speak a type of slang Afrikaans that the Afrikaners wouldn't understand. So when they said 'are you from Fietas?', it means are you from the Free Burg, from Vrededorp ... its all Vrededorp (Pather, 6 September 1995).

I remember the Africans were moved out of Fietas in the 1930s. They were put into trucks and taken to Orlando [a suburb of Soweto]. I remember this well, because it was then that the Indians, Malays and Coloureds came into the bottom side of Fietas (Docrat in Carrim, 1990, p. 100).

By 1940 the forced removals of blacks had left Fietas predominantly Indian. In 1942 the area was officially designated for Indians only, and renamed Pageview after the mayor of the time. Despite this, Pageview remained defiantly mixed. Petrus Radebe, for example, is black and was born in 1941 at 24 Seventh Street, where his family had been living for some time. His overriding memory is of a place where blacks, coloureds, Indians, Chinese 'and even whites' (Radebe, 23 November 1993) lived harmoniously together. He describes a 'squatter' area where rooms, streets and houses were crowded one on top of the other and recalls a 'time of respect' — for parents, for neighbours and for the police, who 'didn't carry guns'. He contrasts this to his present home in Soweto where 'there is too much politics and too many people dying' and the police are figures of hate, ridicule and fear. Radebe's family moved in 1952 to nearby Sophiatown, itself shortly thereafter declared 'white' and obliterated, thereafter to Soweto. Other residents of the time remember

> Being very happy, everybody was uncles and aunties, nobody was very rich and very poor, we were all you know, on one level. We had a lot of friends ... it was very mixed (Ramnarain, 4 May 1995).

> It was too lively, a very mixed area, very congested. People had different relationships in Fietas, they were more close-knit (Sonvadi, 30 November 1993).

The heart of the area is widely recognised and fondly recalled as the lively 'Mecca of shoppers', Fourteenth Street:

> In its own quiet and, if you wish, slummy way, Fourteenth Street in Vrededorp is long overdue for recognition as one of Johannesburg's most famous streets. This street, entirely Indian controlled, does business with people of all races, all walks of life, from Soweto to Mayfair, from Houghton to Japan, India, Europe, England and the United States. (Nakasa, 1975, p. 9)

The closeness and vibrancy was not to last. Crisis came in 1956 when pursuit of the ideal Apartheid City was intensified, and Pageview declared no longer 'Indian' but 'white'. All other race groups became 'disqualified' and were warned to leave under threat of fines or imprisonment. By the end of the 1950s and the beginning of the 1960s all 'non-white' houses had been issued eviction orders and schools were closed down. The community became insecure and frightened. Challenges to the eviction orders gained some time, particularly when residents frustrated the City Council's attempts to survey buildings at every turn. Nevertheless, a number of people were 'legally' evicted while those who refused valid eviction orders were arrested (Carrim, 1990).

> ... because of the laws, people were afraid, and that started fragmenting people...we were fragmented, we were put apart — apartheid — we were pulled apart, and people had to move out by force, you know. That's when all the problems started (Seedat, 9 September 1995).

> We were traumatised by the experience, definitely ... your whole life seems to be torn apart (Bhamjee, 21 September 1995).

For the first time, an outcry of protest was heard from the local media (Figure 4.3). Nevertheless, by 1976, the same year as the milestone Soweto riots, most tenants had been evicted. The last stand of resistance focused on areas where many people were landowners and could not be forced out until, the Group Areas Act stated, 'suitable alternative accommodation' or trading sites had been provided. Banners spread across Fourteenth Street carried the simple but powerful message: 'WE WILL NOT MOVE'. Until the police arrived:

What was really bad and degrading was the way people were moved out. There were dogs and police there. They just threw all the goods onto the street and people were pushed around like animals. I mean how can you even think of doing something like that? (Patel in Carrim, 1990, p. 134).

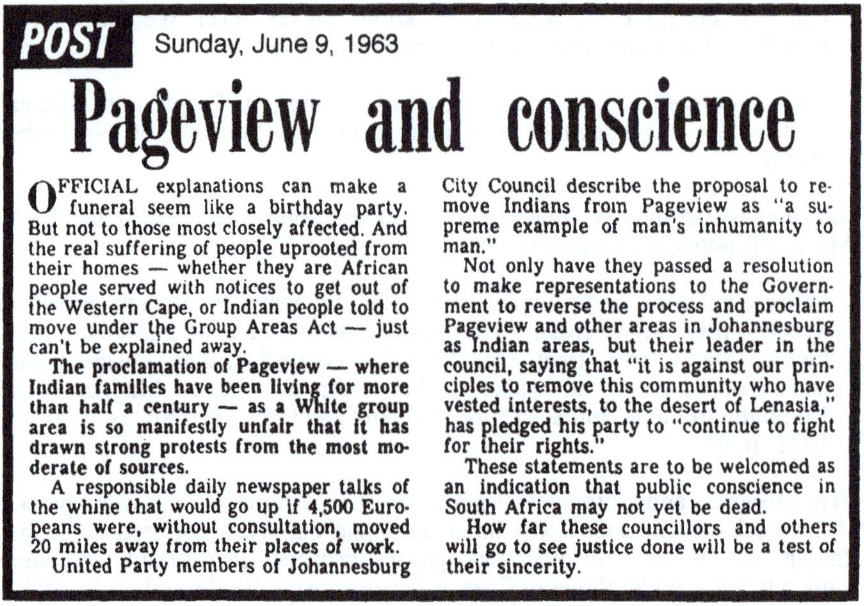

POST Sunday, June 9, 1963

Pageview and conscience

OFFICIAL explanations can make a funeral seem like a birthday party. But not to those most closely affected. And the real suffering of people uprooted from their homes — whether they are African people served with notices to get out of the Western Cape, or Indian people told to move under the Group Areas Act — just can't be explained away.

The proclamation of Pageview — where Indian families have been living for more than half a century — as a White group area is so manifestly unfair that it has drawn strong protests from the most moderate of sources.

A responsible daily newspaper talks of the whine that would go up if 4,500 Europeans were, without consultation, moved 20 miles away from their places of work. United Party members of Johannesburg City Council describe the proposal to remove Indians from Pageview as "a supreme example of man's inhumanity to man."

Not only have they passed a resolution to make representations to the Government to reverse the process and proclaim Pageview and other areas in Johannesburg as Indian areas, but their leader in the council, saying that "it is against our principles to remove this community who have vested interests, to the desert of Lenasia," has pledged his party to "continue to fight for their rights."

These statements are to be welcomed as an indication that public conscience in South Africa may not yet be dead.

How far these councillors and others will go to see justice done will be a test of their sincerity.

Figure 4.3   The media protests forced removals
Source: Sunday Post 9 June 1963

After the eviction of the traders all property in Pageview was expropriated by the incongruously titled 'Department of Community Development', and the Johannesburg City Council. Then the bulldozers arrived. Empty premises were razed. People who lived on the top floors of buildings would have the bottom floors gutted beneath them. Others had adjoining walls of their houses ripped out as destruction proceeded. Finally the roads were scarified to disable access. Only the mosques, granted immunity as religious buildings, and the homes of the most stubborn residents who refused to leave remained in the denuded landscape:

The demolishers went about their task with gusto: bulldozers roared in fury, drills screeched and bit into the concrete; labourers shouted amid falling walls and dust, wielding terrible sledgehammers; trucks roared. When at the

end of the day, the last truckload of rubble was being carried away, a purple reflection flared in Khalid's vision. "Look! Look!" he said to his wife, taking her hand, "The purple lotus!" For an instant the setting sun seemed to concentrate all its fire into the stained glass bloom, infusing it with gemlike splendour. The truck turned and was gone and for a while darkness held Khalid's eyes. His wife felt his hand tremble and heard a soft cry of anguish. For the first time she realised her husbands stoic spirit was not impregnable. For Khalid, the shattered glass lotus had become in that instant emblematically related to a flaw within man.
(Essop, 1989: 'Jericho Again ... And they utterly destroyed all that was in the city. Joshua 6:21') [stained glass was a proud adornment of homes in Fietas; the purple lotus is richly symbolic of residents' attachment to the area]

Almost 90 per cent per cent of Pageview was destroyed.

Deepening the divide

From 1969 onwards various plans for the renewal of Pageview were tabled. Not until the early 1980s however did construction begin on infill housing and modifications to the road grid, only to be halted by court order two years into rebuilding as displaced Pageview landowners challenged the redevelopment rights of both State and City. This legal battle has now intensified with promulgation of the Land Restitution Act 1995 by the new, democratically elected Government of National Unity. This Act has as its explicit intention restitution of land rights to those affected by racist legislation, and its development into policy is being keenly observed by the past landowners.

In the interim large tracts of land remain undeveloped but for a steadily consolidating population of squatters, vigorously assertive of their own land rights, and deepening drifts of litter and weeds. Many of the surviving historic cottages show signs of decay and degradation, the result of insecure residents reluctant to invest in their maintenance and upkeep. In contrast, several bold new homes stand testimony to a premature attempt at pacifying claims for the land of the late 1980s, now contested as illegitimate.

Voices cross the divide — again

While the bulldozers driven by apartheid eventually succeeded in destroying Pageview/Vrededorp, the history of the area still stands as a potent denial of the argument that apartheid was the consolidation of 'traditional' segregation of the races, as well as 'necessary' for avoiding friction between them. The voices which cross that divide are optimistic indicators for forthcoming urban redevelopment, and racial reconciliation. Supporting this optimism are the present residents of the still fragmented environment. They are again mixed, and of the opinion that:

We're going back to the racial tolerance of the 1940s (Molefe, 6 September 1995).

... it has to work (van Rensburg, 6 September 1995).

I do believe its going to happen, but it's not going to be very easy, it's going to take a while (Machava, 27 September 1995).

... but we will have a rainbow nation (Bassadien, 6 September 1995).

5   Conflict, empowerment and planning in post-apartheid South Africa

John Muller

Introduction

The discussion which follows is predicated upon the premise that where there is a substantial inequality in the distribution of resources in a society, that society is likely to be involved in conflict. The nature and extent of conflict has a congruency with the circumstances that have precipitated and sustained the condition of inequality, in which regard the volatile and violent climate that for decades spread through all areas and activities in South Africa can be attributed to the abnormal circumstances that attached to the apartheid doctrine. It is now common cause that doctrine skewed resource distribution on an unparalleled scale. The demise of apartheid in the early 1990s carried with it the hope and expectation that societal conflict would be eradicated, but the disparities created during some forty years of statutory discrimination have proved difficult to dislodge. Conflict, albeit of a genre less hostile than that pertaining previously, remains prevalent around the country. The past is not yet past.

A significant catalyst of the present discord is the enduring asymmetry in the living conditions between the affluent White and disadvantaged Black citizens of South African society:

> The most striking thing about South Africa ... is that the inequalities — in the distribution of power, wealth, income, education, and all the rest of it — have all coincided with each other. There has been a system of accumulated inequalities. The section of society which has been at the top in the power hierarchy has also had the best education, the most income, the most wealth and so on ... (Beteille, 1993 p. 86).

Consequent upon political change, this pattern of cumulative or concentrated inequality will be — and indeed already has partially been — superseded by a system of dispersed inequalities in which those holding political power will not necessarily be pre-eminent in economic or other terms. Democracy does not signify a society free of inequalities but it does suggest a society in which unequal conditions are dispersed rather than concentrated. Equality is taken, correctly in my view, as synonymous with the term 'social justice' and consistent with the principle of universal entitlement (Baker, 1990). Every citizen has a right to justice, to enjoy equal treatment and respect, and to experience life free from arbitrary power and oppression. That such birthrights were vitiated during the barren years of apartheid was voiced with quiet but telling indignation by Sir Colin Buchanan during his visit to South Africa in 1978. Referring to the deprivation of the black citizenry and 'the dignity of man,' he posited the proposition

> that no matter who he is or what may be his colour, he is educated and thus given the chance to develop himself, that he has the franchise and thus a say in the way he is governed, that he can say what he likes, and read what he likes, and go where he likes, and do what he likes, and deploy his talents as best he can and reap the rewards thereof, and marry as he prefers, and that he is neither harassed nor held in subjection with his life spread before him in subservient or menial roles doing the dirty work for others with no chance to escape, and that he can find a reasonable choice of places to live with enough space in conditions free from squalor, noise, pollution, danger and thuggery, and without having to face, every day of his life, glaring contrasts between the standards he has to endure and those which other people enjoy (Buchanan, 1978, p. 9).

These fundamental rights were denied the Black citizens of South Africa when the white supremacist system held sway.

It can now be said that the afflictions set out by Buchanan have, with the advent of democracy, been removed — with the inescapable exception of the last; the 'glaring contrast between the standards he has to endure and those which other people enjoy'. The existential gap separating the haves and the have-nots remains.

Disparities

A report produced in 1995 presents a stark picture of the inequalities that continue to plague the nation. The Human Sciences Research Council reported that 45.7 per cent of the country's population (over 18 million people) lived in poverty — and that 57 per cent of Black citizens were thus categorised, as opposed to the two per cent figure pertaining to Whites. About 13 million rural people are subsisting on the breadline, of which 35,000 are White. Seventy-five per cent of the poverty burden is thus borne by people living in the homeland areas created by the apartheid government. (Whiteford et al., 1995). While the World Bank classifies South Africa, as a 'middle income' country, it is among the 'world's most unequal nations' with regard to income distribution. Blacks earn a per capita disposable income only 13 per cent of that earned by whites.

The disparity in the circumstances of the rich and poor is perhaps most tangible in the field of housing. While almost all Whites live in houses or apartments, 15 per cent of Blacks live in shacks, 14 per cent in huts, 17 per cent in outbuildings in residential areas and 7 per cent in hostels. Although some 45 per cent of Blacks reside in houses, the size and standard of the housing is markedly inferior to that occupied by Whites. Statistics pertaining to public utility services are also revealing: just 34 per cent of Black persons have access to flush toilets while 16 per cent have no ablution facilities. Although South Africa produces 50 per cent of Africa's electricity, approximately one third of the country's population has electricity — 80 per cent of households in the former homelands having no electrical service at all.

Pressure for housing is most keenly felt in the country's larger cities. South Africa's functional urbanisation level, which includes informal urbanisation, is estimated at 65 per cent (Development Bank, 1994) — this in comparison with an urbanisation figure of 27 per cent on the African continent, and the world average of 41 per cent. Some 53 per cent of the Republic's urban population resides in cities of more than 500,000 persons. Perhaps the most significant statistic is that relating to informal settlement: of the 24 million living in urban areas today, at least 7 million are squatters. The shortfall in urban formal housing which was estimated at 850,000 units in 1990 and was probably of the order of one and a half million by 1995, adds impetus to the cycle of squatting which extends sporadically across the urban fringe and the open spaces and backyards of the townships. The shacks occupied by the huge disadvantaged Black sector of South African society, stand in sharp contrast to the substantial homes of the White suburbanites, and starkly illustrate the heritage of an uneven distribution of resources.

Examples

Alexandra, a residential township almost exactly one square mile in extent, was proclaimed on rural land north of the mining town of Johannesburg in 1905. The timing of the proclamation was not propitious: in the depressed economic conditions that followed the Anglo-Boer war, the isolated township apparently had little conventional market appeal — in consequence of which it was placed on the market as a 'Native Township' in 1912. On this occasion the timing was favourable since the township's freehold title provisions anticipated by one year the 1913 Native Land Act that placed severe restrictions on land ownership by Blacks outside the reserves. The demand for the township's 2,500 stands was thus considerable and despite the lack of essential services such as water and electrical reticulation, sewerage facilities and refuse removal, the population of Alexandra reached 14,000 by 1920. With the unabated influx of Black citizens searching for residential land and accommodation, this figure grew to nearly 50,000 by the 1940s (Klein, 1991). The increase in the residential population was accompanied by spreading environmental deterioration and social distress.

At that time Alexandra was the home of the young Nelson Mandala, who has described life in Alexandra as exhilarating and precarious:

> Its atmosphere was alive, its spirit adventurous, its people resourceful. Although the township did boast some handsome buildings, it could be fairly described as a slum, living testimony to the neglect of the authorities. The roads were unpaved, dirty and filled with hungry, undernourished children scampering around half-naked. The air was thick with smoke from coal fires in tin braziers and stoves. A single tap served several houses. Pools of stinking, stagnant water full of maggots collected by the side of the road .... The township was desperately overcrowded; every square foot was occupied by either a ramshackle house or a tin-roofed shack .... [I]n spite of the hellish aspects of life in Alexandra, the township was also a kind of heaven.

As one of the few areas of the country where Africans could acquire freehold property and run their own affairs, where people did not have to kow-tow to the tyranny of white municipal authorities, Alexandra was an urban Promised Land ... (Mandela 1994, p. 71).

That promise was vitiated by the early 1960s, at which time the Nationalist government sought to suppress Black political activity and apply its apartheid ideology with greater rigour by, *inter alia*, transforming Alexandra into a hostel city for some 20,000 male and 5,000 female workers. This led to a mass expropriation of homes by the State and converted private home ownership to rental occupancy. Close to 50,000 residents were displaced and located in distant townships. This did not stem the tide of settlement in the beleaguered township which from the mid-1970s accommodated a growing influx of people — principally in backyard and open ground shacks.

The 1976 Soweto uprising ushered in a modified approach to the development of the township. With the introduction of 99 year leasehold provisions, the suspension of the hostel programme and the production of proposals to redevelop Alexandra as a 'model township' (involving the clearance of shanties), a facade of reform was erected by the government. Lack of authentic commitment by the State and of financial resources to meet the costs of redevelopment has however left Alexandra — which has now reached an estimated population of well over 300,000 — in a state of physical deprivation, environmental degradation and of social disorder and distress.

President Mandela's depiction of Alexandra as a kind of heaven has arguably, and by most conventional measures, greater applicability to the township's affluent neighbour Sandton. Characterised as 'Arcadia' (Bristow, 1994, p. 263), Sandton must in economic and environmental terms rank as one of the most congenial urban centres in the Republic. It was proclaimed as an independent municipality only in 1969 and has since then functioned largely as a dormitory town to Johannesburg although substantial retail, office and to a lesser extent industrial, development is pushing the town toward satellite status. In the years immediately following establishment, the major concern of the new town was the consolidation and conservation of the its natural environment — 'the preservation of the natural beauty of the area' (Carruthers, 1994, p. 66). Enthusiasm for the semi-rural lifestyle declined as the dictates of rates-producing commercial development spawned large shopping centres, office park complexes and higher density townhouse precincts. In less than 20 years, Sandton attracted 47 of the top 300 companies in the country to its sylvan setting (Carruthers, 1994) and its population grew by some 100,000 persons.

Today the gently rolling hills of Sandton provide an undulating carpet of green on which substantial houses on large plots and upmarket townhouse developments sit comfortably. The town covers an area of some 14,200 hectares accommodating a population of 172,000 — this in comparison to Alexandra's figures of 350 hectares and over 300,000 persons. Sandton has a density of 120 persons per hectare; Alexandra has close to 1,000 persons per hectare.

There are, beyond the patent inequalities in the physical townscape of the adjoining settlements, other fundamental issues that separate the two. The first revolves about the matter — indeed the right — of choice. Caught in the web of history and poverty, it seems that the people of Alexandra are condemned to continue their lives in a state of privation and deprivation; to remain trapped in a condition of dependency; to be denied the opportunity of choice which is everywhere available to their privileged neighbours in Sandton. Secondly, entrenchment of the unequal equation appears likely in the light of the self-protective stance of the privileged and powerful sector. While the have-nots are seeking to acquire at least a modicum of the comforts enjoyed by the more affluent, the haves are seemingly intent upon retaining that which they have (in the face of what they discern as a threat and challenge from the deprived). And, it is from the fiction of such issues as choice and challenge that conflict is ignited.

The potential for conflict is manifest most clearly in the interface between black informal settlements and white residential areas; between squatters and suburbanites. From among the cases of inter-community conflict that are currently testing the will of the new democracy, is that of the Zevenfontein informal settlement — the second case study. In late 1991, a group of about 50 families settled on a portion of a farm in the Zevenfontein area on the rural-urban line north of Johannesburg. The community expanded rapidly as growing numbers of homeless families attached themselves to the original group. The presence of squatters in the area engendered concern among homeowners in the vicinity and, as a climate of hostility developed, Zevenfontein became a *cause célèbre* and a testcase.

The entry of the provincial authorities into the altercation fanned the fire of conflict. Their intention to resettle the community in close proximity to the Bloubosrand residential area evoked an aggressive response from the White ratepayers of Bloubosrand, whose protestations were supported by at least eight other groups representing White residents in the area. Their protests took the form of physical confrontation, street blockades, threats of violence and the like. Objections to a subsequent decision to resettle the Zevenfontein community (now numbering some 1,000 families) in the Diepsloot area ended up in the country's Appeal Court — which dismissed an appeal against an earlier court decision that had ruled in favour of resettlement. The community has not yet [1995] moved, the situation remains unresolved and the hapless body of squatters continue to subsist in a state of uncertainty and impotence, of intimidation and imposition. In exposing such issues as homelessness and landlessness, poverty and plenitude, vested interests and racial intolerance, social tension and inter-community conflict, Zevenfontein has cast up questions and problems that are symptomatic of the South African situation and which will test the Republic's — and indeed the planning system's — capacity to respond creatively to the challenges of reconstruction and development now facing the country (Muller, 1994).

Empowerment

The plight of the poor is, possibly for the first time in the history of modern South Africa, being accorded the attention to which it is entitled. The point of convergence of the offensive on poverty is the present government's Reconstruction and Development Programme (RDP). This programme identifies a set of principles and key projects, and includes the following statements that, in my opinion, epitomise the spirit and ethos of the RDP:

the people of South Africa must together shape their own future.
Development is ... about active involvement and growing empowerment

the RDP requires fundamental changes in the way that policy is made and
programmes are implemented. Above all, the people affected must participate
in decision-making

The central objective of our RDP is to improve the quality of life for all South
Africans, and in particular the most poor and marginalised sections of our
community. This objective should be realised through processes of
empowerment which gives the poor control over their lives ...

The RDP reflects a commitment to grassroots, bottom-up development which
is owned and driven by communities ...

Legislation must be rapidly developed to address issues such as tenants'
rights, squatters' rights, the rights of people living in informal settlements ...
land restoration, community participation in planning and development, and
anti-discrimination protection.

RDP is a people-driven programme.

(African National Congress, 1994, pp. 5, 7, 15, 24, 147)

The people-centred, bottom-up, participatory and empowering prerequisites of
the RDP dictate that the professions that are tied to processes of social and
physical redevelopment, notably that of town and regional planning, now adopt
procedures reflective of the quality of humanism that underpins the new national
psyche.
    The need for empowerment and capacity building pertains of course to the
nation's underprivileged and disadvantaged communities — such as those
attached to Alexandra and Zevenfontein. These are the communities that were
calculatedly excluded, disempowered, over the years by State policy and thus by
planning. The planning methodologies of the apartheid era were, in form and
purpose, autocratic and authoritarian. The planning paradigm of the time was of
the rational-comprehensive genre (Muller, 1992) although the exclusionary
nature of apartheid planning rules out claims to rationality. Certainly, the
planning approach was projected as scientifically objective, apolitical, efficient
and centralised — and was in fact the epitome of the top-down model and
mentality. Notions of any involvement of affected black citizens in the planning
process were perceived as inimical to the dominatory ideology of the ruling
regime. The practice of imposition from above has proved difficult to break, as
the Zevenfontein experience illustrates. Here, while the provincial authorities
purported to adopt a participatory approach, the actual procedures were
exclusionary and authoritarian — and did nought to advance the cause of the
disempowered community. Exclusion from decision-making processes is
however no longer acceptable to such communities, the stance of whom is
summarised in a statement of the National Civic Organisation:

The single biggest complaint — greater even than the vociferous objection to getting a toilet and not a house — was about the lack of consultation and participation .... This is not just political rhetoric as some would assume. It is a genuine desire on the part of community organisations to be taken seriously and be given due responsibility for implementation (South Africa National Civic Organisation, 1994, p. 11).

The call for participation is entirely consistent with the ethos of the new South Africa since the primary principle attaching to the proposition of community involvement in decision-making processes is that such involvement is tied to the idea, the ideal, of democracy.

Planning

The democratic imperative requires, as Friedmann has suggested 'substantial departures from traditional planning practice, which is typically imposed from above rather than generated from within the communities of the disempowered themselves' (Friedmann,1992, p. 170). It necessitates, in Healey's view, not that type of planning that 'could be associated with the dominatory power of systematic reason pursued through State bureaucracies' but rather a conception of planning as 'a communicative enterprise (which) holds most promise for a democratic form of planning in the contemporary context' (Healey 1992, pp. 144-5). Drawing on Habermas, Healey holds that 'whereas contemporary social relations reveal deep cleavages of class, race, gender and culture, which can only be resolved through power struggle between conflicting forces', the communicative participatory approach will facilitate debate leading to consensus, choice and action. Communicative reasoning requires acceptance of differences not only in economic and social terms but, importantly, in systems of meaning, in interpretation. Thinking of this sort moves planning away from the rational paradigm — away from naturalist methodologies — and towards anti-naturalist models constructed on the philosophical base of critical theory or phenomenology. Both models are emancipatory in nature, but the latter offers practical opportunities for community input into the planning process — through which community empowerment can be facilitated. It is, in the ultimate analysis, essentially in the empowerment of the deprived that the inequalities will be removed.
A central element in phenomenology — as formulated by the philosophy's father figure Edmund Husserl — is that of human consciousness: the understanding of an individual in the terms of his/her interpretations of reality (Mouton, 1989). It is the interpretation of the people, not of the politician, planner or the powerful, that is crucial since that interpretation is grounded in the values, beliefs and meanings held by them. Husserl, suggests that 'any object of my consciousness, a house, a pleasure, or another person, is something meant, constructed, constituted, that is intended by me' (Stumpf, 1983, p. 456).The meaning that members of a squatter community place upon the phenomenon 'house' is derived from their *lebenswelt* — from their store of experience — which is the source from which their beliefs, values, perceptions and interpretations flow. The free expression of a community's experiential value-based perception is critical if participation in the planning process, leading to

empowerment, is to be achieved. The right to consider options, to express views, to make decisions, is crucial to capacity enhancement. Now, planning does not in itself have the capability to empower communities, but it does have the potential to enable empowerment to be pursued and realised. The potential for enablement resides within the processes, the procedures, the methodologies, devised and employed by planners. Experience shows that the convention of tacking participatory segments onto the rational model does little to liberate the disadvantaged, so that the need is to allow the prerequisites and parameters of authentic capacitating participation to give form to the planning process. A community decision-making model derived from phenomenological precepts should have community enablement potential (Muller, 1994).

Comment

A process providing for decision-making by hitherto powerless citizens must, by engendering in them a realisation of their capacity to build their own future as they perceive it, be enabling in purpose. This will not automatically remove the inequalities particular to the current South African situation and characteristic of a condition of societal conflict, but it will promote fair and equal access to decision-making which will, in turn, advance the cause of community self-development and eventually redress the asymmetry in resource distribution. Empowerment is, in the end, possible only in conditions of freedom and it is not possible to learn about freedom without experiencing it. When planning promotes just participatory procedures which provide rich choices for the people, the spirit of true freedom can be experienced.

Part Three
Other African and Latin American experiences

6 Ethnic communities, access to housing and exclusion: the case of the Haitian immigrants of French Guyana

Eric Gallibour

'Housing and Exclusion' are two terms the definition of which seems obvious today. However, what *common sense* considers excluded most often represents individuals — rather than social groups — not included within society or kept apart from collective or individual benefits produced by the system. Amongst the many reasons put forward to try to explain the exclusion processes are those which no longer hesitate to make the individual responsible for himself and even for his socio-ethnic origin. Social constraints then become 'cognitive' problems and social problems of individual behaviour systems arise from lack of socio-cultural adaptation. Then we need to find ethno-psychological explanations which would make it possible in time to better socialise the individual in order to adapt him to his new social space, the town or city. Therefore the town again becomes — or does not cease to become — a privileged space of delimitation and determinism of the social order which produces socio-ethnic stigmas (Economie et Humanisme, 1993). Media discussions on the exclusion and housing of those least favoured, tend in the vagueness of ethnic social and political representations to relate the image of *the other* to his living conditions. The deviant, the delinquent, the immigrant or the unemployed become excluded and the spaces where they live are 'exclusion zones' (Ballain et Benguigui, 1995).

Today, planning and management of urban areas and outlying urban spaces — made up mainly of composite and heterogenic social and ethnic milieux — confront the various agents in town planning with plural ethnic and poly-migratory spaces where the populations seem not to able to escape from the production and/or reproduction of the process of discrimination and exclusion in terms of living conditions (Behar, 1991). The French political system up to now has practised the rejection of ethnic identities considered as incompatible with the principles of the Republic. In fact, practical approaches to the ethnic question in the social residential situation are taken in terms of inter-cultural relations rather than in terms of socio-ethnic relations. Moreover, community membership and ethnic relations are irredeemably sliding towards an ideological and political debate. The acknowledgement of the existence and (re)production of practices of social and ethnic discrimination in the field of political, administrative and institutional management of the living conditions of immigrants in France, hence calls into question the relevance of a model and its reproduction on the overseas 'French' territories (D.O.M.[1]).

Living conditions and ethnicity in French Guyana

Our socio-anthropological approach to ethnicity in the town or city calls into question at the same time the agents, sites and activities revealing the ethnic dimensions of the question of accommodation in the French overseas territories. The research which we have carried out in French Guyana analyses the means of access and use of social housing by Haitian immigrants. It studies at the same time adaptation of the tools and procedures transposed by the public authorities within the framework of application of a housing policy — that of the town or city — within the *polyethnic model* of Guyanese society and the type of resources mobilised by Haitian residents within the field of cohabitation and/or inter-ethnic coexistence, which is at the core of participation by citizens (Gallibour, 1995).

We take up the question of ethnicity — which can be understood in the literal sense of the term, ethnicity in the city — in order to translate the symptomatic relationship of interdependence which this supports in the practices and regulations of urban planning and local development with the ideas of segregation and social mixing, inter-culturality and territoriality. The social differentiation of towns and cities consists today of superimposition of territories where enclosure within the residential space leads to captive populations. Therefore, mobility and segregation are essentially interlinked (Roncayolo, 1994). Following the lines marked out by Yves Grafmeyer, one may wonder about the various hypotheses which underlie the idea of segregation, the ideological functions it fulfils and the socio-cultural evolutions which change usage and circulation in the urban field (Grafmeyer, 1994). The logic of the ghetto — considered as the concentration of population within circumscribed spaces — arising from a phenomenon of exclusion, may thus express forms of accumulation as proofs of integration and social inclusion (Viellard-Baron, 1991). At the core of residence — between *inter-generational migration*, residential mobility and daily movements — methods of territorialisation are being constructed within an urban space produced by and producing mobility, segregation and social mixing which condition a differentiated and complex relationship to the town (Affandi-Joseph et Gallibour, 1992).

Polyethnicity and town planning in French Guyana

Guyana, which is 8,000 kilometres away from France, covers over 90,000 km^2 (90 per cent of which is covered by Amazon forest) and has 140,000 inhabitants.[2] This French overseas department has 21 districts and one capital city, Cayenne. The population is concentrated in towns and seaside accumulations situated around Cayenne, Kourou and the river St. Laurent du Maroni (Mouren-Lascaux, 1990). The artificial local means of production, dependant on the mother country, regularly undergoes the ups and downs of a restricted economic market receiving infusions where the unemployment rate represents up to twice that of the mother country. The distinctive characteristic of the Guyanese urban microcosm lies in the fact that the stakes relating to migratory practices — many residents in abnormal positions taking part in local activities — and to mobility of populations have a direct share in the orientation of local policies in connection with living conditions and population (Georgeon, 1985). The socio-residential problems of mobility, cohabitation and coexistence in the polyethnic towns of Guyana call into question both the social consensus and the use by the public authorities of tools appropriate to implement education for socio-urban integration (Ripert, 1990). The Guyanese mosaic known as 'creole and polyethnic', made up of both communities and ethnic minorities, has been represented exclusively by the local political elite of 'Guyanese creoles' since departmentalisation.[3]

In terms of French overseas departments, Guyana also has the highest percentage of rented accommodation and the highest percentage of household budgets devoted to housing. If you account for the number of marginal households where the head of the household is out of work, Guyana is also out in front (La Lettre de l'IDEF, 1993). Although the problems of insanitary conditions and shanty towns are concentrated in the town of Cayenne, they affect more than 15 per cent of the stock of accommodation (D.D.E.-Guyane, 1990; D.S.U., 1994). In spite of enquiries carried out by the various State departments, there is no exact knowledge of the level of occupation of unhealthy accommodation on the island of Cayenne. There is no permanent organisation for research into housing in Guyana and very few districts are structured homogeneously either on the ethnic or on the spatial level. The mobility of the residents and the sites that are classed as unsanitary in *diffuse or grouped housing* accentuates the special characteristics and complexity of the Cayenne urban phenomenon. An areolar representation — the vision of a space made up of contiguous but distinct areas (or of polarity centre/suburb) — is replaced by a space traversed by concrete and abstract networks structured so as to move around axes and connection points, spaces made up of entangled discontinuous zones, bordered by imprecise and vague boundaries (De Ruddler, 1990; 1991). The conjunction of dwellings around a courtyard and of apartments on the street distorts a social geography based on the study of addresses, since segregation occurs even within the accommodation itself while additionally the indicators of spatialisation of residents are almost obsolete in a context of mobility. So there is the problem with the socio-spatial construction of social groups, of over-representation of segregation in relation to one social group or one ethnic group — in this case the Haitians.

The anti-diagnosis of town and housing policies in French Guyana

In France, the legal and legislative mechanisms within the fields of town planning and housing policy have been constructed on an ambiguous principle. The laws deal with the problem not from the viewpoint of the housing market but rather from the point of view of its method of occupation characterised by an increasingly strong socio-ethnic concentration. The notion of ethnic concentration however is not based on reliable national statistical indicators. In a commune therefore 25 per cent of the inhabitants may be immigrants but at the same time 60 per cent of immigrants are concentrated in social housing. This leads us directly back to the ideologies on which urban policies in the planning and management of the polyethnic space are based.

Within the framework of housing policy and town planning, a distinction between planning tools (Departmental Plan for the most deprived and the Town Contract) and management tools (District Social Development, Urban Social Development and Subsidised social housing) must be made. These jointly contribute to the Regeneration of Unfit Dwellings. Access to accommodation for the most deprived goes back, in the French overseas departments, as in France, to the problem of the social housing defined 'for' immigrants and hence to the orientation of public policies, and to the production of specific standards and regulations offered to a 'foreign' population. Owing to the make-up of Guyanese society, it is generally agreed that to deal with living conditions is to take into account immigration and the specific nature of the socio-economic conditions of local development. For social housing in Guyana, the public authorities have opted initially to create a Social Housing product which was intended to rehouse immigrants on the basis of self-build, having as an objective to lower construction costs and to make the inhabitants responsible for their building and their living environment. This ideology of building evolved at the same time as procedures linked to urban management developed, and as the geo-socio-professional origin and initial training of representatives of public authorities in the field of urban planning were themselves modified. In the 1950s and 1960s, agents of the State operating in the French overseas territories acquired their experience in the neo-colonial area of Third World countries and Africa. During the 1970s and 1980s, however, they originated directly from the French overseas territories and, from the beginning of the 90s, they have been arriving directly from the mother country to carry out their professional activities. Previously, the strategies were to give land or to build and then to settle administrative problems. Today, in the desire to move on from a social and cultural practice specific to the settlement to the application of French and subsequently European administrative standards, the decision-makers are coming up against resistance. The desire to install a socio-ethnic mix guarantees social integration and harmony — by attempting to correct the gaps left by the social housing 'tool' by a better balance of population in social housing — but it ends up, through a policy of quotas favouring the most deprived, in an ethnicisation of procedures. In Guyana, the social housing crisis has become one of ethnic housing.

French Urban Policy in Guyana and in the French overseas territories, developed by the public authorities as a means of democratic participation in urban development, favours the creation of numerous local associations. But, in applying rules, it is not so much the level of participation of inhabitants that poses a problem, but rather the level of autonomy and the means at their disposal to influence the decision-making processes. Priorities are often defined in advance or imposed by community, institutional or professional representatives in their role as experts. The municipal elected members, in order to obtain local control or a local establishment in the districts, very quickly exerted pressures in order to influence the associations' dynamics. The latter could therefore be the collective expression of inter-ethnic competition or of solidarity within the same residential area. But, the principle of representing the population of a district in the District Social Development measure sometimes led to real power conflicts related to the type of ethnic composition of the district itself (pronounced ethnic mix or pronounced mono-ethnicity), to its kind of housing in terms of differentiations of social and spatial order (crowding or distance between places of accommodation) or sanitary order (generalised or partial insalubrity of the site, running water, electricity). In selling its measures to local collectives, the State aims successively to harmonise, rationalise, energise, then provide a framework for and control local initiatives in urban areas in Guyana. It has not been possible to apply these policies in terms of access to accommodation for the most deprived. The financial crisis of the local collectives played a part, but the main reason seems to be the absolute obstinate determination of the elected members to consider access to social housing for immigrants as a 'political hobby horse'. This bottleneck in procedures is the consequence of something arbitrary: the application to the local context of measures which should theoretically involve all those excluded from housing, but which in the event are mainly directed towards foreign inhabitants, and, what is more, in an abnormal situation — as is the case with the Haitians. Guyanese urban management, therefore, in spite of its special features, remains dependent on models and standards arising from the mother country guideline.

Haitian immigrants and the Guyanese town

Haitian immigration, which began in the 1960s-1970s, was at the start essentially a male phenomenon. Subsequently, its feminisation and rejuvenation modified the composition of the local population — with a considerable presence of couples — and increased its visibility with the increase in births in the region. It has not so far been possible objectively to evaluate the number of Haitian residents in Guyana.[4] Statistics do not provide distributions or time periods, or local dynamics. The reliability of the indicators varies according to the 'ethno-geographic' configuration of areas where censuses have been carried out (Domenach et Picouet, 1988). The margin of statistical uncertainty leaves the field open to absurd social representations which feed xenophobic political debates. The theory — spread by Guyanese political representatives in the 1980s — of 'ethnocide by replacement' of Guyanese creoles by Haitians, is a good example of this (Jolivet, 1986).

Haitian migrants residing in Guyana are mainly from the agricultural departments of Southern Haiti and a minority are from the capital, Port-au-Prince. Illiterate and unqualified, their conditions of life and work are characterised by an overall precarious situation. The *typical* Haitian in Guyana is an 'odd-job man' (*Jobeur*[5]), agricultural labourer or forester in the areas of the interior or a domestic, building worker or gardener in urban areas. He dwells in a run-down urban area situated on the island of Cayenne (the town and its built-up area), or St Laurent du Maroni and Kourou. Very few Haitians inhabit council flats in Cayenne. On the other hand, they sub-let their own plots. The current practice of landlords is to construct dwellings at the bottom of their garden which they sub-let, unless they authorise the migrant to built the accommodation himself — often for his family — against payment of rent. This widespread type of accommodation is found also in residential suburbs or communes. The Haitian 'gardener or odd-job man' is then accommodated in a shed belonging to his landlord and boss.

The dynamics of ethnicity and mix in housing

The territorialisation on the same geographical unit of migrants of multiple ethnic origins implies practices of avoidance, conflict or mutual adjustments. However, as the place of residence is always put together on the basis of opposition towards the outside, the ethnic variable itself generates within inter- and intra- community social relations an ideology of exclusion appropriate to 'ethnic honour' (Weber, 1991). The dynamics of ethnicity in the urban environment in Guyana involve inter-ethnic categorisation where the resultant stigmas and stereotypes of communities arises from the logic of promiscuity. Within the Guyanese territorial microcosm, relations between the residents themselves are in keeping with socio-ethnic space since they are all involved in situations of urban interactions in daily life. The appropriation of towns by migration and the evolution of spatial and social compositions and re-compositions then form invisible and multiple spaces of inter-ethnic social interaction. For Haitian migrants, the town is first of all considered as a space of polymorphic mobility which encourages development and reproduction of spatial behaviours integrated into culturally implied forms of social interaction. To develop his local activities, the Haitian migrant uses the extended family network as the basis for economic strategy. A Haitian shopkeeper provides herself with consumer products in the places where a member of her extended family resides. From Surinam, to Miami, from Haiti to the mother country, from the West Indies to Canada, the family network is involved directly in an international economic circuit. The house — alternatively food business, workshop for making and/or selling clothes — can serve as a warehouse or point of sale.

At the same time, the tenant of rundown sites, who has become the occupant of social housing, often withdraws from his culture and family cell. However, if the accommodation is linked to a feeling of possession of private property, then the district becomes the stake and the expression of specific ethnic characteristics, the person who accedes to it tends to maintain his old urban practices. So we have been able to show that not only new residents — owners or tenants — continue to maintain relations with the population of the shanty town where they used to live, but that the links woven between the shanty town and the new residential district of nationals from the Haitian community were involved in networks which are at the same time emotional (familial, friendly, conjugal or sexual), economic (maintenance or economic exploitation taking the form of sub-letting by the resident of his former dilapidated accommodation), religious (maintaining the initial frequenting of the place of worship with co-religionists) and sanitary (general practitioners and alternative medicine).

The dynamics of ethnic mixing in new districts can have conflicting effects and are not in themselves a guarantee of natural solidarity. On the other hand, we have been able to observe that ethnic groupings were much stronger than neighbourhood forms of social interaction. Conversely, the method of religious congregation can be a way of transcending ethnic divides. Therefore, you have to be wary of believing that if the shanty town favours ethnic groupings on the basis of the socio-spatial segregation which it implies, access to social housing in a residential district — a new space bounded no longer by the inhabitant but by standards which are foreign to him — engenders of necessity an ethnic accumulation. There is no linearity or homogeneity in the phenomenon as urban planners might have thought (Letchimy, 1992). On the other hand, there are a number of correlations between the two methods of living and socialising in accommodation which undergoes an ethno-spatial socialisation since from the start — for Haitians — it is based on a reference to community identity, which leads to urban practices which can come into conflict with the standards imposed by procedures.

Mobility, taken in the sense of polymorphic trajectories for the citizen from both the symbolic and practical points of view, becomes the main characteristic of access to accommodation within a segregated migratory space. The practice of segregation in space sends the Haitian resident back to his own strategy of segmentation and ethnic grouping where spatial and social mobility should serve to avoid the ethno-spatial division of the shanty town. It seems that socio-ethnic segregation is a feature of the *Guyanese way of life*. The various ways of living which are related to sites of coexistence and/or to the social mix only mask the social hallmarks of the ethnic differences which form the inegalitarian foundations of Guyanese society.

The political and ethnic stakes in procedures for Haitians to gain access to social housing

For Haitians, the possibility of benefiting from access to social housing — as owners or tenants — emerged during the period 1985-1988. Arising from the Redevelopment of Unfit Dwelling procedures, three sites: *Fourgassié, Matoury* and *Rémire-Montjoly*, have a total of 350 social housing units in three municipalities on the outskirts of Cayenne. In spite of the low number of units of accommodation proposed and the low proportion of Haitian residents gaining access to this type of residence, access of Haitians to social housing has rapidly become a political stake in Guyana. Procedures were subjected to economic and political bargaining between the operators and the decision-makers — the local elected members and representatives of the State — leading at the same time to delays and modifications in the type and number of units of accommodation initially provided. Access to ownership changed to renting. The procedure in terms of social housing was envisaged at the beginning by the elected members as an electoral trump card, as it involved re-housing populations at the lowest cost on a space under development. Subsequently, the image of a municipality favouring a project for pluri-ethnic cohabitation and social desegregation was very soon replaced by that of a common reception land for *Haitian* owner immigrants 'to the detriment' of the 'Guyanese' electors. For the State, access to social housing was an urgently required response to a policy for the redevelopment of unfit dwellings: evacuation of zones where building could take place or the movement of population in order to install public infrastructure. The movement of population was not envisaged by the public authorities as an anti-segregation procedure intended to disseminate residents into a new space. It was rather a matter of confining a population within a precise spot in order to facilitate its control, for purely practical reasons. Pluri-ethnic grouping was considered as a guarantee of good operation and of local integration. Hence the procedure became a real political stake — 'communal populating' — where the segregationist strategies fed by socio-ethnic representations led to ethnicisation of allocation procedures in terms of social housing, sometimes generating unforeseen effects. So at *Matoury*, where, owing to the composition of incoming Haitian families — essentially made up of women with children and only representing 40 per cent of residents — the mixed couple became a living rule.

These operations showed that State agents use in their decisions social perceptions and ideological judgements on ethno-spatial compositions observed or desired. They take part in maintaining, spreading and (re)producing conflicting social representations emanating from various social agents such as politicians. Certain urban planners go so far as to impute specific predispositions to ethnic differences. Inversely, the collective organisation capacity of populations in situations of exclusion is considered as 'natural', expressed by an organic type of solidarity. In access to ownership, participation in construction of accommodation is a factor of inclusion and socialisation which encourages the emergence of civic responsibilities! It is the fact of resuming traditional practices of constructing accommodation, which will in theory drive a positive dynamic policy for those who gain access to housing. The existence of such beliefs shared by the decision-makers and operators based on the idea of social engineering, presupposing a naturally solidaristic and participative character for certain ethnic groups amongst the most deprived, hides the fact that precariousness constitutes at the same time the way of life and the basis of managing the social time where access to housing is not an end in itself.

Notes

1   D.O.M.: Département français d'Outre-Mer.
2   Estimate by INSEE following the 1990 census.
3   Ethnic communities: 'Créoles Guyanais', 'Métropolitains', 'Noirs Marrons' (Boni, Djuka, Saramaka, Paramaka), 'Amérindiens', 'Brésiliens', 'Surinamiens', 'Haïtiens', 'Antillais', 'Chinois', 'Hmongs'. Ethnic minorities: citizens of the European Community, 'Syro-Libanais', 'Javanais', 'Indiens', 'Africains' and 'Latino-Américains' (Chérubini, 1988).
4   The 1990 census enumerated almost 9,000 Haitians, while the figure put forward in 1985 by the anthropologist Bernard Chérubini is similar to that given by official sources ten years later in 1995 — that being between 15,000 and 20,000 individuals, of whom 60 per cent were 'undocumented'.
5   *Jobeur*: name given to unqualified workers 'moonlighting' in the private sector.

7   Jwaneng: a case study of socio-economic and ethnic integrated town planning

Sergio-Albio González

Introduction

Design of new towns and cities in Africa is basically a result of colonialism and/or industrial development. Major political statements such as Dodoma, Abuja and Lilongwe should not overshadow another reality of African urbanisation, the existence of numerous small and medium sized towns created as result of political, and economic interests or for administrative reasons.

Botswana was considered until independence to be among the least industrially developed countries in the world, and among the 20 poorest, conditions that changed gradually in a remarkable way after the first Tswana elected government came to power in 1966. By independence, Botswana's exports were almost completely (97 per cent) dependent on the cattle industry.

The discovery of copper and nickel ore deposits in Selebi-Pikwe and, later, diamonds in Orapa and Jwaneng, prompted a series of major political decisions and heavy economic investments in the mining sector, which had at the same time a tremendous impact on the country's major infrastructure, facilitating urbanisation at national level.

Botswana has shown an amazing pace of development, building a new town every four years since independence, starting with Gaborone in 1966, Selebi-Pikwe in 1970, Orapa in 1974 and Jwaneng in 1978. The small town of Sua followed 10 years later.

Botswana new towns

Gaborone

For seventy years prior to independence, the Bechuanaland Protectorate constituted a unique case in political geography with its capital or administrative centre, situated some 27 km outside the country's southern border, in Mafeking (Mafikeng, in South Africa's North West province).

The creation of Gaborone was the result of the country's development towards political independence, a driving factor fuelled by South Africa's exclusion from the Commonwealth.

The location of the new capital was selected from among nine possible sites, including the two existing urban settlements, Lobatse and Francistown. The choice went to the small village of Gaborone, a site with significant advantages over the other alternatives:

- it was located within Crownland and had already several administrative offices;
- it was not difficult to reach by six of the eight major ethnic groups;
- foremost, it had a reliable water source in the Notwane River.

Other important factors were the proximity to the Pretoria-Witwatersrand region and the relative density of Gaborone's sub-region: 35 per cent of the total population of the country lived within a 90 km. radius.

Gaborone was built with the assistance of the British Ministry of Overseas Development and designed by British consultants. Botswana's traditional settlements vary in size, from scattered homesteads to villages of significant development, unique in the southern African context. Major villages — rather they should be called rural towns — such as Molepolole, Kanye, Mahalapye and Serowe reach populations of 20-30,000 inhabitants. The settlement pattern results primarily from social interaction and secondly from livelihood premises, income, etc. The fact that land is communal and has been traditionally allocated by the chief, brought settlements a particular form of democratic land occupancy and way of life.

Gaborone was located east of the railway line and was designed on a butterfly-shaped pattern, with striking similarities to Brazil's new capital Brasilia. The urban structure concept was based on a central east-west axis along which the major facilities and features of the capital were located: to the west the Government Enclave contains the main Central Government facilities, ministries, and the National Assembly. The Central Business District (CBD) was located immediately east of the enclave, featuring a pedestrian precinct running along its central east-west axis. Other main facilities, the hospital, the university and the airport were situated further east.

The axial plan structure is reinforced by the development of residential wings north and south of the town's central spine. Supporting radial roads underline the concentric (and symmetrical pattern) of the urban tissue.

As noted above, Gaborone's prospects for growth at the time of independence were dubious. There were no clear, concrete indications for future improvements in the country's economic base. This factor limited the size of the town plan. The planners' prevailing idea was that the town would not grow significantly, limiting the conceived urban structure to accommodate only 20,000 inhabitants. The lack of flexibility in the plan structure and in provision for the town's economic growth potential was soon to be evident with Gaborone's pace of development. Nine years after its original design in 1962, the town had already exceeded the estimated target population.

It is, however, in the conceptual design of the residential areas at town level that the planners most clearly related back to traditional colonial thinking. The town was divided physically into two halves by the central spine, north of which the high income group was developed and with medium and low income located south of it. A north-south drive along the two major ring roads, Independence Avenue and North Ring Road, would demonstrate the gradual succession of income levels in housing areas, from high to medium to low to site and service to the squatter area of Naledi.

Gaborone continues growing with a population currently reaching 200,000 and development stretching far out towards the west across the railway line encompassing the village of Gabane, and east across the Notwane river, incorporating the village of Tlokweng.

Selebi-Phikwe

The discovery of large copper-nickel ore bodies in an area between Selebi and Phikwe south of the village of Mmadinare in eastern Botswana, resulted in a join venture between Bamangwato Concessions Ltd. and the Botswana Government to develop a mine. The recovery of the minerals required the development of a new town to accommodate the projected mine working population of 2,700, and a total of 13,000 in its final phase as far as the mine-related population is concerned. Population projections for new towns are difficult to forecast, specially when there are few statistics available, as was the case with Selebi-Phikwe. Time has shown in Botswana, that forecasts are normally overtaken by development. In Selebi-Phikwe new residential areas have been added to the original town plan and the town boundaries have been extended to encompass new areas including the squatter settlement of Botshabelo.

The original town plan for Selebi-Phikwe had to be designed in three months, a condition that possibly dictated the future shape of the settlement The scarce time for designing it dictated solutions based on conventional planning, in order to achieve quick implementation and economical results. This fact cannot, however, overshadow another circumstance that might have influenced even more the shape of the town — the same consultants that designed Gaborone were commissioned to plan Selebi-Phikwe.

There is a striking similarity between the two towns. The limited time available for designing Selebi-Phikwe may have been the underlying factor causing the planners to copy the basic plan layout of the Capital.

The exact orientation and form of both towns' road networks is not the only major common feature they have. Residential areas are, as is the case in the Gaborone Plan, divided into two halves by the Mall area. The low income housing for mine workers is located north of the east-west axis and closer to the mine and the low-lying and subsiding zone. Across the Mall and the major axial feeder roads, the medium and high income housing are situated, on higher ground. Major facilities such as the hospital, hotel, police station and town park, surround the Mall area, increasing the separation between the residential areas.

Orapa

After years of prospecting, kimberlites containing significant amounts of diamonds were found in the sandveld of central Botswana, far from any major settlement. The kimberlites' remote location and the tremendous mine potential required the construction of a new mining town. The Architecture Department of Anglo American Corporation was commissioned to design it and the plan was ready in 1974. Orapa is a small town with a built-up area covering no more than 100 ha. that has a special peculiarity — it is a 'closed' town i.e. visitors need to get an entry permit. The whole town including the mine, is screened by a fence, a measure necessary to increase security against illegal diamond buyers.

Orapa town plan has however other features that give it a different character. Designed by South Africans for South African management and technical personnel as well as for Batswana labour, the conceptual layout design reflects the values applied by Anglo American and De Beers in their mining communities.

Housing areas for the basically white personnel are located apart from the mine workers residential areas, being separated by open spaces and service facilities. The Government of Botswana, through the Department of Town and Regional Planning (DTRP) started the process for opening up Orapa, incorporating other facilities and making possible a transition to normal community life.

Jwaneng

In search of a model town

After prospecting for four years in Southern District, in 1973 De Beers Mining Company discovered the existence of several major kimberlites of sufficient size and quality to be exploited commercially. Soon it was realised that the pipes were of such significance that the mine would become one of the biggest of its kind in the world. The kimberlites were discovered in a remote area in the Kalahari sandveld 30 km. from the closest existing earth road linking Kanye with Ghanzi, and 80 km. north-west of Kanye. The development of such a mine in such a situation required major undertakings by the development company, Debswana, a joint venture by the Government of Botswana and De Beers, each holding a 50 per cent shares stake. The implementation of the project required provision of major infrastructure including upgrading and tarring of the Lobatse-Kanye road, a completely new road between Kanye and Jwaneng, new railway sidings in Lobatse, a new town, a small airport and the development of wellfields 40 km. north of the mine.

Jwaneng's study

Up to 1977, growth studies and structure plans for towns and major residential developments were commissioned from private consultants. This situation changed when the Department of Town and Regional Planning (DTRP) was entrusted with preparing the structure plan of Jwaneng in spite of De Beers' insistence that it should be done through the Anglo American Corporation (AAC) Architecture Department. The latter was to be consulted during the plan preparation process.

The AAC Architecture Department had a staff of about 80 and included planners, architects and engineers who were responsible for planning and building the international corporation's projects within South Africa and abroad.

The relationship between the planning team and leadership of DTRP and Anglo American representatives was not smooth all the time, the latter trying to impose views on how the new town should be designed. A draft plan presented by the AAC Architecture Department at a meeting with DTRP showed their traditional view on land use separation.

The proposed draft plan indicated the town's basic land use needs in the first stage of development, with the Company's residential areas far from other housing such as that for squatters and also from site and service provision locations. They were also separated by a central road along which the commercial centre, hotel, hospital, etc. were located. The AAC Architecture Department draft plan was discussed and shelved without further action.

The Jwaneng planning team started work by studying Selebi-Phikwe and Orapa through site visits and interviews with local authorities and mine management.

The methodology used for the preparation of the Jwaneng Structure Plan was fairly conventional, with a first stage of research, information and data collection followed by the formulation of the town's development policy where Jwaneng's possible roles in the region were studied and evaluated in relation to the National Development Plan IV as well as to other relevant district and regional plans. A third stage included data analysis and correlation with the development policies and strategies, conducive to a draft structure plan. The various stages of the plan preparation process were documented in Working Papers, widely distributed for information and comments. The twelve subjects studied in the Working Papers included the following: location study, existing conditions in Jwaneng, experience with Orapa and Selebi-Phikwe, mining activities, existing conditions in Jwaneng, regional development policy, regional policy for development of Jwaneng, design principles and urban standards, proposed development of Jwaneng, employment and population in Jwaneng and Jwaneng housing. This last paper outlined future housing needs including spatial requirements, standards and phasing.

Verbal presentations were made to various authorities at local, district and national level in addition to the circulation of Working Papers. Regular and frequent meetings with the AAC Architecture Department and with Botswana Government agencies provided good ground for constructive discussions on which the structure plan work developed confidently.

The Jwaneng Plan

The proposal for the location of the town was discussed by Department of Town and Regional Planning staff in a meeting where six possible alternatives were presented. They showed the interrelation of the mine, town, highway, airstrip and the existing croplands. The chosen alternative located the town in the tree belt area, offered unlimited expansion possibilities south and no interference with existing croplands. The location also offered the shortest possible access links between the highway and the mine and the town. Access to the airstrip was acceptable for the mine and the town. The decision on the location of the town was taken in January 1978. It was to be built five kilometres south of the mine lease area, at a maximum travelling time of 20 minutes and on an area that would not present conflict with future mining operations.

The following stage was to design the town itself, and for this purpose the Chief Designer prepared eight different urban model structures with the purposes of achieving an open discussion, facilitating liberty of thinking and a better understanding of the advantages and disadvantages of the preferred alternative. The selected plan structure is shown in Figure 7.1.

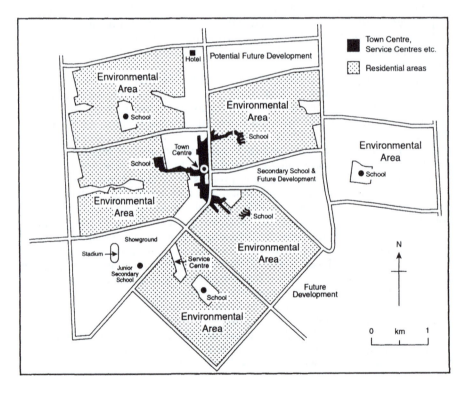

Figure 7.1   Jwaneng's Environmental Areas as planned

Design principles

The planning team established a series of design principles that were the starting point for creative work. They derive from national policies and objectives:

- Adaptability and flexibility for growth.
- Adaptation to the site and provision of a good living environment.
- Non-polarisation of socio-economic groups.
- Easy access to services for most of the people.
- Facilitation of Botswana's traditional cultural activities and social interaction.

Furthermore, the application of the above criteria should ensure a functional, efficient, rational and economical plan for Jwaneng.

As Figure 7.1 shows, the structure of the town plan derives from a modular concept: self-contained neighbourhood units denominated Environmental Areas (EA) in the Structure Plan. The Plan follows closely the design criteria described above, and through the creation of EAs, the elements of adaptability and flexibility for growth as well as provision of easy access for the majority of people, are pursued.

The Environmental Areas

The EA concept of self-containment facilitates the growth of the town without abnormal distances to basic social infrastructure and services. The area of each of these units is approximately 70 ha. (700 m. by 1,000 m.) accommodating a population of some 3,000 inhabitants, enough to sustain a 2-stream primary school. Other planned services in the EA include service centres and corner shops. The former provide space for public and private services, small scale manufacturing and informal activities, including a market place.

The service centres have not been developed to date (which explains the complaint of shortage of plots for churches). The Jwaneng Town Plan establishes, however, their functional significance:

these service centres are not located in the geographic centre of an area but rather in the population centre with good contact with the main centre and the main pedestrian network. The intention is to reinforce the function of the main centre and not to compete with it.

The buildings should be of modest standard to facilitate low rent, attracting the relocation of informal activities, normally carried out within residential plot boundaries.

In search of linkages with tradition

One of a planner's greatest challenges when designing a new town in a country with strong traditional life patterns and characteristic physical environment is to create a plan able to channel and enhance people's quality of life in their living environment as opposed to social alienation and a sense of non-belonging to the local community. To achieve this goal, the chosen size and zoning of the EAs play a crucial role.

The form of housing groupings: the cluster concept. A look at traditional villages, specially at the central areas of the major ones — Serowe, Kanye, Molepolole and Mahalapye — show in their oldest parts, particular spatial patterns deriving from traditional community life: clusters of 'plots' group around an open space, the *patlelo,* of special significance in village people's interaction.

The cluster-local open space concept, together with traffic separation criteria form the basic elements from which the EA layout derives. (see Figure 7.2). In traditional villages, plots cluster around *patlelos*, in numbers of approximately 40 households, a figure used as a reference for the design of housing clusters in Jwaneng.

The local open spaces created in the EA are surrounded by approximately 20 plots and were intended to be used for social interaction — meeting place and play ground for children, and for pedestrian and cycle movements, as is the case in traditional villages. The rear of the plots face the open space which conditioned gate locations and easy access from plot rears to the common open space. This experiment in urban planning thinking was new in Botswana and could in case of controversy and opposition be defended, arguing that, in most of cases, the open spaces could be converted into pan-handle plots.

Focusing on pedestrians. The rich pedestrian network patterns of villages have been a starting point for the EAs' walkway system. The local open spaces of the housing clusters are connected to the central open space, where the primary school is located and where sports facilities may be developed. Pedestrian crossings of vehicular roads have been kept to a minimum.

In search of non-polarisation

One of the most controversial issues discussed during the planning preparation process, was the mixing of residential plots for households with different income levels. Income levels as defined in the Structure Plan included high, medium and low for company housing and high, medium, low and site and service for non-company housing.

Housing clusters with their respective open spaces contain the same income level households and are ordered in such a way that each income group is in proximity to the next higher and lower income household groups: there is a gradual transition from one income group to the other. Across the central open space, the principle of gradual income level grouping is equally applied. The resulting disposition of housing clusters show that, for example, distance between the two extreme income level housing groups — high income and site and service — can be as short as 100 m.

Infrastructure can be more cheaply upgraded in low income areas due to greater proximity to medium and high income areas with higher standards, as and when the aspirations of low income households can be met. In addition the population of the EA shares common grounds and schools easily accessible by foot.

Site and service and low cost housing were located closest to the town centre, thus facilitating easy access to the services at short walking distance. These two housing categories, with the smallest plot sizes (450 square m.), surround the town centre and comprise the densest populated areas of Jwaneng.

High income housing clusters were, on the other hand, placed farthest from the centre. It was considered that transportation to the shopping areas is usually done by car.

Lessons to learn: successes and failures of the planning concepts

Almost two decades have passed since the Jwaneng Structure Plan was prepared and building started. To the two and a half EAs that formed the original town plan, other detailed EA plans prepared by DTRP were added, following population growth demand.

The full extension of Jwaneng's six EAs is shown in Figure 7.1. The two most recently developed EAs do not follow the original detail plans prepared by the Chief Designer. By the mid 1990s Jwaneng's population was of the order of 15,000-20,000.

- Green areas at EA level — the central and the local open spaces within clusters — are considered too generous in extent and consequently, the total area has been reduced in the latest designed EA, from 15 to 10 per cent.

- The Town Council has, for economic reasons, neither developed nor maintained the open spaces of the EAs. No landscaping has taken place and only one sports ground has been developed.

- The local open spaces within clusters, as a result of lack of maintenance, are overgrown and are only used by pedestrians and bicycles and not as playgrounds for children.

- Land prices are too high. To attract investments, they should be lowered. Industrial development lags behind.

- The existence of single quarters generates social problems, an issue that has to be addressed by the Town Council and the mine management in consultation with DTRP.

- The Service Centres are not developed and consequently, there is a shortage of civic and community plots, particularly for churches.

- The central and only developed market is not functional, and its location is far from the bus terminal.

- The road network system with peripheral feeder roads causes annoyance to car owners who tend to drive across the central open space, short-cutting the driving distance.

Of the above criticisms, only the last two represent planning 'failures'. The others reflect unforeseeable political priorities of the Town Council, and possibly an overoptimistic view of Council financial assets. It is important to note that the plan continues to provide the option to develop the open spaces, recreation facilities and service centres. This option together with the planned woodlot areas north of the town and several other minor components give Jwaneng the possibility to pioneer in practice the concept of the sustainable city.

However, it is considered that the main planning concept — that of achieving a non-polarised community at EA level — has succeeded. In general, it is felt that there are no resentments between the various income and ethnic groups sharing an EA. The design of these areas has managed to mix the different income groups and at the same time successfully separate them in terms of open space, footpaths and roads. The mixture of housing categories also pays dividends in that it fuels a healthy competition in terms of plot development.

Related reading: The following provide material relevant to the matters discussed in this chapter: Dix, (1965); Best, (1970); Ford, (1975); Letsholo, (1980); Various authors (1980).

Part Four
The United States:
principles and practice

8 From civil rights to national rights: the development of race as a nationality concept

James Upton and Rebeka Maples

Americanised cultures

Cultural diversity, that is, racial, ethnic, gender, and other pluralistic relations, has received increased attention in higher education over the past ten years. At the same time, there is increased discussion and evidence of racial and ethnic conflict in the world. This has led to renewed recognition that racial, ethnic, gender, and other minority group divisions still create serious problems for countries such as the United States (US). Many Americans have been sensitised to conflicts in other countries, for example, South Africa, Rwanda, former USSR and Yugoslavia, and Northern Ireland. It is more and more apparent that unresolved differences have the potential of tearing apart even a modern industrialised nation. As a result, greater attention is being given to cultural diversity and multiculturalism in order to avoid and diffuse volatile situations.

The study of multiculturalism offers an outline of stratification patterns for recognising the heterogeneity of American society. By studying the inner dynamics of a culturally diverse society, and the nature of its minority group relations, with all the corresponding socioeconomic, psychological, and political overtones, we gain a better understanding of the structure and significance of such relationships (Vander Zanden, 1983). For instance, the exclusion of women (of all races and ethnic groups) from full participation in society has contributed to the marginalisation of half of the world's population based on gender. Thus, in an analysis of gender relations or a critique of increasing violence and abuse against women in society, this is essential information. In this regard, the study of racial, ethnic, gender, and other pluralistic relations helps create a more harmonious and equitable society based on the recognition, respect, and dignity due to all people.

In this chapter we discuss race as a nationality issue in the context of the diversity of American society. This includes examining the unique development of the term 'American' based on an ideology of racism and Anglo hegemony over American nationalism. It is a study of the union between beliefs and power in the formation of a racially stratified and unequal society. Even though the US is a nation of immigrants, its cultural diversity has been ignored, for the most part, by the dominant Anglo culture. That is, ethnically and culturally the US is an amalgamation of diverse people, but the 'typical American' continues to be a white, Protestant, Anglo American male. This perspective is presented in American history books, classrooms, television, movies, magazines, newspapers, etc. So that being white and male is seen as 'normal' and anyone else is abnormal or deviant, that is, the 'Other' (see de Beauvoir, 1989).

Racism in American society functions as an ideology. Historically it has been used to justify white/Anglo superiority and black/African inferiority. Innumerable theories and rationales have been offered as 'proof' of a 'natural' hierarchy of Anglos over the Other. Peter Fryer (1988) indicates, there is no scientific validity to the division of people by race (or skin pigmentation); it is a political construction for domination. Furthermore, Fryer claims it is a 'delusion' to assume that physical or cultural characteristics have anything to do with the mental capacity of people. W.E.B. Du Bois also argues that any classification system that places people in superior or inferior categories is 'ludicrous' (1992b, p. 539). In spite of these refutations of racist ideologies or pigmentocracy, 'scientific' arguments are still offered as explanations for racially based or politically motivated problems (Herrnstein and Murray, 1994). For instance, poverty, unemployment, crime, teen pregnancy, or other socio-economic problems in the African American population are often blamed on race, not on the institutionalised barriers created by racism. On the one hand, it is absurd that the amount of melanin or pigment in human skin is even used to explain socioeconomic problems in modern nation-states. On the other hand, it is amazing that the arguments have survived through centuries of scientific advancement, intellectual and otherwise. Although there are numerous interconnected factors that function to produce various cultural phenomena, we are concerned with identifying a few variables that reinforce the racialised constructs of American nationalism. First, as Beverly Tatum (1992, p. 5) notes, race and racism are considered taboo topics for discussion, especially in racially mixed settings. The irony is that even though the US is a racially stratified society, with a racial caste system (see Du Bois, 1965), it is not socially acceptable to acknowledge it. Americans become self-conscious of race in early childhood when they learn that most questions about race produce anxiety in adults. The avoidance of these topics, then, is a subtle but effective way to solidify racial divisions.

Another social mechanism for perpetuating racism stems from the common American belief that the US is a meritocracy. Most Americans believe that the US is a just and fair society, where individual efforts are rewarded (Tatum 1992, p. 6). Cose refers to this belief as the 'myth of meritocracy' which permeates all levels of society; so confusion or anger occurs when the belief is challenged (1995, p. 34). In university courses on cultural pluralism, students often become uncomfortable or hostile when new information challenges their precritical assumptions about 'the way it is'. This overlaps with one final way that racism is maintained in American society — through the denial or ignorance of history. By this we mean the deliberate ignoring of the past. For instance, many American students are often surprised when they learn about the diverse immigrant history of the US. The general information on American history goes something like this: after Christopher Columbus 'discovered America', a few Europeans (or 'Pilgrims') travelled in a ship to Plymouth Rock and had a 'thanksgiving' dinner with some 'Indians'. Then, slaves were brought from Africa but were later freed. Now everyone in the US is free and equal. The story receives near-biblical status and any attempt to change this 'historical' scenario is treated as a personal attack on white Americans (for example, see Feder, 1992, p.3d). Thus, the early indoctrination into racialised views of the world later presents a challenge to multicultural programmes which seek to accommodate cultural/pluralistic differences.

The effect of 'Americanisation', on the many different immigrants who settled in the US has been to forget their non-American ethnicity, in order to assimilate into the early American 'nativist' tradition (Easterlin, et al., 1982, pp. 75-105). This tradition stems from an Anglo American movement by 'nativists' in the early 1800s who saw themselves as the true 'native' Americans. They ignored the existence of indigenous Americans who were dehumanised with the same superiority/inferiority arguments applied to Africans (Brown, 1970; King, 1967, p. 80). The nativists even tried to apply multiple origins theories to justify Anglo superiority over other European immigrants. However, with the onslaught of the Civil War, and since European distinctions were difficult to identify and nearly impossible to sustain, the arguments did not last (Higham, 1968). The nativist arguments, though, can still be observed in American society with each new wave of non-white immigrants.

The nativist claims for power and superiority are further reflected in the formation of a national racist ideology with the justifications and rationalisations that were proposed in defence of slavery. The claims that Africans were 'non-human', 'uncivilised', 'savages', are well documented in American and British history (see Fryer, 1988; Du Bois, 1992b). In its earliest stages, the goal of American slavery was to supply a permanent labour pool that would guarantee privilege and wealth to the white/settler population. The state of slavery meant continual degradation of a group of humans relegated to the status of property. It is this past condition that continues to prevent the granting of full citizenship rights to African Americans in the twentieth century. As Du Bois explains, segregation laws in American society were an attempt to reinstate the racial caste system imposed during slavery (1992b, p. 539). The logic for this coincides with other racial classification systems proposed in theories such as evolutionism, social Darwinism, plantocracy, pigmentocracy, etc. (see Fryer, 1988), in which degradation of social condition corresponds with physical characteristics (Du Bois, 1992b).

W.E.B. Du Bois has analysed American racism with a yet unmatched eloquence and accuracy. His life's work (of thousands of manuscripts, essays, and poems) was devoted to exposing the decadence and violence of racism in American society. He deciphered the intricate details embedded in the logic of racial beliefs and laws as a way of dismantling racist ideologies. In 1909, he saw signs of degeneration in the social, physical, and spiritual fabric of white American society. He develops an argument that the white race seeks to protect itself from the outside but 'its most dangerous fate is deterioration from within' (1992b, p. 546). In some ways, this statement is more applicable in the mid 1990s with white militia terrorists threatening white government forces and institutions (Morganthau, 1995, pp. 36-9). With attempts to avoid economic and social equality by maintaining horizontal and vertical barriers between races and classes, the US reaffirms its centuries-old nativist-style nationalism. In this regard, it becomes even more crucial to reconstruct the core of American nationalism as a race concept for African Americans. In the following discussion, we examine some key philosophical works in African American political thought. These analyses provide important insight on American racism that connect race with nationality.

African American social and political philosophy

In reviewing the literature on African American social and political philosophy, we find that most of it is idiographic[1] (descriptive) rather than nomothetic[2] (probabilistic) in its approach to causation. The nomothetic model of explanation attempts to seek out law-governed processes in the development of different philosophical and ideological outlooks, which conform to laws of social movements.[3] There is need for extensive study of recurrent themes in reference to all social phenomena, in order to generalise about the democratic tendencies in social and political movements. Hence, in this chapter, we discuss two of these recurrent themes, justice and equality, in the context of American (that is, US) democracy.

We approach these terms from both historical and logical (that is, logic of substance) points of view, since the structure or forms of thought should approximate the content of the subject matter which we are examining; that is, the lived experiences of African American people in history (as objective processes governed by laws of social movement or social change) should be in conformity to the forms of thought that attempt to describe and explain the history or lived experience (Du Bois, 1992a, pp. 484-5). In addressing the terms justice and equality, we identify two major democratic tendencies in African American political philosophy — liberal and national democracy — which are not mutually exclusive and are sometimes conflictual. The resolution of the undergirding tension has been the source of nearly all debates by African American philosophers, from the Booker T. Washington-W.E.B. Du Bois antipodes, through Martin Luther King Jr-Malcolm X, up to the present. We use the word antipodes to characterise the debate around the question of integration versus separation as two opposing strategies for overcoming national (racial) oppression. Interestingly, the respective protagonists were not antagonistic on all questions. As Malcolm X notes: (Breitman, 1966, p. 51)

Integration is only a method that is used by some groups to obtain freedom, justice, equality and respect as human beings. Separation is only a method that is used by other groups to obtain freedom, justice, equality or human dignity.

While there is a plethora of works that deal with integration-separation themes in a historical-descriptive way, we focus on only a selection of these writers: W.E.B. Du Bois, Anna Julia Cooper, and Martin Luther King Jr. This literature delineates the recurring democratic trends in African American social and political movements, that is, liberal and national democracy. Our purpose here is to discuss equality and justice in the context of liberal and national democracy.

The different forms of democracy that have been espoused by many African American leaders within the US have been liberal and national democracy. Both forms of democracy are concerned with the nature of the state. For example, democracy (or representative rule) is a milder form of domination by the state, while militarism (or totalitarian rule) is a harsher form of state domination (King, 1967, p. 35).

The major distinction between liberal and national democracy that under liberal democracy the masses of people do not participate in state construction except at election time, voting being the predominant form of political activity.[4] The other exception is during times of revolution (for example, the American Revolution, the US or American Civil War, and Civil Rights Movements). Although the Civil Rights Movement of the 1960s was small in numbers,[5] demands for maximum feasible citizen participation, community control, and community self-determination emerged.[6] Martin Luther King Jr contended that the granting of civil rights (through the 1964 Civil Rights Act and the 1965 Voting Rights Act) to African Americans would positively affect the whole atmosphere in which remaining inequalities were considered problems. Legal or civil rights would not cause, for example, economic and social disparities to disappear.[7] It is interesting that for both proponents and opponents of equality, economic and social equality are beyond civil rights. Opponents of social and economic equality argue in favour of meritocracy or class status for claims to equality, while proponents of equality argue in favour of race for citizenship claims and equality.[8] King believed that if the civil rights movement had become a national movement rather than a regional movement (confined to the southern US), it would have become a threat to liberal democracy which only extends to legal emancipation.[9] As a solution to limited civil rights, King advocated the passage of a 'social and economic Bill of Rights to supplement the Constitution's political Bill of Rights': (King, 1967, p. 200)

> The new forms of rights are new methods of participation in decision-making. The concept of democracy is being pushed to deeper levels of meaning — from formal exercise of voting, ... to effective participation in major decisions.

Liberal democracy is formal democracy (legal emancipation or civil rights) as distinguished from national democracy (power-sharing on the basis of nationality representation).

Liberal democratic (Lockean) principles for representation in the US are based on population and territory, or majority rule. African Americans do not have the numerical strength to muster a simple majority. Hence, they have been democratically excluded from social, political, and economic arenas since the granting of citizenship in 1867 (Guinier, 1994). Under the Lockean principle of liberal democracy, majority rule permitted the removal of Native (indigenous) Americans to reservations as a way of solving the 'Indian problem', (Spicer, 1982, pp. 176-203). In addition, southern states used the majority rule principle to maintain segregation laws in the South even with the onslaught of black political insurgency and federal civil rights mandates.

According to Joseph Scott (1984, p. 175), the US began as a libertarian democracy *in rhetoric*, and became a totalitarian democracy *in practice* — with differentiated and prescribed race privileges. This legal pluralism came to mean separate and uneven statutory prescriptions and proscriptions for Africans, Asians, Native Americans, and women (of all races and cultures). Scott (1984, p. 176) maintains that if the social ranks of various groups in the US are purely the outcome of competition and acquisition, they are 'economic class' statuses. However, if the social ranks are ascribed through legislative, judicial, and executive decrees, without regard to marketplace efforts or acquisitions, then they are 'political class' statuses. Therefore, since the founding of hereditary racial slavery and the introduction of legal pluralism in the US Constitution, African and European Americans have been separate, statutorily recognised political classes, black and white, respectively. Thus, the US practices liberal democracy for white Americans and totalitarian democracy for black Americans (1984, p. 176). Scott concludes (1984, p. 177) that prescriptive pluralism (which led to the creation of racial castes) came to mean separate and uneven development between the races (a type of limited and qualified citizenship for African Americans). The establishment racial castes also set off a protracted political-race struggle over legal status and civil and economic rights; because black and white Americans occupy different hereditary (racial) statuses, they have contested each other over racial equality for five centuries.

National democracy, on the other hand, introduces into the formula for representation the nationality principle (or category), which translates into a race principle for African Americans (Cooper, 1988, p. 159). The nationality principle does not equate to a nationalistic principle for domination, but it is a universally recognised democratic construct for nation-states of mixed origin which extends democracy to categories of gender, age, race, class, religion, national origin, etc.

The dilemma of democracy: justice or equality

King maintains that the passage of the Civil Rights Bill in 1964 and the Voting Rights Act of 1965 represented the first phase of the civil rights movement. He contends (1967, pp. 3-4)

... the first phase — had been a struggle to treat the Negro with a degree of decency, not of equality. When Negroes looked for the second phase, the realisation of equality, they found that many of their white allies had quietly disappeared.

King further claims that black and white Americans have fundamentally different understandings of equality, 'there is not even a common language when the term "equality" is used' (1967, p. 8). He argues that with the exception of a small number of whites who genuinely support equality between the races, the majority of whites in the US 'have declared that democracy is not worth having if it involves equality' (1967, p. 11). By 1967, King's views underwent a philosophical transition on civil rights for African Americans as he became more and more disillusioned with liberal democracy:

Ever since the birth of our nation, white America has had a schizophrenic personality on the question of race. She has been torn between selves — a self in which she proudly professed the great principles of democracy and a self in which she sadly practised the antithesis of democracy (King, 1967, p. 68).

King faced the crisis that many black and white liberals faced at that juncture in the civil rights movement — the inability of liberal democracy to solve the race question beyond legal emancipation (that is, justice or decent treatment). According to King (1967, p. 90):

The white liberal must affirm that absolute justice for the Negro simply means, in the Aristotelian sense, that the Negro must have 'his due' ... It is as concrete as having a good job, a good education, a decent house and a share of power ... I am aware of the fact that this has been a troublesome concept for many liberals, since it conflicts with their traditional ideal of equal opportunity and equal treatment of people according to their individual merit.

King gradually shifted from advocating liberal democracy (or formal democracy — the extension of civil rights laws to black Americans) to supporting national democracy (or substantive democracy — a policy of affirmative action and the extension of power-sharing to black Americans). This is illustrated in one of King's analyses before his death:

But this is a day which demands new thinking and the reevaluation of old concepts. A society that has done something special against the Negro for hundreds of years must now do something special for him....In our kind of society liberation cannot come without integration and integration cannot come without liberation....Integration is the mutual sharing of power. I cannot see how the Negro will be totally liberated...until he is integrated, with power, into every level of American life. (King, 1967, pp. 90, 62)

King asks the question (1967, p. 4): 'Why is equality so assiduously avoided?' In his response, he directs our attention to the works of W.E.B. Du Bois, who prophesied in 1903 that 'the problem of the twentieth century will be the problem of the color line' (1967, p. 173). According to King, 'now we stand two-thirds into this exciting period of history we know full well that racism is still the hound of hell which dogs the tracks of our civilisation' (1967, p.173).[10] The issues of racism that Du Bois addressed early in the century are still unresolved as we near the next century.

In one of his classic essays (1992a, p. 483; Lewis, 1995, pp. 20-7), Du Bois provides further insight into the significance of race in US politics. He asks the question: 'What, then, is a race?' (1992a, p. 485), and replies by telling us that 'political reality forces us to discuss skin color, hair texture, facial features and even language as means of drawing distinctions between races'. (1992a, p. 486). Du Bois argued in 1897, what some scientists have only recently acknowledged, that these criteria are contradictory and non-mutually exclusive.

He maintains that the noted physical differences between people do not explain the differences in their history or intelligence:

> the whole process which has brought about these race differentiations has been a growth, and the great characteristic of this growth has been the differentiation of spiritual and mental differences between great races of humankind. (Du Bois, 1992a, p. 486)

As (racially) differentiated groups of humankind come into closer contact with one another, their physical differences diminish but hostility and prejudice based on those physical differences intensify. Du Bois captures the essence of these dynamics by identifying a dilemma that all black people in America face. He rhetorically asks:

> What after all, am I? Am I an American or Am I a Negro? Can I be both? Or is it my duty to cease to be a Negro as soon as possible and be an American? If I strive as a Negro, am I not perpetuating the very cleft that threatens and separates Black and White America? .... Does my black blood place upon me any more obligation to assert my nationality than German, or Irish or Italian blood would? (Du Bois, 1992a, p. 488)

Resolutions with the 'other'

The dilemma that Du Bois describes is the dual existence of being: 'an American, a Negro; two souls, two thoughts, two unreconciled strivings; two warring ideals in one dark body' (Franklin, 1965, p. 215). The duality of black Americans in the US sensitised Du Bois to minimise the nationalistic (racial) side of the nationality question and maximise the democratic (pluralistic) side of nationality.[11] In Du Bois's view, because of this dilemma African Americans would play a dramatic role in bringing about world democracy. He argues: (1992a, p. 487)

> ... the advance guard of the Negro people ... must soon come to realise that if they are to take their just place in the van of Pan-Negroism, then their destiny is not absorption by the white Americans. That if in America it is to be proven for the first time in the modern world that not only Negroes are capable of evolving individual men like Toussaint, the Saviour, but are a nation stored with wonderful possibilities of culture, then their destiny is not a servile imitation of Anglo-Saxon culture, but a stalwart originality which shall unswervingly follow Negro ideals.

The end result of African American striving is 'to be a co-worker in the kingdom of culture' (Franklin, 1965, p. 215), 'in order that some day on American soil two world-races may give each to each those characteristics both so sadly lack' (p. 220). Du Bois remains optimistic and concludes that unless modern civilisation is a failure, it is possible for the white and black races in the US 'to develop side by side in peace and mutual happiness, the peculiar contribution which each has to make to the culture of their common country' (1992a, p. 491).

Anna Julia Cooper, a nineteenth century African American woman, also writes about African American dualism which predates Du Bois's work (1988, p. 225). She describes her concern for what she believes is the dilemma of African Americans (1988, p. 112): '[The negro in America] merely asks to be ... allowed to pursue his destiny as a free man and an American citizen ....' Whereas Du Bois describes the dilemma as the plight of African Americans to be both African and American, Cooper expresses it as being both 'free ... and an American citizen'. From these two perspectives, the duality or tension of being both one (American/citizen) and the Other (African/Negro) stems from European American resistance to understanding and appreciating African Americans as human beings, who, like all Americans, have a dual heritage. In other words, the claims of Cooper and Du Bois are congruent in that one can be both African/black and an American. As Cooper states: 'Be true to yourself' (1988, p. 226), to the self that is an American citizen and the one that is a Negro.

To the student of African American history and literature, the terms 'dualism' and 'double-consciousness' are central because they represent the voices and experiences of the Other which have been historically and systematically silenced. Cooper describes the black male as a 'muffled chord' and the black woman as the 'mute and voiceless note' of the race, with no language but a cry (1988, p. xxix). Because their voices were silenced it does not indicate their works are now of less value as primary philosophical or literary sources. Rather, their views are representative expressions of the duality or 'twoness' that has always characterised US citizenship (for all Americans). It is the denial of this trait in American nationality that concerns Cooper and Du Bois. Cooper implores African Americans: (1988, p. 172)

> ... but don't let them argue as if there were no part to be played in life by black men and black women, and as if to become white were the sole specific and panacea for all the ills that flesh is heir to — the universal solvent for all America's irritations.

Indeed, Cooper claims it is the retention of one's uniqueness that halts the goals of domination by any one particular race over another:

> The supremacy of one race — the despotism of a class or the tyranny of an individual can not ultimately prevail on a continent held in equilibrium by such conflicting forces and by so many and such strong fibred races as there are struggling on this soil (Cooper, 1988, p. 167).

Conclusions

In conclusion, Cooper and Du Bois's nineteenth century discourses are uniquely significant, as they foreshadow current multicultural discussions. In her prophetic prose, Cooper argues that the inclusion of 'others' will create a more vibrant and progressive civilisation, one that fosters tolerance and appreciation for humankind (1988, pp. 149-74). Through multicultural studies we have an opportunity to prepare for and benefit from a changing world, instead of merely reacting to it (see Chism and Pruitt, 1995). The interdependence of the world economy and our modern electronic age link people together in new ways everyday (King, 1967, p.181). Those of us who study, work, and live with people (male and female) from other cultures and races have the opportunity to enjoy more success in school, on the job, and in our neighbourhoods. This means learning new ways of thinking, speaking, and acting. Communicating across cultural (racial, ethnic, and gender) lines provides myriad possibilities for creating new models of interaction. It can be frightening, frustrating, or even painful in the beginning. But, ultimately, it will be exciting, enriching, and affirming. At one time, only sociologists or anthropologists talked about cultural exchange. Now, all of us must join in the dialogue. The more we value cultural diversity, the more we learn how to accommodate our differences and to avoid a violent clash of cultures.

Notes

1   The idiographic model of explanation attempts to explain the sequence of events through (descriptive) enumeration of the many considerations that support a given event (Babbie, 1992, p. 70).

2   The nomothetic model of explanation involves the isolation of those relatively few considerations that will provide a partial explanation of a given event (Babbie, 1992, p. 71).

3   Just prior to Martin Luther King Jr's assassination, he underscores the following observation: (King, 1967, p. 137-8) 'People struggling from the depths of society have not been equipped with knowledge of the science of social change. We found a method in nonviolent protest that worked, and we employed it enthusiastically. We did not have leisure to probe for a deeper understanding of its laws and lines of development. This is where the civil rights movement stands today'. Also, W.E.B. Du Bois (1992a, p. 484) asks, 'What is the real meaning of Race; what has, in the past, been the law of race development, and what lessons has the past history of race development to teach the rising Negro people'?

4   Carole Pateman (1970) makes this same observation. She draws a distinction between representative democracy and participatory democracy. Also, see Frances Fox Piven and Richard A. Cloward (1977).

5   Martin Luther King Jr (1967, pp. 9, 20) acknowledges that there were millions of sympathisers; however, 'only a modest number were actively engaged, and those were relatively too few for a broad war against racism, poverty and discrimination'. Although the active number of participants was small, King argues that the civil rights movement had a diverse mass base representing all aspects of United States society.

6   The limitation of liberal democracy can be characterised by its representative form of rule, i.e., one brings pressure to bear on the state to force it to implement reforms rather than implementing them yourself. Hence, Daniel Patrick Moynihan (1970) presented his book as an argument against extending democracy.

7   See King (1967, pp. 10, 11, 34-5, 79, 82); also for an in depth discussion see James N. Upton (1994, p. 198)

8   For proponents of the ethnic group model of race, see Nathan Glazer (1975), and Thomas Sowell (1978). According to Betty Watson and Willy

Smith (1987, pp. 271-6), both Glazer and Sowell 'frame race as a variable which operates in a fashion parallel to ethnicity'. Watson and Smith contend that Thomas Sowell, William Julius Wilson (1981) and Glenn Loury (1985; 1986) use socio-cultural and/or class models regarding race based socio-economic differences. Thus, a logical extension of such an analysis is that race-based policies have no functional role in the public arena (Watson and Smith 1987, p. 272). Proponents of racial claims for first-class citizenship or equality utilise what many refer to as the institutional racism model. This model argues that socioeconomic differences result from institutional exclusion and marginalisation of African Americans based on their race and/or colour (Watson and Smith, 1987, p.273).

See Martin Luther King Jr (1967, pp. 10-13, 17, 35).

Also see, Derrick Bell (1992); and Andrew Hacker (1992).

Maximising the nationalistic side of the nationality question in multinational nation-states can lead to the intolerance of other nationalities (e.g., national oppression by a militaristic or police state). Anna Julia Cooper (1988) critically directs our attention to this problem. According to Cooper, 'that exclusiveness in a nation is suicidal to progress ... One race predominance means death' (1988, p.160). While on the other hand, minimising the democratic side of the nationality question in multinational nation-states can lead to the loss of national identity. In reference to African American people in the US, Du Bois argues 'then their destiny is not absorption by the white Americans ... then their destiny is not a servile imitation of Anglo-Saxon culture, but a stalwart originality which shall unswervingly follow Negro ideals' (1992a, pp. 487-8). For further elaboration of this discussion, see E.U. Essien-Udom (1962, pp. 27-30).

9   Opening housing opportunities: changing Federal housing policy in the United States

John Goering

Introduction

A series of intellectual and policy critical events have occurred in the areas of race, immigration, and housing policy in the United States over the last several years that powerfully affect the potential for accommodating differences within metropolitan societies. These interrelated policy and political realignments help set the context for Federal Government interventions and demonstrations aimed at the desegregation or integration of persons of colour within the larger community.

The purpose of this chapter is to describe recent initiatives undertaken by the US Department of Housing and Urban Development to address the racial and economic isolation of the poor, with research presented on the scale of these problems as they affect the continued effectiveness of these programmes.

Critical events

Federal Government retrenchment

The ability and relevance of the US Federal Government to function effectively in the interest of the public has recently been severely challenged by popular and political resistance to governmental intervention into a variety of domestic social problems — including social welfare policy, housing, and civil rights interventions. The unwillingness to pay the cost of increasingly intransigent problems extends to doubts about the continuation of entitlements for the poor, including subsidies to immigrant and non-immigrant minorities. As of December 1995, there were certain to be substantial reductions in the size or rate of growth of most domestic welfare and housing related programmes over the next decade that would inevitably affect the ability and relevance of central government interventions to assist in economic or racial deconcentration (Kazin, 1995).

A long-term decline in real incomes

This has been experienced by the less-wealthy citizens of the US over the course of the last two decades and appears linked to a collapse of hope and optimism of a large portion of the population for whom the slope of life is downwards (Edsall, 1995; Pearlstein, 1995; Glater, 1995). The downward slope of life chances often results in resentment of and resistance to programmes whose objective is to offer the poorest families in society a chance of moving 'upwards' into communities bent on defending their dwindling prerogatives and life chances. Public polices, which aim at redistributing opportunities to the poor, continually encounter fragmented and vulnerable communities whose incomes are only slightly higher or more stable than those of the poor (Rieder, 1985; Anderson, 1990, p. 145).

Race, immigration and demographic balkanization

There is evidence that two different versions of America are emerging based upon the shape of economic opportunities facing immigrants and racial minorities. The declining number of working class blue collar jobs potentially results in what Portes and Zhou (1994, p. 23) call an 'hourglass economy':

> The new 'hourglass economy' created by economic restructuring means that the children of immigrants must cross a narrow bottle-neck to occupations requiring advanced training if their careers are to keep pace with their US-acquired aspirations.

Some immigrants manage to assimilate into segmented economic niches with the potential for upward mobility while many others are 'assimilated' relatively quickly and directly into a world of felt discrimination, criminal career opportunities, and underclass behaviour.

Urban underclass areas are becoming home to both poor disenfranchised blacks and newer immigrant groups of colour. Increasing numbers of Latin and Asian immigrants appear connected to white flight from the larger cities housing immigrants, with the result that two Americas are emerging:

> ...the first, ageing, largely white, nonmetropolitan and small metropolitan communities in the Midwest; the second, young, vibrant, multicultural metro areas in the South and West (Frey, 1991 p. 8; Frey, 1995).

Anti-immigration sentiments often flourish in such conditions as exemplified by Peter Brimelow's *Alien Nation* (1995) which argues against America become more multi-ethnic. American interests, according to Brimelow, are as a 'white' nation. Unwanted immigration policies have been, he laments, 'bringing about an ethnic and racial transformation in America without precedent in the history of the world — an astonishing social experiment launched with no particular reason to expect success' (p. 9). Such analyses are mirrored in statements of major political figures who support English-only legislation and strict enforcement of immigration border controls as a solution to stemming the 'browning' of America.

Race apathy, burnout or 'racial fatigue' — a deep 'weariness of things racial' (Steele, 1990 p. 23) — has accompanied fears, among blacks and whites, of the urban pathologies of drugs, violence and gangs. Middle class African American's '... lives are more integrated that they have ever been before. Race does not determine our fates as powerfully as it once did, which means it is not the vital personal concern it once was' (Steele, 1990, p. 23).

At the same time, scepticism about the legitimacy of Federal Government efforts to end discrimination and promote desegregation seriously undermine efforts at cross-racial dialogue and policies. An African American school board member from Kansas City, Missouri recently said: 'I think desegregation is dead and should have died a long time ago, if the focus is on trying to have a physical mixing of the races' (Hentoff, 1995).

As the goal of 'racial integration' has become an unusable part of public policy debate among blacks and whites, it has left the analysis of America's racial future conflicted over the nature of black culture, the implications of 'diversity', and the limits of affirmative governmental actions to create a perfected racial future.

The popular and political assessment of the role of the Federal Government in anti-discrimination and affirmative policies is affected by current judicially and Presidentially mandated efforts to re-think the role of 'permanent' affirmative action programmes (Stephanapoulos and Edley, 1995). At the same time 'federal' programmes appear more likely to become administered through states and localities, placing centrally administered civil rights policies in potential conflict with other centrifugally-driven federal programmes.

At the level of urban jurisdictions, a variety of forms of NIMBYism and defensive localism have emerged opposing federal or local efforts aimed at introducing most forms of subsidized housing for the poor or near poor. Neighbourhood-based organizations act quickly to thwart or minimize policies aimed at race or income dispersal and accommodation. And while race-based prejudice can be treated, there are currently few means available to the Federal government to address the neighbourhood and 'family' based panic that emerges when the prospect of 'exceptional' neighbours moving into the social fabric arises.

The persistent problem of housing segregation in the United States and the United Kingdom

Central to the frustrations felt by both policy makers and citizens about options to promote desegregation has been the scale, density and intransigence of the racial and economic isolation of public housing tenants. Tables 9.1 and 9.2 briefly display some of the key similarities and differences between the segregation of public housing residents in the United States and the United Kingdom. The tables illustrate the differences in historical and demographic patterns which are central to the successful implementation of new forms of intervention. (for additional detail see Goering, 1993; 1994). The following section provides new research evidence on the scale and form of the

Table 9.1
Key background characteristics on race and housing in Britain and the United States

Characteristic	Britain	USA
• Minority population: % of total	2.5 million: 4%	59 million: 24%
• Arrival of ethnic minorities/undocumented	Immigration: 1950s 50,000; earlier communities	Slavery: 1790 (757,000); post World War; 1965 Immigration Law
• Percent owner occupied	65%	66%
• Public housing started	1919 (1949)	1937/49
• Public housing units: number and % of rental	4.7 million: 73%	4.1-5.2 million: 16%
• Tenant ownership	Increasing	Minimal
• Public housing authority autonomy	Moderate	Moderate/declining
• Major form for delivery of new housing assistance	Housing Associations	Rental Assistance (Section 8)
• Level of racial prejudice	Moderate/increasing	Moderate/new forms
• Level of segregation	Moderate/stable?	High/declining slightly
• Civil rights laws enacted	1968/1976	1964/1968/1988/1990

racial and economic isolation of public housing residents. In the next section research data reveal the lessened patterns of concentration in HUD's (Housing and Urban Development) current, major housing assistance programmes (Section 8 Rental Assistance). The following section briefly describes a number of specialized housing mobility programmes which have encouraged even greater racial and economic mixing.

The purpose of this section is to briefly describe current US patterns of racial and poverty concentration in the neighbourhoods or census tracts within which public ('council') housing residents live. Programme design is important for understanding the racial and poverty characteristics of public housing projects

Table 9.2
Key issues affecting public housing racial segregation in Britain and the United States

Issue	Britain	United States
% Minority public housing tenants	Low	High
Built on segregated basis	Initially no	Initially yes
Level of segregation	Low-moderate	High
Underclass impacts	low/increasing?	Moderate/unclear
Segregative mechanisms	Home visitors; tenant selection; Choice; White resistance	Site and tenant selection conditions; White resistance
Level of enforcement	Weak	Weak/variable
Minority data reporting	Voluntary/uneven	Mandatory/ improving

because projects designed for families or elderly households have different patterns of distribution throughout metropolitan housing markets.

Using weighted values for all family and elderly households, Table 9.3 summarizes the average or typical experience of African American, white and Hispanic tenants living in either family or elderly low-rent public housing developments.

For family developments, for example, the typical African American lives in a project that is 85 per cent African American, eight per cent white, with 80 per cent of tenants below the poverty level, 25 per cent working, and 53 per cent single female headed households with children. They also live in census tracts that are 68 per cent African American, 25 per cent white, 47 per cent poor.

The average white family household lives in a project that is 60 per cent white, 27 per cent African American, 74 per cent below poverty level, with 27 per cent working, and 47 per cent single female headed households with children. They live in a census tract that is 78 per cent white, 15 per cent African American, 26 per cent poor, and 89 per cent working.

For elderly developments, the typical African American household lives in a project that is 72 per cent African American, 20 per cent white, with 69 per cent below the poverty level and they live in a census tract that is 53 per cent African American, 40 per cent white, 38 per cent poor, and 83 per cent working.

For elderly developments, the typical white household lives in a project that is 78 per cent white, 14 per cent African American and live in a census tract that is

Table 9.3
Location of typical white, African American and Hispanic households in public housing projects

		Live in Public Housing Projects where:				
		% Af/Am	% White	% below Poverty	% Working	% SFWC*
Typical African American Households	In Family Projects	85	8	80	25	53
	In Elderly Projects	72	20	69	26	33
Typical White Households	In Family Projects	27	60	74	27	47
	In Elderly Projects	14	78	47	11	14
Typical Hispanic Households	In Family Projects	25	12	65	38	33
	In Elderly Projects	22	25	58	25	28

* SFWC=Single Female Headed Households with Children

83 per cent white, 10 per cent African American, 21 per cent poor, and 91 per cent working.

The typical Hispanic family lives in a project that is 59 per cent Hispanic, 25 per cent African American, 12 per cent white, with 65 per cent below the poverty level, 38 per cent working, and 33 per cent single female headed households with children. The average elderly Hispanic household lives in a project that is 50 per cent Hispanic, 22 per cent African American, 25 per cent white, with 58 per cent of residents below the poverty level, 25 per cent working, and 28 per cent single female headed households with children.

This synthesis makes it easier, for example, to see that a majority of all African American, white and Hispanic tenants live in projects where they are in the majority, whether they are in family or elderly projects. Only elderly Hispanics are likely to be living in projects where a greater number of the their neighbours are whites. African American tenants live in projects with half the level of working families experienced by Hispanics, much higher levels of households living in poverty, and majority African American populations living within their project and in their surrounding neighbourhood. Elderly families are, in general, substantially less likely to be living among higher concentrations of households living below the poverty level when compared with residents in family buildings, regardless of which racial or ethnic group they are in. The lowest levels of poverty concentration are experienced by both elderly and family white tenants.

The data confirm that African American residents living in family projects are housed in segregated projects in deeply poor neighbourhoods. The majority of African Americans living in public housing projects in the United States are living in poverty-concentrated areas, while the majority of public housing white tenants — both families and the elderly — are living in neighbourhoods with substantially lower poverty rates.

Racial and economic isolation in the Section 8 rental assistance programme compared to public housing

This chapter provides the first examination of the forms and patterns of racial and economic isolation that are imbedded in the traditional public housing programme, contrasted with those found in Section 8 rental assistance, where households are provided with certificates and vouchers which enable the renting of modestly priced housing anywhere in the private market. This comparison reveals that Section 8 housing programmes are better able to overcome the racial isolation inherent in American housing markets than is the case with traditional public housing developments.

Here we make use of newly available administrative data gathered by the US Department of Housing and Urban Development and the General Accounting Office, linked to 1990 census tract data. The discussion employs newly available data from four metropolitan areas on the distribution of Section 8 rental assistance households among census tracts of varying racial concentrations and poverty rates. The limitations of these data bases are described in Goering, Kamely and Richardson (1994).

As of 1993, there were approximately 1.4 million units of conventional public housing located in roughly 14,000 separate projects throughout over 3,200 public housing agencies (PHAs) (Bratt, 1994, p. 13) and a roughly comparable number of rental assistance recipients. The current data include the census tract locations of over 23,000 white, African American, and 'other' Section 8 rental voucher and certificate recipients in four metropolitan areas: Washington, DC; Wilmington, Delaware; Seattle, Washington; and Oklahoma City, Oklahoma. (For purposes of this report, no distinction has been made between certificate and voucher recipients, nor between movers and those who qualified in place.) Of the total households in the GAO study, roughly 45 per cent were African American, 41 per cent were white, and nearly 14 per cent were designated as 'other', a category that includes Hispanics.

The information in Table 9.4 reveals that nearly 85 per cent of white Section 8 rental assistance recipients live in census tracts where fewer than 20 per cent of the residents are African American, compared to only 36 per cent of African American recipients. For black Section 8 recipients, 25 per cent live in tracts where 70 per cent or more of the residents are also black; the comparable figure for public housing residents is 59 per cent.

The comparable figures for whites and African Americans in public housing are 82 and 17 per cent, respectively. Forty per cent of African American rental

Table 9.4
Location of Section 8 and public housing households by tract African American population, four Metropolitan Areas

Per Cent Tract African American	Per Cent Distribution Heads of Household with Section 8 Assistance				Per Cent Distribution Heads of Household in Public Housing			
	White	Af/Am	Others	Total	White	Af/Am	Others	Total
<5	57	10	15	30	63	7	32	32
5-9	16	12	7	13	15	5	13	9
10-19	12	14	9	12	4	5	11	6
20-29	8	14	6	11	8	9	20	10
30-39	3	10	7	7	7	9	20	10
40-49	2	5	3	3	1	1	1	1
50-59	1	6	5	4	0	4	0	2
60-69	0	4	2	20	0	1	0	1
≥70	1	25	46	18	2	59	3	29
Total %	100	100	100	100	100	100	100	100
N	9,709	10,712	3,249	23,667	8,197	14,967	3,555	26,719

assistance recipients selected housing in areas that were 40 per cent or more African American, making them more than 10 times more likely than assisted white families to live in such neighbourhoods. However, this likelihood is much higher for public housing project residents (about 22 times); 65 per cent African American compared with three per cent white in census tracts that are 40 per cent or more African American.

Table 9.5 provides information on the incidence of poverty in areas where Section 8 and public housing households are living. Relatively few white Section 8 recipients reside in high-poverty census tracts (poverty rate higher than 30 per cent). Overall, only 9 per cent of all families selected housing in

Table 9.5
Location of Section 8 and public housing households by tract poverty rate, four Metropolitan Areas

Per Cent Tract Poverty	Per Cent Distribution Heads of Household with Section 8 Assistance				Per Cent Distribution Heads of Household in Public Housing			
	White	Af/Am	Others	Total	White	Af/Am	Others	Total
<5	15	11	13	13	5	1	2	3
5-9	34	21	36	28	30	10	17	28
10-19	35	31	40	34	31	16	29	24
20-29	12	22	8	16	16	21	13	18
30-39	3	11	2	6	9	25	24	19
40-49	1	3	1	2	6	22	5	13
50-59	0	1	0	1	3	3	10	4
60-69	0	0	0	0	0	2	0	1
≥70	0	0	0	0	0	0	0	0
Total %	100	100	100	100	100	100	100	100
N	9,709	10,712	3,249	23,667	8,197	14,967	3,555	26,719

such tracts in the four MSAs (Metropolitan Statistical Areas), four per cent of all white Section 8 recipients, compared to 14 per cent of African American recipients. In the same MSAs, a much higher percentage of public housing residents live in high poverty tracts.

Most Section 8 recipients — of all races — obtained housing in areas with less severe concentrations of poverty. Forty-one per cent of all recipient families (49 per cent of whites and 32 per cent of African Americans) in the four MSAs selected housing in census tracts with poverty rates of less than 10 per cent. Another 47 per cent of whites and 53 per cent of African Americans live in tracts where between 10 and 30 per cent of the population is poor.

Viewed from this metropolitan perspective the improvement in locational outcomes associated with HUD rental assistance is impressive. According to the 1990 census, only 4.5 per cent of the US metropolitan population live in tracts with a poverty rate of 40 per cent or higher, but such neighbourhoods are home to 36 per cent of metropolitan area African Americans (Jargowsky 1994). Public housing residents are even more likely to live in concentrated poverty. The sample of roughly 23,000 families receiving Section 8 rental assistance displays a general tendency toward racial concentration similar to that found, to varying degrees, among other segments of the population: whites were more likely to select largely white neighbourhoods; the more heavily African American an area, the less likely that white Section 8 recipients would be found living there.

Section 8 mobility options

This part of the chapter describes current programmes that use Section 8 rental vouchers or certificates combined with various forms of counselling and housing search assistance to promote city-wide or metropolitan area-wide residential mobility for low-income and/or minority households. These programmes are located in Chicago; Boston; Cincinnati; Dallas; Memphis, Tennessee; Hartford, Connecticut; Las Vegas, Nevada; and Yonkers, New York.

Information on a number of housing mobility programmes was compiled between the spring and early fall of 1994 through written and telephone contacts with the administering Public Housing Agencies (PHAs) and/or the relevant non-profit organizations. These agencies provided a current description of the services and assistance that families typically received through their mobility counselling programme, as well as data on the census tract location of families assisted under both their conventional Section 8 and housing mobility programmes. This includes information on major court-ordered and voluntary housing mobility programmes currently in operation.

Section 8 recipients enrolled in a mobility programme typically move to less segregated portions of the housing market than Section 8 households that do not receive additional counselling and assistance. This effect is directly tied to the requirement attached to such mobility programmes that the vouchers or certificates are only usable within less-segregated areas. The effectiveness of mobility programmes increases with their longevity, as programmes tend to start up slowly and gain momentum as the first families have successful experiences and more landlords become aware of the programme itself.

A small body of existing research provides compelling evidence that mobility programmes, to the extent that they enable low-income households to consider low-poverty or suburban locations previously inaccessible to them, open the way to expanded opportunities for personal, social, and material growth. Peterson and Williams (1994, p. 9) comment that:

> Mobility should be thought of as a long-term investment with a potential for long-term payoff. It generates immediate benefits in household satisfaction and safety. It is relatively inexpensive and generates some short-run benefits to offset the short-run costs of administration. The potential rewards are to be found in the lives of children and in the longer-run adjustments that families make.

The persistent argument for metropolitan dispersal policies: themes for current demonstrations

The concentration of the poor into ghetto enclaves or underclass areas has been commented on and decried for nearly three decades in the United Sates, with analogous forms of commentary in the UK. Social analysts, such as Daniel Patrick Moynihan (Moynihan, 1971, pp. 132-33) presciently described — nearly three decades ago — the core urban problem in America:

> The poverty and social isolation of minority groups in central cities is the single most serious problem of the American city today. It must be attached with urgency, with a greater commitment of resources than has heretofore been the case, and with programs designed especially for this purpose.

In the late 1960s, the Kerner Commission described two options for redressing the 'division of our country into two societies; one, largely negro [sic] and poor, located in the central cities; the other, predominantly white and affluent, located in the suburbs and in outlying areas' (US National Advisory Commission, 1968, pp. 21-22). The first option would be to enrich or improve the quality of ghetto life while abandoning integration as a goal. The preferred option they argued for was to combine ghetto 'enrichment' with policies which encouraged African-Americans to move out of central city areas.

For over twenty years, no Congressionally authorized, Federally funded efforts were made to address this critical flaw in urban communities. The need for such efforts is driven by the major role which federal housing programmes and policies have played — directly and indirectly — in fostering large concentrations of poor and black residents within American cities (Bickford and Massey, 1991; Massey and Kanaiaupuni, 1993; Wood, 1957; Taeuber and Taeuber, 1965, p. 49; Hirsch, 1983; Flournoy and Rodriguez, 1985; Bauman, 1987; Bratt, 1994, p. 15).

After the enactment of the civil rights acts of 1964 and 1968, a growing number of Federal court suits sought to reverse the patterns of racial discrimination and segregation in federally assisted public housing projects by using Section 8 rental assistance to counterbalance the racial isolation associated with large scale projects (Pynoos, 1986; Goering, 1986, pp. 197-207; Massey and Kanaiaupuni, 1993; Hirsch, 1983, pp. 265-6). Beginning in 1990, research on the Gautreaux programme indicated a glimmer of hope; desegregated housing opportunities facilitated through the Section 8 programme had led to notable improvements in the lives of parents and children who moved out of segregated, inner city neighbourhoods.

This research (Rosenbaum and Popkin, 1990; Rosenbaum, 1993; 1994) led to the political and legislative endorsement of a new 'demonstration' aimed at assisting families living in poverty to move to better neighbourhoods. In 1992, the Clinton Administration stated a commitment ' ... to ensuring that people are not trapped and isolated in predominantly poor neighborhoods for lack of options' and authorized a number of small scale demonstration programmes to address the twin goals of inner city neighbourhood redevelopment and opportunities for deconcentrated housing.

The Urban Revitalization, or 'HOPE VI' programme, is aimed at demolishing large scale inner city developments and rebuilding in place smaller scale, mixed income complexes (Pressley, 1995). In addition a major demonstration — the Moving to Opportunities demonstration, aimed at the economic deconcentration of inner city public housing residents — has begun using HUD's main housing assistance programme (Section 8 Rental Assistance) as the funding vehicle (Drier and Atlas, 1995). The Moving to Opportunity for Fair Housing (MTO) demonstration, which is now underway in five metropolitan areas, provides approximately 2,000 families living in distressed inner-city neighbourhoods with Section 8 rental certificates and vouchers, as well as counselling and other assistance for an experimental group, to aid them in moving to low-poverty areas.

Designed after the enactment of major civil rights laws, the key evaluation issue is: can these new programmes achieve more racial and economic desegregation than their predecessor? Can any federal programme — including one which relies upon private landlords — escape the segregative tendencies within America's housing markets? (Massey and Denton, 1993; Farley and Frey, 1994). Indeed there has been recent argument that, despite its promise of greater housing opportunity, the Section 8 Rental Assistance programme is cloning the segregative patterns of traditional federal housing programmes by fostering racially segregated sub-markets (Finkel and Kennedy, 1992; Bratt, 1994, p. 17).

Conclusions

One of the primary questions concerning the continued viability of housing dispersal efforts is the extent to which there can be federal control over the problem of housing opportunities and integration; whether there will remain an active, centralized concern by the Federal Government over the many forms, symptoms, and systemic effects of concentrated poverty (Mayer and Jencks, 1995). In local communities, the tension between ethnic and neighbourhood rights and accommodation issues may increase friction between minority and white residents (Clark and Morrison, 1995) and reduce enthusiasm for and tolerance of federal intervention.

Such social conflict can quickly refocus public policy at the national or local levels to emphasize family values and education or to press for remedial programmes and resources. It is uncertain which direction will be sought in the future. Elijah Anderson (1990, p. 254), at the end of his assessment of racial and class tensions in Philadelphia concludes with his view of the future, should no sustained change be made in current practice:

> If these suggestions are not heeded, we face growing incivility and crime ... This poverty of the city itself will accelerate the breakdown of community and the exodus of middle-class residents, leaving their former neighbors even more isolated. The city will be ringed by the white middle and upper classes, who will venture in only when absolutely necessary. And the urban neighborhood will become less and less habitable.

HUD rental certificates and vouchers offer one remedy to this isolation if assistance is provided so that low-income families can use them to rent modestly priced housing anywhere in the private market.

The Section 8 certificate and voucher programmes have already enabled very low-income families — many of whom were previously homeless or living in crowded or inadequate housing — to obtain affordable, higher quality rental units. The data from four metropolitan areas confirms that Section 8 families are less likely to live in racially and economically isolated neighbourhoods than public housing residents. Moreover, the housing mobility programmes profiled in this paper have been generally even more successful in facilitating housing opportunities within neighbourhoods and communities not typically used by Section 8 rental assistance recipients.

It is, however, essential to bear in mind the limited, complementary role housing mobility plays in efforts to achieve a comprehensive set of housing options. Mobility programmes may not meet the needs of every community and may not affect the locational choice made by every family receiving HUD rental assistance. The role of mobility programmes is simply to foster conditions under which families long trapped in economically distressed and racially segregated inner-city neighbourhoods can freely choose among a full range of residential options, including the option of remaining within the inner city community they have been raised in.

HUD's ongoing data collection and evaluation activities will help to answer these and other important questions, including a 10-year evaluation of Moving to Opportunity which will yield detailed longitudinal data on the impact of neighbourhood on social and economic opportunity. Hopefully MTO will prove that it has taken to heart the lessons of the past and Nicholas Lemann's (1991, p. 352) sage advice:

> The most straightforward way for new federal programs to win acceptance is to show that they work, not in the sense of dramatically eliminating the underclass overnight, but in the sense of being demonstrably honest, well run, committed to mainstream values, and devoid of the punitive, ram-it-down-their-throats quality that the shortest-lived reforms have had.

The MTO experimental demonstration is only one component of the Clinton Administration's effort to promote the balanced desegregation of American cities by offering poor families the choice to either remain in and rebuild inner city neighbourhoods or to move into the private rental market in non-poor communities. This is the first serious commitment by senior political officials in roughly 30 years. It can only be hoped that the institutional and political forces outlined in the first section of this paper will permit them to fulfil their promises.

Acknowledgements

The author would like to thank Dr. Ali Kamely, Abdollah Haghighi, Todd Richardson, Reynolds Farley, Joe Feagin, John Yinger, Roderick Harrison, and Robert Benjamin for their assistance with this research project. Mr. Thomas Noon, of GAO, kindly provided access to their data files on Section 8 households. The opinions expressed in this paper do not reflect the views of the US Department of Housing and Urban Development or the Federal Government.

10 Racial and ethnic diversity in US urban communities: challenging the perceived inevitability of segregation

Michael Maly and Philip Nyden

Introduction

By the middle of the 21st century, 'minorities' will comprise nearly one-half of the American population (O'Hare, 1992). However, examples of America's 'melting pot' are hard to find at the neighbourhood level, where a pattern of racial and ethnic segregation has been the rule. Will the US become a nation of co-existing, co-operating groups sharing ample resources, or will it become an even more segregated society with heightened tensions between diverse groups?

Residential segregation by race remains a fundamental feature of US urban areas. However, there are a number of communities around the country that have been able to swim against the tide and sustain diversity. The purpose of this chapter is to examine several communities that have sustained diversity. This essay will concentrate on local policies and strategies of urban communities that have and can bring about greater diversity in American cities.

We examine alternatives to segregated communities. We explore possible strategies, policies, or processes, which local neighbourhood residents, institutions, and community groups have used to maintain racially diverse communities. After examining the extent of racially diverse neighbourhoods in Chicago from 1980 to the present, six neighbourhoods from that city are selected for a closer examination.

Past research on segregation and diversity

The dominance of residential segregation in urban America has been documented by many researchers (Taeuber and Taeuber, 1965; Lieberson, 1980; Massey and Denton, 1993). In the 1960s this persistent segregation led the Kerner Commission (a federal body established to investigate the causes of inner city riots in American cities in the late 1960s) to conclude that the US was 'moving toward two societies, one Black, one White — separate and unequal' (US National Advisory Commission on Civil Disorders, 1968). Sociologists Nancy Denton and Douglas Massey refer to the concentration of African-Americans in inner city neighbourhoods as 'hypersegregation'. Blacks are twice as isolated and segregated as Latinos and Asians (Denton, 1994). One-third of all Blacks in the US are living under conditions of intense racial segregation (Massey and Denton, 1993). Although metropolitan neighbourhoods are becoming more multiethnic (Denton and Massey, 1991), racially diverse neighbourhoods are a rarity in the US (Sorenson, Taeuber and Hollingsworth, 1975; Taeuber, 1983).

While some have argued that no amount of local intervention is likely to reverse the process of transition from white to black neighbourhoods (Molotch, 1972), others provide evidence of 'successful' attempts at maintaining racial diversity (Goodwin, 1979; Saltman, 1990). The latter approach, an 'interventionist model', challenges the notion that racial succession and segregation are inevitable. Interventionist theorists argue that community-based organisations can sustain racial and ethnic diversity if sufficient resources (such as support from churches, business, block clubs, local elected officials, and even real estate investors) are developed early enough to pressure other decision makers into adopting pro-diversity strategies. Strategies include marketing the neighbourhood to underrepresented groups and improving community social and economic infrastructure — such as schools, community safety, and public services (Keating, 1994; Saltman, 1990; Taub et al., 1984; Nyden et al., 1992; 1993; Nyden and Adams, 1996). This research does caution that the maintenance of diversity requires constant attention by community leaders (Smith, 1993; Wiese, 1995).

Research rationale and methodology

We use a combined quantitative and qualitative approach in studying diversity. While necessary for understanding the national dimensions and institutional backbone of segregation, the unintentional effect of some quantitative work is to de-emphasise the role of local communities in determining their futures. In describing national trends and institutional racism, local communities are seen as powerless to counter the forces of segregation. Passage of federal laws and intervention by federal agencies are held up as the primary solutions to neighbourhood segregation.

However, while federal laws are critical tools for local groups, much of the social processes of integration or segregation are processes that play themselves out in real everyday interactions at the neighbourhood level — from the construction of public perceptions of neighbourhood stability to real estate broker steering. Qualitative studies on diverse neighbourhoods compliment segregation studies by focusing on how *local* institutions and individuals are not only affected by structural forces, but also how the day-to-day decisions of individual residents and local leaders define the texture and quality of urban life (Taub et al., 1984; DeSena, 1994). This perspective sees community groups and individuals as vital actors in neighbourhood outcomes. The negative impact of broader forces, e.g. redlining and patterns of disinvestment, are not accepted as inevitable.

Rather than focusing on what produces segregation, our study focuses on *what produces diversity*. Here we combine quantitative *and* qualitative approaches in understanding what produces stable, diverse communities in the city of Chicago. First, we identify census tracts that are racially and ethnically mixed. Defining stable diverse neighbourhoods as those clusters of tracts that approximate the breakdown of the overall city averages for both the 1980 and 1990 Census years (that is, were approximately 43 per cent White, 38 per cent African-American, and 19 per cent Latino in 1990), we identify which community areas are stably diverse. (A more detailed explanation of this methodology is provided in the short methodological note at the end of the chapter.) Having identified these positive examples of diversity, we then completed interviews with community leaders in these communities to gain a better understanding of the social, political, and economic forces that have contributed to the creation of stably diverse communities.[1]

Findings

Quantitative analysis:

Not surprisingly the data show that segregation is the standard in Chicago. Diverse census tracts are the exception. In 1990 only 7.9 per cent of the 852 census tracts were racially diverse, 35.7 per cent were moderately segregated, and 56.5 per cent were segregated. These percentages were remarkably stable from 1980 to 1990. Of the 68 diverse tracts in 1980, 40 remained diverse in 1990, 25 had become moderately segregated, and only 3 had become segregated. Of the 497 segregated tracts in 1980, 430 remained segregated, 66 became moderately segregated, and only 1 had become diverse in 1990. Table 10.1 displays these findings and indicates that the racial composition of tracts in 1980 is strongly associated with the racial composition in 1990 (Gamma = .93, $P < .001$).

Table 10.1
'Diversity' and 'segregation' tracts, Chicago: a 1980-1990 comparison

1980

1990	Diversity	Moderate Segregation	Segregation	N
Diversity	40 58.8%	26 3.5%	1 0.2%	67 7.9%
Moderate Segregation	25 36.8%	213 74.2%	66 13.3%	304 35.7%
Segregation	3 4.4%	48 16.7%	430 86.5%	481 56.5%
N	68 8.0%	287 33.7%	497 58.3%	852 100%

Diverse tracts tend to cluster together (see Figure 10.1). With only a few exceptions, these tracts are concentrated in nine community areas.

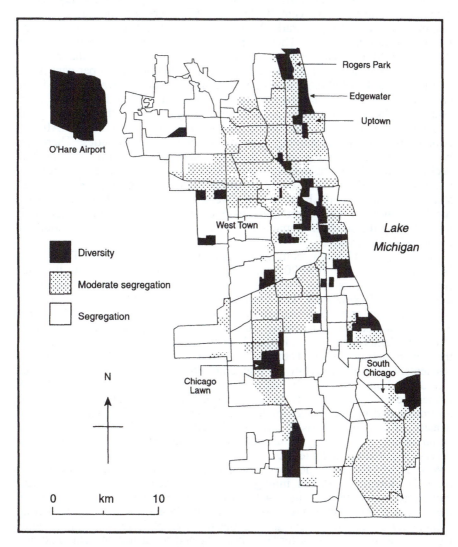

Figure 10.1 **'Diversity' and 'segregation' census tracts, Chicago, 1990**
Source: US Bureau of the Census

Using the quantitative analysis as a guide for our qualitative analysis, we selected six of these community areas for more detailed qualitative study. These six areas contained 47 per cent of Chicago's 67 diverse census tracts. The six communities were Rogers Park, Edgewater, Uptown, West Town, Chicago Lawn, and South Chicago. These community areas each have populations in the 60,000-90,000 range.[2] Rogers Park, along the lakefront at the northern boundary of Chicago is characterised by a dense population, 85 per cent living in rental units. In 1990 more than one-third of its population was foreign born, compared to a 17 per cent figure for the entire city. In addition to a more established White ethnic older population, in-migrants over the past 20 years include Russian Jews, Pakistanis, Asian Indians, and younger African-Americans and Latinos moving from other Chicago communities. There has been a large increase in the size of these two latter groups, with a concomitant decline in the White-Anglo population. However, while change is occurring, wholesale 'flight' or 'panic' by White groups is not taking place. Rogers Park shares a boundary with Evanston, a diverse Chicago suburb with a strong residential and commercial economic base. Loyola University's main campus is located along the southern boundary of this community, spanning its southern border with Edgewater.

Edgewater and Uptown, community areas just south of Rogers Park, have been diverse for more than 20 years. The public high school serving this area reports that students come from families speaking 65 different languages or dialects. Like Rogers Park, close to a third of the 120,000 residents of these two community areas is foreign born. Ethnicities range from older Irish and Swedish homeowners to more recent Nigerian, Ethiopian, Vietnamese, Chinese, Cambodian, Romanian, and Mexican residents — to name a few of the new immigrant groups. There are a significant number of African-American residents. Uptown has a relatively high concentration of government-subsidised affordable housing. In both communities, neighbourhoods of single-family homes are in close proximity to more dense high rise developments — both affordable and middle-income high rises. Edgewater and Uptown have a high density of community-based and social service organisations serving the communities and playing an active role in promoting and maintaining the diverse populations and interests.

West Town, two miles northwest of Chicago's central business district and once the domain of Polish immigrants, experienced an influx of African-Americans and Latinos in the 1970s. Despite some recent tensions between these three groups and newly arrived White middle-income gentrifiers, strong community organisations representing the interests of lower-income residents have been able to protect affordable housing and a balance of economic and ethnic diversity has been maintained (Huebner, 1994).

Chicago Lawn, on southwest side, is a working class neighbourhood, with moderately priced single-family housing stock, located in what is referred to as the 'Bungalow Belt'. In the past, Chicago Lawn was viewed as one of the strongest centres of White resistance to African-American 'infiltration'. Also known as Marquette Park, this community became the focus of national media when Martin Luther King attempted to confront Chicago's segregationist housing practices in the 1960s (Pacyga et al., 1991). Although there is still a dramatic contrast between this community and the very poor, virtually all-African-American community to the east, an Anglo-Latino diversity with a few African-American residents has developed in recent years. Chicago Lawn is a community working to survive in the middle of an old industrial area which has experienced a significant shift from manufacturing to a service employment base. Its location adjacent to again-expanding Midway Airport and the connection to downtown Chicago stores and offices through the new 'Orange Line' rapid transit, have been economic benefits.

The sixth community studied, South Chicago, is also at the heart of former industrial Chicago. Like Chicago Lawn, single-family home prices in South Chicago are well below the city average. The steel mills had attracted a diverse ethnic and racial workforce that lived in segregated communities within a broad radius of the mills. Traditional Black-White-Latino boundaries have changed in the past two decades. The diversity we see in South Chicago exists within a community devastated by the complete shutdown of a number of steel mills and the loss of thousands of well-paying union jobs.

In analysing the six communities, it is clear that different dynamics and forces face each of these neighbourhoods. The three lakefront communities to the north have fewer single-family homes and more foreign born residents. At this moment, West Town is a community successfully battling gentrification and racial change, although of all the communities studied it is the most vulnerable to the gentrification process which could displace low-income, predominantly minority families. The two southside communities have more single-family homes, more working class residents, and are facing the effects of economic shifts. While each community has its unique history and features which may make maintaining diversity more problematic or more manageable, as the case may be, nonetheless key common factors emerge. Thus, rather than analysing each of these communities separately — implying that each has its own unique explanation for stable diversity — we have analysed interview data and pulled out key factors which contribute to diversity maintenance overall

Diversity through the eyes of community leaders

In contrast to the inevitability of segregation that is implicit in many academic researchers' emphasis on ecological and structural forces, community leaders in diverse urban neighbourhoods focus on the ability of community organisations, block clubs, and other grassroots organisations to affect the future of the community. The approach used by the organisations studied is predominantly a *community-building* strategy. Just as racism and ethnocentrism are the products of manipulation of perceptions, so too can diversity or integration be a product of a countervailing manipulation of perceptions.

The need for a strong commitment to community is seen as basic among most of the leaders of pro-diversity community organisations. A tenants rights committee member articulated this well when he said:

> ... our main goal is to involve people to improve this community, to improve it so that they work with other residents in the area in doing that. It

wouldn't help if out of the sky came big beautiful stores, if the community didn't discuss it. If we didn't argue about what should go here or how it should happen, it wouldn't help. That wouldn't be community building, it has got to come from the hearts and souls, spirits of the community ... and the struggles of the community ....

Organisations build community in different ways and focus on different issues in the process. For example, one organiser states that efforts need to be culturally inclusive: 'We try to involve everybody in issues of the neighborhood. You know we do practically all of our literature in English and in Spanish and there are cases we do it in other languages as well, including French'. Including those individuals who speak different languages indicates an effort to be inclusive in community building in a diverse area.

As more diversity is present in the community, community-based organisations (CBOs)[3] see a need not only to keep a sense of 'community' strong, but to get people to tolerate and, in some cases, celebrate, ethnic, and racial differences. Respect and understanding, it is argued by one organiser on the far north side, must be conscious. He explains:

we try to involve, educate [and] show them what power ... they have working together ... There has to be a conscious [effort] not only to celebrate the diversity, but ... to get [people] to know each other. To know who they are, where they came from, and to begin to respect that, even if you don't like it.

Each of these efforts attempts to create community building based on shared values and understandings. A director of a youth organisation in Chicago Lawn provided a good overview of these ideas when she stated:

So what's happened now is that we have Latinos, Arabs, Christians, and Jewish people, all coming to the Lutheran church for basketball. So, *what you are doing is creating a community* that is working together and crossing those different lines. It has been very important.

Organisers are stressing social links between members of diverse populations.

Pro-diversity community organisations are challenging the 'common sense' notion that diversity means instability. Most Americans assume that racial and ethnic diversity do not typically work. Diversity is seen as a sign of imminent change — an indicator of instability.[4] Thus, for a community organisation to facilitate the development of a *stable* diverse community, the common sense notion that 'diversity equals instability' needs to be challenged. Creating stable diversity means manipulating perceptions about the community and even aggressively marketing the community. As one community leader put it: 'there are two different types of people who talk about diversity, [one] because they are afraid of it and how are we going to control it and contain it. And there are those who talk about diversity, because they really believe that we want to create a community of equals'.

To many of the community leaders, stable diversity has come about because communities have been able to put a 'positive spin' on diversity. In the case of one northside community, diversity is favourably described by saying 'what we have in common are our differences'. A high school principal in Edgewater echoes this sentiment by stating that 'most people, since you know they chose to live here, see [diversity] as a strength of the community ... as an asset'. Further north in Rogers Park, a group of developers has hired a marketing firm to advertise the community's diversity and stability. It is only logical that in a capitalist society where marketing and advertising is used to promote everything from candy bars to Congressmen, that advertising could be effective in promoting positive images of neighbourhood diversity.

Basic issues beyond manipulating perceptions

It is *not* only the manipulation of perceptions that has kept these communities diverse and stable. Addressing basic issues such as economic development, housing, community safety, and education have also been central.

Economic development

Because many of these diverse urban communities are ageing city neighbourhoods, continued investment in the local economy and infrastructure has been vital. A key interest among leaders is maintenance of quality shopping centres and other amenities. The head of an economic development organisation in Chicago Lawn explains that his community is not only fighting the forces of racial succession, but is 'fighting disinvestment'. He adds that this is a 'keep-even' battle, because 'fighting the negative doesn't produce the positive, it just stops the negative. It's kind of like if you amputate the arm it might stop the cancer growth, but you still don't have an arm'.

His organisation has been effectively shepherding a major economic development programme that is revitalising a main traffic and commercial artery in his community — a street that also borders West Englewood, a majority African-American community that has fallen victim to major business disinvestment. This business area acts as a 'seam' to sew together diverse groups not only within Chicago Lawn, but also between Chicago Lawn and its neighbouring community, allowing for a 'diversity of uses' instead of a detrimental border.[5]

In their economic strategy, Chicago Lawn leaders realise that they are involved in marketing their community. The leader of the Greater Southwest Development Corporation (GSDC) explains that leaders started asking questions: 'Why [do] neighborhoods deteriorate? Why do they go from okay places ... maybe not the greatest in the world, but adequate — a good place to raise your kids, go to church, and sleep?'. His conclusion is that this transition occurs through a vicious disinvestment-lower confidence-more disinvestment cycle.

Recognising that this is a combination of larger institutional decisions, e.g. decisions by banks, realtors, large employers, as well as by individual residents, he explains that neighbourhood decline and resegregation 'is about choice', about 'people who could choose to be there don't choose', about 'lenders not choosing to lend', about 'businesses not choosing to invest', and about 'home owners not choosing to buy'. The conclusion he draws is that saving the neighbourhood means 'creating a market' for that neighbourhood among both homeowners and businesses. As he puts it: 'It means competing in the large economy of neighborhoods that compete for people who have money to invest. That is producing the positive'. Here it is understood that while subjected to structural forces (e.g. discrimination, lack of governmental support), groups can intervene by attracting investment and creating a market for themselves. The GSDC did just that by influencing the opening of a new rapid transit line which makes their community more attractive (and affordable) to downtown commuters. The GSDC's intervention is aggressive, amazing considering a history of racial tension. Community economic development agencies in other communities studied are also engaged in building a positive image to promote investment and increase the worth of existing businesses and housing.

Full range of housing

Because racial and ethnic diversity in urban neighbourhoods is often congruent to economic diversity, provision of a broad range of housing options is also at the foundation of the diverse communities studied. Although it is common for 'trendy' and 'up and coming' urban neighbourhoods to change from low-income minority communities to middle income White neighbourhoods, many of the areas we studied have not experienced this wholesale gentrification. This is due largely to a mix of affordable housing and middle-income housing.

The mix can be created in different ways. The presence of single-family dwellings *and* apartment buildings (with a broad range of rents) can be one way in which the mix gets established. Another way in which a mix is often created is through the efforts of affordable housing advocacy groups that 'lock in' affordable housing (e.g. in the form of community-development managed buildings or tenant owned buildings) in a community when the community is 'down' and housing and land values are cheaper (Nyden and Adams, 1996). When middle-class investment in the community does occur, low-income residents are not displaced.

Bickerdike Development Corporation — a not-for-profit affordable housing group working in West Town has been involved in exactly such a 'locking in' process. West Town's proximity to the Loop has made it a prime target for gentrification. Bickerdike is attempting to stave off the displacement that has often accompanied gentrification, and in doing so is also involved in sustaining diversity through the provision of affordable housing to groups of various social levels.[6]

Community safety

Community safety is another key factor affecting residents' perceptions about the stability of a neighbourhood. However, it is not a simple relationship where perception of increased criminal activity equals increased instability. Each area we studied has experienced increased crime. However, respondents are more likely to analyse crime according to the extent to which it could be 'controlled' versus the extent to which it is 'out of control'. It is assumed that crime rates are on the increase everywhere; the threat to community stability is more related to any ineffectiveness in *controlling* crime than the existence of crime itself.

Crime prevention efforts not only increase the collective feeling that crime is 'under control', but also are effective organising opportunities that can create a stronger sense of community control. At the foundation of community safety efforts are block clubs. Each of the communities studied had fairly active block club networks. Block clubs are groups that meet to discuss problem areas and watch over what happens on their block. The director of the United Neighborhood Organization in South Chicago described these efforts as follows: 'The operating dynamics that we have is that the world is a very large place. I can't control what is happening globally. If you want to, you should be able to control what goes on your block'.[7]

Organisations involved in community policing prefer to describe their efforts as 'community safety' and 'community governance' initiatives — emphasising a community's ability to control its own quality of life (Friedman, 1994). A director of a youth collaborative project in Chicago Lawn put it this way: 'The issues come down to quality of life. That is what humans strive for. Is there a good quality of life here? Is it safe for their kids? Do they have facilities? Is there gangs that are problems? That's what human beings are looking for no matter what color they are'. Two other community leaders recognise that crime is an issue that has to be addressed if diverse neighbourhoods are to be sustained. The director of a community organisation on the southwest side observes that

> ... while crime is a problem in maintaining the diversity, it is also an issue that the overwhelming majority of people of all ethnic backgrounds agree on, that they want a safe neighborhood. And so it becomes a point of unification and we have seen that consistently in our work in the neighborhood.

The leader of a housing initiative in Rogers Park agrees that crime is an issue around which pro-diversity CBOs and networks can organise:

> ... it is a reality and if crime is not addressed then you are never going to have a stably diverse neighborhood. That's a problem threatening diversity but is also a unifying factor. Because 99 per cent of the people in this world disapprove of that sort of behavior and are willing to work together to stop that. So it is a paradox. What is a threat, might also be the hope. Because if that kind of diverse community can unite and work together to successfully address that problem ... you might have a permanent stable diversity.

The importance of schools

Schools follow closely after safety as an essential factor in positive or negative perceptions of a community and residents' commitment to a community. Although schools are a critical factor in keeping young families with children in or attracting new families to a particular neighbourhood, the image of schools affects the entire neighbourhood. Neighbourhoods often demonstrate their attachment to the positive image of local schools by accepting the school name as their own identifier. Conversely, when schools are seen as the organising point of gang activity, the entire neighbourhood suffers a blow to its reputation. Past research has shown that schools are very important institutions in shaping the community's attitudes toward racial, ethnic, and economic diversity (Orfield et al., 1996; Nyden et al., 1992).

In addition to shaping a community's broader image, schools can promote greater co-operation among children from different backgrounds. This contact can also provide the basis for stronger co-operation and cultural co-operation among adult parents. Although inattention to racial tensions can make schools a spark for disharmony within a community, they can be the place where intergroup co-operation is developed. As a parent and director of a housing development corporation reflects, 'I really believe in education. My children have been able to shirk most of the stereotypes in race and culture, because they've been raised in this community. In their educational setting, it is the children that draw the parents together'.

Local social networks and diversity maintenance

Block clubs and community organisations with direct contact with residents are the social building blocks of diverse neighbourhoods. These are the intermediary organisations that link residents to or bring residents in contact with larger organisations or larger social institutions, e.g. local government, economic development associations, businesses, or citywide fair housing organisations. These intermediate groups give residents a voice in decision making in these larger groups and networks.

However, these organisations and social networks serve as more than simple units in a hierarchy of political influence. These groups serves as *filters* for information and *circuit breakers* that stop potentially damaging negative information coming in from outside the community. Given the perceptions that diverse equals unstable, there is a critical and constant need in diverse communities to counter this assumption. In the diverse communities that we studied, neighbourhood-based networks provide a way in which residents can bolster each other's confidence in their neighbourhood. The networks provide a filter through which neighbourhood events, e.g. the purse snatching on the corner, the trash on the 1800 block of Elm Street, or the store closing on First Avenue, can be interpreted as being the work of an 'outsider', the result of a 'careless homeowner', or the result of 'poor business management'. These explanations can counter more neighbourhood threatening explanations such as crime is increasing, homeowners are all giving up on the community, or businesses are moving out of the neighbourhood.

These networks can also serve as circuit breakers, countering negative stereotypes of their community that exist in the minds of individuals outside the community. Past research has found that diverse neighbourhoods have been frequently perceived by outsiders as 'dicey', 'crime infested', and 'drug-ridden'. At the same time 'insiders', the residents themselves see the neighbourhood as a 'safe', 'family-oriented' community (Nyden, 1988).[8]

Conclusions

There are two threads in our analysis. One is a methodological thread looking at how approaches to research on racial and ethnic segregation can affect the conclusions of the research; the other is an analytical thread, looking at how grassroots organisations promote stable diversity. In terms of methodology, in examining diversity or segregation there is a need for a multi-faceted approach. Quantitative studies focusing on national or metropolitan area statistics often overlook critical neighbourhood level social dynamics. Emphasis on national and metropolitan area statistics can misdirect policy-making and future research projects toward national and regional institutions, ignoring the importance of community-level social institutions. While the impact of broader social institutions, e.g. federal, state, and city legislation; national and regional banking practices; and national or regional business trends, does influence residential patterns, these institutions are not the only factors affecting housing patterns. Grassroots-level organisations from community-based organisations to block clubs can also have an effect on the racial and ethnic patterns in urban communities. Although they are swimming against the American stream of segregation, communities in our case studies have demonstrated that local-level intervention can be effective in bolstering and promoting racial and ethnic diversity. Research that does not take this into consideration is providing only part of the picture.

The second thread in this chapter is an analysis of how local-level groups and organisations can influence the character of their neighbourhoods. Although much of the housing segregation literature has focused on macro-level institutions, we have found *local* activities to be effective in shaping the character of a neighbourhood. Much of this activity revolves around the manipulation of perceptions — perceptions about the current quality of life in diverse neighbourhoods and perceptions of where diverse communities are headed. In a society focused on selling goods and services by creating 'needs' through advertising, perceptions are the currency of social life. The real estate industry and fair housing advocates have long been aware of the central role that perceptions play in defining a neighbourhood as 'desirable' or 'not desirable'. Negative perceptions of a community can erode confidence for both long term and potential residents; positive perceptions are the foundation for economic and social vitality.

Our finding that the actions of community-based groups can influence the character and stability of a community has implications for understanding the future of American cities. While urban sociologists have increasingly focused on the national and global forces affecting individual cities, we should not retreat into a research-induced fatalism about the future of American communities. We are going to see a more diverse US population in upcoming decades. Will this lead to an America with more segregated communities or will we see the building of more stable, diverse communities in our cities? The answer to this question is as much in the hands of urban communities and local political leaders as it is within the control of national or global forces.

Methodological note

Measuring the extent of racial and ethnic diversity is a difficult methodological issue. We know what is *not* diverse, yet we often have difficulty conceptualising and thus, measuring what *is* diverse. Is there *a* proportion of racial and ethnic mixing in a neighbourhood that can be defined as diverse? Various measurements of diversity have been used (see White, 1986). For purposes of this paper, we argue that diversity is a continuum, from slightly to substantially integrated. We place tracts along this continuum based on the overall racial composition in the city.

We define diversity as the statistical mix represented by the city-wide proportions of racial and ethnic groups in a given year. For example, in 1990 the racial and ethnic breakdown of the Chicago city population was 43 per cent White, 38 per cent Black and 19 per cent Latino. Therefore a 'perfectly' diverse tract in 1990 would have been 43 per cent White, 38 per cent Black and 19 per cent Latino. Our measure takes into consideration the racial and ethnic characteristics of the overall population. We recognise that statistical diversity does not translate into social diversity, i.e. social interaction between people of different races and ethnicities. That is why we have included that qualitative component to not only determine what social forces have produced the statistical diversity, but to determine the nature of social interaction between various racial and ethnic groups.

The measure includes three racial or ethnic groups (White, Black, Latino) and is based on a comparison with the overall percentages of each group in the city.[9] The logic of the measure is fairly simple. The population composition of the tract is compared to the city average for that year (1990: White=43% Black=38% Latino=19%) (1980: White=46% Black=40% Latino=14%). The formula used to calculate spatial differentiation is:

$$1/2 \left(|CW - TW| + |CB - TB| + |CL - TL| \right)$$

Where C is a racial group (i.e. W=White, B=Black, and H=Latino) percentage for the whole city and T is the racial groups percentage for the tract. The sum is divided by two to measure in-flow and out-flow of the three groups. The range of scores for 1990 is between 0 and 81. The high-end of the range is determined by the tract furthest from the city average, in this case a tract that is 100 per cent Latino. For our purposes, a tract with a score closer to 0 is more diverse and conversely, one with a score closer to the high-end is segregated. Thus, this measure does not indicate the percentage of a certain group that would have to move to achieve evenness, all that is known is that *a percentage of the three racial groups* would have to move.

After calculating an index of diversity score for each tract, tracts were divided into three categories: diverse, moderately segregated, and segregated. These categories are based upon the mean index score and the standard deviation of all tracts in a given year.[10] Tracts with a score 1 1/2 standard deviations below the mean are considered diverse. Tracts between the diverse cutpoint and the mean are considered moderately segregated. Tracts above the mean index score are considered segregated. The mean was selected as the basis of division given that as a measure of central tendency, it considers the overall environment in which tracts are situated. Because the city of Chicago is highly segregated, we define diverse areas as those 1 1/2 standard deviations below the mean to ensure that we pick up tracts which are the most racially and ethnically diverse and not merely diverse relative to a segregated city.

We define as stable a neighbourhood that is in the diverse category for two consecutive Census years. Since most communities have experienced racial resegregation in shorter time spans than 10 years, our ten-year measure to determine stability is sufficient for our purposes of identifying stable, diverse communities. Also as noted in this chapter, most of the communities studied have actually been diverse for longer than ten years. Population data comes from the US Bureau of the Census, STF1A, for both 1980 and 1990.

The quantitative analysis provides a demographic overview, identifying diverse neighbourhoods. The qualitative analyses is of racially diverse residential areas. Our analysis involves a series of open-ended interviews with community leaders in areas identified as stably diverse from 1980 to 1990. A snowball sample of 38 community leaders and informants in each of six community areas were selected. Interviewees were selected in each community to represent a cross-section of community-based organisations, educational institutions, financial institutions, housing providers, youth services groups, and religious groups.

Notes

1   Of course, 'stability' is a relative term. We are not saying that the communities studied have been diverse for 50 years or will be diverse for 50 years (although in most cases, the communities studied have been diverse for at least 20 years). However, compared to most American urban and suburban communities the communities studied have remained diverse for longer periods of time.

2   Using research data from Chicago School studies in the 1920s, Chicago has been divided into 77 community areas which represent socially, economically, and geographically distinct areas created by natural and manmade boundaries (e.g. the lake, the river, interstates, large parkways, forest preserves, and large factories).

3   Community Based Organisations (CBO's) are not-for-profit organisations governed by boards, elected by local residents concerned with improving living conditions in a particular subarea of a city. Community-based organisations may serve a variety of constituencies ranging from the general population to specific groups such as women, African-Americans, or tenants (Nyden and Wiewel, 1992, p. 43).

4   In talking about the meaning of 'diversity' in American culture, we could borrow from the logic of the 'incivilities thesis' developed by criminologists to explain what causes people to socially and economically stop investing in a community and even move out of a community. The thesis argues that residents look to the surrounding social and physical environment for reinforcement of what they feel are desirable public norms (Lewis and Maxfield, 1980; Skogan and Maxfield, 1981; Wilson and Kelling, 1982). If the norms displayed in the neighbourhood environment are not viewed as positive, residents' commitment to the neighbourhood drops, i.e. their willingness to invest volunteer time in the community or home improvement money in their property might decline. This withdrawal from investment is often the prelude to flight. Authors of

the thesis give examples of signs of incivility: public drinking, abandoned buildings, graffiti, litter, poorly kept up parks, and/or children out of control. If we see diversity as a 'violation' of a public norm — i.e. the expectation that neighbourhoods 'should' be racially or ethnically homogeneous — then diversity could be seen as an incivility that leads to personal and institutional disinvestment in the community.

5   The concept of social 'seams' was developed by Jane Jacobs in *Life and Death of Great American Cities* (1961, p. 267).

6   Investing in affordable housing can be a tricky process. Over investment can not only overwhelm a community with low-income housing, but also overextend affordable housing groups. In the current hostile political and economic environment in the US, affordable housing organisations can find themselves on financial thin ice. One such housing development corporation on Chicago's far northside, People's Housing, went bankrupt within the past two years and has left the community with a high concentration of poorly maintained multiple family units housing hundreds of low-income tenants. This has not contributed to stability in the northern section of Rogers Park.

7   Of course if a community does not address residents' concerns with crime, it frequently experiences out-migration of residents and related disinvestment in local businesses (Taub, 1984; Skogan, 1990).

8   Although we have described how neighbourhood networks can be used for pro-diversity purposes, we want to caution that the mere existence of such groups does not produce tolerance and stable diversity. Like any other social mechanism, it can be used for varying purposes. In other communities, indeed in some of the same communities that we studied, such grassroots-level networks have been used to bolster segregation and attack pro-diversity efforts. Marquette Park, now one of the diverse communities studied, was the site of white supremacists, anti-integration activities in the 1960s and 1970s. Some block clubs and grassroots organisations fed racism at that time. However the growth of a more tolerant diverse community in the 1980s and 1990s was an outgrowth of actions by the active intervention by Catholic parishes among other forces.

9   American Indians, Asians and the 'other' category are included in the 'White' category in order to include all groups. Asians comprised less than two per cent of the Chicago population in 1990; Native American less than one per cent of the population. Because the index is simply a preliminary tool to enable us to complete more detailed qualitative research of specific communities, this statistical amalgamation or oversight of groups is balanced by subsequent analysis. In fact in the communities studied (particularly Uptown) Asian and Native Americans are both represented as ethnic/racial groups. In terms of the US Bureau of Census definitions of 'White', this includes individuals defining themselves as non-Hispanic, White; 'Black' represents those describing themselves as non-Hispanic Black.

10   In 1980: Mean=47.5, STD=11.6. In 1990: Mean=48.3, STD=12.7.

Part Five
Israel: seeking the 'New Jerusalem'

11 Some socio-spatial perspectives on co-existence between Arabs and Jews in five mixed cities in Israel

Ghazi Falah

Introduction

For some time now the focus of research on quality of life (QOL) in cities has been associated with material factors. Traditional indicators such as average *per capita* incomes, unemployment rates and cost of living indexes were often adopted to measure the 'overall health' of a nation and the well-being of its citizens. This approach for conceiving QOL came into its own in the late 1980s. A different set of criteria — largely non-material — was also put forward (Kuz, 1978; Pacione, 1982; Grayson and Young, 1994), ultimately redefining our view of QOL. As Shook (1982, p. 17) notes '[q]uality of life is not necessarily a direct result of high income and material wealth! Rather, it is a summing up of a city's or region's perceived value for the people who reside or who may contemplate moving there'. This definition is consistent with Grayson and Young's (1994, p 10) observation: '[t]he emergence of the quality of life debate can itself be seen as signifying the transition to a post-materialist society in which other values and the meeting of less basic needs increasingly shape people's actions'.

This chapter deals with the case of Arab and Jewish residents in the five mixed Arab-Jewish cities in Israel — Acre, Haifa, Jaffa, Lydda and Ramla (Figure 11.1). It seeks to examine the co-existence experience between the two groups there. I suggest that the perception of degree of co-existence can be better conceptualised as a non-material signifier of QOL. It in turn is generated or informed by various social, political, cultural factors bound up with the surrounding social environment. I also argue that co-existence between Arabs and Jews in the mixed cities and in the state of Israel more generally has a marked geographic expression, interlinked with the attributes of place and the conflicting expectations inherent in the minority-majority relationship.

The remainder of the paper presents: first, a background theoretical discussion including the application of adaptation theory to the study of Arab-Jewish relations, followed by a second section focusing on the study area and methodology; a third section examines how Arab and Jews in mixed cities

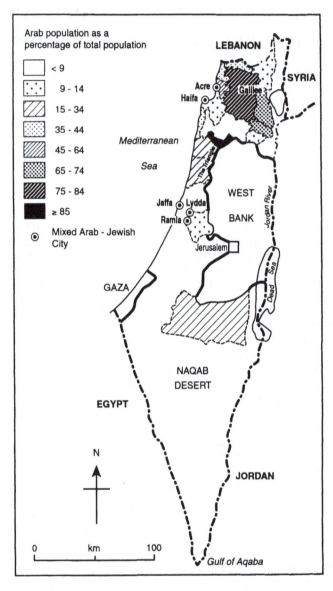

Arab population as a
percentage of total population

☐	< 9
⋯	9 - 14
▨	15 - 34
▨	35 - 44
▨	45 - 64
▨	65 - 74
▨	75 - 84
■	≥ 85
⊙	Mixed Arab - Jewish City

LEBANON

SYRIA

Acre
Haifa
Galilee

Mediterranean

Sea

Jaffa Lydda
Ramla

The Triangle

WEST

BANK

Jordan River

Jerusalem

GAZA

Dead Sea

NAQAB
DESERT

EGYPT

N

JORDAN

0   km   100

Gulf of Aqaba

Figure 11.1   The spatial distribution of Arabs in Israel's natural
regions, 1990 (excluding East Jerusalem)

assess co-existence in the state and in their cities. The fourth section explores co-existence as a manifestation of people's attributes. This is followed by some concluding remarks.

Adaptation theory and the discourse of Arab-Jewish relations

This paper draws on Helson's (1964) adaptation-level theory and certain concepts from psychology. In brief, this theory maintains that for any specified dimension of stimulus variation the individual establishes an AL (adaptation-level) which determines his/her judgmental or evaluative response to a given stimulus located on that dimension. Wohlwill (1974, p. 134) draws on Helson's (1964) adaptation-level theory in defining adaptation as a 'quantitative shift in the distribution of judgmental or affective responses along a stimulus continuum, as a function of continued exposure to a stimulus'. Harvey (1966, pp. 7-8) uses the term system (instead of organism) in his discussion on adaptability. For Harvey, adaptability implies the notion of accommodation to a given pressure emanating from the environment. According to him (1966, pp. 7-8), there are at least two ways in which a system could accommodate to deviant or pressureful environments. One way entails altering the environment; the other, changing the system in the direction of conformity to the environmental press. In turn, according to Harvey (1966, p. 8), accommodation via system change can be accomplished in two very different ways. One results in a loss of the integrity of the system and capitulation of it to the pressureful impingement. The other allows for maintenance of the system through articulation of new alternatives within it and the expansion of the boundaries of the system to include the previously deviant element. While in the first choice the system is better described as conforming or adapting to the condition emanating from the environment, the second choice is essentially an adjustment process because it has some influence on the environment and sometimes brings about certain changes within its premise.

To make adaptation theory a useful conceptual framework for our case study, we need first to clarify our terminology. Here the term 'environment' is used for all Jewish-related entities that have a relationship with or influence the existence of the Arab minority in Israel. This may include state government, local authorities, Jewish population, and Zionist institutions and organisations. Clearly, the kind of environment referred to is social and is the product of human construction. This environment is also seen here as a system and a subject of change. Sometimes roles can even be switched with the Arab minority; that is to say that the Arab minority becomes an environment and exerts an influence on the Jewish community (organism or system). From this perspective, a stimulus emanating from the Jewish environment has no absolute influence on the Arab minority. This statement means that our discussion is not grounded in environmental determinism of any sort. I note that adaptation theory is rooted traditionally in Darwinism (Helson, 1964, p. 37) and there is always the risk of its application being viewed as deterministic.

Both the 'organism' and the 'system' that are impacted by the environment are associated with the Palestinian citizens of Israel in its pre-1967 boundaries, better known as the Arabs in Israel or Israel's Arab minority. They made up some 15.5 per cent (or 846,700 persons) of the total population of the state in

1994. The size of the Arab population in the five mixed Arab-Jewish cities for the same year is 72,210 or less than 9 per cent of Israel's Arab minority population (based on Israel Central Bureau of Statistics, 1995). In applying adaptation theory to their case, it should be borne in mind that this group should not be viewed as passive consumers of whatever comes from the Jewish environment. Nor should one view the stimulus emanating from the Jewish environment as if it could have the power to impact on all Arabs equally. While they are loyal to state laws and orders they are not all prepared to express solidarity with state policies and majority aspirations. At the same time, in their response to conditions dictated by both the state and the Jewish majority, the Arab minority endeavours to maintain its integrity and bonds with the wider Palestinian nation with whom their state (Israel) has been at war for several generations. Thus the Arab minority has to demonstrate a double loyalty: to the state of Israel as citizens and to the Palestinian nation. In short, the Arab minority must adjust and modify their political aspirations in order to comply with the ideological structure of the dominant and defining Jewish environment.

A brief note on the study area and methodology

The term 'mixed cities' is a translation of the Arabic *Al Mudun Al Mukhtalata*, and the Hebrew term *Ha 'Areem ha Mua'uravot* and often is used in popular writing and in daily communication in Israel to describe those few cities where the Arab residents in them form a significant portion. Notwithstanding, these cities do not acquire any specific official designation for being 'mixed' and from the state's perspective these cities are conceived of as 'Jewish cities', like many others in the state. It should also be noted that the word 'mixed' is merely used in the Israeli context to reflect an ethno-demographic reality and not an actual residential pattern. Both Arabs and Jews continue to live in highly segregated residential areas; they have their own separate school system and religious service facilities. Using statistical data from the 1983 census return, Falah was able to calculate the five cities' index of dissimilarity (ID). His findings show that Haifa and Ramla were the highest with an ID of 0.776 and 0.718, respectively; Jaffa (ID= 0.669) came next; Acre (ID=0.654) and Lydda (ID= 0.647) were the lowest ones (Falah, 1996, p. 830).

Historically, all the five cities under investigation were defined as Palestinian cities with an almost absolute majority of Arab population residing in them over many centuries. Shortly before 1948, the three cities of Acre, Lydda and Ramla had an absolute majority of Arab residents and none of these could be regarded as mixed cities in that period. Haifa and Jaffa were turned into mixed cities before the establishment of the state of Israel. Haifa contained a fairly large Jewish majority, while Jaffa was regarded as having an Arab majority with a relatively large Jewish minority. The 1948 war wrought drastic changes in the demographic balance. Of more than 170, 000 Arabs in these cities before 1948, only some 20,000 persons remained after the war: in 1951, that was equal to only 11.6 per cent of the original Palestinian population of the cities. By 1990, that is within a period of 45 years, the Arab population of the five cities had tripled. The changing political circumstances in 1948 and after had a direct impact in the (re)production of people's choice of dwelling.

Let me now briefly explain the field research procedure by which empirical data for the present study was gathered. Based on two comprehensive surveys carried out during the period March-May 1991, I introduced a set of questions related to the topic of co-existence between Arabs and Jews. The interviewers who worked on this survey (i.e. Arab and Jewish students in Israeli universities) were instructed not to impose their own values and not to explain to the interviewees the various perceptions involved in the term co-existence. Each interviewee had to have his or her own understanding. Despite the various interpretations that may have been made by the interviewees, there is still a fairly good account of the common denominator that the term signifies. Both Arabs and Jews perceive co-existence as a positive enterprise grounded in the principle of *sharing place*. The two surveys, involving random samples of 600 and 570 questionnaires respectively, were distributed among the Arab and the Jewish populations in the five mixed cities. The number of questionnaires delivered to the Arab households was apportioned to reflect the size of this community in each of the five cities, based on 1983 census figures. In the second survey (i.e. the Jewish households survey), the apportioning of questionnaires to the Jewish population was done according to the same criterion as used for the Arabs. However, the apportioning of the number of questionnaires for each city was not made proportional to the size of the entire Jewish population of the city, but corresponded to the size of the Jewish population in areas of Arab concentration. It could be argued that the answers given by the Jewish respondents do not precisely represent the total Jewish population of the city. However, it does represent a segment of the Jewish majority exposed to social interaction (or similar familiarity of place) with their Arab neighbours more than it does any other Jews in the city.

For the purpose of this chapter, only those questions that are relevant to the present theme were analysed. While some reported answers consisted of rank scores from 1-5 (see below), because of the large sample size and because mean scores were of interest, it was reasonable to obtain approximate results using Analysis of Variance (ANOVA).

In order to assess the impact of place attribute (or the social environment) on the perception of both Arabs' and Jews' feeling about co-existence, I examine the configuration of answers for the two questions: (1) 'To what extent, in your opinion, is there co-existence between the Jewish and Arab citizens in Israel (within the green line border)?' and (2) 'To what extent, in your opinion, is there co-existence between the Jewish and Arab citizens in your city?' (along two geographic scales: the city and city sub-areas). Perceptual differences between Arabs and Jews are examined here by analysing the difference in mean answers (using Least Squares Means or adjusted means) in a given city, in a sub-area and for the ethnic group. The mean value here indicates a qualitative measurement of feeling of co-existence: it is a figure that points up the satisfaction level along a rank of 1-5: 1 equals 'To a very high extent', 2 = 'To a high extent', 3 = 'To some extent', 4 = 'To a low extent', and 5 = 'There isn't any coexistence'.

Co-existence in the state versus co-existence in the city

Discussion in this section will examine two types of co-existence foci: the wider Arab-Jewish co-existence in the state of Israel (within pre-June 1967 boundaries) and the experience of living together in urban centres. The first may involve some abstract assessment of the overall political dimensions of the relation between the two ethnic groups; the latter centres on the actual experience of the participants in their respective places. In what follows I furnish empirical assessment of perception of feeling about co-existence and draw certain conclusions about the way in which co-existence has been conceived.

With regard to 'co-existence in the state', Arab and Jewish score means were 3.42 and 3.53, respectively. However, for coexistence in the five cities combined, the Arab and Jewish score means were 2.94 and 2.75, respectively. In other words, while co-existence in the state perceived by both groups stands at approximately the mid-point between 'To some extent' and 'To a low extent' values, coexistence in the cities is much more positive: it stands at a point between 'To a high extent' and 'To some extent' values, but the point is closer to the latter. This suggests that both ethnic groups are consistent in attributing a higher level of co-existence in their respective cities than in the state in general. This finding is salient for the present analysis and can be attributed to several aspects of adaptation theory. First, the city provides the meeting ground for both groups and increases the prospects for interaction and integration. More than any other place in the country, intervening opportunities for meeting is extremely high in the mixed cities. People become more tolerant toward each other by belonging to the same place, and it follows that both groups are likely to conceive co-existence as possible and, indeed, a positive venture. In essence, this explanation is closely linked to what Sommer (1966, p. 64) calls a 'confinement' situation. Tellingly, living in a restricted space, dwellers control their emotions because they are in face-to-face contact for extended periods. Sommer (1966) illustrates this by an example of a situation where men at Antarctic stations keep a tight rein on their emotions because each member has no choice but to see the same faces every day and therefore must learn how to tolerate others — otherwise, living together becomes impossible. By analogy, Jews and Arabs living in mixed cities are arguably 'confined' in a broad sense to their cities. In due course, they crystallise their attitudes toward each other in relatively better terms than in other localities where Arabs and Jews live apart and do not meet on a daily basis. Of course, city dwellers have more options to deal with environmental stress than do teams of scientists in Antarctic stations; this could occur through the suburbanization and migration counter-reaction (Sonnenfeld, 1966; Wolpert, 1966). Alternatively, one may also suggest that, because both Arabs and Jews have been living together in the same localities for a long time, they have consciously or unconsciously been experiencing an adjustment to their environment, accepting the permanent presence of the other group and eventually becoming less sensitive to the danger of communal conflict or the ideological dogma of place purification. One may also submit that each city has its own specific attributes that have helped in cultivating peaceful relationships between the two ethnic groups. Such place attributes, which vary from city to city, could include the different composition of individuals in terms of their personal and neighbourhood characteristics as well as their backgrounds. In addition, each city has a different history of Arab-Jewish relations, a wide range of local institutions, and leadership that has inevitably contributed to the emerging levels of perceptual co-existence.

Table 11.1 summarises co-existence means for each group in the five cities and also documents the rate of their perceptual differences. Here the picture gets

Table 11.1
Co-existence means in the 'state' and in the 'city', by city and by ethnic group

City	Co-existence in the State		LSD p-value	Co-existence in the City		LSD p-value
	Arabs	Jews		Arabs	Jews	
Acre	3.48	3.20	0.0353	3.63	2.15	<0.0001
Haifa	3.65	3.29	0.0003	2.54	2.58	0.6381
Jaffa	3.68	3.61	0.9484	2.75	2.79	0.7175
Lydda	3.10	3.70	<0.0001	2.75	3.28	0.0002
Ramla	3.27	3.88	0.0010	3.09	3.02	0.7105

Co-existence: 1=to a very high extent; 2=to a high extent; 3=to some extent; 4=to a low extent; 5=there is not any co-existence

more complicated and each city has to be treated separately. Looking first at respondents' means of co-existence for the state, Figure 11.2 indicates that the Jews score relatively higher rates than the Arabs in Acre and Haifa, and have equal rates with those in Jaffa. In Lydda and in Ramla the reverse is true: the Arabs score the higher positive rates. The differences between Arabs and Jews in the four cities of Acre, Haifa, Lydda and Ramla are statistically significant (see Table 11.1). Figure 11.2 also indicates respondents' mean co-existence scores between Arabs and Jews in the city in which they reside. Here we arrive at a different picture: in the three cities of Haifa, Jaffa and Ramla, the Arab and the Jewish mean scores are almost equal (though both differ from one city to the other; no significant statistical differences were recorded). But, Acre and Lydda have maintained the same pattern that had appeared earlier in assessing co-existence for the state: namely, the Jews score higher positive rates than the Arabs in Acre; while the reverse is true in Lydda. The differences between the two groups in these two cities remain statistically significant (see Table 11.1). It should be noted that Jaffa also maintained the same pattern it had earlier (Figure 11.2). Here, Jews and Arabs have scored similar means for their city and for the state.

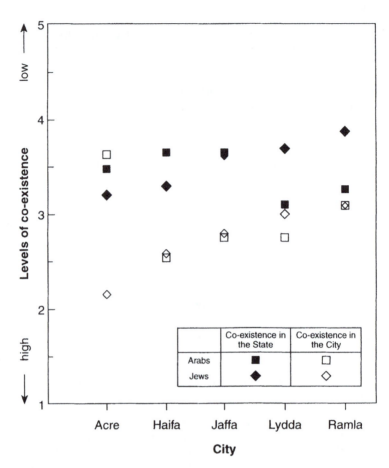

Figure 11.2   Co-existence in the 'state' and in the 'city', by city and by ethnic group

Variation in ethnic mixing

In order to establish some causal links (or at least some direction) between place attribute and co-existence, I examine respondents' perception in relation to spatial homogeneity of the place. To this end, the 'statistical areas' in the five cities were grouped under three ranges of ethnic mixing: 'Arab majority' is an area in which the Arab residents form 60 per cent or more of the total population of the statistical area (based on 1983 census figures). In 'equal mixing, the Arabs form between 40 and 59 per cent of the statistical area and, in an 'Arab minority' area, the Arab residents form less than 40 per cent. This grouping procedure is intended to create a similar set of ethno-spatial and demographic conditions within the residential environment and to test how such spatial arrangements could impact on the perception of co-existence.

Looking first at respondents' means of co-existence for the state, Figure 11.3 indicates that the Arabs recorded a higher positive means of co-existence (i.e. 3.00, 3.22 and 3.28) than the Jews in all three groups. In the two groups of 'equal mixing' and 'Arab majority' areas, the differences between Arabs and Jews are statistically significant at p=0.0004 and p=0.0152, respectively. Of

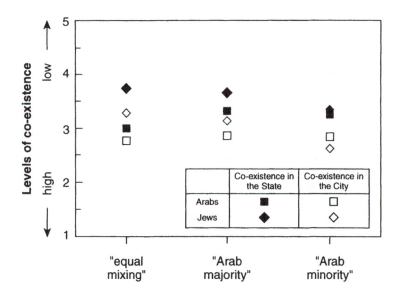

Figure 11.3   Co-existence in the 'state' and in the 'city', by type of mixing and by ethnic group

special interest are the changing means for the Jewish respondents: they change from 3.76 to 3.66 and to 3.36 as they move from 'equal mixing' to 'Arab majority' to 'Arab minority' areas respectively. This means that Jews perceive their most favourable situation for co-existence where there are only a small number of Arabs living in their residential areas. This pattern is even more pronounced when we examine co-existence in the city. Here the Jews have assigned the highest means for co-existence, 2.6, for the group 'Arab minority', compared with the means of 3.28 and 3.15 for the other two groups 'equal mixing', and 'Arab majority' areas, respectively. It appears that areas of 'equal mixing' are the least favourable for Jews. This finding can be explained by looking at the geographical characteristics of these areas in the city. Equal mixing areas are traditionally known as the least desirable residential places. These areas are also known for having an unstable population, that is, turnover of population there is frequent. This results in closing of apartments or housing for a lengthy period of time. Closed apartments are a target for vandalism, and the entire area is then perceived as an unsafe place. It should be noted that our discussion on 'equal mixing' areas is limited to three cities, as Acre and Jaffa have no such areas. Central to our argument is that 'equal mixing' areas do not furnish enough duration of residence for Jews to conceive co-existence in favourable terms.

Unlike those of the Jews, the Arabs' means for co-existence in the city are close to each other in value (2.77 versus 2.86 versus 2.83), and this suggests that ethnic spatial homogeneity does not play a major role in influencing Arab judgement for conceiving co-existence in the city. Other reasons should be explored. It is my thesis that these reasons are mainly related to the way in which both central and local government treat the Arabs and make them feel equal as citizens (see Falah, 1999).

Of course an Arab presence does not explain all of the Jewish conception of co-existence. However, the above finding suggests that such presence is perceived by Jews as a negative one. This is not the case for the Arabs with regard to a Jewish presence. A Jewish or Arab presence, whatever its level, does not seem to influence the Arab conception of co-existence. One possible reason for that is related to the nature of Arab-Jewish conflict in Israel, which is characteristically non-militant. Acre, Haifa or Jaffa never produced the violence of a Belfast or a Los Angeles. One researcher has noticed that the source of Jewish intolerance towards the Arabs is based on the perception of what the Arab might do to the Jews if they took control. (Shamir and Sullivan, 1985). This conclusion clearly fits the present empirical finding where the Jews do not like to see so many Arabs in their city sub-areas (see also Falah, 1997). Yet, the suggestion is that Arab intolerance towards the Jews is based on things that have already been done to them, things that they experience in their every day life. From the Arab perspective, it is the state and its local agents and not the Jewish citizens (or neighbours) at large, who are harassing them and trying to determine their destiny. Contexually, the barrier to achieving better terms of co-existence is not created by Jewish individuals but by the state institutions and associated policies towards the Arabs. This probably explains the absence of any strong link between Arab responses on co-existence and the grouping of statistical areas in terms of degree of spatial ethnic mixing.

Co-existence as manifestation of people's attributes

This section focuses on the question of co-existence in the city. Co-existence in the state as a manifestation of people's attributes will not be dealt with below. Central to the present analysis is an examination of the way in which people of different personal, social, economic and political orientations perceive co-existence. Generalisations here are based on a positivist analysis of relevant questions that were incorporated into the two questionnaires mentioned earlier. Differences related to sex, to social group and to religious denomination are examined. Then religious practice, class and affiliation to political parties will be analysed in that order (Table 11.2).

The gender dimension

Probably women have greater concern (as well as sensitivity) when it comes to maintaining peaceful relations with neighbours. Women who are not working often stay at home with their children and must assure that the home is a safe,

Table 11.2
Co-existence means, by city, by ethnic group and by selected personal variables

Personal Variable	All Cities		Acre		Haifa		Jaffa		Lydda		Ramla	
	Arabs	Jews	Arabs	Jews	Arabs	Jews	Arabs	Jews	Arabs	Jews	Arabs	Jews
Sex												
Male	3.05	2.77	3.62	2.09	2.40	2.82	2.89	2.82	3.06	2.86	3.37	3.33
Female	2.90	2.69	3.63	2.18	2.61	2.37	2.71	2.77	2.64	3.50	3.00	2.74
LSD P-value	-	-	0.9692	0.5770	0.0593	0.0024	0.3055	0.7706	0.0299	0.0043	0.1147	0.0653
Social/Religious Group												
Ashkenazis	-	2.78	-	2.14	-	2.77	-	3.27	-	3.23	-	2.63
Sefardis	-	2.62	-	1.85	-	2.47	-	2.69	-	2.89	-	3.33
Israeli Origin	-	2.74	-	2.15	-	2.37	-	2.63	-	3.53	-	3.18
Moslems	2.94	-	3.60	-	2.63	-	2.85	-	2.65	-	3.04	-
Christians	2.90	-	3.69	-	2.50	-	2.43	-	2.96	-	3.08	-
Religious Practice												
Religious	-	2.82	-	2.29	-	2.48	-	2.95	-	3.25	-	3.00
Traditional	-	2.84	-	2.20	-	2.81	-	2.63	-	3.53	-	3.17
Secular	-	2.76	-	2.15	-	2.58	-	3.08	-	3.02	-	3.03
Observe	2.93	-	3.48	-	2.52	-	2.87	-	2.75	-	3.09	-
Observe a little	2.93	-	3.60	-	2.50	-	2.77	-	2.76	-	3.07	-
Do not observe	2.94	-	3.70	-	2.64	-	2.59	-	2.74	-	3.13	-
Income Level												
High	2.99	-	3.67	-	2.49	-	2.57	-	2.80	-	3.10	-
Middle	2.83	-	3.61	-	2.47	-	2.83	-	2.42	-	2.89	-
Low	2.99	-	3.12	-	2.69	-	2.90	-	2.88	-	3.41	-
Party affiliation												
Religious	-	-	-	2.28	-	1.61	-	3.00	-	4.99	-	-
Labour-centre	-	2.67	-	2.18	-	2.39	-	3.53	-	2.58	-	2.81
Right-wing	-	2.97	-	2.13	-	2.67	-	2.64	-	3.78	-	3.86
Left-wing	-	2.22	-	2.47	-	2.17	-	2.61	-	2.33	-	1.61

Co-existence means: 1=to a very high extent; 2=to a high extent; 3=to some extent; 4=to a low extent; 5=there is not any co-existence secure place. In essence, much of their behaviour involves a continuous adjustment to stimuli within and outside the home. This sense of security at home is likely to be extended into and to inform the overall feeling of co-existence in the city.

As Table 11.2 indicates, the Jews demonstrate behaviour that differs markedly from that of the Arabs. There are salient differences from city to city. In both groups, the female scores (2.90 and 2.69 for Arabs and Jews, respectively) show slightly higher positive means than the male scores (3.05 and 2.77 for Arabs and Jews, respectively). In Haifa, Jaffa and in Ramla, Jewish females perceive co-existence as positively higher than their male counterparts. Differences in Haifa and Ramla are statistically significant. Only in Lydda do Jewish males perceive co-existence in more favourable terms than their female counterparts (2.86 versus 3.50) and differences are significant at $p = 0.0043$. For Jaffa differences between females and males are quite minor and not significant.

Looking at the Arab respondents' scores, Table 11.2 indicates that females score a higher positive means of co-existence in Jaffa, Lydda and Ramla but, statistically speaking, only in Lydda are differences significant (at $p = 0.0299$). It was only in Haifa that Arab males perceived co-existence more favourably than their female counterparts (2.40 versus 2.61), although differences here are not statistically significant. It should be noted that Acre scored the most favourable levels of co-existence for Jews (2.18 and 2.09 for female and male, respectively) but for Arabs the obverse picture is true (3.63 and 3.62 for female and male, respectively). In sum, one may say that females in both groups perceive co-existence in more favourable terms than do their male counterparts. Moreover, since Table 11.2 indicates that inter-city differences are more pronounced, it is evident that place still plays a significant role in shaping both male and female perceptions.

Social subgroups

Do perceptions of co-existence change according to subgroup? In order to examine this hypothesis, the Jewish respondents were grouped into three social groups: the Ashkenazis (originating from Western countries), Sefardis (Oriental Jews) and those of Israeli origin (i.e., they or their parents stem from the pre-state population of Palestine); (culturally speaking, the latter two groups are closer to the Arabs than are the Ashkenazis). The Arabs were grouped by religious denomination: Moslems, Christians and Druze. The Druze do not live in mixed cities and therefore were excluded from the discussion.

It is clear from Table 11.2 that in all the cities, there is no particular social group among the Jews that can be identified as having a consistent higher (or lower) positive rate of co-existence. For all groups, Acre is the most favourable city followed by Haifa then Jaffa. The least favourable cities are Lydda and Ramla. As Table 11.2 indicates, differences between cities are more pronounced. In short, co-existence is not an intra-Jewish group issue, but rather a city one.

With regard to the intra-Arab group variation (Table 11.2), the pattern is quite similar to that of the Jews; i.e. there is significant variation from city to city and no particular subgroup is associated with having a more favourable term of co-existence across all cities.

The religious dimension

Is there are any moral or religious dimension behind people's feeling of co-existence? This question has been examined by asking both Arab and Jewish respondents to what degree they practice religion. While Jewish respondents were grouped into religious, traditional and secular, the Arabs were divided into observance, little observance and no observance. As evidenced from Table 11.2, it is striking to learn that religious practice or moral obligation does not have any real link to co-existence. The way in which the above sub-groups have clustered their means close to each other in a single city and how the sub - group rank order is changing from one city to another, suggests that co-existence is perceived almost on an equal basis for all groups in a given city. Yet, as Table 11.2 illustrates, differences between cities are clearly emerging. This once again suggests that it is place or city attribute which is the salient issue at stake, and not religious practice.

Class and income

Class or income level are other factors which have a possible link to co-existence; these are examined below. There are some limits to systematic comparison between Arabs and Jews, or among the Jewish respondents themselves, as far as class is concerned. This is because the Jewish questionnaire does not include questions that address incomes. Class division in Israeli Jewish society is by and large structured around two social groups: the advantaged Ashkenazis versus the disadvantaged Sefardis. The former are better off than the latter (Tamarin, 1980; Massad, 1996). Yet comparison between Ashkenazis' and Sefardis' perception of co-existence that can be viewed from a class perspective is possible by utilising the data presented earlier in Table 11.2. Looking once again at the Table, the Sefardis are seen to record positively higher rates of co-existence than the Ashkenazis in four cities, but the differences are not statistically significant. In one city (Ramla) the Ashkenazis score a positively higher mean than the Sefardis, but the differences are not statistically significant either. Because of the lack of real differences in a statistical sense it is hard to attribute these findings to a class linkage. It may be that we have here some combination of class and cultural solidarity attributes that makes the Sefardis group appear as having a more favourable feeling of co-existence with the Arabs than do the Ashkenazis. After all, many Sefardi Jews migrated to Israel from Arab countries, and some of them also speak the Arabic language.

Co-existence as a manifestation of class is examined for the Arabs by obtaining relevant empirical data on household income. Three groups of income levels were identified during conduct of the field survey: high income (in which a household's total income is 1,601 and more New Israeli Shekels (NIS) per month), middle income (monthly income ranges between 1,001 and 1,600 NIS) and low income (monthly income is equal to 1,000 NIS or less). As Table 11.2 indicates, each city has its own unique characteristics, and each income group has to perform accordingly. No specific income group can be identified with consistency over all five cities. With such a result, one must conclude that class does not play a salient role in shaping Arab perceptions of co-existence.

Political party affiliation

The last attribute to be examined as having a possible link to co-existence is political party affiliation. The concrete question in the two questionnaire surveys that addressed this issue is 'To which of the political movements and parties are you most close in your political thinking ?' Based on the list of political parties who ran for the previous Knesset election (1988), the Jewish respondents' answers were classified under four groups: the right wing parties, the labour-centre parties, the religious parties and the left parties. The Arab respondents' answers were grouped into supporters of Zionist parties (including Jewish religious parties) and supporters of non-Zionist parties. About 40 per cent or more of Arab votes go to Zionist and Jewish parties in each national election.

Table 11.2 illustrates the distribution of Jewish groups' means. One may point to a pattern of co-existence here if the religious group is excluded from the comparison. The religious group behaves very differently from one city to another and also differs from the other groups in the same city. For example, this group generates similar scores to the other groups in Acre. In Haifa it scores the most favourable means and in Lydda the least. The group does not exist in Ramla and in Jaffa its scores locate at a point between the centre-labour and the left or the right group. Looking at the behaviour of the remaining groups, the left scores the most favourable means in four cities (i.e. Haifa, Jaffa, Lydda and Ramla). In the fifth city (i.e. Acre) the left has the least favourable scores but, statistically speaking, it has almost an equal value to (or is at least very close to) other groups' scores. On the opposite end of the political continuum, the right wing group contrasts with the left because it views co-existence to the least favourable degree. Based on what has been said, it is possible to confirm an existing causal relationship between people's affiliation to political party and perception of coexistence. The pattern suggests that it is the left which perceives co-existence most favourably, followed by the centre-labour, while the right is the least favourable. This pattern is not consistent for all cities. Place attributes intervene, play a moderate role and pull the pattern in different directions. This can be seen from the behaviour of the religious group, from the scores for Acre (which are almost equal for all groups) and from inter-city differences.

The results of the Arab respondents' scores provide further evidence with regard to the possible linkage between party affiliation and perception of co-existence. As Figure 11.4 indicates, in all five cities Arab supporters of the Zionist parties score higher positive means than the non-Zionist party supporters. In Acre and Jaffa the differences between the two groups are significant at $p=0.0066$ and $p=0.0405$ respectively. Place attribute also plays an important role as evidenced by the differences between city-to-city scores. It is not surprising to see that Arab respondents have performed in such a pattern where those who support Zionist parties perceive co-existence more favourably than others. It follows that this group has more contact with the Jewish counter-partner, and eventually such contact is translated into mutual benefits. Having adopted the political agenda of the Zionist political parties, the Arab supporters have in effect made a major step in adjusting their needs to those of the Jews. It follows that co-existence with their fellow Jews is perceived as a positive reality. The same can also be said in the case of the Jewish left. For their part, the left has adopted some of its Arab partners' claims and thus has established better terms of contact as well as co-existence with the Arab population than it has with the rest of the Jews.

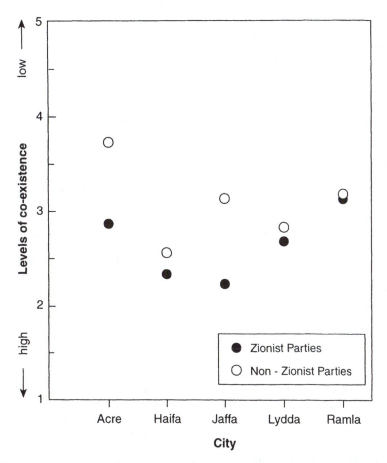

Figure 11.4   **Arab perception of co-existence in the 'city', by city and by political party affiliation**

Concluding remarks

This chapter has examined the relation between Arabs and Jews in Israel. Utilising the fruitful concept of adaptation theory, we were able to explore the scope of co-existence between the two ethnic groups. Three major findings emerge: (1) both Arabs and Jews agree that the extent of co-existence in their respective city of residence is much more positively developed than in the state as a whole; (2) more than any other factor, place attribute plays a central role in determining the scope of co-existence; (3) co-existence between Arabs and Jews is inseparable from the wider political issue as evidenced by the configuration of co-existence means along the lines of political party affiliation.

A further dimension is the nearly total absence of direct linkage between co-existence and other independent variables such as sex, social group affiliation, religious practice, class or income level. This finding is salient here since it underscores the role of the place (i.e. the city) in shaping people's sense of co-existence with each other. The city has its own environmental autobiography that impacts all groups. This latter reflection is important partly because it refutes some of the myths often present in Israeli popular writing. For example, the Christian Arabs are frequently seen as the Jews' potential 'allies' and have been privileged by the state over the Moslems. One might thus expect them to come up with more favourable co-existence means, but our findings did not support this. The same can be said about the Sefardi Jews who are seen by many as the natural supporters of right-wing political parties. Therefore one would expect them to be less enthusiastic about co-existence with Arabs. This was also not borne out by the findings. What seems to matter here is the city in which the Arab-Jewish encounter takes place. How does this city provide the appropriate environment for people to interact with each other and feel a part of the place? This is the central issue.

How then can the society progress from here and what are the prospects for better terms of co-existence? What are the concrete steps that must be taken so that, for example, people will feel co-existence at the level of the state has reached that perceived at the more local levels in the city. And how can co-existence in the city be further enhanced? In order to make practical suggestions, I suggest utilising Harvey's (1966) reflection on the interaction between the system and the environment. From the Arab perspective, achieving an optimisation means that the environment must be significantly altered — thus, Israel and Israeli society must change many of its hegemonic codes. For example, Israel should cease to be defined as a Jewish state but rather as a state for all its citizens. The Arabs have to be seen as full partners in nation-building and the state must take concrete measures and act as a kind of social engineer, making sure that the Arab citizens are integrated fully into state affairs. This option is hard to achieve (but not impossible) since most of the state resources are in the hands of Zionist organisations that allocate them exclusively to the Jewish segment of Israel's citizenry. In addition, the Jewish majority will not readily accept such changes in their environment since it will most likely affect their material well-being. Looking at the situation from the Jewish perspective, in order to achieve full optimisation the system (i.e. the Arabs) must either be rejected (i.e. transferred externally) or assimilated into the environment. While the first option entails high political risk and will not be supported by the international community, the latter has never been seen as a desirable option because of religious reasons at the very least. What remains is a double option that allows the maintenance of the system (i.e. the Arab identity) while creating several 'openings' within the Jewish environment so that the system could be actively integrated within it without the risk of being undermined. To put this in terms of the current Israeli reality: there is no shortage of governmental and non-governmental organisations that are currently advancing Arab-Jewish co-existence in Israel. Yet not all of these bodies can be very credible, at least from the Arab perspective, since their activities include elements aimed at containing the Arab citizenry. By and large, only 'pre-approved' Arab members can join their activities. In other words, the system has to be adapted to a state-supported hegemony. The Israeli authorities and the Jewish majority must be aware that co-existence with the Arab minority cannot be attained by force. As Frank (1989) notes, 'man does not live by bread, nor even by GNP, alone'. He needs among other things '... reasonably clean air, feelings of participation and community, and an atmosphere of security and trust within and among nations' (Frank, 1989, p. 75). Israel must assure its Arab citizens that they are not strangers in their own homeland. Past mistakes must be corrected, resources that have been appropriated from Arabs and given to the Jews must be returned. A new set of co-existence codes (and what is 'non-biased' discourse and imagery) should be established. Arab participation must have power and should not be limited to matters only of concern to Arabs. Access to state jobs must be based on equity. The list of possible suggestions is far too long to be presented here. The bottom line is that the situation for Israel's minority (and its imagery in the media and public mind) must be drastically improved. That both Arabs and Jews have rated co-existence in the state to a point between 'To some extent' and 'To a low extent' should alarm the government and signal the need for change.

To improve co-existence in the city is much easier. There is always a spillover effect, whether the measurement was taken in the city or in the state. In the city, Arabs and Jews are both resident. There is no need to travel long distances to create joint activities. To be sure, any concrete measurement to improve relations between the two groups can be quickly felt and monitored and useful lessons can be learned. After all, adaptation theory is based on learning. Local government could play a major role in bringing the two groups to feel at home in their city. In concrete terms, local government could develop an effective communication system and deliver messages on a daily basis so that residents can be exposed to each other's cultures and needs. Local cable systems in which members of both groups participate would be helpful to disseminate information, exchange opinions, and participate in improving mutual images. The local government could undertake concrete activities during Moslem and Christian events and holiday celebrations to make its citizens feel welcome and full members of the community. Municipal budget and place allocations must be made available. No less than the Jews, the Arabs too need to demonstrate and enjoy the elements of their civil religion. The status of the Arabic language must be improved and should be made equal to Hebrew in any official communications between local government and the Arab residents of the city. These suggestions are not exhaustive. Others are welcome and although one can conceive of these as revolutionary or utopian, they can be justified by the spirit of Israel's Proclamation of Independence. Of course, there are always many ways to bypass fundamental obligations and portray Israel's situation as an exceptional case in which the current status quo is unalterable. Be that as it may, cities will remain the best evidence for co-existence as a reality and a dream, foreshadowing needed changes on a possibly not so distant horizon.

Acknowledgements

This paper was written while the author was visiting the Centre for Urban and Community Studies, University of Toronto. The support of the Centre is gratefully acknowledge. I am also most grateful to the Ford Foundation (New York) for a grant (No. 890-0439) to finance the research on relations between

Arabs and Jews in ethnically mixed Israeli cities on which this chapter is based. I also wish to express many thanks to the numerous Arab and Jewish students who were involved in distributing questionnaires and conducting interviews.

12 The Jewish-Arab struggle for the environs of Jerusalem

Elisha Efrat

Introduction

Few cities evoke such strong emotional response from so many people as does Jerusalem. Sacred to at least three major religions, Jerusalem has long been a source and a scene of contention among the adherents of these faiths and their political sponsors. During the past half of the 20th century, each of the three religions, represented by a Christian, a Jewish, and an Islamic polity, has attempted to determine the orientation of development in the city. Each effort has had only limited success. The particular physical characteristics of Jerusalem and the religious aspects of the settlement have produced a unique combination of factors that affect decisions by politicians and planners, regardless of the controlling administration. These conditions are likely to remain influential in the future.

Since 1948 Jerusalem has usually been discussed in terms of a threefold division: the Old City and East Jerusalem (both under Jordanian control until 1967), and Israeli West Jerusalem (Figure 12.1). The Old City comprises five areas: the Armenian quarter, the Christian quarter, the Jewish quarter, the Moslem quarter, and the Temple Mount which, depending on religious orientation, is also known as Mount Moriah, Dome of the Rock, or Haram esh-Sharif. The Old City is conveniently and precisely defined by its impressive encircling walls, built during the reign of the Turkish Sultan Suliman the Magnificent early in the sixteenth century.

East Jerusalem usually refers to the parts of the city to the north, east and south of the walls of the Old City. The population of East Jerusalem is now about half-Arab, half-Jewish. In West Jerusalem the population is predominantly Jewish (Efrat and Noble, 1988).

The neighbourhoods in the city

The uneven topography of the Jerusalem region profoundly affects the settlement and growth patterns of the city. Hillocks and isolated interfluves

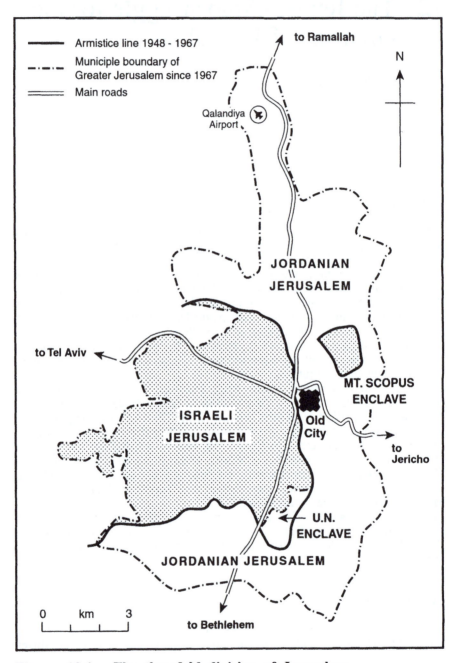

Figure 12.1   The threefold division of Jerusalem

alternate with winding valleys and scattered basins. These lower-lying areas originally were used for agriculture and for access, and on the steeper slopes were wastelands, forested parks, cemeteries, and public open spaces. The high elevations became the locations of residential neighbourhoods and independent villages that were subsequently absorbed by the expanding city. The mosaic of residential clusters separated by agriculture, open or institutional zones emerged as the standard pattern of settlement in late 20th century Jerusalem.

The long-established neighbourhoods beyond the Old City developed through years of accretion. Instead of displaying the conventions of modern city planning they often reflect the personalities of their founders and original inhabitants who generally had a common origin and who formed a close-knit social group. In contrast with the modern practice of neighbourhoods or towns, planned by central governmental authority that are settled with heterogeneous inhabitants who must undergo social education to adapt to new surroundings and neighbours, these old communities began with residents of relatively similar background, experience and orientation. Settlements of this type were associated with each major religion.

More than thirty such residential neighbourhoods had emerged in Jerusalem prior to World War II. The Jewish settlements were mostly west of the Old City. A further impetus to the proliferation of distinctive residential neighbourhoods emerged solely in the Jewish community. Jews often refrain from mixing with their neighbours, a tradition that reflected centuries of discrimination in widely scattered areas. Most Jews who arrived after 1918 were not as bound by the conservative religious traditions, and conflict and tension soon arose between orthodox and liberal groups. With continued population growth, crowding and congestion in the Jewish settlements eventually led to the planning and the erection of neighbourhoods in western architecture styles prevalent in the 1920s and the 1930s. However, the established neighbourhoods were largely unaffected by new trends. Gradually long-term residents who were less bound by conservative religious interpretation migrated into the westerly parts of the city, and the buildings thus evacuated in the old quarters were taken by the expanding orthodox Jewish communities.

The neighbourhoods of East Jerusalem are more likely than ones elsewhere to be outgrowths of independent villages that coalesced. These neighbourhoods tend to be traditional in orientation and unpatterned in layout. As with other parts of the Muslim world they shared rigid ideas about neighbourhood form and housing to ensure maximum privacy of women and to deflect casual traffic from private spaces (Costa and Noble, 1986).

The divided city

From 1948 to 1967 Jerusalem was a politically and a religiously divided city. The armistice line in 1949 confirmed the division of the city and created a neutral zone between the Jordanian and Israeli military positions, to be administered by the United Nations (Figure 12.2). That no man's land comprised seven areas, but along most of the dividing line, hostile positions were immediately adjacent to each other. The armistice line ran through land

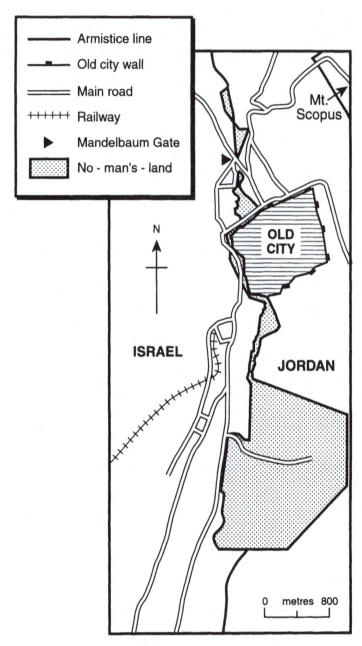

Legend:
- ——— Armistice line
- ■■■ Old city wall
- ═══ Main road
- ++++++ Railway
- ▶ Mandelbaum Gate
- ▨ No - man's - land

N

Mt. Scopus

OLD CITY

ISRAEL

JORDAN

0   metres   800

Figure 12.2   The armistice line in divided Jerusalem, 1948-1967

that was open, undeveloped, or occupied by former roadways. The Jordanian army occupied the Old City and East Jerusalem, and the Israeli army controlled Mount Zion, West Jerusalem, and an important enclave on Mount Scopus.

The division symbolised by the armistice line worsened during the next nineteen years. Each political sector in the city underwent separate development with different orientations. Connections between eastern and western Jerusalem were effectively severed, because streets were often blocked by cement walls as a protection against snipers, and prominent buildings near the line were fortified. In the central area, the Jordanians had the advantage of occupying the massive 16th century walls.

The portion of Jerusalem under Israeli control was oriented to the narrow corridor connecting it with the rest of Israel and ultimately the Mediterranean coast. Arab Jerusalem was generally focused eastward, especially toward Amman, the capital of Jordan. The population of the city was almost totally segregated on the basis of ethnicity: virtually no Arabs, either Muslim or Christian, lived in West Jerusalem, and no Jews inhabited East Jerusalem. Immediately after the division, the occupants of the Jewish quarter in the Old City were forcibly evacuated to Jordan, but they were released nine months later. Most of the Arab residents in West Jerusalem fled at the outbreak of hostilities.

In 1948 and immediately thereafter, Israel authority in Jerusalem seemed to be better organised than the Jordanian counterpart. The former quickly recognised that effective claims had to be based on physical control. By December 1949, the Israeli government began to shift offices from Tel Aviv to Jerusalem, and on January 1950, the Knesset averred that the city has always been the Israeli capital. In many circles that move was considered to be a contravention of the UN resolutions that had decreed the international status of the city. Most foreign governments did not transfer their embassies from Tel Aviv to Jerusalem. Nevertheless, Jerusalem has functioned as the de-facto capital since 1950.

The Arab sector of Jerusalem did not enjoy the level of organisation and efficiency that characterised the Israeli portion. Part of the situation was the confused political circumstances that marked the fate of the Arab Palestinian territory and advocacy. The Arab state projected in the UN resolutions about post-war Palestine did not materialise, and the central Arab Zone was ultimately absorbed by Jordan. The political change implied an economic one. The absorption of the West Bank by Jordan shifted the orientation of commercial activities eastward to Amman. Merchants in the Old City, previously wholesalers and suppliers for the East Bank, became dependent on imports from Amman. The eastward orientation affected the physical layout of Arab Jerusalem and encouraged its spread eastward onto the difficult terrain of the Judean desert as well as along the road to Jericho and toward Ramallah on the north. Another highly significant aspect was the increased pressure to develop the eastern flanks of the Temple Mount, the Qidron Valley, and the Mount of Olives, areas whose use was especially sensitive because of their Jewish and Christian associations.

Expansion of Arab Jerusalem was also hampered by a general lack of suitable space for rapid urban development. Areas to the east and south-east not only introduced archaeological considerations, but had also unsuitable terrain for expansion. Little expansion occurred to the south, because the direct connection to Bethlehem had been severed. The winding road subsequently built on the eastern flank of the Jerusalem hills was hardly an urban thoroughfare. Expansion was consequently channelled along the saddle in the hills, on both sides of the Jerusalem-Ramallah corridor on the north.

The reunified city of Jerusalem

The Six Day War began on 5 June 1967. Shortly after its conclusion, Israeli annexation of East Jerusalem and the Old City brought Jerusalem under a single political control. For security reasons, military officials and politicians made hasty decisions about the exact location of the new boundaries of the reunited city. Two goals guided those decisions: military considerations, especially the inclusion of heights to facilitate defence, and a desire to maximise the amount of territory but to minimise the size of the Arab population. Difficulties of achieving the latter were reflected in the fact that between 60,000 and 70,000 Arabs were included in the united city that was approximately three times larger in area than the exclusively Jewish pre-1967 portion controlled by Israel.

The boundaries of Jerusalem, which were delineated in 1967, were expedient rather than logical (Efrat and Noble, 1988). They included too much mountainous area and too many Arab neighbourhoods and suburbs which had never before belonged to the city. By delineating these particular boundaries, Israel's purpose was to include all the hills and ridges from which Jewish Jerusalem had suffered artillery shelling by the Jordanians. The boundaries of reunified Jerusalem extend up to the western fringe of the Judean Desert in the east, to the airfield of Qalandiya in the north, and to Bethlehem in the south. Jerusalem comprises an area of 108 square kilometres, 2.8 times greater than that of the city before the Six Day War. Only the western boundary abuts territory which was part of Israel between 1949 and 1967 (see Figure 12.1).

Among other techniques, the reunification of Jerusalem was accomplished by confiscation of Arab land, and by a rapid construction of seven new Jewish neighbourhoods. These residential settlements were built at strategic locations partially encircling the pre-1967 city. On the other hand, no new Arab neighbourhoods have been established in East Jerusalem since 1967, and no institutions for the benefit of the growing Arab population have been created.

Israel's intention, following the reunification of Jerusalem, was to prepare the urban area as a capital to which many Jews would immigrate and increase, thus providing a counterweight to the rapidly expanding Arab population in East Jerusalem and its surrounding area. Since 1967 the Arab population has gradually increased, but the efforts made by the Israelis to populate Jerusalem with Jews have not kept pace with the Arab natural increase.

The Jewish-Arab struggle in the city

Since the Six Day War unprecedented building activity has been conducted in the Jerusalem area with Arab financing and co-ordination between landowners, former mayors, heads of village councils and 'mukhtars'. Areas that were neglected were now cultivated, and every month dozens of houses were erected in the vicinity of the city.

The demand for workers from among the Arabs of the occupied territories grew in the course of time and the inhabitants of Judea, especially from Mount Hebron, began streaming to the building sites in Jerusalem, and gradually moved into the Old City of Jerusalem with their families, despite its crowded conditions. The original residents then moved into the Old City suburbs. The Arab population of Jerusalem has more than doubled itself since 1967, and by 1995 amounted to about 160,000.

At the same time the demographic balance in the city has changed. The annual increase in the Jewish population was about half of the Arab and the ratio of 73.3 per cent Jews to 26.7 per cent Arabs in 1967 shifted to 72 per cent Jews and 28 per cent Arabs in 1995. This trend has obtained since 1969, and figures have accelerated with the government assisted move of Jerusalem residents to nearby towns beyond the 'Green Line'.

In recent years Arab construction in Jerusalem, has also acquired a political tinge. The National Guidance Committee of the Arabs of the occupied territories has urged the inhabitants to plant trees and erect buildings in every place designated for Jewish settlement. The Arab villagers of Judea and Samaria made no distinction between State land and private land. For them both were lands to which the occupation authorities had no right. The areas never operated according to an overall plan, had a long tradition of unauthorised building, and lack awareness of planning, so that the application of construction regulations there was extremely difficult (Efrat, 1988).

In the north-west villages of Jerusalem a few thousand new buildings have been erected since 1967. On the mountainside north of Jerusalem also a few thousand have been added since then. In East Jerusalem the spread of Arab construction and the acquisition of land for building purposes was obvious. South of Jerusalem the pace of growth has been smaller, but there too several hundred units were added.

This accelerated Arab construction had implications for the future planning and development of Jerusalem. Some routes had to be changed due to this speedy Arab construction that interrupted the continuity of Israeli spread in many places. Arab construction had spatial and political implications, involving the occupation of considerable territory by a relatively small population, control of important roads connecting Jerusalem with the environs, the placing of obstacles between sites of Jewish development, and the creation of difficulties in providing services.

These developments impelled the Israeli authorities to take preventive measures in the form of confiscating land. Jewish private individuals and public bodies have been acquiring hundreds of acres of land, occupying as much territory as possible in order to ensure orderly construction and development of the region in the future. The settlement and development authorities claimed that, within one or two decades, the settlement policy of the government would prove to be a solution to the establishment of rural and semi-urban settlements, based on a comprehensive regional plan, to the east of the Arab population. It will be effective and be able to compete in size with other Arab concentrations.

The Jewish-Arab struggle in the environs

In regard to the Jewish areas of settlement in the region, in many places around Jerusalem Jewish settlements were erected. The townlet of Givat Zev, for instance, houses about 7,100 inhabitants. East of Jerusalem is the town of Maaleh Edummim, being rapidly populated, with about 16,000 inhabitants by 1995. The Jewish expansion over the region was designed to ensure control of access to Jerusalem, there being no desire to return to the pre-1967 situation, when Jerusalem was a cul-de-sac, cut off from its environs.

The Jewish-Arab struggle for the Jerusalem area has a demographic aspect as well. At the end of 1994 Jerusalem had about 552,000 inhabitants. The Jews numbered 393,000 and the non-Jews 159,000. Furthermore, the Jewish population of the city is ageing, while the Arab population is becoming younger.

The 160,000 Jews who now live in East Jerusalem comprise a third of the total Jewish population in the city. By the extension of the municipal boundaries from 9,500 acres before 1967 to 27,500 acres after the Six Day War, about 4,250 acres of land have been confiscated by the Israeli authorities for the establishment of seven new Jewish neighbourhoods which were built later on in the 1970s. Jewish settlement in East Jerusalem was seen as a political act with the aim of stabilising the enlarged municipal boundaries. The official guidelines were 1) not to settle Jews in high-dense Arab areas; 2) to keep the permanent demographic ratio between Jews and Arabs around 72:28; 3) to occupy maximal land with minimal Arab population, and above all 4) to prevent the division of the city in the future. Most of the confiscated land which was added to the city was taken from 28 neighbouring Arab villages, and partly from the towns of Bethlehem, Beit Jala and El-Bire. As a result, 17 Arab villages were by this act bisected by the new municipal boundary (Figure 12.3).

It should be indicated that thousands of Israelis reside not only in East Jerusalem, but also in suburbs and settlements adjacent to the northern, eastern and southern municipal boundaries. While inside Jerusalem a third of the population is Arab, in the near periphery of the city, between Ramallah in the north, Bethlehem in the south and Maaleh Edummim in the east, or in the so-called Jerusalem metropolitan area, there live about 750,000 people, half of them Jews and half of them Arabs, in separated communities mingled in the area as a whole.

The Israeli authorities were interested in a rapid construction of housing in Jerusalem and its environs and in a fast Jewish populating of the added areas in the town and its periphery to prevent the closure of Jerusalem by Arab building in the south, east and north. In the so-called 'influence zone' of Jerusalem, between Ramallah in the north, Hebron in the south and Bet Shemesh in the west, which is much wider than the above-mentioned metropolitan area, there reside about 1.125 million inhabitants, 55 per cent of them Jews. In Jerusalem itself there live 47 per cent of the total 'influence zone' population, among them 72 per cent Jews and 28 per cent Arabs. It is considered that by the year 2010 the Arab proportion of the population might increase to 31 percent — as against 69 per cent for Jews. In the 'influence zone' of Jerusalem, except the small part of the western mountainous corridor, 90 per cent of the inhabitants are Arabs.

The Israeli policy in that case was twofold: to increase the Jewish population

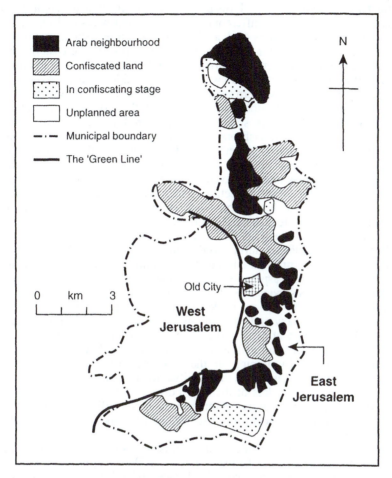

Figure 12.3   Confiscated lands in East Jerusalem, 1995

in Jerusalem by rapid housing and encouragement of new immigrants to settle there, together with an increase of Jewish population in the periphery, which consists of the metropolitan area and the zone of influence, by establishing and populating new settlements which belong to the occupied area of Judea. It was intended, actually, to develop an axis of Jewish urban sprawl from Maaleh Edummim to Jerusalem to Givat Zev to Ramot, and another one from the Etzyon Bloc to Betar and Jerusalem.

Jerusalem is also an example of the political problem which has led to the Palestinian uprising. Twenty eight years of reunification, and eight years of the Arab 'Intifada' uprising in Jerusalem, can be examined from the perspective of the functional interrelationship between Jews and Arabs, mainly in services and related occupations (Romann and Weingrod, 1992). As regards functions there are still two separate cities in Jerusalem, inhabited by two different peoples with two different religions, different cultures, different ways of life, and with different political orientations and aspirations. In more than a quarter of a century since 1967, no major Jewish business has shifted to the eastern section of the city, excluding the Jewish quarter of the Old City, and no Arab business moved to Western Jerusalem. Arab workers, who reside in East Jerusalem, are employed by Jews in the western section, but no Jews are employed by Arabs. There are two systems of public transportation in the city, one Arab and one Jewish. A central Arab bus station is located in East Jerusalem, opposite Damascus Gate, while a Jewish one is located in the western section, without any functional connections between them. Health services, first aid stations and medical clinics exist separately for Jews and for Arabs. Separate restaurants, coffee-houses, cinemas and playhouses exist for Arabs in East Jerusalem and for the Jews in the western section. Arabic newspapers are printed and distributed only in East Jerusalem, while Hebrew ones circulate only in the western city and in the Jewish neighbourhoods in the 'East'.

Different systems of education function in Jerusalem. The Arab system is still based upon that established during Jordanian rule, while the Jewish system is based on Israeli governmental education programmes. The Israeli government does not supervise any aspect of Arab education, nor provide any funding. Welfare and religious services are also separate.

Despite considerable efforts made by the Israeli government and the municipality to create new and modern city facilities, the artificial reunification of the city has not been effective. The Arabs are not impressed with what has been achieved in the city during the last three decades, and they have expressed their attitude clearly by joining in the uprising. During the conflict the artificiality and basic weakness in the reunification of Jerusalem came as a great surprise to the Jewish leaders of the city. Former Mayor Teddy Kollek, often cited elsewhere as a great unifying force in the face of divisions, even had to admit that the delicate peaceful coexistence between the Jews and Arabs in Jerusalem had died.

Because of the uprising of the Arabs, Jerusalem suddenly regressed many years. Along the seam line between East and West Jerusalem, where the armistice line and an open no-man's-land once divided the city into opposing sections, Arabs attacked Jews with stones, and passing through the streets of East Jerusalem by Jews became dangerous. As a result, fewer Jews visited the Western Wall in the Old City, and none entered the Dome of the Rock which has become a focus of Arab nationalism.

Without a declared war, and only after a relatively short time of unrest, the artificial fabric of unity was torn by demographic, geographic and political realities. Although Jerusalem has been decreed a reunified city, during the uprising it returned to its earlier status as a divided city, sundered along the so-called 'Green Line'. The Israeli illusions of a Greater Jerusalem and a reunified city for the two peoples vanished, probably for ever.

These facts indicate, that the Jerusalem environs are a site of a demographic and physical struggle between two populations, aiming at substantive achievements, each with the clear political purpose of holding and controlling the environs of the city.

13 The dilemma of public housing in a multi-ethnic society

Arza Churchman and Gilbert Herbert

Introduction: the dynamic trend

Changes in the social and economic order, in science and technology, in population growth and urban concentrations, in knowledge bases and value systems are a dominant characteristic of all dynamic industrial and post-industrial societies. Our times are marked not only by this universality of change, but by the phenomenal increase in the rate of change. The dynamic process, instead of the stable situation, has become the norm. Instead of living in a traditional environment of familiar situations, enduring objects, and known facts, we experience today, to an ever-increasing degree, situations of novelty and unfamiliarity, an explosion of new knowledge. Our greatest challenge is to plan for diversity and complexity in a dynamic fashion; to reduce complexity to manageable proportions, to allow for diversity through the options of choice, and to create an orderly but flexible framework for change.

Transience may be the essence of our civilisation, and we are moulded by the forces of change; but for our psychological well-being, as well as the management of the pragmatic agenda of our daily lives, we need, now more than ever, those elements of stability which will serve us as a fixed frame of reference within which to cope with the dynamics of change.

The role of the dwelling in a changing world

In a physical sense, the built environment constitutes such a frame of reference, within which we act out our lives. In our urban world, some facets of the built environment are relatively stable and enduring, others are changing and transient. Between the relative permanence of a great monument and the transience of a street advertising hoarding, lies a whole environmental spectrum of stability and change. Within this spectrum the home has a special, unique place. It is, paradoxically, both the flexible stage on which are enacted the dynamic events of family life and, simultaneously, the familiar, enduring physical framework, the cornerstone of stability in the flux of that dramatic unfolding.

What is the meaning of the term 'dwelling'? The dwelling may be regarded as an environmental setting appropriate for the complex series of behaviours which together constitute the everyday functions of life in the home. These life functions, which concern the community and the family, as well as the individual, fall into a number of categories (Depres, 1989; Churchman, 1991). We will relate here to two of them, the pragmatic and symbolic, which in turn reflect two different levels of meaning of the concept 'dwelling'. The first meaning is contained in the imperative of shelter: that is, the dwelling as a mechanism for ensuring survival, health, and a reasonable level of comfort and convenience. The second meaning is concerned with the imperative of identity: dwelling as a reinforcer of a sense of person, a sense of family, a sense of community, and a sense of location in both time and place. These two levels of meaning, overlapping and interacting, are inseparable.

In defining the dwelling, we have used the term 'an appropriate environmental setting'. What do we mean by 'appropriate'? The physical environment is not deterministic; that is, it does not prescribe how a dweller behaves. However, it is usually more than a neutral container. The built environment has the capacity to either inhibit or support desired patterns of human behaviour. Environments which support behaviours are appropriate, or congruent, environments. It is the basic supposition of our approach that the built environment should be supportive of the imperatives of shelter and identity; that is, that there should be a congruence, or 'fit', between the dwelling and the direct and symbolic behaviours which constitute the user's desired pattern of living.

In considering the problem of housing, we are thus confronted with a paradox. The general conditions of dynamism which typify our age are of course relevant to where and how we live: that is, our homes are of necessity an environment which must accommodate change. Environmental congruence, or fit, must be maintained over long periods of time, even in the face of changing dwelling needs, behaviours, and circumstances. On the other hand, the dwelling, both in its connotations of shelter and as a reinforcer of identity, must be an enduring event, a stable setting which gives the dweller a sense of security, order, belonging, orientation. However pressing the need to cater for change, the basic characteristic of 'dwelling' nevertheless remains its 'fixed' nature, its relative stability (Pawley, 1968).

The problem of the adaptation of a relatively stable dwelling to the pressures of change exists in all dynamic societies. It is a problem which exists, even when the potential user, defining with greater or lesser precision the desirable starting conditions, can initiate a design or choose between available options, in order to optimise at least the initial congruence of the dwelling to his/her dwelling needs. The problem is exacerbated a hundred-fold when, as in public housing, the intended user is not known, except in a generalised, statistical sense. The problem is further compounded in a multi-ethnic society; and it is magnified to almost intractable proportions in a country facing unpredictable waves of immigration from diverse cultural origins.

Complicating the problem even further is the fact that ethnic groups are not monolithic entities. There is variability within each of these ethnic groups which has implications for the nature of the housing they require or prefer. The differentiation necessary or relevant may be based on developmental stages: children, teenagers, middle agers and the elderly; it may be based on socio-economic status; it may be based on social role: women and men; it may be based on household type; it may be based on health; and it may be based on values and life-style. Some of the variability may cut across other groups, such as developmental differences which exist in all societies. Others, such as caste distinctions, may exist only in particular countries. And others may be more or less relevant to the issue of housing, depending on the social and cultural interpretation given them within a given society.

Housing policy and immigration

The housing policy approach adopted within a society is a function, among other things, of its attitude towards immigration and immigrants. Some countries welcome immigrants, others discourage or even forbid their entrance. Even those that allow their entrance into the country may view them differently: they may be viewed as a necessary evil, as a humanitarian gesture, or as a blessing. They may be offered support of various kinds when they arrive, or they may be left to sink or swim on their own. This attitude is in turn related to the way in which the process of migration is viewed and its results anticipated. If the immigrants are perceived as a group with an inferior culture, they are expected to give up their former customs and way of life and become one with the host culture. Under these circumstances there is no need to consider their special needs, since these needs are expected to disappear as quickly as possible. However, many countries have gone through a process of attitude change in the recent past, which recognises the legitimacy of different cultures and is willing even to 'celebrate' those differences and allow them to flourish.

Israel can be characterised as an immigrant welcoming country; one that views immigration as one of the major reasons and justifications for its existence, and one that takes active steps to encourage immigration. Indeed it has over the years mounted heroic operations to bring large groups of Jews out of dangerous situations. Witness the operation in 1990 to bring 20,000 Ethiopian Jews into the country within two days. No restrictions are placed on Jewish immigrants, not in terms of economic circumstances, age or health. Immigrants are given many kinds of assistance, varying over the years in nature and scope depending on the needs of the immigrants and the economic resources available to the country at that time.

For many years the words used to describe the process after migration were 'absorption' and 'melting pot', reflecting the notion that the immigrants should adapt themselves to the reigning European-influenced culture. This, indeed was the conscious and subconscious housing policy adopted by the Israeli government in the early years of the State. However, Israel has become more and more sensitive to the ethnocentrism of this approach and has begun to accept the legitimacy of the differences between ethnic groups.

Housing needs in an ethnically diverse society

Israel for the last century has experienced successive waves of immigration of Jews from remarkably different cultural backgrounds: from Eastern Europe up to the 1920s; Nazi Germany in the 1930s; Morocco, Yemen, and other Arab states after the establishment of the State of Israel; and from the Western democracies. In the early 1990s the country's population increased by more than 10 per cent within three years, due to the unanticipated and emergency immigration from the Soviet Union and from Ethiopia (Oelsner, 1995).

Every wave of immigration has provided a challenge to the authorities dealing with the housing problem. First and foremost this is a challenge in terms of producing a sufficient quantity of dwellings, within endemic constraints of time, resources and budget, essentially the imperative of shelter. The solutions have been ad hoc and short term. They have admirably provided newcomers with the first priority, a roof over one's head.

They have less successfully addressed the more intransigent question of housing quality, especially in terms of the imperative of identity; that is, in terms of generating the specific dwelling types desired by each group as a reinforcer of their sense of self, family, community and location in time and place. Complicating the matter is the fact that migration is a process and there are differences between groups and within groups in the degree to which they wish to retain their ethnic identity and the degree to which they wish to remain together as a group, geographically or culturally (Hasson, 1991). For most migrating groups, there is over time a process of culture change that manifests itself in the adoption by the new group of some or all of the ways of the host society. It is not clear how long that process takes, or whether there are actions that can be taken to facilitate it, should that be considered desirable (Churchman and Mitrani, 1994; Abelson, 1992).

The basic objective of government housing policy in Israel has always been to provide adequate housing to families and individuals without a home, usually meaning to assist them to own their apartment. Over 70 per cent of the housing units are owner occupied and over 70 per cent are in multi-family buildings. An historical overview of housing policy in Israel indicates a trend of steadily declining governmental involvement and an increasing reliance on the private sector (Fialkoff, 1993). During the first two decades after the establishment of the State in 1948, housing and related services were constructed directly by the centralised and welfare-oriented government (Oelsner, 1995). This policy changed in the 1970s , and instead of supporting the supply side of the housing market, the government improved assistance schemes on the demand side, thus allowing households much more freedom of choice in terms of the location , size and design of their dwelling (Ginsberg, 1993).

In the mid 1980s the government relied on market forces and operated within a framework of a privatisation policy . The share of public housing — i.e. units constructed directly by government bodies — dropped from 80 per cent to less than 30 per cent in 1985. While in the past, public housing meant units that were initiated, planned and constructed directly by governmental bodies, the term is currently used when the initiative is public, while most of the planning is carried out by the private companies (Carmon and Czamanski, 1990). Housing prices are set by the private market and residents are free to choose the location and type of apartment they buy. Neighbourhoods are designated for development among the country's settlements and the production of housing is tendered to private developers. A government plan for the neighbourhood is part of the tender, and housing is subsidised by the government through the price of land, the provision of services and urban infrastructure and through the financial assistance available for its purchase (Oelsner, 1995). In other words, even though the role of the government has greatly decreased, it still maintains a say in various aspects of the housing built. Most of its attention has been directed at the neighbourhood level, although there has also been some suggestion that structures be planned with the potential to upgrade the apartments to higher standards in the future according to changing family needs (Drinberg, 1992).

In terms of the design of the dwellings, the role of the government is limited now to ensuring that minimal standards of room size and such are adhered to, but this is a very minor role in the larger scheme of things.

In parallel, the immigrant absorption policy changed from one of giving immigrants a dwelling unit, without necessarily allowing them to choose where or what kind it would be, to one where they are given a mortgage or a rent subsidy and the choice to live wherever they desire.

During the periods when the government controlled the design and planning of housing, it was possible for it to take a position on design strategies and issues, to try out new ideas or to remain with the tried and true. It was the public and not the private sector that was usually the leading force in innovative design (Carmon and Czamanski, 1990). The Ministry of Housing initiated many experimental housing projects, and also funded research projects whose mandate was to study the housing needs of various population groups and to examine strategies such as flexibility (Herbert, Keren and Kalay, 1978; Churchman and Frenkel, 1992; Herbert, Churchman and Poreh, 1991). However, when the government stepped out of the picture, leaving the design of the dwellings to the private market, the degree of fit obtained became a function of the sensitivity of that private market to the needs of different groups within the population, and the ability of each of the groups to make their needs visible. Unfortunately, there are indications in Germany and Israel that the private market may not be able to cope with situations of great change and extreme fluctuations in needs. Furthermore, despite the present-day popularity of notions of privatisation and market forces, it can be argued that governments must still have social housing policies. It is highly unlikely that the poorest and weakest groups will be provided for by the private market, and the government's responsibility for providing decent housing for all cannot be abrogated (Churchman and Ginsberg, 1991).

Housing strategies for an ethnically diverse society

How can a government housing authority in an immigrant welcoming society provide appropriate long-term (as against emergency) solutions for such a diverse population, with such varied housing needs? While realising that within prevailing constraints, any such attempt can only partially meet the problem, nevertheless three theoretical options suggest themselves, a priori, for consideration.

The most obvious strategy is that of specificity: the attempt to define the specific needs and desires of various ethnic groups, and to tailor-make, as it were, housing types to suit these requirements. On the face of it, this strategy would appear to be highly desirable, but in point of fact it does not answer many questions. In deciding on this strategy, we are confronted with some obdurate problems:

Quantity: Where immigration is largely unpredictable, how many dwellings should be provided?

Timing: When should this housing be provided: in anticipation of a wave of immigration, as an on-going process, or after immigration materialises?

Definition: How does one determine specific housing needs? Do you ask the newcomers, or do you examine their previous housing? Is existing housing in the country of origin a true indicator of housing preferences, or the outcome of existing constraints and conditions? Is there uniformity or diversity, even in one ethnic group?

Location: Where do you put this housing: where there is land and infrastructure available; where national priorities require new population concentrations; where there is already a population of the same ethnic group; where there are job opportunities?

Cost and efficiency: Does the provision of special types increase the cost of public housing? When there is a limited housing budget, does the search for specificity come at the cost of fewer numbers of dwellings?

Stability of demand: Do ethnic housing preferences remain unchanged over time? Is there a desire to assimilate with the existing population? Do prevailing housing types of the settled population become the model for emulation?

Looking at these problems realistically, it would appear that the strategy of specificity is of very limited applicability, and is an approach so costly in nature that it is contra-indicated in any programme of state-subsidised public housing.

An alternative approach, more convincing, is what we might call the strategy of diversity, by which a limited variety of housing-type options are provided at any one time, providing a reasonable range of choice to potential dwellers. This strategy meets some of the problems raised above by diversifying, and not putting all one's eggs in one basket. Problems of location and quantity are diminished, in an overall sense, but they may be exacerbated in a local sense, with over-provision in some areas and under-provision in others. Timing here is essentially met by building in advance, not always feasible in a fluid and unpredictable situation, but the commitment — the precise matching of housing need to housing provision — is much less restrictive. The problem of definition is reduced, by limiting the range of housing models to certain well-known generic types, rather than attempting to custom-make each type to fit each ethnic ideal. Problems of cost and stability remain. However, there are some clear advantages in this strategy of diversity: diversity implies choice, and choice is a valuable commodity in a free, dynamic, and highly mobile society. Choice, moreover, is an inherent characteristic of flexible systems, and the advantages of diversity may be amplified if this strategy is allied with that of our final approach, discussed below.

Our third option is the strategy of flexibility, by which is meant the provision of housing so designed as to facilitate, either before or during occupation, changes of plan arrangement or increase of total floor area, to provide adaptability in the face of different needs or changing circumstances. The potential of the strategy of flexibility to meet the requirements of an ethnically diverse and culturally dynamic society is worthy of serious study. It cannot be the sole, or universal, approach, nor is it a panacea for all ills, but it may offer a solution to some seemingly intransigent problems. Uniform starting conditions, which provide more or less open-ended options for development in various directions, may minimise the risk of premature commitment and misjudgement by a housing authority in situations of indeterminacy, of what, where and when to build. In the face of traditional rigid approaches to public housing, it provides an unconventional, but not unknown, alternative direction (see Herbert, 1978, for a theoretical analysis of the flexible dwelling).

The strategy of flexibility has its advantages also because normal changes in the standard of living, in norms and expectations, in values, in household size and composition make housing a process rather than a static condition.

A strategy of flexibility

The ideal of flexibility is not a simple one to attain. Many questions arise, such as what are the aspects of the dwelling that people wish to be flexible — what can they accept and deal with as flexible aspects? How can we ensure that the dwelling remain habitable and acceptable at all points in time, regardless of whether or not the flexible options are applied?

In order to illustrate the complexity of the issue, we will briefly present the results of a research project undertaken at the request of the Israel Ministry of Construction and Housing (Herbert, Churchman and Poreh, 1991). The research brief given us was to develop a method for evaluating the performance of apartments designed for expansion according to a particular expansion strategy. The project was defined as a high-rise residential building, containing apartments designed for expansion. The defined expansion strategy was one where the total building structural frame would be completed at the start, leaving the enclosing elements of the envelope and part of the internal space unfinished and designed for completion by the residents themselves at a later time.

Not convinced of the advisability of such an expansion strategy, we took upon ourselves to develop an evaluation method that could apply to this as well as other strategies. We focused on the individual apartment, determined that under any condition it must meet basic minimal requirements of housing quality. We examined the advantages arising from the built-in expansion possibilities and the relative saving achieved by the shape and organisation of the apartment. However, we also included criteria relating to the building as a system, both in terms of the initially defined options and in terms of the interactions between the apartments during the dynamic process of expansion.

A set of eleven criteria were specified, four relating to the building as a whole and seven to the individual apartments before and after expansion. Since the research project was a theoretical one, these criteria are intended for evaluation of the plans and thus rely solely on analysis of these plans, and not on the attitudes and behaviour of the residents. Each of the criteria stands on its own, enabling various kinds of weightings of the relative importance of a given issue.

A. The building as a whole

A1. Choice of Size — Initially Defined Options: How many different apartment types are offered the buyer.

A2. Choice of Size — Reciprocal/Varied Options: Does the plan allow for exchanging space between adjacent apartments?

A3. Level of Independence During the Expansion Process: Do the characteristics of the expansion process affect the relationships between the residents of that apartment and those of the other apartments in the building?

A4. The Appearance of the Building until the End of the Expansion Process: Will the appearance of the building be satisfactory at all stages of the process — initially, in the intermediate stages and in the final stage?

B. The apartment as a separate entity, before and after expansion

B1. Fulfilment of Minimal Performance Requirements: Does the apartment at all stages fulfil the minimal requirements as defined in Herbert, Churchman and Dokow (1984).

B2. Quality of the Spatial Allotment at the Initial and Expanded Stages, in Comparison with Defined Norms: To what extent does the space allotted to various activity areas meet the norms defined in our previous work.

B3. Quality of the Functional Organisation: Connections — the effectiveness of the organisation and the connections between the functional spaces within the apartment.

B4. Choice of Plans — Configurations/Combinations: The dynamic qualities of the apartment plan, in terms of choice and flexibility.

B5. Saving Achieved by the Plan: In terms of the relationship between the length of the building envelope and the gross size of the apartment.

B6. Saving in Cost: 1) Minimising excess in terms of Stage One elements that are unnecessary in Stage Two. 2) Minimising oversupply that provides elements in Stage One that are useless until Stage Two.

B7. Minimising Discomfort During the Expansion Process: To what extent are the daily lives of the apartment residents disturbed by the expansion process?

Conclusion

Regardless of the strategy adopted, it will be necessary to base the specific planning and design details on systematic and up-to-date information as to the size and nature of the ethnic groups that must be considered, and as to the design and planning parameters that are relevant to the ethnic distinction. One would need to know 1) which design issues cut across ethnic groups and which do not and 2) for the latter, what is the nature of the relevant differences. Even a strategy of flexibility must be based on an understanding of the areas in which flexibility is probably necessary and the areas in which it is probably not necessary or even not desirable. Where there has been research, there are certain design issues that have been found to be differentially relevant for different groups. However, we are limited in our knowledge to the research that has been done and the questions addressed within it, and unfortunately, it is very sparse. The task, therefore, is a complex, but critical one and research is urgently needed that can assist governments, architects and planners to better understand the appropriate ways of meeting the housing needs of their increasingly diverse and demanding populations.

14 Housing solutions for a mass population of immigrants: the Israeli experience

Adam Buchman

Summary

During the period 1990-1995 the state of Israel had to provide housing solutions for some 680,000 of immigrants who had arrived without any capital. For a state with a population of 4.5 million (in 1989) this has comprised a substantial effort which, in retrospective, has been successfully met. The process required the solution of a series of problems which related to the nature of the immigration and also to the economic situation, availability of land and infrastructure etc. at that time in Israel.

The measures applied varied in respond to changing conditions. During the first years 1990-1992 the emphasis was on creating a large stock of housing, with massive government involvement and rent subsidy being the main tool on the demand side. In 1993 the supply of housing became the private sector's task and the government supported the demand with soft mortgage loans. The provision of planned land by the government became its main tool on the supply side.

The housing policy and its implementation has proven successful in providing housing solutions for most of the immigrants without almost creating slums, and in expediting integration into the existing population at reasonable cost. Furthermore, the continuous demand for housing has triggered a substantial growth in the Israeli economy. The Gross Domestic Product doubled from US$43 billion in 1989 to US$87 billion in 1995 and the per capita GDP grew from US$10,400 to US$15,500.

During the process various measures have been applied and there are some conclusions to be drawn and some mistakes to be avoided:

a: Government must take most of the risks at the initial stages of a huge national effort to provide mass housing.
b: It calls for mobilisation of efforts and granting extended authority to a single body.
c: In some case tax breaks can provide fast solutions at low cost.

d: Private contractors respond quickly and effectively to financial incentives. This rule does not necessarily apply to public sector suppliers of infrastructure and services.
e: Infrastructure must be given priority and a larger share in its execution given to the private sector.
f: A large stock of planned land should be prepared in advance in order to deal effectively with a sudden rise in housing demand.
g: Temporary housing solutions (like mobile homes) should be avoided. It is economically unviable and socially unworthy.
h: Subsidising directly the eligible ones — 'soft loans' — is in most cases the most cost effective and socially worthy measure.

Background

Definition of the challenge

The arrival of the first waves of immigrants in the last months of 1989 created a need to provide housing urgently in large scale. The challenge that faced the government was to provide proper housing while (a) avoiding creating slums, (b) integrating the immigrants into the existing population, (c) applying economically viable measures and (d) without discriminating against young couples and other needy families in the existing population.

Immigration's characteristics

The characteristics of the immigration comprised problems such as:

   - Irregular schedule of arrivals and varying number of families. (Figure 14.1)
   - The newcomers arrived without any capital. Their expected income during the first years was quite limited.
   - Special needs of ageing population, single parent families etc.
   - Some newcomers had completely different attitudes and standards of living.

The situation in 1989

In 1989 Israel was a country with a population of 4.5 millions, a per capita GDP of US$10,000 and unemployment rate of 8.9 per cent. The economy had slowed down to 1.1 per cent growth in the GDP and a low rate of investment. The construction industry had been recovering from a crisis and was operating on a low scale with 20,000 dwelling starts per year. However the sharp decrease in the long term interest rates raised the demand for housing and a price hike of 12 per cent (in real terms) was recorded.

The most critical barriers on the expansion of housing construction were:
   - Limited financial resources.
   - Limited planed and available land.
   - Regional planning inadaquate for large development.
   - Lack of proper infrastructure.
   - The mismatch between available land and employment opportunities.

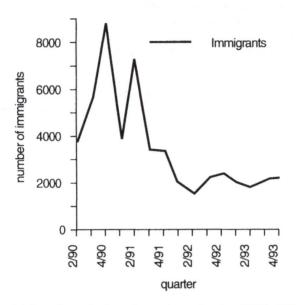

Figure 14.1   Israel: immigrant arrivals, 1990-1993

Measures applied

General

The measures applied varied over time and responded to the changing conditions. During the first years 1990-92 the emphasis was on creating a large stock of housing on the supply side and rent assistance on the demand side. In 1992 a new government came to power and changed the policy from massive direct involvement on the supply side to private market orientation and a direct support to the eligible families with subsidised loans.

It must be noted that circumstances changed. The number of newcomers decreased from 200,000 per year in 1990-1991 to 60-80,000 in 1992-1995 as the immigrants of the first wave were successfully absorbed and started to shop for permanent housing.

Supply side

Tax exemption for rent income had been the first and most effective measure taken. It assisted in providing some 60-80,000 unoccupied dwellings to the market that housed the first waves of immigrants.

Direct government building was applied mostly in the peripheral areas where the marketing risks were considerable. The government used its direct involvement to promote new techniques that had been considered not acceptable in the market.

Purchase guarantees were applied in new neighbourhoods and peripheral areas where the demand had been considered low. The government had to purchase over 20,000 dwellings and to sell them later at under cost price.

Speeding up incentives were applied to both private and public housing construction in order to accelerate the supply of houses. However, no effective measures had been applied to speed up the provision of infrastructure for those dwellings.

Temporary housing in mobile houses provided housing for some 20,000 households. Since 1993 the government has put a great effort into moving these neighbourhoods' residents to permanent housing. So far about 70 per cent have been provided with alternative solutions.

Supply of developed land to the private sector became, after 1992, the main target of the government — this in conjunction with the withdrawal of the government from direct involvement. The process has been slow and in 1993 only 20,000 land units were supplied. The turning point came in 1994 when a land for over 50,000 housing units was marketed. In consequence, the number of housing starts in 1995 grew to nearly 60,000 all financed and marketed by the private sector.

Demand side

Subsidised rent: A substantial grant (diminishing in 3 years) to each household upon arrival has been the initial tool in housing the newcomers. Most of the families rented a house on the private market as a temporary solution in the first two to three years

Trade-in of rent subsidy for mortgage payment assistance was applied to encourage fast transfer to permanent housing solutions.

'Soft mortgages' have been the main tool in providing housing solutions for most of the immigrants. Between 1991 and 1995 some 128,000 households purchased homes within this scheme. The scheme enables the loans of more than one eligible household to be combined to enable the purchase of one housing unit (mostly an elderly parent with his or her family).

Public housing has been provided for elderly people, single parent households and other weak families.

Results

Housing solutions

The housing policy and its implementation has been proven successful in providing solutions for most newcomers without creating slums. It has also aided integration into the existing population and at a reasonable cost.

By mid 1995 70 per cent of the families originating from the CIS lived in their own houses. The figure ranges from 38 per cent for the 1994 arrivals up to 79 per cent for those who arrived in 1990.

Other housing solutions include public rented housing, hostels for the elderly population and rent assistance. The housing solutions for the immigrants from Ethiopia are characterised by a higher share of public housing .

The housing density of immigrants has been reduced dramatically from 1.6 households per dwelling unit at the end of 1991 to an estimated 1.2 in 1995, a figure not far from the 1.04 for the general Israeli population

In general, homelessness has not been known even at the peak of the immigrant wave. Four years later the housing standards of the immigrants were closing on the Israeli standard.

The big demand for housing has strongly affected the prices of houses and rents. During 1989-95 the prices of dwellings rose by 56 per cent in real terms. However, since mid-1994 the rate of change was reduced to between two and four per cent in real terms on an annual basis.

The construction industry

The need to provide housing, public services, commercial facilities and infrastructure has had a dramatic effect on the construction industry. The investment in building and construction grew from US$4 billion in 1989 to an estimated US$11 billion in 1995. The share of the industry in the GDP rose from 9 per cent to nearly 13 per cent in the same period. In fact the construction industry proved to be the locomotive that pulled the entire economy. Even more dramatic was the change in the private sector's activity. While in 1990-92 public sector investment was the main contributor to the industry's growth, since 1993 the private sector has taken over and by 1995 was financing over 80 per cent of the total activity.

The economy

The continuous demand for housing solutions triggered a substantial growth in the Israeli economy. Between 1989 and 1995 the total GDP doubled from US$43 billion to an estimated US$87 billion. In that period the per capita GDP grew from US$10,400 to estimated US$15,500. The total investment grew in volume and its share in the GDP grew from 17 per cent in 1989 to an estimated 25 per cent in 1995. Although part of the large investment has been financed with foreign and local debt (and foreign grants) the relative size of the national debt as part of the GDP was reduced.

The net external national debt grew from US$15.1 billion in 1990 to US$16.5 billion in 1995 but thanks to the rapid growth in the economy its share of GDP decreased from 30 per cent to 22 per cent in the same period.

The fast growth in the population and the working force due to the immigration waves have increased the rate of unemployment from 8.9 per cent in 1989 (compared to 6.4 per cent in 1988) to a peak of 11.2 per cent in 1992. A reduced immigration and a rapid growth of the economy lowered this figure to 6.2 per cent in 1995 (Figure 14.2).

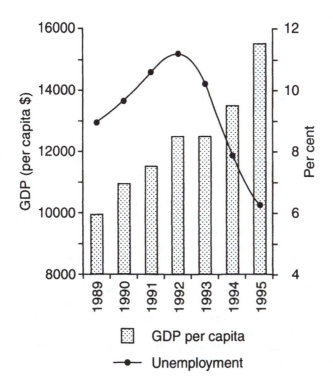

Figure 14.2   Israel: GDP and unemployment, 1989-1995

Unresolved problems

The elderly population comprise most of the unsolved cases among the immigrants. They are not qualified for long term mortgages that could enable the purchase of a house — so the solution lies in rented housing. Public housing is limited so the main tool is rent subsidy. The problem is that in Israel there is no housing to hire on a commercial basis. The renters must shop for houses let to hire by households, in most cases on a yearly basis. Lately the Ministry of Housing commenced construction of hostels for elderly population.

Housing prices in terms of income are very high. Between 1989 and 1995 the cost of an average dwelling unit has risen by 56 per cent in real terms. While in 1989 the average 2.5-3 rooms dwelling (including the living room) sold for the equivalent of 57 month's salary, this had risen to 82 month's salary by 1995. This required heavy long term borrowing and necessitated governmental assistance to first time home buyers. However, commencing in the second half of 1994 there was a significant decrease in the rate of housing price change.

Conclusions: general

The absorption of the mass immigration of 1990-1995 has been demonstrated to have been very successful. Adequate housing solutions have been provided and in the process the Israeli economy has made very substantial progress. During the process various means have been applied and there have been some changes in policy and in policy instruments.

There are some conclusions to be drawn concerning the relative roles of government and the private sector, the various tools applied and the timing.

Government involvement

When the mass immigration started the government expected the private sector to respond to the new housing needs with a large scale construction of housing. But the private sector was reluctant to take the risk. It was made clear that there is a strong distinction to be made between *Needs* and *Demand.* The penniless immigrants were not able to transform their needs to an active demand. Thus, at least in the first phase, the government had to carry the risks. From 1990 till mid-1992 most of the additional housing was either financed directly or indirectly — with purchase guarantees — by the government.

Only at the end of 1992, when the immigrants commenced employment, were they able to utilise the soft loans (with government subsidy) and thereby appeared in growing numbers as a demand element in the housing market.

On the *supply side* the volume of private sector production consistently expanded to meet demand and in time took over from the public sector.

The conclusion is clear: **Government must take most of the risk at the initial stages of a national effort to provide mass housing.**

Mobilisation of efforts

The arrival of 380,000 immigrants, who comprised 8 per cent of the population within just two years, increased housing needs dramatically. It required unconventional measures and means of bypassing existing procedures.

This called for **mobilisation of efforts and the granting of extended authority to a single body** (Ministry of Housing and Construction).

Tax breaks — an effective measure

The tax exemption of income from rent for residential purposes has been a major factor in the re-emergence of unoccupied apartments in the housing market. In fact this was the buffer which absorbed the first waves of immigrants. Thus, in some cases, **tax breaks can provide fast solutions at low cost.**

Conclusions: the supply side

Speeding up construction — financial incentives

In order to speed up completion of housing units various financial incentives were applied. These incentives proved to be very effective in their impact on the private contractors who made a major effort and reduced average completion time from 23.5 months in 1989 to 14.3 months in 1992. Although the target of speeding up construction was met it did not achieve its purpose of increasing available housing stock in a short time. In many sites the infrastructure and services were not ready in time to enable occupancy of the completed dwellings.

It appears that while the **private contractors respond quickly and effectively to financial incentives, this rule does not necessarily apply to public sector suppliers of infrastructure and services.**

Infrastructure and services

Lack of proper infrastructure has been in many cases the most effective constraint on housing development. The process of planning is more complicated and time consuming and needs co-ordination with many public sectors organs. As mentioned above, public sector organs are less responsive to financial incentives than is the case with the private sector.

Given its nature, **infrastructure must be given priority** and the private sector should have a larger role in its execution.

Location

The location of much of the dwellings constructed in 1990-1992 was determined by the availability of planned land, rather than by the anticipated demand for housing. The implications of the lack of planned land in the 'demand areas' were quite severe. The creation of large unsold stocks of dwellings in peripheral areas did not ease the over-demand in the 'demand areas' which, in turn, brought about a hike in housing costs during 1993-94.

In 1993-94 about 16,000 dwelling units, out of 40,000 units built or purchased by the government, were sold below cost. The estimated cost to the government was around one billion dollars.

A large stock of planned land should be prepared in advance in order to deal effectively with a sudden rise in housing demand.

Temporary housing

Temporary housing — the use of mobile homes — proved to be economically unviable and socially unworthy. It required almost the same investment in infrastructure as was the case with permanent housing in terms of money and time. The temporary housing neighbourhoods turned into slums and its residents had to be evacuated within three to four years with additional substantial costs.

Although the first decisions concerning the application of this measure had been taken at the peak of the immigration wave — an annual rate of 400,000 —

the government has been too slow in reversing its decisions when the conditions changed. **Temporary housing solutions should be avoided.**

Conclusions: the demand side

Soft Loans and rent subsidy

Subsidising directly eligible households — immigrants in our context — is, in most cases, the most cost effective and socially worthy measure. It does not affect directly the decisions of the suppliers and the buyers concerning the locations, standards, prices, range etc.

Since subsidisation does not give preference to new dwellings over second hand ones, it assists in the integration of new immigrants into existing neighbourhoods. In addition the possibility of trading-in the rent subsidy for payment of mortgage gave flexibility in the timing of moving from temporary to permanent housing.

Acknowledgement

The author wishes to acknowledge the valuable contribution of Sason Avudi to this paper.

Part Six
The United Kingdom: immigrants and natives

15 Addressing the housing needs of minority ethnic communities: towards a pluralistic ethnic housing policy

Richard Tomlins

Introduction

The need for an ethnically sensitive housing policy has been highlighted by academic research which has documented the differential housing outcomes experienced between ethnic groups within national boundaries. A particular cause of concern has been the housing inequalities of minority ethnic communities, who are often concentrated in parts of urban areas which are neglected by the private market, and where other social welfare goods face pressure from high demand. State intervention is often the response to these 'problems', however it may take divergent forms. For example the advocacy of the distribution of additional state resources from the political left, and the advocacy of social control from the political right.

These approaches often appear to be paternalistic majority ethnic 'solutions' on behalf of, and for 'the other'. An alternative approach is offered by grassroots activism within minority ethnic communities. Demands for greater resources, but also significantly for more community control over resources, provide an important challenge to the future construction of social policy. They assert the primacy of empowerment and self help over paternalism, and question the validity of social engineering which may emanate from top down policy implementation.

In terms of a pluralistic ethnic housing policy, a fundamental issue concerns the right of minority ethnic groups to express identity through residence. Current perceptions of ethnicity highlight the benefits for minority ethnic communities of choosing ethnic residential segregation, and formulating a self-defined ethnic housing policy. Modood (1990, p. 86) suggests that ethnicity describes a 'group's internal structure, values and understanding of itself'. This provides a potential which in the form of ethnic residential segregation offers group resources (Boal, 1981, p. 235) which might otherwise be lost by spatial dispersal, and particularly by forced dispersal.

Social policy has been slow to respond to the potential value of ethnicity as a resource. However the growing acceptance of sociocultural and political pluralism (McLennan, 1995) and the growing celebration of postmodernity, offer the scope to embrace diversity and provide the user led perspective which the complexity of ethnicity demands. Nevertheless Soja and Hooper's (1993, pp. 193-4) suggestion that postmodernism is revealing the resource of diversity, might be clarified by the coda that it is demonstrating to majority ethnic communities, that which has long been known to minority ethnic communities.

Conventional debates on ethnicity and housing

Conventional debates of ethnicity and housing within social policy have accepted that there are differential housing outcomes amongst minority ethnic communities, and between those communities and majority ethnic communities. In Britain, in so far as generalisations can be made, Brown's (1984) conclusions that minority ethnic communities experience poorer quality housing than the majority white community have been validated by the 1991 Census (Owen, 1993). Throughout Europe (Blauw, 1991, p. 49; Body-Gendrot, 1993, p. 81; Lindén and Lindberg, 1991; Owen, 1994, p. 28) and the United States, (Goldberg, 1993) there also appears to be a degree of residential segregation between ethnic groups.

Spatial distance between ethnic groups has typically been characterised in a negative way. For example as a barrier to social contact (Boal, 1976), which has been developed in a pathological way by the political right to construct minority ethnic identity as a 'racial other' to the 'norm' and a threat to existing order (Smith 1989, p. 120). Ethnic residential segregation can also be seen as central to the continuing socio-economic disadvantage of minority ethnic communities:

> segregation is not a neutral expression of cultural preference. It is, rather, the fulcrum of racial inequality — in the labour market, in the housing system and, consequently, in access to a wide range of opportunities and life chances (Smith, 1989, p. 18).

Nevertheless the causal link between residential and employment positions may be complex. In the United States, economically advantaged African Caribbeans in professional occupations, often still live in ethnically segregated suburbs. Whilst this may reflect an element of choice, it also seems to be because of continuing discrimination and white abandonment of areas once a 'tipping point' of African Caribbean residence is reached (Huttman and Jones, 1991).

A further contentious area of discourse surrounds the causes of differential housing outcomes within ethnically diverse communities. Do they reflect the preferences of particular minority ethnic groups or the constraints of housing providers? For example in Britain, it is still not clear whether the relative concentration of Indian households in the owner-occupied sector, and the relative concentration of Black-Caribbean households in the social sector (both ethnic groups as defined by the 1991 Census) are a product of choice or constraint. In practice the majority of academic research has concentrated upon the constraints which minority ethnic households face. This reflects the starkness and obscenity of discrimination as well as the interests of researchers predominantly drawn from majority ethnic groups. The current academic consensus is articulated by Sarre, Phillips and Skellington (1989). They suggest that minority ethnic communities have some freedom of housing choice within a system of constraints. However these restrictions may well prevent access to the range of opportunities available to the majority white community.

The widely observed discriminatory attitudes of organisational gatekeepers (for example Henderson and Karn, 1987) and the biases of institutional policies (for example Commission for Racial Equality, 1988; 1989), do require a continuing commitment to tackle direct and indirect discrimination within the housing system. Nevertheless within a pluralistic ethnic housing policy, there is clearly also a need for an assessment of the housing preferences and opportunities available to minority ethnic communities. Equally in the spirit of diversity it is palpable that if pluralistic ethnic housing policies are to be achieved throughout Europe, then British experiences cannot be treated as the norm. For example Dutch research places a greater emphasis upon particular explanatory factors. Continuing differential housing experiences between ethnic groups in the Netherlands have been perceived as a 'mismatch' between supply and demand (Lower House of the States General, 1994, p. 49), although some findings might alternatively be interpreted as indicating the existence of institutional racism. Recent study trips by this author have also highlighted a greater emphasis upon employment disadvantage, rather than discrimination, within the Dutch housing system as an explanation for minority ethnic housing inequality. Nevertheless the British example may still be instructive because of the wealth of detailed research into particular causes of housing disadvantage, such as indirect discrimination.

One common theme across many national housing policies has been the aim of assimilating or integrating minority ethnic communities into 'mainstream society' through spatial engineering. In Britain:

> Our white liberal 'friends' of the time knew of course what was best for us; they knew that it was in our best interest to be dispersed; that our aggregation was synonymous with ghettoization; that as black people we will obviously be flattered to be placed among white people rather than having to live in communities in which the majority of people are black. They knew our needs better than we ourselves did. Our 'friends' and enemies were at one in ignoring alternative views (James, 1993, p. 261).

As James notes the implications of these actions went far beyond housing outcomes through an attack upon the resource of community which residential concentration can offer.

The pervasive desire to 'get a better racial mix' (Rex, 1981, p. 40), and to see the minority ethnic community reproduce the social and spatial 'norm' of the majority ethnic community has also been seen in other European countries (Blauw, 1991; Mik, 1991; Arin, 1991; Lindén and Lindberg, 1991). It also arguably remains the convention in the United States:

> This picture of positive attributes of clustering and the negative effects of assimilation (and loss of one's life style) — causing, Barou feels, social isolation and loss of a positive identity — is not discussed in most contemporary American housing segregation literature; that integration is positive is a given by most writers, except for a few who are minority and organisation leaders (Huttman, 1991, p. 33).

Whilst Boal (1976, p. 75) argues that by the mid 70s the value of separate communities was being recognised, and initiatives to forcibly disperse minorities were falling out of favour, Marcuse (1994) continues to see a danger that ethnic residential separation provides a cover for continuing inequality. In addition Nanton (1989, p. 561) echoing Sivanandan (1985) suggests that policies targeted upon particular communities lead to a retreat into 'defensive ethnicity'.

Towards a pluralistic ethnic housing policy

Smith (1993, p. 137) provides a pessimistic perspective of the way in which postmodernist agendas are being applied to minority ethnic housing experiences in Britain. She believes that the neo-liberals' desire to preserve traditional social and moral 'norms', will lead to a justification of inequitable ethnic residential segregation, as an expression of free market diversity. The cultural and moral homogeneity of majority ethnic areas will be preserved by 'assimilating' minority ethnic communities to the marginalised sectors of society. Whilst the majority move towards the diversity and flexibility of 'new times', minority ethnic communities will be trapped in areas which are divorced from access to resources.

However the emerging debates around housing differentiation between ethnic groups, provide opportunities for empowerment as well as dangers of exclusion. Thus the choices of minority ethnic communities to spatially concentrate need not lead to marginalisation, if they are backed by policies and financial resources to ensure that the life chances within those spatially differentiated areas are comparable to those within 'mainstream society'. Therefore a pluralistic housing policy is likely to be most successful when it is developed as part of a pluralistic social policy, addressing structural inequality and assessing all governmental measures for their impact upon minority ethnic communities. For example in the context of housing, funding for property improvement and new building in areas of minority ethnic residence must be linked to the employment of local labour. Positive action should also be taken to ensure that employment opportunities within the wider urban area are available to minority ethnic communities. In addition social welfare services must be proportionate to need across the urban milieu. Through a combination of measures, social contact on the grounds of ethnicity need not be constrained by a minority ethnic preference for residential segregation.

Further community empowerment can be achieved by ensuring that at least some of the services targeted upon areas of minority ethnic residence are controlled by the communities receiving the service. Whilst this might occur through representation within 'mainstream organisations', the provision of services by separate organisations controlled by particular minority ethnic communities also has an important role to play. Ensuring continuing improvements in access to mainstream provision, alongside the development of separate organisations will prevent the development of an apartheid system of provision. This means recognising that provision by majority ethnic communities for majority ethnic communities will have a very different power dynamic to minority ethnic provision for minority ethnic communities.

The 'black housing movement' in England provides one positive example of separate provision within a universalistic framework. Black housing associations are identified by the Federation of Black Housing Organisations (Harrison, 1991, p. 3) as those where seventy five per cent of the organisation's staff and committee members are black (non-white). As Crawley and Lemos (1993) note, they are essentially a community response to the inequalities which minority ethnic communities experience in access to accommodation and employment opportunities within the social housing sector.

Black housing associations are projected to have received capital allocations of £417 million between March 1992 and March 1996, sufficient for the production of 10,230 homes (Misra, 1995). However as generally small organisations their prospects of growth have suffered from changes to housing association funding systems following the 1988 Housing Act, coupled with government reductions in capital housing expenditure (Singh, 1991; Crawley and Lemos, 1993). This is demonstrated by the reduction in the funding for social rented housing received by black housing associations from £91 million in 1994-95 to £43.77 million in 1995-96. Nevertheless black associations continue to receive a notable share of state funding for new social rented housing, with an increase from 9.12 per cent in 1994-95 to 10.44 per cent in 1995-96.

Whilst mainstream housing associations have improved their race equality performance in response to the development of black housing associations (Harrison, 1992, p. 435), separate organisations continue to offer important benefits to society:

> People will tell you that it is no longer necessary to have black organisations, that we are part of the society and that we don't need organisations of our own. Everywhere people need to value the hyphen. That is to say that it is perfectly possible to be an enthusiastic patriot of the country in which you are born, in this case Britain without devaluing your origins (Wood, 1992, p. 6)

Separate self-provision can therefore be seen as a key part of a pluralistic ethnic housing policy.

Realising a pluralistic ethnic housing policy

Whilst it is relatively easy to advocate a new pluralistic ethnic housing policy within an academic article, it is less easy to foresee the realisation of processes of change where individual organisations are characterised by inertia. The attitudes of representative housing bodies, and national governments can also be barriers to initiatives. For example it will be difficult to realise a pluralistic ethnic housing policy in countries which have reacted to ethnic diversity by promoting assimilationist models. Castles argues (1995, p. 299) that in France 'special policies for ethnic groups and recognition of their leaderships are seen as potential hindrances to integration', whilst Schönwälder (1995, p. 423) argues that there are still objections within key sections of the German political establishment to the recognition of ethnic plurality. Furthermore Swyngedouw (1995, p. 326) reproduces research which suggests that almost half of the

Dutch population believe that 'minorities should integrate themselves (virtually) entirely into Dutch culture'.

State financing of minority ethnic housing organisations is likely to be particularly contentious where the extreme political right is attacking ethnic diversity. For example directing state resources towards housing associations run by and for France's Islamic community would undoubtedly be controversial, given the Front National's stated concern to prevent the 'Islamification of France' (Layton-Henry, 1992, p. 228). Indeed there is no legal mandate for positive discrimination or provision for ethnic difference within France (Costa-Lascoux, 1994, p. 372). Blanc observes:

> Because there is a risk of provoking new urban segregation by funding specific housing for 'immigrants,' some suggest that it is better to fund housing organisations, public or private, in order to encourage them to accept ethnic minorities. This orientation tends to prevail, but its justification is unclear (Blanc, 1991, p. 151).

Advocates of pluralistic provision might respond with Castles' conclusion that:

> countries with pluralistic policies actually achieve a much higher degree of economic, social, and political integration than do countries which explicitly set out to assimilate immigrants (Castles, 1995, p. 306).

In essence if the legitimacy of a particular community's ethnic identity is denied by the wider political culture or if it feels in danger of racial harassment, it may fold in upon itself (*le repli sur soi*) and become inward looking.

Whilst locating the control of housing resources within specific communities might in the short term provide the freedom to choose to segregate, it may increase other opportunities for social contact. For example Johnson and Ward (1985) note in their study of the effectiveness of the Birmingham Inner City Partnership, that 'black' led organisations are frequently more inclusive than 'white' led ones. Therefore minority ethnic communities have a critical role to play in achieving pluralism through demanding influence in housing policy and local politics, in addition to arguing for improved housing conditions.

In so far as academic debate can have an impact, conferences such as that held in Belfast in 1995 (International Federation for Housing and Planning) offer the opportunity to disseminate ideas and create a new paradigm for policy implementation. The growing precedence of postmodernist recognitions of the existence of diversity, also offer an opportunity to create a pluralistic framework for the future construction of housing policy. Advocates of pluralism can aim to influence key thinkers within government and representative organisations, so that the virtues of minority ethnic self-provision are recognised and promoted. However it should be emphasised that there is also an important role for the individual housing worker within these processes. Even at a relatively junior organisational level s/he can act as a 'change activist', to try and advance equal opportunities and engage institutional support for pluralistic principles.

Conclusion

The essential condition of any housing policy is the recognition of, and provision for, minority ethnic housing need. This should mean pluralism and universalism, with separate provision augmenting sensitive provision from the mainstream.

This will involve ensuring that mainstream provision is nondiscriminatory and meets any particular needs and demands of minority ethnic communities. In Britain, social housing organisations have begun to develop more sensitive management policies through training, monitoring and the provision of translated material. They have also begun to recognise that some minority ethnic communities may have specific requirements of properties which will increase their satisfaction with the dwelling. In so far as these innovations increase the variety of the total housing stock, they are also likely to directly benefit majority ethnic communities, who have in any case in Britain historically sought to import many vernacular architectural styles. These include forms which are now commonplace such as the bungalow and the verandah.

This is not to say that all minority ethnic communities will have specific requirements of dwelling design and/or management, or that particular minority ethnic communities will always continue to have specific requirements. However in a genuinely pluralistic system responsive provision is essential. Therefore there is a need for greater research into the housing needs of minority ethnic communities, although this does not remove the need for existing practitioners to evaluate and improve the equity of their current performance. Indeed the British experience has been that even where direct discrimination has been eliminated, a litany of rules and regulations, (for example residence qualifications, preference given to sons and daughters of existing residents, dwelling type and design), act as barriers to minority ethnic access to good quality housing.

Minority ethnic communities must also be given a greater influence over their own housing outcomes as part of a pluralistic housing policy. The increased involvement of minority ethnic communities within mainstream housing organisations, particularly at senior organisational levels has a key part to play in this process. However there is also a need for generous ring fenced funding for minority ethnic organisations. Whilst the prospect of a racist backlash to separate provision cannot be ignored, the successes of the black housing movement within a relatively hostile English political environment offer an indication of realisable potential. Therefore it must be concluded that a pluralistic housing policy is not only desirable, but is clearly realisable.

16 Housing preferences and strategies: an exploration of Pakistani experiences in Glasgow

Alison Bowes, Naira Dar and Duncan Sim

Introduction

Issues of housing preference and the promotion of choice have dominated recent centralgovernment policy-making. Such policies may, however, be largely irrelevant fordisadvantaged groups in society who have little opportunity to exercise choice in thehousing market, or whose housing is determined by forces largely outwith their control. British South Asians, for example, have long suffered from discrimination in housing, but it is important to avoid the determinism of approaches which portray them as pawns, unable to resist the forces which control their lives (cf. Ballard, 1992). While accepting that there are considerable limitations on housing choice, this paper recognises, with Ballard and also Sarre, Phillips and Skellington (1989), that social actor agency is a vital component influencing life-style and life chances.

Issues are further complicated by problems in previous research. Firstly, South Asians have tended to be stereotyped and there has been little recognition of the heterogeneity of Indian or Pakistani 'communities'. Secondly, differences in housing policy and housing structure in different parts of Britain have often been ignored; in fact, Scotland has a different institutional and legal structure, a distinct housing tenure pattern, and a different set of minority ethnic groups (Miles and Muirhead, 1986).

Thirdly, South Asians have generally been considered to prefer owner-occupation, and little attention has been paid to those who are, and may prefer to be, council tenants. Robinson (1980), for example, showed the extensive use made of local authority housing by East African Asians who had entered Britain as refugees, while many younger, UK-born Asians are increasingly willing to consider renting as a tenure.

Finally, much of the data collected by the various studies of minority ethnic communities has been quantitative, thus fitting categories predetermined by researchers. There is very little good, recent, qualitative material available, which explores the decision-making processes within minority ethnic families. Shaw's (1988) research is qualitative but does not focus specifically on housing.

There is a literature on housing choice, such as Clapham, Kintrea and Munro (1987), who examined choices by first time renters and buyers, and Forrest and Murie (1988), who have examined choices regarding the 'right to buy' council housing. We would argue, however, that an important missing element in much of this work is the study of action by householders, the realisation (or otherwise) of preferences, the consequences of various actions, and the cumulative results of actions in facilitating or restricting choice. Social actor agency therefore requires further investigation.

The study

Our study aimed to develop a life history interviewing technique to investigate the housing strategies of Pakistanis in Glasgow. To ensure that respondents had a reasonably long housing history, those interviewed were aged at least around 40; they were likely to have grown up children and this would allow the collection of data on the possible dispersal of households. A sample of nineteen families, in different forms of tenure, was interviewed, contacted through personal introductions from community organisations.

The interviews were carried out by Dar in the language of the respondents' choice. Most were tape-recorded, then translated, if necessary, for transcription. Generally, the interviewees were the female heads of household, two male heads being interviewed. On seven occasions, more than one household member was present and added their comments to the interview.

A semi-structured schedule was used, focusing on housing preferences, housing moves and experiences. Interviews began by focusing on the present home and its characteristics, household composition and on other relatives who might live locally. The next topic was the move to the present house, with particular reference to the exercise of choice, difficulties in achieving that choice and the levels of awareness of alternatives. The interview then explored the same factors in relation to the previous home. This focus on recent housing experiences was important, as it has been argued by Dex (1991) that life history interviews should begin by discussing issues and events which are easily recalled.

Respondents were then asked to look back to their first marital home, a standard starting point of household formation; in fact, several preferred to refer back to their first home in Britain, following migration from Pakistan. From the first marital home, interviewees were asked to talk about the sequence of homes, the same factors being covered in each case. The final part of the interview concerned aspirations for the future.

After transcription, the interviews were used to construct a chart of each household's history. The transcripts were indexed and sorted to produce collated comments on various aspects of these histories. It was hoped that the life history approach to interviewing would lead to an appreciation of agency and move interpretation away from a deterministic view.

Results

Current and previous housing

Of the nineteen households interviewed, twelve were currently owner-occupiers; seven were tenants, two with Glasgow City Council, four with private landlords, and one with a housing association. Eight households were living in tenement flats, six in semi-detached housing, two in modern, walk-up flats, and one each in terraced, detached and multi-storey housing.

The Pakistani families interviewed showed a general willingness to move, as household size changed. On average, those interviewed had lived in between three and four different houses since marriage and moved house approximately every five years. This contrasts with the findings of Sarre, Phillips and Skellington (1989) in Bedford, where 40 per cent of Asian families (mostly Indians in this case) stayed in their first home for at least ten years. Generally, the chief factor influencing a decision to move was space, with many families living in overcrowded conditions. Sometimes households changed tenure, buying a house to get the space they required:

> I decided to buy our own house, because you know we were sharing the house with someone else, sharing the kitchen, sharing the bath and it was difficult, you know. Every day I always ended up cleaning the kitchen and toilet and all this. I was pregnant, so it was difficult to stay with two children in one bedroom, you know. So we bought another, one-bedroomed flat in Govanhill and we were very pleased we got something, you know, of our own.

In their search for appropriate housing, Pakistani families showed themselves willing to move around Glasgow, in sharp contrast to the pattern of moves for white families which shows a tendency to move within areas but not between them. It is comparatively rare for white movers to cross the Clyde (Forbes, Lamont and Robertson, 1979).

Household composition

All nineteen households contained children. At the time of interview, the average household size was 5.2 but, at its maximum, had been 5.7; there were instances where older children had moved out. This compares with the average household size for the Pakistani population in Glasgow, at the 1991 Census of 4.8 — and an average for whites of 2.4. In our desire to interview families with older heads of household and, therefore, longer housing histories, we had clearly ignored some younger, smaller households and this accounts for the above-average household size in our sample.

Thirteen of the nineteen households had, at some time, had other members of the family staying there. In seven instances, it was a brother or sister while, in four cases, older sons had married and a daughter-in-law had joined the household. Only one household had grandparents living in the house while, in three cases, friends had lodged with the household.

Children were seen as important, partly because there was an expectation that, in later life, sons would take responsibility for looking after elderly parents, and, consequently, they were seen as having an important role to play in decisions about the household's future. Relatives too were important as part of the wider social network and helped to influence some locational decisions. Ten of the nineteen interviewees had relatives living locally, while a further two had relatives living just outside Glasgow.

Organising household moves

Decisions regarding household moves were sometimes taken by the male head of household but mostly it was a joint decision. Once taken, a variety of methods were used to find the right house. Seven households had used an estate agent but, generally, this was only where the house was purchased from a white family. It is possible that Pakistani families tend to avoid estate agents. Sarre, Phillips and Skellington (1989) found that many estate agents stereotyped Asians as being unreliable and devious in property transactions and two openly admitted excluding Asians from their services. The Pakistani families in our sample clearly saw no reason to use them, except where absolutely necessary.

There was some concern expressed that, in looking to obtain a house, Asian families would be unable to buy in certain areas:

> They didn't say anything but I lost almost six, seven houses in this area, then I had a good offer. Later on, somebody told me, and she is Jewish, and she said, 'Mrs. A____, you are not the only one. Thirty, forty years ago, when we were trying to buy the houses in this area, the people didn't like to sell to us at that time. Now, it's happening with Asians, that people don't like to sell the houses to Asians, because they know, instead of the Jewish, now the Asians are taking over'.

Perhaps because of such difficulties, personal contact seems to have been the main way in which households found houses to which they later moved:

> I was in Govan and I used to come to visit my aunt's daughter and she used to tell me to try and move house, and there was a friend that I used to meet and I told her and she said that my relatives, they're moving soon — in a month or two — and I'll talk to them for you. And I said, 'Please could you do that', and she said, 'I'll let you know in the morning'. So she spoke on our behalf and they said, 'That's fine. We're moving out on this date and you can come that day'.

For owner-occupiers, a wide range of sources of finance was used to fund such moves. Only one household appeared to have made use of a building society loan, although three had obtained a loan from their bank and a further two had, at different times, obtained home loans from the City Council. In three cases, households had paid cash for the property and two households had used private loans from friends or relatives.

Relatively common within the Pakistani community is the operation of a system of savings clubs, usually known as 'kametis' (Shaw, 1988) and

173

reference was made to them by our interviewees. Individual households pay into them at a rate which they can afford and the money is invested; they are then allocated a number indicating their position on a list. When that number is reached, it is then their turn to take out the money they have saved. Clearly, households may save through a kameti for any item of expenditure, but some use it to save for either the deposit on a house or, in the case of cheaper inner city property, perhaps the whole asking price. The operation of the kametis is not unlike the early 'terminating' building societies, into which individuals paid and from which they drew enough to build a house: when everyone had been housed, the building society was wound up or 'terminated' (Boddy, 1980). A key difference here is that, unlike the early building societies, the Pakistani kametis are characterised by a strong degree of anonymity and individuals may not know which other households are involved.

Another method of funding, used by two interviewees, was deposit-and-instalment. Such schemes involve the purchaser in paying a deposit to the seller of around 10 per cent of the purchase price, followed by monthly instalments. They are usually arranged privately and the title deeds of the property are not transferred to the purchaser until the last instalment has been paid. The use of such schemes, once relatively common in parts of inner city Glasgow, where building societies refused to lend, may indicate difficulties in accessing more usual forms of loan.

When households did not seek owner-occupation, the organisation of their moves involved approaching either private or public landlords for a house. Four households in the sample currently rented privately, all from Asian landlords and had obtained the housing through personal contact; there was thus a relative absence of formality in the relationship. While this may be seen as a positive thing, such informality may mean that households have an incomplete knowledge of the responsibilities of their landlord; a number of households, who had experienced private renting, referred to this.

Of increasing importance in recent years, is the use of council housing by Pakistani families and Bowes, McCluskey and Sim (1989) demonstrated an increasing orientation towards the local authority housing sector in Glasgow, especially amongst younger households. This is a trend which has been observed elsewhere, for example by Robinson (1986) in Blackburn.

In our sample, two households were council tenants and a third had previously been housed by the District Council as homeless. We found considerable ignorance, however, concerning the allocation system and, even those who had been successful in obtaining a council house, had failed to understand it.

Importantly, for Pakistanis, with larger households than white families, the Council seemed unable to offer appropriately sized accommodation. In the case of a family housed by the Homeless Persons Unit:

> I asked them but the Council said they are all small houses here, and they said for us, you need one room each for your children and you should have a separate room for the husband and wife. We don't have a house like that for you, so you have to look for one for yourself privately. Then I found this house, my children are happy ....

The problem of a lack of suitably sized accommodation is not peculiar to Glasgow, although Bowes, McCluskey and Sim (1989) calculated that only 3.2 per cent of council housing in Glasgow had four or more bedrooms; as a result, there was evidence that Asian families were being forced to under-estimate their needs in order to obtain a house. The situation had become even more serious by 1993, with the proportion of council stock which had four or more bedrooms falling to 2.6 per cent (Glasgow City Council, 1994). Because this shortage of large houses has a disproportionate impact on the Asian communities, the Association of Metropolitan Authorities (1988) has suggested that this constitutes indirect discrimination under the race relations legislation.

Pakistanis seemed to have complex attitudes towards council housing and there was a view that the public sector was in some ways merely a safety net, rather than a form of tenure to be sought in its own right. In part, this rather ambivalent attitude appears related to a concern that the allocation system is not geared towards the specific needs of the minority ethnic community. There was, in particular, a feeling that Pakistani families might be allocated a house in an area where they might be vulnerable to harassment:

> That's what most people in our Asian community view, you know, it's not worth applying and you never manage to get a house of your own choice. You always get offered where you can't survive - Castlemilk [an outer estate], Gorbals and things [both areas with small Pakistani populations]. If you don't have transport, if you can't speak the language, if you don't have any extended family to give you some kind of help, then obviously you prefer to stay within the community, so you can make friends, you can get help from them, instead of staying on your own. If you took ill and you have two children, who is going to phone the doctor or do things for you?

The sense of isolation is undoubtedly heightened if heads of household are unable to speak fluently in English or if the local authority has no Urdu or Punjabi speakers in their local housing offices. There was some anger at a local authority which was prepared to offer accommodation but seemed unable to offer follow-up support and advice:

> What happened was ... my in-laws got a house, a council house, it's only been one or two weeks since they got the house ....It was very difficult for them because they couldn't speak English. Then they were told that they could get a council house and they got angry. They said, 'We can't speak English, so what are we going to do with a council house; what we need is help'.

These problems of communication, particularly in terms of language were highlighted by Bowes, McCluskey and Sim (1989) but it would appear that they have not yet been resolved.

The evidence from our sample suggests that the allocation policy in Glasgow has not been particularly sensitive. In a particularly serious case, in the North Govanhill area [an inner city Council estate]:

> the day we put our things in the house, they got stolen. They made a mess, they spread flour all over the flat, they didn't leave anything, they broke

everything. My children were young as well, so I got really scared and I left the house that day and rented a place [privately]. I asked them to give me another place — I still ask them — but they haven't yet. They said your points have been greatly reduced because you left that house and that was our only setback, but we're OK just now. You know, they give you houses in areas that aren't very safe and I get scared. They're all-white areas.

In at least three cases, families had moved from the public to the private rented sector because of similar difficulties.

Housing associations

The relationship between ethnic minorities and housing associations in Glasgow is not a satisfactory one, and their record in housing minority families is not impressive. Partly this reflects the background to the establishment of associations in Glasgow, which were set up primarily to rehabilitate tenemental housing. The houses acquired were therefore already tenanted and the turnover of tenancies was too slow to make much impact on their waiting lists. It was only as the rehabilitation programme declined and associations undertook more new build, that there were greater opportunities for rehousing families (including minorities) from the waiting lists.

The slow progress made by associations became a matter of concern for the Commission for Racial Equality (CRE) who funded a major study which examined four associations (Dalton and Daghlian, 1989). More recently, the CRE launched a national study of housing associations and racial equality, and the Scottish associations fared poorly, in terms of racial equality policies, ethnic monitoring and minority ethnic representation on committees (Commission for Racial Equality, 1993).

Unsurprisingly then, associations did not emerge very positively from our study. Indeed, the only housing association tenant in our sample actually believed the house was rented from the local authority; we were able to establish later that this was not in fact the case. Two other households had applied to associations but had not been offered a house, mainly because of an insufficient number of points. One complained that she had been rudely treated by the Allocations Officer at the association in question and had felt threatened.

Housing likes and dislikes

Not surprisingly, a proximity to Asian facilities was seen as being particularly important in housing search strategies, although it was not the only factor. Generally, the presence of good neighbours, of whatever ethnic origin, was essential. A great deal of importance was attached to the existence of a good local school and transport was also important, to enable interviewees, mainly women without access to a car, to travel to visit family and friends and to reach shops. Proximity to Asian shops, to doctors and to the Mosque were all positive attributes of interviewees' housing.

A number of households had actively sought a property on the ground or first floor, because of an elderly relative in the family. Four households liked the house they were in, because of its size, while the presence of a garden was beneficial to those households with children. One important advantage of a large house, for some, was that it allowed families to have separate facilities for men and women:

> I like two rooms downstairs, and sitting and dining separate. I like, because in our families, we like men separate and ladies sit separate .... I feel I don't like only one room. Sometimes two families come and they have to sit together, and I don't enjoy it ... with men.

No matter how accessible facilities might be and how appropriate the housing was, the key issue for many respondents was the safety of their family within the area. Freedom from fear and harassment therefore transcended other factors influencing a choice of house and families distinguished quite carefully between the characteristics of the house and those of its surroundings.

Conclusions

Our study allows several conclusions to be drawn. The first is the continuing difficulty experienced by Pakistani families in funding household moves. While accepting that some families will seek a loan other than from a building society, this in itself is indicative of the suspicions which many households have of the agents who control house buying and house exchange. The frequency with which Pakistani households made use of personal loans (such as through the 'kameti' system) and of deposit-and-instalment schemes for house purchase suggests difficulties in obtaining normal building society mortgages. The reluctance of societies to fund mortgages for Pakistani families may simply reflect the 'redlining' of inner city housing areas. But, given that these are often the areas in which Pakistanis are looking for housing, then this policy is having a discriminatory effect.

Some inner city housing is undoubtedly of poor quality, but for most people that we interviewed, the area is more important than the house itself. This then is a second, clear conclusion — that there are still large areas of Glasgow where Pakistani families feel unsafe and where they are reluctant to live. Proximity to Asian shops, the Mosque, good schools and transport and, above all, good friends and neighbours, were the key factors in finding a suitable house.

A third finding is the continuing failure by the local authority to meet the housing needs of the Pakistani community, by allocating housing in appropriate areas and of appropriate sizes. Indeed, the provision of suitably-sized local authority accommodation is actually worsening. For some households, the private rented sector has proved a suitable alternative but, given the decline of this sector, the option of rented accommodation is not easily available to Pakistani families.

Fourthly, the issue of racial harassment continues to be serious. In certain parts of Glasgow, notably the peripheral local authority housing estates but also certain inner city estates, Pakistani families are treated in a hostile fashion. This is still an issue waiting to be tackled thoroughly and effectively.

In addition to the basic survey findings, it is important to identify those conclusions which have emerged from the particular type of methodology used.

177

The life history interviewing technique allowed us a proper sense of how often households had moved and the factors which were important to them in their move. We have already referred to the importance of area characteristics in choice of accommodation; the interviews allowed us to assess the extent to which households indulged in 'trade-offs' between a particular area and a particular house, or indeed between different tenures. The private rented sector, for example, has tended to be seen by many white households merely as a stepping-stone on the way to the majority tenures and not as a long term destination (Crook, 1992). Pakistanis in our sample, however, appeared willing to move from a secure tenancy in the local authority sector, into private rented accommodation in order to get a house of the right size in the right place.

The life history interviews also enabled us to assess the cumulative nature of choices; thus, the choice made by a household at a particular point may in time constrain further choices. Households which over-reached themselves financially found themselves constrained in terms of their future options. In the council sector, Pakistani families had frequently discovered that they had insufficient points to obtain a house of their choice but had lacked the knowledge of the system to apply earlier, a decision which might have earned them some points for waiting time. It is only through studying a household's life history that the longer term impacts of these decisions can be appreciated.

Another area which was explored by life history interviewing was the way in which the composition of the household changed over time. Changing household size clearly had an important impact on the frequency of moves and Pakistani families showed themselves willing to move around the inner city, rather than keeping to particular geographical sectors.

One of the most important gains from the life history technique is in the avoidance of stereotyping. While it may be true that the majority of Pakistanis are owner-occupiers and the majority live in the inner city, it is essential that those households with needs and aspirations which depart from this 'norm' are not ignored. The interviews demonstrated clearly that Pakistanis, like white people, have widely varying attitudes and aspirations and these change as housing policies change and as knowledge changes.

Finally, we believe that life history studies help to tackle the missing element in much previous housing work, namely the actions which have been taken by householders themselves. While recognising that there is a difficulty in making precise connections between individual experience and wider social processes, we believe that the technique allows us to observe how individuals and households operate within the wider constraints which exist in housing. Thus, our understanding of the role of agency in the development of patterns of housing and individual housing careers, is substantially deepened.

Acknowledgement

The research reported in this chapter was funded by the University of Stirling's Internal Research Fund.

17 Living apart in Belfast: residential segregation in a context of ethnic conflict

Paul Doherty and Michael Poole

Introduction

Belfast is the dominant urban centre in Northern Ireland. From 1891 to 1981 at least twenty per cent of the population of what in 1921 became Northern Ireland have lived in Belfast County Borough or its successor Local Government District. This proportion fell to 19.3 per cent in 1987 and 17.7 per cent (279,237 persons) in 1991 as people moved out to the surrounding suburbs and towns. Looking beyond the political boundary, since 1945 upwards of 32 per cent of the province's population has lived in the built-up area of the city (Compton, 1990, p. 20).

It is also significant that the major part of the recent conflict in Northern Ireland has taken place on the streets of Belfast: an analysis of the 1969-1993 period (Poole, 1995, pp. 31-3) showed that 54.5 per cent of fatal incidents took place in the city, and these high levels of violence have been historically a recurrent feature (Hepburn, 1994). Belfast can be accurately described as 'the urban encapsulation of a national conflict' (Boal, Murray et al., 1976, p. 77).

A spatial outcome of this struggle is the residential segregation of Protestants and Catholics that exists in much of the city today. The purpose of this paper is to provide empirical evidence as to the intensity of the segregation. We will seek first to provide a historical perspective, using census data from 1871 to 1991, and second a spatial perspective on the variation in segregation levels within the contemporary urban area.

In the early 1970s the view was developed that the religious division in Northern Ireland was essentially an ethnic split (Poole and Boal, 1973, p. 11). According to this conceptualisation, it was contended:

> First that the conflict in Belfast can only be understood if it is viewed both in ethnic group terms and also in national terms, and second, that residential segregation is a key index of the level of the conflict itself (Boal, Murray et al., 1976, p. 77).

Our discussion follows this widely accepted conceptualisation of the conflict in Northern Ireland as being essentially ethnic, in which the two ethnic groups may be identified by their religious affiliation, Catholic or Protestant (Doherty and Poole, 1995).

It has been suggested that residential segregation existed in Belfast from the early 17th century, when it received its first effective plantation of English settlers, and obtained its charter. Emrys Jones suggests that the first map of Belfast shows the native Irish living outside the walls of the town, at what is today the apex of the main Catholic sector of the city running along the Falls Road (Jones, 1956). While there is historical evidence for the existence of segregated areas (Hepburn, 1992), we do not have any statistical evidence until the census of 1871, which for the first time provided figures for the religious groups for the five wards into which the city was then divided. The 1871 census therefore provides the starting point for the analysis presented here.

Our discussion will use a single statistic, the dissimilarity index D (Duncan and Duncan, 1955), which is the most frequently used measure in the research literature. D measures the unevenness dimension of segregation (Massey and Denton, 1988). It expresses the dissimilarity between two percentage distributions across a set of subareas, one distribution being the minority group, and the other the majority. The statistic ranges from zero, when all the subarea minority percentages equal the city-wide percentage, to 100 when all the subarea minority percentages are either zero or 100. Thus a D value of zero means a perfectly even population distribution, while 100 indicates a very uneven distribution — a situation of total segregation.

The dissimilarity index, like other spatial statistics, is profoundly influenced by the spatial framework from which it is derived. This means that it is hazardous to compare indices that have been calculated using differing spatial frameworks. In the present discussion, three distinct spatial frameworks will be used, which are a consequence of the ways in which the various censuses from 1871 have published their data: five wards for 1871-91, fifteen wards for 1901-71, and 157 one kilometre grid squares for 1971-91. While statistics from one of these frameworks cannot be compared directly with statistics derived from another, they do indicate something of the changing levels of segregation within their particular time periods.

The 1871 to 1891 censuses

The first three censuses, 1871, 1881 and 1891, used a very crude spatial subdivision into five rather large wards. The city population increased 46.7 per cent in just twenty years. Belfast was industrialising and attracting population in from its rural hinterland (Bardon, 1982). Growth was greater for Protestants than for Catholics, so the proportion of Catholics declined from 31.8 per cent to 26.3 per cent. The D values (Figure 17.1) are low, as might be expected because of the small number of subareas. However there is a clear upward trend in segregation levels with D rising from 13.2 to 21.6, a fairly substantial increase from an initially low base. The implication is that in this period of dynamic urbanisation, the in-migrants were tending to move to areas of like ethnic identity, possibly to be with friends or family, and this was serving to increase the overall level of segregation. Furthermore, as new housing was being built it tended to intensify the exclusivism. For example, the expansion of the Catholic Falls Road sector has been identified as an outcome of riots in 1872 (Hepburn, 1992, p.44). These riots were accompanied by evictions which also firmed up the religious divide (Bardon, 1982, pp. 144-6), a common sequence of events in Belfast's troubled history.

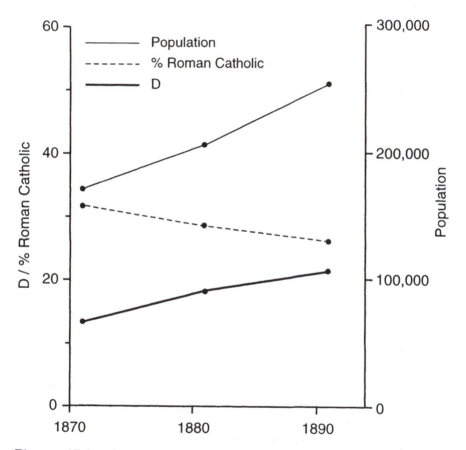

Figure 17.1 Segregation levels in Belfast County Borough, 1871-1891

The 1901 to 1971 censuses

In 1896 the city boundary was extended and fifteen wards were introduced. This provided the spatial framework for the censuses from 1901 to 1971. Figure 17.2 shows that the population of the County Borough increased from 349,180 in 1901 to 443,671 in 1951, then fell back to 362,082 in 1971. Against this background of considerable numerical variation, the number of stated Catholics as a percentage of total population only varied slightly, from a low of 23.0 per cent in 1926 to a high of 27.5 per cent in 1961. The segregation levels however reveal interesting trends. The D values show a constant level from 1901 to 1911, followed by a steep increase of ten percentage points between 1911 and 1926. The increase can be directly attributed to the Troubles of 1920-1923, which were related to the partition of Ireland. This period was one of particularly severe inter-communal conflict that resulted in the deaths of 453 persons in the city (Bardon, 1982, p. 202).

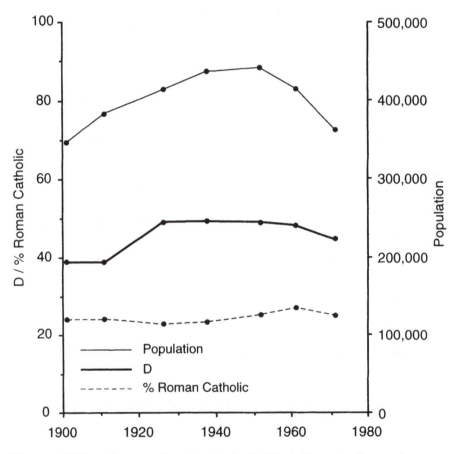

Figure 17.2   Segregation levels in Belfast County Borough, 1901-1971

The spatial outcome of the conflict was again increased segregation. Districts which had already acquired an ethnic identity had that identity strengthened by the population movements which followed sectarian riots and intimidation. Once an ethnic identity became established in an area, it tended to be perpetuated, and reinforced during periods of conflict. A map of the religious groups of 1926 found the sectarian geography to be clear, and shows much that is familiar in the city today: 'the outstanding fact is the 90 per cent concentration in two wards, and the high proportion of Catholics (40 per cent) in the centre of the city' (Evans, 1944, p. 25).

From 1935 to 1968 the city experienced a period without major conflict, a lull before the storm that was to break with the outbreak of the most recent Troubles, a storm which had its eye in the city. Rioting reached the streets of Belfast in May and June 1969, and this marked the commencement of the most severe and sustained period of violence the city has ever experienced.

Figure 17.2 shows a plateau in segregation levels between 1926 and 1951, with D values just over 49. This is followed by declining values from 1951 to 1971. The D value in 1971 was lower than had existed for fifty years, but it still had not fallen back to the level of 1911. This leads to the conclusion that while segregation falls when there has been a period free from conflict, it does not fall back to where it had been before the preceding outbreak of violence, and therefore the overall trend is inexorably upward. This has been described as a 'ratchet effect' (Smith and Chambers, 1991, p. 112), by which segregation rises in a stepwise fashion, only falling back after an extended period of tranquillity. The 1971 D value was obtained after almost two years of civil disturbance, and we might therefore reasonably assume that had this outbreak of violence not occurred, the D value would have been lower. We can only speculate what the segregation level might be today had there not been the past 30 years of violence.

The 1971 to 1991 censuses

In 1973 the boundary of the city was further extended and the new Local Government District was subdivided into 51 wards. However the 1971 census was the first Northern Ireland census to be geocoded, and this enabled data to be obtained from it (and from subsequent censuses) for a system of 1 kilometre grid squares. It also enabled data to be obtained for the entire built-up area of the city, as opposed to being restricted to the political boundary (County Borough) as heretofore. The built-up area of the city is clearly defined by a Stop Line on growth (Matthew, 1964) which delimits the Belfast Urban Area. This grid square system has been used for more detailed analysis of the 1971, 1981 and 1991 censuses (Doherty and Poole, 1995)

Both the 1971 and 1981 censuses were subjected to politically motivated campaigns to encourage non-response to the religion question, and to disrupt the implementation of the census (Compton, 1993, pp. 345-7). In 1981 this was particularly serious, so that 'not even the size of the population of Northern Ireland is accurately known ... let alone the breakdown of the population by religious denomination' (Compton, 1985, p. 203). The figures presented here for that year are therefore based on estimates of the Catholic and Protestant numbers (Doherty, 1989, pp. 157-8). The problems surrounding the use of religion statistics as an indicator of ethnicity are discussed by Doherty and Poole (1995). the statistics given here are considered to represent best the true position with regard to the segregation of the two groups, in the light of these problems. Figure 17.3 shows the relevant data for the three censuses in question.

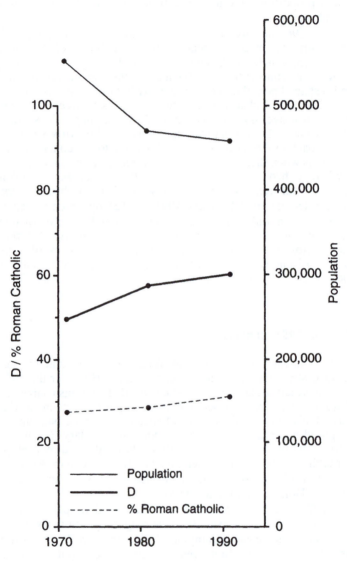

Figure 17.3   **Segregation levels in the Belfast Urban Area, 1971-1991**

Over the twenty year period the population of the Urban Area fell by 17.2 per cent. This was due to the decentralisation of housing and population from Belfast (Compton, 1990), a trend found elsewhere in the United Kingdom and beyond. In part this may be explained by the availability of attractive and affordable housing in the surrounding commuter towns, but the Troubles have also had an impact in contributing to the outflow of population from Belfast. It is no coincidence that the steep decline in population numbers during the 1970s occurred in the period when the urban violence was most intense.

Throughout the twenty year period the proportion of Catholics in the Urban Area rose steadily, particularly within the Local Government District where it is now around forty per cent. The proportion Catholic has also increased in the suburbs, but these remain much more Protestant. So even at this very basic level the city is segregated.

The increase in segregation at grid square level is clear from Figure 17.3. It is worth noting that the D value for 1971 calculated on the basis of 15 wards is 44.9, while the value calculated on the basis of 157 grid squares is 49.6. This is entirely to be expected due to the change in spatial framework: the finer the spatial resolution, the higher the dissimilarity index will be. It underlines the point made earlier, that statistics calculated from different spatial frameworks should not be directly compared. The graph shows a fairly steep rise in D value from 1971 to 1981, followed by a gentler increase to 1991.

The 1971 figure of 49.6 relates to census night in April of that year. During the summer of 1971 the situation in the province deteriorated substantially and internment of terrorist suspects without trial was introduced on 9 August (Bardon, 1982, pp. 284-7). This action by the Government was an attempt to calm a rapidly worsening situation, but it was to prove the catalyst for even greater violence which resulted in large scale population movements within Belfast. A report into these movements stated that 'the most significant trend observed in the movements of August 1971 was the re-sorting of mixed areas into segregated areas, the continuation of the patterns of 1969 and 1970' (Darby and Morris, 1974, p. 2). The report provided evidence of the forced movement of 8,000 families from their homes in the Greater Belfast area, but suggested that the actual figure could be as high as 15,000. This represented between 6.6 and 11.8 per cent of the population of the Urban Area.

The steep rise in segregation levels in the 1971-81 period can be attributed to these major movements, and subsequent lesser ones. The period from 1981-91 did not experience major population movements, but there were nonetheless continued instances of intimidation, whereby members of the minority in an area (either Protestant or Catholic) would be intimidated from their homes. In addition, more normal housing market movements, while not directly occasioned by intimidation, tended to see families move into areas where they were members of the majority and as a consequence felt more secure. Large scale movements were succeeded by a gradual drift of households into their ethnic heartlands. These movements served to increase further the segregation level, to its present D value of 60.2 for the Urban Area as a whole.

Segregation variation within the city

It must be noted that these segregation levels are not uniform throughout the city. The Urban Area has been subdivided into nine units (Doherty, 1989). A tenth unit may be added to these (Figure 17.4), the Urban Area Extension, which contains housing developments which were permitted beyond the Matthew Stop Line, to relieve housing pressure in the 1980s. Five of these units

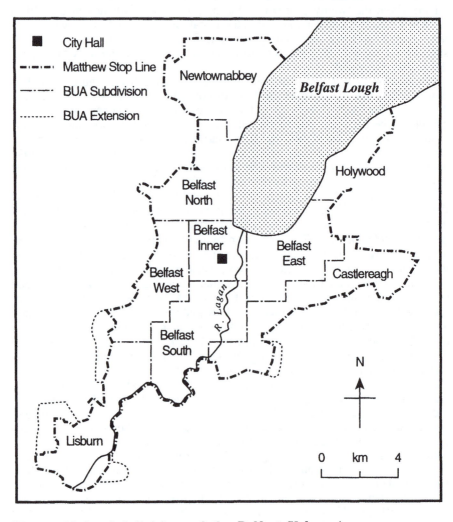

Figure 17.4   Subdivisions of the Belfast Urban Area

lie within the Belfast Local Government District, the remaining five are
suburban and are parts of the surrounding LGDs. Table 17.1 presents the
relevant statistics for these subdivisions.

Table 17.1
Segregation measures (D) for the subdivisions of the
Belfast Urban Area, 1991

	Population	% Roman Catholic	D
Belfast LGD	271,789	40.2	57.0
Belfast Inner	34,787	47.3	36.2
Belfast North	58,325	39.3	38.1
Belfast West	67,691	74.7	63.9
Belfast South	48,525	32.3	33.4
Belfast East	62,461	6.0	46.8
Belfast Suburbs	193,904	19.2	52.0
Newtownabbey	57,540	15.4	45.6
Lisburn	57,889	30.4	58.9
Castlereagh	59,574	8.4	55.5
Holywood	11,243	18.1	16.0
BUA Extension	7,658	47.7	90.4
Urban Area	458,035	31.2	60.2
Urban Area + Extension	465,693	31.5	60.7

Source: Doherty and Poole (1995)

Of these ten subdivisions of the Urban Area, only Belfast West has a Catholic
majority, and that majority is substantial. The other subdivisions vary
enormously in the size of their Protestant majority. This majority is particularly

high in Belfast East and the contiguous area of Castlereagh. Other subdivisions lie between these two extremes. The subdivisions within the Belfast LGD tend to have larger Catholic minorities (40.2 per cent overall), while the suburban divisions have smaller such minorities (19.2 per cent overall), with the exception of the BUA Extension.

The variation in the Catholic share of population between the subdivisions is to be expected, given the existence of residential segregation in the Urban Area. What is perhaps more surprising is that the intensity of segregation itself varies considerably between subdivisions, as is apparent from the dissimilarity indices. These range from 16.0 in Holywood, to the recent extensions of the Urban Area, which have a value of 90.4.

The figures for the Belfast LGD are comparatively moderate, although the Catholic heartland of Belfast West is substantially higher than the others. In fact, the unweighted average D value for the Belfast LGD subdivisions is 43.7, which is almost ten percentage points lower than the corresponding suburban average of 53.3. Thus not only is the ring of suburban subdivisions more Protestant than the Belfast LGD subdivisions, but it is also more internally segregated according to this approach to measurement.

On the other hand, if segregation in the Belfast LGD is expressed as the deviation from the Catholic proportion in the LGD as a whole, instead of from the series of five local proportions used to calculate the five separate dissimilarity indices in Table 17.1, then a profoundly different conclusion emerges. This generates a Belfast LGD index of 57.0, which is boosted by the fact that it is measuring segregation between the five subregions as well as within them. The corresponding approach in the ring of suburban subdivisions, however, yields an index of 52.0, which is hardly altered because there is so little segregation between these suburban divisions to raise the new index. Thus one approach to measurement finds that suburban segregation is higher than city segregation, while the other demonstrates the opposite. Both are answers to valid, but different, questions on the relative intensity of city and suburban segregation. This emphasises the importance, in segregation analysis, of defining precisely what it is that needs to be measured.

The same methodological effect, illustrated here for Belfast LGD, impacts upon the dissimilarity index for the entire Urban Area, for the latter is higher than those for all but two of its subdivisions. This is because the BUA index is measuring not only the segregation within subdivisions, but also the considerable segregation between them.

Conclusion

There is good reason to believe that Belfast has been segregated since its beginnings. It has been demonstrated that the overall trend in dissimilarity indices from 1871 to the present day has been upward, and once segregated areas develop they tend to be perpetuated. This is a clear example, at the intra-urban level, of the localised social reproduction which has been argued elsewhere to be a fundamental part of the processes generating the geography of both residential segregation and political violence at the inter-urban level in Northern Ireland (Poole, 1995, pp. 40-3).

Segregation in Belfast is a direct spatial outcome of violence: violent episodes such as occurred in the early 1920s and 1970s were followed by marked increases in segregation. This segregation increase has been demonstrated at the level of suburbs/inner city, at the ward level, at the kilometre grid square level, and is also demonstrable at street level (Boal, 1982), where the impact of residential segregation on daily life is most evident. While segregation tends to fall back after a peaceful period, there is no evidence to suggest that it returns to its previous level. Rather, a ratchet effect occurs whereby segregation rises inexorably in steps after violent episodes and only moderates slightly in more peaceful times.

Even when violence is not high, there is a tendency for segregation to be perpetuated through the operation of the housing market. In Belfast, the highest levels of segregation are to be found in public sector housing, which has become increasingly polarised and partitioned by the operation of segregated migration flows (Keane, 1990). The extensions to the Urban Area which were permitted in the 1980s contain new-build developments which are almost totally segregated (see, again, Table 17.1).

Segregation levels in contemporary Belfast are at an all-time high following a conflict of unprecedented length and intensity. Earlier this century a period of 25 to 30 conflict-free years elapsed before a slight decline in segregation levels could be observed. It must therefore be concluded that a similarly lengthy period must go by before there is any significant desegregation from the present levels, and should there be a resumption of violence segregation will once more begin to rise.

Acknowledgements

The authors wish to gratefully acknowledge the financial assistance which enabled them to purchase the various data sets used in this analysis. The 1971 data were purchased by the Department of Geography, Queen's University, Belfast. The 1981 data were purchased by the Department of Environmental Studies, the University of Ulster. The 1991 data were purchased using a grant from the European Social Fund Training Programme in Research Methods, and have been adapted from the Northern Ireland Census 1991 grid square small area statistics by permission of the Controller of HMSO and the Department of Finance and Personnel.

18 Belfast's peace lines and potential directions for local planning

Brendan Murtagh

Introduction

> Barbed wire protects, but it imprisons; stockades protect the invader, but confine as well; stucco walls and wrought iron fences provide a sense of identity but reflect insecurity and betray vulnerability as well (Marcuse, 1994, p. 50).

The ambiguities and contradictions embodied in Belfast's peace lines provide the central empirical focus for this chapter. The acceleration of segregation after the outbreak of civil disorder in 1969 was characterised by a desperate spatial sorting process that left jagged and uncomfortable edges to ethnic territory. The use of walls to manage the worst of these is one of the most enduring social and physical images of violence in Northern Ireland. In his attempt to classify urban walls, Marcuse drew a distinction between functions of oppression, isolation and control and those of protection, insulation and community reinforcement. This chapter locates Belfast's peace lines in the latter context.

Survey data is used to build a profile of life in the interface and argue that these locales need to be better understood by policy makers. Despite the complexity and spatial significance of peace lines there are few coherent statements from planners or housing managers on how to deal with them. The very 'wickedness' of the problem is part of the explanation for this but so too is the professional reluctance by planners to move away from the core technocratic values, particularly in Northern Ireland where such a departure holds real dangers for the independence of professionals and the state. But in a process of global economic, social, technological and spatial restructuring the need for coping strategies that cross the conventional boundaries of land use planning might seem fruitful. Community responses to the issue are evaluated as one possible point of departure in that task and the chapter concludes by arguing for an engagement of ethnic issues in general and peace lines in particular in local planning debate and analysis.

The peace lines

Belfast has always experienced high rates of ethno-religious segregation (Boal, 1982). However, the most dramatic period of population movement, as result of ethnic turmoil in the city, was between 1969 and 1973 when an estimated 60,000 people left their homes (Brett, 1986). That movement tended to be concentrated in the working class areas of North, West and inner East Belfast. The particular ethnic patchwork of Catholic and Protestant neighbourhoods in North Belfast experienced the worst of the internecine conflict, population flight and starkest division of territory. The consequence was fifteen peace lines, where a physical barrier has been used to separate the respective communities (Figure 18.1).

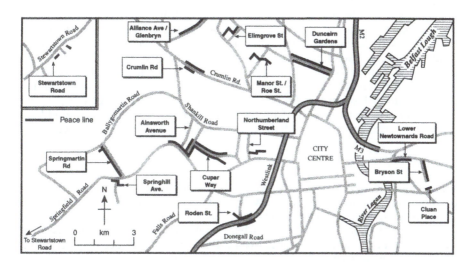

Figure 18.1   Belfast 'peace lines', 1996

Social and demographic life

The analysis below profiles community life at the interface. It is based on household survey data in three case study areas representing different relationships between Protestant and Catholic communities. Suffolk, in West Belfast, contains a small Protestant community physically surrounded by largely Catholic housing. The opposite circumstance exists in the Short Strand where that Catholic community is numerically outweighed by Protestants in the lower Newtownards Road. In Ardoyne in North Belfast Protestant and Catholic communities are in roughly even numeric and spatial proportions. A total of 450 households were surveyed during 1994 in each case study area.

   Indicators of social deprivation illustrated the extent of the problem among peace line communities. For example, if the case study areas are considered typical of peace lines zones, then 69 per cent of the community earn less than £5,000 compared to 45 per cent of Northern Ireland as a whole. The unemployment rate for Northern Ireland as a whole was 11 per cent but at the interface, it is nearly three times that (31 per cent). High benefit dependency underscores the nature of poverty at the peace line. Forty-one per cent of households in total receive Income Support compared with half that for the Province as a whole (21 per cent). In addition, twelve per cent of the population of Northern Ireland achieved Advanced level standard as their highest qualification and the same proportion a university degree (12 per cent). The comparative figures for the peace line communities were two per cent and one per cent respectively.

The population mix of peace line communities is linked to the different demographic profile of Protestants and Catholics. Protestant demographics are characterised by lower fertility rates, family sizes and an elderly profile whilst Catholics demographics are typified by larger than average family sizes, a younger age profile and higher than average fertility rates. This has direct implications for housing provision in these areas as the Catholic community is correlated with higher waiting lists, lower dwelling void rates and a more equitable match between household size and property size. For example, 27 per cent of the households in Protestant Suffolk were equal to the 'bedroom standard' measure of dwelling occupancy compared to 46 per cent on the Catholic side of the line. In Ardoyne and Short Strand nearly half (43 per cent and 44 per cent respectively) of Protestant households are classified as elderly compared to one-quarter of Catholic households (26 per cent) in each area.

Economic life

What is significant is the extent to which the two communities share a common position in the social hierarchy. Low head of household income is a feature of all areas with almost identical statistics for each locality whether they are Protestant and Catholic. Similarly, when employment data are considered, it shows a degree of variation between peace line communities but relatively even profiles within each zone. In the Short Strand, 17 per cent of household heads on the Protestant side of the line are in full-time work compared to 16 per cent on the Catholic side.

The survey also showed that communities that are in a minority in one area experience significant problems in daily life activities such as getting to work, to see friends and relatives, to health services and to recreation facilities. For example, 28 per cent of Catholics in the Short Strand said that accessing monthly shopping was a problem and 11 per cent of residents in Protestant Suffolk had a problem getting to a leisure centre. Taking the peace lines together, the research showed that 25 per cent of residents had problems with vandalism, 24 per cent with stone throwing and 13 per cent with local rioting.

Social distance

The research also explored the attitudes of the communities who live at peace line to their own identity (the 'in' group) and that of the community on the opposite side of the peace fence (or the 'out' group). Most Protestant communities described themselves as 'British' (Suffolk 60 per cent, Ardoyne 58 per cent, Short Strand 39 per cent). The next most common description for all three communities was 'Protestant'. Similarly Catholics were more likely to call themselves 'Irish' and secondly, 'Catholic'. However, there was some degree of agreement on a Northern Irish identify as, in Protestant Ardoyne, 8 per cent identified themselves as Northern Irish while 9 per cent of Catholic Ardoyne used the same label.

However, positive opinions and attitudes were also prevalent at the peace line. For example, 81 per cent of the total sample would allow a member of the out group to join their clubs and societies. This figure progressively rises when entry into neighbourhood (90 per cent), country (94 per cent) and visiting rights to area (94 per cent) are considered. However, a constant theme across all case study areas is the lower rate of acceptance of Protestant communities compared to Catholics. In Suffolk, 88 per cent of Catholics would allow a member of the Protestant community to marry into their family compared to 60 per cent of Protestants. While 90 per cent of Suffolk Catholics would allow the peace line Protestant community to 'live in their street as neighbours' the equivalent figure for Suffolk Protestants was 70 per cent . Similarly, 79 per cent of Protestant Ardoyne would allow Catholics to live in their street as neighbours compared to 97 per cent of Ardoyne Catholics. It is argued that these trends are the product of a community under a prolonged period of actual and perceived threat. As housing pressure from the Catholic community grows and as dwelling void rates increase in the Protestant estate, any incursion would be perceived as the beginning of the end for the resident community. In these areas attitudes are a product, not of an irrational historic bigotry, but of very genuine fears for the future of their territory and all that this means for community survival. The implication is that before cross community initiatives can be realised, the communities themselves must feel confident about their own identity and future sustainability.

Community initiatives

The processes of segregation have cemented a geography and a mind-set that will not be easy to break down, even given the context of uncertain peace. Three peace lines have been strengthened, heightened and lengthened and a new one built since the 1994 Republican and Loyalist cease-fires. The Northern Ireland Community Relations Council (CRC) surveyed community representatives in peace line communities one year after the 1994 cessation of violence. This showed that issues such as policing and traditional marches are still key concerns among local people and there is strong resistance to any tampering with the peace walls themselves. The report concluded that 'the mental barriers have to come down before the physical ones' (CRC, 1996, p. 5). However, the survey emphasised the need for structured dialogue between communities over matters of mutual concern. The need to build up community infrastructure particularly for families and young people, the problems of drug abuse and the structuring of cross-community contact around contentious issues, such as traditional parades, have been identified as priorities.

In 1995 CRC launched the Belfast Interface Project to take some of these issues forward at community level. The primary objective of the Development Worker appointed to the Project is to harness public, community and private sector resources to address the following key themes:

community development
employment
policing
marches and parades
researching interface communities including health, transport and services and facilities for children
humanising communities including support for victims and survivors and measures to improve internal community identity and security.

It is too early to gauge the impact of the project or to attempt even a preliminary evaluation of the work to date. But many of the themes in the approach and the emphasis on community based analysis and problem solving could be embraced by the wider policy sector. Three case studies illustrate some of the thinking and methodologies within the community sector that may have potential as learning experiments.

The origin of the Woodburn Interface Project, West Belfast lay in the violence among young people between Protestant Suffolk and Catholic Lenadoon in the late 1980s (McCorry, 1991). Conceptually, the project lies in the problem of social control and young people in areas affected by accentuated violence:

> The overall image of an estate was determined by what were usually quite small sections of the community which the study called 'toughs'. With the general weakening of social controls in the community the adults were increasingly unable to influence the youth from whom the 'toughs' were mainly drawn (Hamilton et al., 1990, p. 19).

The response was to establish a youth project in the area that aimed to promote a culture of mutual security, interests and needs and the creation of attitudinal change in adolescents with a concentration on perceived young toughs. The project was based on a neutrally located building that acted as the focus for a series of joint workshops. Here, the emphasis was on mediation skills with the mediator attempting to build mutual respect and understanding among young people in the area. Whilst the early part of the programme was focused on a separate analysis of the two communities, the longer term objective was the achievement of mutually beneficial contact between Protestant and Catholic young people in the area.

The Ballynafeigh Project was operated by the Community Relations Council and explored life in the Ballynafeigh area of South Belfast. The rationale for the selection of the area was that it is sensitively balanced in terms of its religious composition. Pressure from a nearby Catholic area coupled with housing opportunities for Protestants in new suburban developments has meant that the resident Protestant population felt increasingly vulnerable. The CRC initiative in Ballynafeigh examined the factors that could create or encourage community stability. Their research for example, identified problems in the Protestant community linked to the closure of the local Primary School at the same time as a new Catholic Grammar school was opened to serve the Ballynafeigh catchment. The CRC approach called for government support to maintain services and facilities that could help to stabilise the resident Protestant population. This would include finance to continue to operate marginally uneconomic schools. CRC argued that the concept of building and maintaining the community infrastructure in a way that would enhance community stability could represent a central element in any planning approach in these areas.

The EXTERN Neighbourhood Disputes Initiative, North Belfast was significant because it represents a comprehensive analysis of disputes at a neighbourhood level. In the *Report of the Extern Working Party on Neighbourhood Disputes in Northern Ireland* (EXTERN, 1987) the organisation reviewed the meaning and variety of neighbourhood disputes. The report defines a neighbourhood dispute as 'disagreement over aspects of residence between non-kin living in close proximity' (EXTERN, 1987, p. 4). One case study selected was Duncairn and in particular, the conflict between the Protestant Tigers Bay and the Catholic New Lodge. The research had the following objective:

> In view of the sectarian conflict in Northern Ireland, to look at the continuum between individuals and groups and to consider the role and limitations of a Neighbourhood Dispute Service in the area of sectarian conflict (EXTERN, 1987, p. 6).

With regard to Duncairn, the analysis concluded that the response to the formation of a mediation service would be very slow. However, as with other voluntary sector initiatives, the emphasis was placed on the benefits of a formal mediator who would act as a facilitator in dispute resolution:

> This encourages positive attitudes towards conflict in the future, giving mediation services a general educative role. The process itself is very flexible and can be adopted to suit particular circumstances or cultures (EXTERN, 1987, pp. 25-26).

The methodology advocated was broken down into four distinct stages:

Stage 1 Introduction: Get the neutral environment and agree the ground rules with disputants.

Stage 2 Story telling: Explain the situation from their own view point. At this stage the mediators role is simply to separate fact from the emotions that surround them.

Stage 3 Problem Solving: This stage involves framing the issue and generating the solutions. The thrust of the mediators role is to generate formal thinking and concentration on areas of potential future agreement.

Stage 4 Resolution: This may involve joint written or verbal agreements.

This approach demonstrates that the skills in dispute resolution, using discursive techniques can be applied to help communities define their own problems and work through locally relevant solutions. In mediating between competing interests in the use and development of land, planning methodology can learn much from the application of specific approaches in localities where space is highly contested and where the inclusion of all relevant interests is necessary to validate planning outcomes.

Planning and the peace lines

Tomlins (1995) drew significant parallels between circumstances in Belfast and problems developing an ethnically sensitive housing and planning policy in Britain. He characterised much of current thinking and policy initiatives on the segregated housing as paternalistic and argued that 'a fundamental issue concerns the right to express identity through residence, indeed to choose continuing ethnic residential segregation and a self defined ethnic housing policy' (Tomlins, 1995, p. 1; see also Tomlins, this volume Chapter 15). Thus, he argued, the choice of minority ethnic communities to spatially concentrate need not be a process of marginalisation, if it is backed by policies and finance to ensure that the life chances within those areas are compatible with those within mainstream society.

> Recognition of difference can also be used to further justify separate provision, which can lead to further empowerment by ensuring that services are controlled by the communities receiving the service (Tomlins, 1995, pp. 11-12).

This type of analysis and prescriptive agenda has significant implications for Belfast. It recognises a realism which places constraints on, but also opens opportunities for effective policy development. For example, an 'ethnic audit' could complement traditional land use surveys upon which development planning is based and could set out the ethnic balance of the locale and the constraints or opportunities this places the development of planning strategies. 'Ethnic impact assessments' could ensure that new developments are sensitive to ethno-spatial considerations and that they do not have wider negative effects on the stability of communities and areas. All of this should lead to an output that addresses the physical, economic and social development of interface areas. What is called for here is the infusion of an explicit community relations agenda into the development of such initiatives. By addressing these concern through surveys at the start of the planning making process, community relations issues will not become a bolt-on to traditional proposals for local development. Greed (1994) argued that planners should embrace ethnographic techniques to understand complex dynamics at community level. A more complete understanding of the realities of life using this methodological approach is, she argued, a fundamental prerequisite to building effective planning strategies.

The approach suggested requires the development of a different range of skills than those normally associated with land use planning and mainstream housing management. The starting point for such a development would rest with the accredited professional institution responsible for planning education. The role of planners as mediators of conflicting interests in land, is a recurrent theme in the planning literature (Healey, 1989). One of the major conflicts in the use of land in Belfast revolves around the issue of territoriality. Yet this reality and how planners should respond to it, does not seem to inform the range of skills or specific techniques that students are taught at accredited planning and housing courses. Critical learning from and reflection on the experience of community experiments might offer a practical starting point for such a development.

Conclusions

Healey (1989) has reflected the wider shift in planning ideology away from a techno-rational paradigm to one where skills of argument, debate and consultation among relevant stakeholders are central. Coping with post-industrial restructuring has redefined the substance and methodology of land use planning and new issues, priorities and techniques now find a role in local regeneration strategies. That context of change could also provide for a clearer analysis of ethnicity and the inclusion of those marginalised in ethnic space in planning processes and decision making. The development of a pluralist housing and planning agenda for Belfast would reflect the reality that has shaped the social and physical fabric of the city since the Eighteenth Century. Such an agenda could face criticism as an apartheid strategy. However, as Marcuse, Tomlins and the community initiatives have emphasised, such criticism can only be sustained if segregated planning is used as an instrument of community control, discrimination in the allocation of resources, or as an enforced strategy. But approaches that respond to human and community desire for a certain lifestyle, that has an explicit commitment to an equitable allocation of resources and ensures that communities have access to the services, facilities and resources necessary for sustainable living would represent a consumer led response to urban policy priorities in Belfast.

19 Owner occupier residential search in a divided city

John McPeake

Introduction

The research reported in this chapter is part of a wider study concerned with developing a better understanding how residential decisions are made in a segregated urban housing market. The study is set in the Belfast Urban Area (BUA), an area recently described as one of the most highly segregated in Europe if not in the world (Keane, 1990). While perhaps a little overstated, Belfast undoubtedly experiences a high degree of segregation with the principal division being by religion. Religious residential segregation in Belfast is particularly entrenched and bound up with the wider issue of the 'Troubles', a polite euphemism for the sectarian conflict that has engulfed Northern Ireland for much of the past 30 years.

Access to housing and inequalities in housing provision have been identified as issues that sparked the current 'Troubles' (NIHE, 1991; Singleton, 1995), and in spite of the recent cease fires, segregation and religious tensions remain important dimensions of the social geography of Belfast. Against such a background, understanding how households decide where to move is of relevance to scholars and public policy makers alike. As Clark has observed, '... the decision to choose a house and to relocate is made at the level of the individual household, but the consequences are felt at the level of the society' (Clark, 1987, p. 12).

Residential mobility plays a key part in shaping the development of urban areas. For more than three decades, various authors have drawn attention to the two-way relationship that exists between mobility and urban form (eg. Ford and Smith, 1981; Moore, 1966; Pritchard, 1976; Waldorf, 1990). This chapter addresses the search process, an aspect of residential decision making that remains comparatively under researched. The main concern is the manner in which households organise and engage in search against the background of a segregated housing market. Elsewhere, I have argued that the patterns of segregation in the BUA have more in common with those in American than in European cities (McPeake, 1995). Given this similarity, it is further suggested that Catholic search behaviour in the BUA will mirror black household search in urban areas in the United States. This is the basic proposition that underpins the research reported in this chapter.

Following these introductory comments, the chapter is structured into four parts. We open with a review of the empirical evidence on residential search in general and racial differences in search behaviour in particular. This is followed by a discussion of the study area, the data, hypotheses, and research approach. In the next section, the results of the analysis are presented and discussed. The chapter ends with a brief summary of the key findings.

Empirical evidence on residential search

The general literature

Over the past 15 years, the literature on residential search has grown spasmodically, but two issues are commonly addressed: the amount of 'search effort' expended by searchers, and information acquisition and use during search.

In terms of the first of these issues, whilst it appears that there is no common definition of 'search effort', various measures have arisen. These include the duration of search, the number of dwellings considered, and the number of areas searched. The general consensus is that searchers examine a small number of vacancies, over a short period of time, and they concentrate their search in a small number of areas (e.g. Hartshorn, 1992). In terms of the second issue, most studies acknowledge that the housing market is a complex market in which information plays an important role (Smith and Mertz, 1980). Households are faced with imperfect information on potential housing opportunities and must, therefore, search for information upon which to base their choices. From the outset, studies of residential search have noted that search is essentially about the collection of information and its use in order to reduce uncertainties (Barrett, 1976; Hemple, 1970; Silk, 1971). Potentially there are a wide number of information channels available to searchers and a succession of empirical studies suggest that the most important channels are newspaper advertisements, estate agents, personal contacts and personal observation of 'For Sale' signs usually by 'driving around', although the relative significance of each varies from study to study.

Racial differences in search behaviour

Whilst interesting in themselves, characteristics of such search effort and information use become more important when one seeks to understand how they differ between groups within the population. Variations according to factors such as the social, economic, and demographic characteristics of the searchers and the nature of the dwellings purchased are well documented (e.g. Hemple, 1970; Michelson, 1977). Perhaps surprisingly, however, with some important exceptions, race and ethnicity have been largely ignored in studies of search behaviour. As a result ' ... there is almost no empirical evidence with which to compare ... the search characteristics of minority and white home seekers'

(Newburger, 1995, p. 446). The information that is available is briefly reviewed in the following paragraphs.

Racial differences in search effort

One of the earliest sources of information on racial differences in search behaviour is the US Government's Housing Allowance Demand Experiment (HADE) (Kennedy, 1980). Using these data, Cronin (1982) reports that minorities searched for longer but examined fewer dwellings than non-minorities. In a more rigorous analysis of the same data, Vidal (1980; 1982) confirms the finding in terms of search duration, but he shows that the difference in the number of inspected dwellings was not significant. Both authors agree that black search is more spatially restricted than that of white households. Cronin (1982) notes that minority households tend to search in those areas with higher proportions of minorities in the population in general. Similarly, Vidal (1982) writes that both black and white households 'restricted their search in ways that tended to reinforce a racially concentrated pattern of housing' (p. 63).

Lake's (1981) investigation of owner occupier search in New Jersey, USA provides the most detailed information on racial search behaviour. In terms of search duration, he found that black households spent significantly longer than whites thinking about moving and slightly longer in active search. Differences also emerged in terms of the number of dwellings considered — minority households 'looked at' fewer dwellings than whites, they 'internally inspected' fewer than whites, but, overall, blacks and whites 'seriously considered' the same number of dwellings. In respect of areas searched, blacks were found to search significantly fewer areas than whites.

Lake's work is important because he recognized that differences in search effort might be explained by background socio-economic, demographic and other differences between the two groups. Using regression methods, he controlled for a host of background variables and found that race continued to exert an independent effect on search behaviour. The 'racial effect' was especially strong in terms of search duration, with blacks spending half as long again thinking about moving and 24 per cent longer in active search than whites, all other things being equal. In contrast, when background factors were taken into account, the differences in the number of dwellings considered and the number of areas searched disappeared.

More recently, Newburger (1995) produced results that are broadly consistent with Lake's study — blacks were found to search for longer than whites, examine fewer vacancies than whites, and search in fewer areas than whites. As with Lake's (1981) study, her analysis confirms that race exerted an independent effect on search behaviour.

Racial differences in information acquisition

The empirical literature on racial and ethnic differences in search information is rather limited. Most of the major search studies (e.g. Hemple, 1970) do not disaggregate their results according to the race of the searcher. One of the first general studies of racial differences in information use during search was conducted by Zonn (1980). He was interested in whether black households had 'a form of information acquisition that differs significantly from that of the white population' (p. 43). He found that blacks relied more heavily than whites on certain channels (real estate brokers, newspapers, and driving or walking around) and that they used more channels than whites.

In contrast, Lake (1981) reports that the most surprising result of his analysis is that 'startlingly little differences are discernable in either the information sources used or found helpful by black and white homebuyers ...' (p. 145), although nothing is said about the volume of information use. His data indicate, however, that minorities rely more heavily than whites on informal sources. In common with Zonn, information from estate agents was also more important to blacks than whites.

Further insights into racial differences in information use may be obtained from the HADE data. Cronin's (1982) analysis showed that whilst differences were evident according to race, the pattern was not consistent across the two study areas. In terms of the effectiveness of the information source, however, a much clearer pattern emerged. In both of the HADE study areas and for both groups, personal contact with friends and relatives emerged as the most effective source. Vidal's (1982) analysis confirms that minorities are more extensive information users than non-minorities.

Another important aspect of racial and ethnic differences in information in search is the extent to which particular sources have differential impacts on search outcomes. Such impacts may range from the relatively benign to the outright discriminatory. For example, it is possible that the use of information derived from personal contacts may have a differential impact according to the race or ethnicity of the searcher. As personal contacts are likely to share a searcher's attitudes and circumstances the range of choice generated by such contacts is likely to be relatively narrow. Thus, if the searcher is from a minority community that is highly segregated then search behaviour is likely to be more spatially restricted.

More overtly discriminatory practices are also possible. It is well established that estate agents are important information providers and the preceding review shows that black households rely heavily on this source. It is equally well established, that estate agents can and do engage in racial steering. As Palm (1976) points out, households that rely on estate agents are 'making use of a highly structured and spatially limited information source' (p. 28). The fact that some agents engage in such activity does not, of course, mean that they all do. Nevertheless, more recent research by Turner and Mikelsons (1992) confirmed that racial steering continues to be an important feature of many urban housing markets in the United States.

Summary of the empirical evidence

In summary, the empirical evidence on search behaviour suggests that most households engage in relatively modest search, concentrate in a limited number of areas and examine a small number of dwellings over a relatively short period. A variety of information channels are employed in this process, but estate agents and informal information sources consistently appear as important. Although largely ignored in the general literature, race is an important segmentation variable. Black households search for longer than whites and in fewer areas.

The evidence on the number of dwellings inspected is less clear cut. Some studies report no differences whereas others indicate that blacks examine fewer dwellings. No studies have reported instances where minorities examine more dwellings than non-minorities. Most studies acknowledge that minority households are more intensive information users than non-minorities.

The study

Study context

Belfast, the principle city of Northern Ireland, has a population of some 280,000 people, although the built up area has extended beyond the city boundaries forming the larger Belfast Urban Area (Figure 19.1). This larger area contains almost half a million people, or about one third of the total Northern Ireland population (DHSS, 1992).

The nature of the division. Most commentators now accept that the essence of the Northern Ireland problem lies in the conflict between the two communities rather than a continuing colonial involvement of Britain in Ireland (Boyle and Hadden, 1994). In basic terms, the conflict is reflective of an ethnic division between the nationalists, comprising primarily the Catholic descendants of the native Irish population, who 'aspire to unity with the Irish Republic' and the unionists, comprising mainly the Protestant descendants of the plantation settlers, who 'wish to maintain the political separation of Northern Ireland from the Irish Republic' (Boal et al., 1976, p. 80). The chief political issue that underlies the 'Troubles' is the nature and purpose of the State itself. In essence the legitimacy of the current political and constitutional arrangements is supported by the unionist majority and disputed by the nationalist minority. Seen in this context, the conflict is not about religion per se. Indeed, Belfrage (1988, p. 406) writes that religion is best regarded as a 'badge of identification to describe two traditions, two perspectives on the past, two views of cultural superiority ...'. In short, Northern Ireland is a divided community in which it has become convenient to use religious affiliation as a label to describe two distinct ethnic groups, but these divisions that are marked by religion run very much deeper. One of the most obvious divisions occurs in the housing market.

Religious residential segregation in Belfast. There is a long history of religious segregation in Belfast, dating back at least two hundred years (Boal, 1994). A number of scholars have pointed to the relationship between inter-community conflict and intensified segregation in the city (Smith and Chambers, 1991). The origins of the contemporary 'Troubles' in Northern Ireland are related to the emergence of civil unrest in the late 1960s. In August 1969 inter-community violence was widespread in Belfast so much so that by September of that year the so called 'Peace Lines' had been erected to keep the two communities apart. The Northern Ireland Housing Executive, the body responsible for all public sector housing in Northern Ireland, recognised the existence of 14 such peace lines in Belfast (NIHE, 1987) — though by 1996 this number had increased to 16.

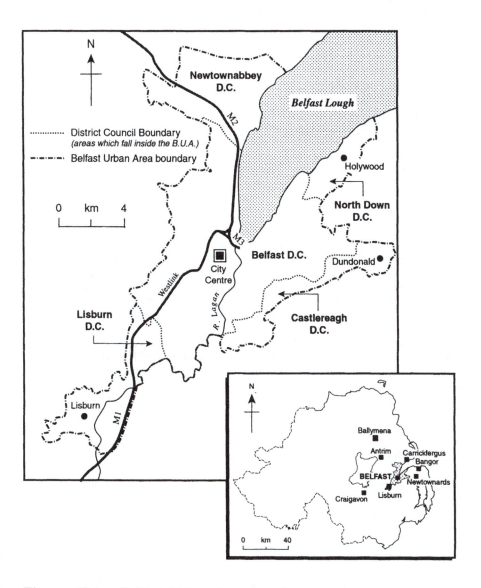

Figure 19.1   Belfast Urban Area location map

Throughout the past 25 years segregated space in Belfast has been 'purified' and consolidated such that the ethnic boundaries have become more clearly defined. Keane (1990) shows that segregation increased in all tenures, but especially in the public sector. Nevertheless, in the owner occupied sector, widely regarded as the tenure of choice, the great majority of all households live in highly segregated streets. By 1991, of the 117 wards that make up the area, the Census shows that 62 are more than 90 per cent Roman Catholic or Protestant. Clearly, as far as housing is concerned, Belfast is justifiably described as a divided city.

The BUA housing market. As in Northern Ireland in general, most households in the BUA own their own homes (57 per cent). One third of all households rent their homes from the Housing Executive. Just seven per cent rent from private landlords, with the remaining three per cent living in other tenure categories, including housing associations. In general, owner occupation increases from less than 10 per cent in some of the core wards of inner city Belfast to more than 90 per cent in suburban wards. The 1991 Census reveals that Roman Catholic households are under-represented in the owner occupied sector (DHSS, 1992).

Data and hypotheses

The data employed in this study are from a survey of households that purchased an owner occupied dwelling in the BUA during the first 9 months of 1993. A sample of 770 addresses was selected, from which 571 usable responses were achieved. All surveys were conducted face-to-face. The questionnaire covered a range of aspects of the housing search and choice process, together with information on the socio-economic and demographic characteristics of the households concerned.

As previously indicated, the basic proposition that drives the research presented in this chapter is that Catholic search in Belfast will be similar to black household search in segregated settings in the United States. Following from this proposition, and based on the literature on racial differences in search behaviour, five hypotheses were developed, each of which relates to a specific measure of search behaviour. The hypotheses are as follows:

H1:   Roman Catholic households will search for longer periods than non-Catholic households, all other things being equal .

H2:   Roman Catholic households will examine a similar number or fewer vacancies (but no more) than Non-Catholic households.

H3:   Roman Catholic households will search over fewer areas than non-Catholic households.

H4:   Roman Catholic households will make more extensive use of existing information channels, and will rely more heavily than non-Catholics on non-market sources and estate agents.

H5:   Roman Catholic household religion will be positively related to the Catholic population composition in the ward of purchase.

In investigating these hypotheses, the research progresses in two stages. In the first stage, each of the measures of search is examined within a bivariate framework, thus enabling an analysis of search according to household religion, on the one hand, and the religious composition of the purchase area on the other. Although useful, this analysis does not permit the isolation of the *independent* effect of any particular variable on search. Thus, in the second stage of the analysis, search behaviour is examined within a multivariate regression framework in which a wide range of potential correlates of search are included with religion as an independent variable. The conceptual framework for this analysis, which is based on studies of consumer search behaviour and the work of Beatty and Smith (1987) in particular, is summarised in Figure 19.2.

Figure 19.2   A conceptual model of search

Results

Descriptive analysis

In this section, we focus on a univariate and bivariate analysis of search behaviour. Results are presented separately for search effort, information use in search, and the outcome of search.

Search effort. In keeping with the standard literature on residential search, three measures of search effort are examined in this study: search duration, the number of dwellings inspected, and the number of areas searched (e.g. Hemple, 1970; Clark and Smith, 1982).

Search duration was measured as the number of weeks between the time that the household decided to move home to the time at which their offer on the house that they eventually purchased was accepted. This is interpreted as the period of active search. The number of dwellings inspected was defined in terms of the number of dwellings visited in person and viewed internally and externally. Dwellings identified and rejected without personal visits were excluded. Areas of search were defined in terms of 'community districts', a classification that is applied by the Housing Executive in its analysis of the private housing market within the city. Each area contains relatively homogeneous housing.

The results of the analysis indicate that households typically engage in active search for around 22 weeks, during which time they inspect about nine dwellings in just one or two areas. There is, however, considerable variability in the level of search effort. For example, almost one-fifth of households searched for four weeks or less but five per cent searched for more than one year. Similar variability was observed in terms of the number of dwellings inspected, but not in terms of spatial search.

In terms of religious differences in search effort, it was found that Catholic buyers searched for significantly longer than non-Catholic buyers (p<0.001). For example, 30 per cent of Catholic households searched for less than three months (0-12 weeks) compared to 43 per cent of non-Catholic buyers. Similarly, Catholic households searched in a smaller range of areas than non-Catholics, a finding that was again highly significant (p<0.001). Thus, three-quarters of Catholics searched in just one area compared to just over half of non-Catholics. Both of these findings, which are mirrored in terms of the religious composition of the purchase ward, are consistent with hypotheses H1 and H3. However, the results for dwelling inspections are not as expected. The bivariate analysis indicates that Catholic households inspect significantly more dwellings (11.7) than non-Catholics (6.9). Similarly, the mean value for inspections reaches a peak of 13.8 for wards of 90 per cent or more Catholic composition. These findings run counter to hypothesis H2.

Information acquisition and search. Following Hemple (1970), information channels were broadly grouped into two categories: market sources and non-market sources. Within the BUA, market sources were the most frequently employed, with more than 90 per cent of buyers indicating that they had used such sources. Not quite so many households used non-market sources (79 per cent). Overall, the most common source of search information was estate agents (76 per cent) closely followed by property magazines (66 per cent). These are both market sources. The third most common source was 'driving around' (50 per cent), followed by information from work colleagues (48 per cent), newspaper advertisements (34 per cent), and visiting show houses (32 per cent). Less use was made of friends (23 per cent), relatives (12 per cent), and journey to work (12 per cent) (Table 19.1)

Significant differences were found between Catholic and non-Catholic searchers in terms of information use. For eight of the 13 sources examined, Catholic use significantly exceeded non-Catholic use. Overall, Catholic households employed an average of 4.3 channels compared to 3.4 on the part of non-Catholics, a difference that was significant at better than the 99.9 per cent level of testing. Similarly, information use appears positively related to the extent of the Catholic population in the ward of purchase.

For both groups, the most commonly used source of information was estate agents. Although, as had been hypothesised (H4), Catholics (81 per cent) made greater use of this channel than non-Catholics (74 per cent), the difference was not significant. Nevertheless, there were significant differences in terms of the use of non-market sources. Catholic searchers were significantly more likely to have employed sources such as friends and work colleagues than non-Catholic searchers, a finding consistent with hypothesis H4.

The outcome of the search. Having searched for alternative accommodation, households move to their new homes. Given the context for this study it is interesting to briefly examine the nature of mobility following search.

It has already been noted that search is spatially constrained and that important differences exist in terms of household religion. It is clear that these differences are directly translated into different spatial relocation patterns. In particular, Catholic households are seen to move home over much shorter distances than non-Catholics. For example, almost one-third of Catholic households moved less than half a mile from their previous address compared to just 12 per cent of non-Catholics. At the opposite end of the spectrum, one-quarter of non-Catholics moved more than five miles compared to just 12 per cent of Catholic households. At the ward level, Catholic mobility is much more focused on intra-ward or adjacent ward movement than is the case for non-Catholics. Thus, 59 per cent of Catholic households moved from within the same ward or to an adjacent ward compared to just 40 per cent for non-Catholics (Tables 19.2a; 19.2b).

Regression analysis

The preceding analysis provides considerable support for the basic proposition and the specific hypotheses that underlie this study. Catholics are seen to search for longer and in fewer areas, and, at the same time, they use more information channels than non-Catholics. However, contrary to expectations, Catholics inspected more dwellings than non-Catholics. In order to explore these

Table 19.1
Differences in information use

Channel	Religion RC %	Other %	Total %
Market Sources			
Newspaper Ads	46.3	28.6	34.4
Property Magazines	73.4	63.0	66.4
Estate Agent	80.6	74.0	76.2
Show Houses	29.0	33.7	32.2
Lenders	7.6	7.7	7.7
Any Market Source	91.6	91.2	91.4
Non-Market Sources			
Driving Around	58.1	46.5	50.3
Relatives	16.5	9.7	11.9
Friends	37.5	16.2	23.1
Work Colleagues	61.7	41.1	47.8
Non-Market Sources (cont.)			
Journey to Work	13.8	11.3	12.1
Other Journeys	32.1	25.3	27.5
Previous Knowledge	32.1	20.8	24.4
Other Source	2.5	3.1	2.9
Any Non-Market	87.7	75.4	79.4
Mean Number of Channels	4.30	3.41	
Number of Cases	186	385	571

Table 19.2a
Spatial aspects of owner occupier relocation behaviour: spatial concentration

Spatial concentration	Religion RC %	Other %	Religious composition of ward (% RC) 0-9.9 %	10-29.9 %	30-49.9 %	50-89.9 %	90+ %	Total %
Within ward of origin	22.6	10.8	12.2	7.8	15.8	23.9	47.2	14.7
Contiguous ward within same sector	25.1	21.1	18.7	22.1	36.6	20.6	9.2	22.4
Non-contiguous but within same sector	8.9	16.3	15.7	17.6	11.5	8.3	—	13.9
Contiguous ward in different sector	11.2	8.3	6.0	13.8	1.6	21.6	8.4	9.2
From elsewhere in the BUA	24.8	22.5	26.3	19.8	24.2	19.5	23.2	23.2
From outside the BUA	7.4	21.1	21.2	18.9	10.3	6.2	12.0	16.6
	χ2=16.51 p<0.005					χ2=31.38 p<0.05		
Total responses	186	385	223	162	96	59	31	571

Table 19.2b
Spatial aspects of owner occupier relocation behaviour: distance moved

Distance moved	Religion		Religious composition of ward (% RC)					Total
	RC %	Other %	0-9.9 %	10-29.9 %	30-49.9 %	50-89.9 %	90+ %	%
0 - 0.5 miles	32.7	11.8	13.1	12.7	28.4	41.6	16.0	18.6
0.6 - 1.0 miles	21.7	21.6	18.3	27.2	14.6	15.7	42.8	21.6
1.1 - 2.0 miles	16.4	19.2	16.8	20.0	14.5	23.1	23.2	18.3
2.1 - 5.0 miles	17.4	22.2	25.1	17.9	26.0	9.9	6.0	20.6
>5.0 miles	11.8	25.2	25.7	22.3	16.5	9.7	12.0	20.8
	χ^2=35.67 p<0.001				χ^2=48.89 p<0.001			
Total responses	186	385	223	162	96	59	31	571

relationships more fully, each of the measures of search was regressed on a series of independent variables organised within the broad conceptual framework presented earlier. The variables employed in this stage of the analysis are detailed in Table 19.3.

Model fit is best for the religious composition of the purchase ward (R^2 = 0.53) and search duration (R^2 = 0.51). In both cases, more than half of the variation is explained by the model. The fit is less good for the number of dwellings viewed (R^2 = 0.35), the number of areas searched (R^2 = 0.31) and the number of information channels employed (R^2 = 0.19). Nevertheless, individual model performance compares very favourably with the earlier studies by Clark and Smith (1982) and Lake (1981).

The regression analysis confirms the importance of household religion in understanding owner occupier residential search behaviour in the BUA. After controlling for a wide range of possible correlates of search, religion continues to exert a strong and independent effect on search behaviour. All other things being equal, Catholic households use more information in a search process that extends over a longer period of time but in a more restricted spatial field than their non-Catholic counterparts. Importantly, there is no significant 'religion effect' on the number of dwellings inspected, a result that stands in contrast to the earlier bivariate analysis but which is consistent with hypothesis H2. Taken together, these results imply that Catholic search is much less efficient than non-Catholic search. The regression analysis also shows that household religion is strongly related to the religious composition of the ward of eventual purchase. Overall, therefore, the analysis confirms each of the five hypotheses and leads to the conclusion that Catholic household search in the BUA mirrors black household search in segregated cities of the US.

Summary and conclusions

This chapter began by suggesting that Catholic search in the Belfast Urban Area would be similar to black household search in segregated settings in the United States. In order to assess this proposition, five hypotheses were developed on the basis of the empirical literature on black household search. Using survey data from 571 households that had recently purchased an owner occupied dwelling in the BUA, these hypotheses were examined first within a simple bivariate framework and second, within a multivariate framework in which religion was one of many possible explanatory factors.

The bivariate analysis provided a wealth of information on the association between the household religion and search behaviour. Roman Catholics were seen to search for longer, examine more dwellings, search in fewer areas, use more information channels and be more likely to have moved to Catholic areas than non-Catholic households. Although instructive, the bivariate analysis is weak in that other possible explanatory factors are ignored.

To compensate for this deficiency, a series of regression models of search behaviour were constructed. The rationale behind this is that by controlling for a range of correlates of search, it would be possible to isolate the independent effect of religion. This analysis confirmed that there are significant differences in the search behaviour of Catholics and non-Catholics in the BUA and that

Table 19.3
Variables employed in regression analysis of search behaviour

Category	Variables	Description
Dependent Variables	DURATION	Duration of active search in weeks
	VIEWED	Number of dwellings viewed inside and outside
	AREAS	Number of 'community districts' in which household searched
	NCHANS	Number of information channels used in search
	RC_WARD	Percentage of Catholics in ward of purchase
Market	SETSIZE	Number of sales within searcher's stated price range during first nine months
Environment	SALETIME	Time taken to sell previous home (weeks)
	COMPETE	Searcher found properties sold before could view or were sold when wanted to revisit
Situational	DWGNEW	Dwelling newly constructed
Factors	DWGSIZE	Dwelling floor space in square feet
	DWGPRICE	Dwelling purchase price in £
	SAFETY	Searcher encountered a neighbourhood where felt unsafe or discriminated against
	ECONMOVE	Searcher moved home because of job-related reasons
	WARDMOVE	Searcher moved within same ward or from an adjacent ward
	RC_PREV	Percentage Roman Catholic of previous ward location
Potential	SATISFY	Searcher very satisfied with new home
Payoff	OUTCOME	Searcher believes search went 'better than expected'
	DISCOUNT	Searcher purchased dwelling for less than asking price
Knowledge and	FTB	Searcher was a first time buyer
Experience	RMOVE	Searcher had lived at previous address for less than 30 months
	UNCERT	Searcher indicated initial uncertainty over what was wanted from search

Table 19.3 (cont.)

Category	Variables	Description
Individual Differences	HOHAGE	Age of head of household in years
	HOHEDUC	Number of years head of household spent in full-time education
	FSIZE	Family size
	PCHILD	School-aged children present in family
	INCOME	Household had above average income
Religion	RC_HHLD	Household self-classified as Roman Catholic
Conflict and Conflict Resolution	CMIND	Searcher admitted to changing mind about fundamental issues during search
	DWELPROB	Searcher admitted had problems in deciding which (if any) dwelling to buy
	CONFLICT	Differences of opinion between partners over what was important in a new home
Costs of Search	LACKTIME	Searcher expressed presence of time pressures in search
	LACKCASH	Searcher experienced financial problems in course of search

Catholic search behaviour displays strong parallels with black search behaviour in the US. Direct support is found for all five hypotheses. After controlling for the background factors, household religion maintains an important independent effect on search behaviour in the city. Catholics are found to employ more information channels in their search which extends over a longer period but which is focused into a more restricted spatial area than that for non-Catholics. At the same time, religion is found to be directly associated with the religious composition of the ward of purchase; Catholics gravitate to Catholic areas and non-Catholics to non-Catholic areas. Finally, as hypothesised and in contrast to the bivariate results, no significant differences are found in the number of dwellings inspected according to religion.

Aside from religion, a variety of influences on search behaviour were identified. Interestingly — with the exception of religion — the most important tend not to be related to the characteristics of the household itself or the attributes of the dwelling purchased, variables which have tended to provide the explanatory factors for most previous studies of residential search behaviour. This implies that many former studies of residential search behaviour, by focusing on the characteristics of the household and the nature of the housing purchased, may have missed some of the most influential factors in explaining search behaviour.

Part Seven
The European 'mainland': managing heterogeneity

20 The rise and fall of the 'City of the Future'

Wicher Nieuwenhuis and Glenn Willemsen

Introduction

After the Second World War the Netherlands were faced with an enormous housing shortage. This was the reason why, in the 1960s, the city of Amsterdam embarked upon what, at that point in time, was considered a unique urban planning experiment — the construction of a 'functional town', in which living, working, traffic and recreation were separated. The planning theory which underlies the Bijlmer's construction stems from the Swiss architect Le Corbusier. Following his concept, the apartments were build mainly in the form of high-rise (10 storeys) deck access apartment blocks in a honeycomb pattern. Thirty modern high-rise buildings, containing 13,000 of the 18,000 units that were built, were constructed this way, with large 'green spaces' between the blocks, where bicycle and pedestrian routes were also created. On a higher level motor vehicles were led to multi-storey car parks while metro lines crossed the roadways.

Now, 25 years later, the urban planner's dream has turned into a nightmare. What was supposed to be the City of the Future, now fills many with horror. Dismal, run-down apartment buildings in an unsafe area where unemployment is high and segregation on the basis of income and ethnic origin is visible. An area where an extremely high percentage of people move, where the privileged will leave as soon as they can, and where the school results of most children lag behind the national or Amsterdam averages.

Many fear that this part of town will become a ghetto if the vicious spiral of decline is not stopped through drastic, integral measures. The Bijlmermeer is therefore undergoing a large scale renewal operation.

In this chapter we will sketch the rationale behind the strategy of renewal of the Bijlmermeer, and we will try to show that what on the surface seemed to be a housing and profitability problem, on closer examination appears to be part of an underlying, social dynamic related to processes of international migration and the demand for diversity in society.

Lack of occupancy and management

Like London, for instance, Amsterdam is divided into districts. Of Amsterdam's 700,000 people, almost 100,000 live in Amsterdam Southeast — and in the Southeast there is an area that is called the Bijlmermeer.

The Bijlmer was planned and built for people with a middle class income. In 1968 the first apartments were completed and Amsterdammers started to move into the Bijlmer. Many came from small flats and were given space in 'the town of the future'. The size of the apartments (often 100 m²) and the promised comfort appealed to many.

After completion of the first apartments, there were several developments that affected the social climate in the Bijlmer. At national level the policy of 'overspill towns' was launched; tens of thousands of houses and low-rise apartment buildings were constructed in the vicinity of Amsterdam. A large number of people thought these much more attractive than the apartment blocks of the Bijlmer. Also the population grew more slowly than was predicted. Combined with the high rents in the Bijlmer, and the problems in and around the high-rise blocks, these other developments resulted in many empty units in the early seventies.

The population of the Bijlmer grew but not as the planners had expected. There were fewer (traditional) families than foreseen. Instead there was a relatively large number of single-parent families, people living alone, and couples without children. The Bijlmer became an area for people, often with a low income, who could not find anywhere else to live and who often left again as soon as they got a chance.

Between 1970 and 1975 the Bijlmer underwent a major change when many people from the Caribbean came to the Netherlands, largely as a result of the decolonisation of Suriname, until that time a Dutch colony. The policy was to concentrate the people from Suriname in the Bijlmer, because the Bijlmer was available and they could easily find a place to live there. Later on, large numbers of immigrants from the Dutch Antilles settled in the Bijlmer. After that new groups of immigrants arrived from all over the world, for instance from Ghana, Nigeria, Pakistan, Dominican Republic and recently from Eastern Europe. So we see that the population of the Bijlmer, which was planned as a functional city to accommodate the 'migration' of the Amsterdam middle classes, now mainly consists of people from Third World countries. Consequently the Bijlmer is now the most multi-ethnic and multicultural urban neighbourhood in the Netherlands.

In the whole of Amsterdam Southeast more than half of the inhabitants belong to an ethnic minority group; in the Bijlmer this percentage rises to 71 and in the high rise blocks to 81 (Table 20.1).

Table 20.1
Percentage of ethnic minorities

Location	Ethnic minorities (%)
Amsterdam	31.6
Amsterdam Southeast	55.3
Bijlmermeer	71.1
Bijlmermeer High Rise Blocks	81.0

Profitability

The first apartments in the Bijlmermeer were completed in 1968, the last in 1975. However, even by the beginning of the 1970s, the housing corporations in control drew attention to growing problems.

The Bijlmer was planned as a spacious, park like area and the ratio between buildings and public area (mainly green spaces) is 20 per cent to the former, 80 per cent to the latter. Consequently there are large stretches of undefined public and semi-public area, which in itself creates a residential area that (to a large extent) is difficult to control and where there is no social control — ideal conditions for unsafety, filthiness, vandalism and high criminality. Among the inhabitants and the authorities of the Bijlmer, and also in the media, doubts rose about the 'functional town'. The reputation of the Bijlmer got worse and worse, the percentage of leavers rose and remained high. Therefore it was decided not to construct the rest of the Bijlmer in the same way, but to return to urban principles developed earlier. This led to the construction of four-storey apartment buildings and houses.

But in the high-rise area the problems remained and even grew worse. In 1984 the housing corporations jointly founded the housing corporation called 'New Amsterdam', which gained control of almost all the apartments in the Bijlmer. The new corporation was given 150 million dollars to reduce the lack of occupancy by making the apartments and the nearby area more attractive. After two years it was already clear that this amount of money was insufficient. The cost of management remained too high and in spite of the commercial approach to renovations and improvements there was still little demand for these apartments. In short, the management and profitability problems of the housing corporation were not solved, nor was any progress made in forming a stable and differentiated society. Too many middle class people left the area.

The functional town, which was constructed with so many ideals, has deteriorated and threatens to become a ghetto. The signs are there — segregation, high unemployment, under-achievement in schools, a breeding place for vandalism, addiction and social unsafeness.

Integral approach

As a result of the high rate of unoccupied apartments and the high cost of management, New Amsterdam's losses mounted rapidly. To stop this, a new, bigger and structural investment was needed.

So the three elements:

1   the weak position of the high-rise apartments on the market,
2   the weak position in society of its inhabitants, and
3   the weak position of this form of city life.

led to a major renewal operation. Three partners were involved:

1   the New Amsterdam Housing Corporation,
2   the City of Amsterdam, and
3   the District Council of Amsterdam Southeast.

In 1990 a Steering Committee for the Renewal of the Bijlmer was instituted (Stuurgroep Vernieuwing Bijlmermeer, 1992). This Steering Committee set up a renewal strategy based on three elements:

1   Physical Renewal
2   Social Renewal
3   Renewal of Management

Physical renewal

The idea is to create a vital neighbourhood. The key words are 'mixing of functions' and 'diversity'. The Bijlmer area should have several functions, so that its buildings and streets are used all times of the day. In an area called Ganzenhoef (Goose Farm) two apartment blocks will be demolished. The inhabitants are given a choice to either remain in the Bijlmer or move to another part of Amsterdam. The nearby shopping centre will also be demolished and replaced by a new shopping centre. The combination of demolition and combining functions on one level will create a continuous area where some 1400 modern units will be built, most of them so-called 'urban villas'.

Social renewal

Social Renewal is the package of activities aimed at strengthening the weak position of the Bijlmer's inhabitants, both socially and culturally. According to the planners, Social Renewal is at least as important as physical renewal (Frieling, 1993). In order to create a neighbourhood with a strong and broad based social structure, education and work are important to promote the inhabitants' participation in society. Unemployment, which is a major problem in the Southeast (37 per cent), should be reduced at least to the level of the Amsterdam average (18 per cent). Newcomers should be attended to and made familiar with the Dutch language and Dutch society and culture.

The question here is how to improve the living situation in the high-rise buildings and to combat vandalism and social unsafeness. The large amount of (semi) public area, and the large and overgrown green spaces, create unsafe situations. In addition maintenance of such spaces requires too large a portion of Southeast's financial means. In co-operation with the people who live there, activities are being developed to improve the atmosphere through apartment improvement projects and restructuring the (semi) public area.

The assumption is that these three pillars (physical, social and management renewal) form part of an integral approach, aiming at demolishing parts of the functional town in the renewal process. For now the choice was made to demolish 25 per cent and renovate 75 per cent. The estimated budget for the projects that should bring about this renewal, is about one thousand million dollars. The renewal process is to last 10 to 15 years.

What, then, is the rationale behind this strategy? It is assumed that strengthening the three pillars will initiate processes that will be mutually reinforcing, creating so-called 'win-win' situations. An example: restructuring the public area contributes to a better social safety and reduces vandalism. This will bring down the cost of maintenance and make it more attractive to live in the Bijlmer. Social Renewal aimed at reducing unemployment will lead to a better income for the people and a stronger social structure. This should create a society that acknowledges its inhabitants and respects its diversity.

How did the policy makers structure this process? First a framework of project groups was set up to encourage participation by the inhabitants. Then the three co-operating parties initiated regular discussions in which the national government was also involved. They actually managed to get the Bijlmer's problems on the national agenda. At the 'Bijlmertable', which is held three times per year, the progress of the renewal operation is discussed with the ministries involved and the European Commissioner for the Urban Programme. These meetings should be mutually profitable for both local and national government.

Social structure

The renewal process has now been underway for several years but the question remains whether a strategy has been found that will lead to greater urban vitality. To answer this question, we should take a closer look at the planning process itself in relation to the social structure of the Bijlmer, where segregation is visible and processes leading to ghetto formation are underway.

If we look at the current reality, it may be said that of the three pillars mentioned, Social and Economic Renewal lags behind, both in a material and non-material sense. As for now, it seems that the renewal process (again) will be dominated by a physical and spatial point of view. The main assumption of this perspective is the belief that by changing the physical, planological environment the behaviour of people and the way in which they will treat their surroundings will also change. It seems that politicians and planners are more prepared to spend money on this aspect, since, for this part of the renewal operation, nearly a thousand million dollars has been set aside whereas it was with a great deal of effort that a mere twenty million dollars were made available for Social and Economic Renewal, and this within the scope of the European Urban Programme (Speerpunt Vernieuwing Bijlmermeer, 1995). The financial contribution for Social and Economic Renewal is disproportionally low. The question, therefore, is this: is the untoward emphasis on Physical and Spatial Renewal not obstructing the solution to the problems rather than promoting it?

The social structure of the Bijlmermeer is full of paradoxes. The Southeast region is known as an economic area of relatively high quality. There is much business, especially in the service industry. The fact that business premises are available at a reasonable price and are within easy reach of both public and private transport, is very attractive, a point emphasised by the large number of national and regional head offices. This feature of the Southeast is reflected in the personnel structure of the established businesses.

The companies in and around the Bijlmermeer are characterised by a relatively high number of positions for well-educated people, while the number of jobs for unskilled labourers is relatively low. In recent years the amount of jobs in the region has grown at five percent per year. Within the Netherlands, the Southeast area is one of the fastest growing business areas.

So one can say that, in one sense, the policy in this field has been successful. Unfortunately the increase in employment is not suitable for most of the unemployed from the Bijlmermeer, who as a rule are not highly educated. Thus there is a gap between the residential area of the Bijlmermeer and the adjoining business area — more than three quarters of the employees there come from suburban areas around Amsterdam, which is illustrated by the fact that only 20 per cent of the employees in the Southeast area also live in the Southeast. Only 7.5 per cent of the total number of jobs in the Southeast area is filled by people from ethnic minorities. Seen in the light of the large proportion of ethnic minorities in the labour force, this therefore only vaguely reflects the local labour market.

This image is a good illustration of the segregation process ongoing in the Bijlmermeer. The questions remain — how can this be solved and what part can government play? Should one leave the solution to this problem to market forces or should the government intervene and regulate? A hard choice is put before us when we try to answer this question.

The predictions by the OECD for the Netherlands and the rest of Europe mention growing unemployment in the short term and in the long term a growth that is too slow to reduce unemployment to an acceptable level. Therefore it is our belief that market forces alone will not be able to solve the problem of extremely high unemployment among ethnic minorities in Southeast (65 per cent). We think that a trade-off would be more favourable — more freedom for the market forces, more flexibility, less regulations and a decrease in the financial burden should be compensated by more jobs for the people, especially for the ethnic minorities from the Bijlmermeer. This brings us to another element of the social structure of the Bijlmer: activation of the available potential.

We think that empowerment of the population should play a major part in the social and economic renewal strategy of our inner cities. Empowerment takes the self-regulative processes of our society as a starting point. One can do this by emphasising the strong points of a community and especially of its inhabitants and make these the starting point of policy. In other words not emphasising the less favourable points of, for instance, the Bijlmer but emphasising the potential, the possibilities and opportunities. Empowerment therefore focuses on the strong points of the inhabitants. It challenges people to stand up for themselves. Empowerment puts the responsibility back where it belongs: in the hands of the people.

We need to adjust our policy to the wishes and the needs of the people. This way we should encourage people of all backgrounds to regard the authorities once again as 'their' government. The ivory tower where, according to many, our politicians and policy makers sit, should be taken down. It is time to reconnect the government to the people. If we are serious about reinventing government, then let us start by revitalising distressed communities and empowering them (Mullard, Nimako and Willemsen, 1989).

We may recall that one of the assumptions of the functional city is the idea that society can be 'made'. The government was to do everything, offering in an almost collective way not only housing, but also schools, nature, and social and cultural facilities. Although this concept has been abandoned, the Bijlmermeer is still confronted with the physical and spatial consequences of this concept. To really empower the people, the remnants of this train of thought must be abolished and we must create space for people's own initiatives and for more opportunities to acquire private ownership of apartments.

The concept of empowerment requires another approach, based on co-operation. The strict division between the market forces on the one hand and an intervening government on the other, must vanish. Government, market forces, citizens and their organisations need to cooperage and initiate activities to stimulate the vitality of our towns. Empowerment builds on power, on co-operation, and therefore includes forms of public-private co-operation.

Another feature of multicultural Bijlmermeer society is that there are communities from more than one hundred different cultures, but few interrelations. It was mentioned before that the inhabitants, both indigenous and ethnic minority, will usually leave the Bijlmer for a 'better' neighbourhood at the slightest chance. Because of this removal rate, which is high even for a big city (more than 15 per cent), social structures are difficult to establish and, if they are established, are delicate and short-lived. If people do organise themselves, either formally or informally, it is usually on an ethnic basis rather than on account of mutual interests. Multi-ethnic interrelations between the people of the Bijlmer are rare. The many ethnic groups live next to each other but not together. Apparently their own ethnic networks have more influence than inter-ethnic social contacts in the area. A multicultural society, in the sense of a community where people from different cultures live closely together, still seems a long way off. It may rather be seen as a sort of island society — ethnic groups form little, autonomous islands without solid interrelations.

Conclusion

In conclusion, we can sketch the following picture. In the 1960s the Bijlmermeer was built according to the principles of Le Corbusier as a functional city for Amsterdam's middle classes. Now, a quarter of a century later this 'city' shows serious signs of social decline. One of the things that escaped the planners was that from the point of view of planning the idea of Le Corbusier was outdated by the time it was applied to the Bijlmermeer. The expected white middle class did not come. Instead the Bijlmer became a 'city' where low income migrants from all over the world were concentrated. It seems that the planners and policy makers could not cope with these demographic and economic changes. To stop the vicious spiral of decline and segregation, the Bijlmer is undergoing an integral renewal process. The process is only a few years underway but it is being dominated by a physical and spatial approach. Social and economic renewal has had a difficult start and threatens to stagnate. A coherent strategy still needs to be worked out as part of a move to integration and real multiculturalism. (Nimako and Willemsen, 1993).

21 Colourful districts: west European cities moving towards multi-ethnicity

Hugo Priemus

Introduction

Formerly we thought that North America and Australia were the continents of immigration and that Western Europe was one of emigration rather than immigration. Meanwhile we know better. Although the proportion of the West European population in the world is systematically declining, Western Europe is now confronted with net migration. In addition, for the years to come it is expected that extensive flows of immigrants from Africa, Eastern Europe and Russia will settle in Western Europe.

Three factors play a leading part in this. Firstly, many West European countries have committed themselves to taking in political refugees. It looks as if there will be political and humanitarian reasons for taking in immigrants in the future too. Secondly, the difference in prosperity between Western Europe on the one hand and Eastern Europe, Russia and above all Africa on the other will in the years to come remain so great that Western Europe will continue to exert a magnetic effect on surrounding regions. Economic and political/humanitarian considerations will also continue to be closely interwoven in the future. Finally, the demographic 'pressure' from Russia and above all Africa will be very great in the years to come, whereas the population of Western Europe is 'greying' and is not managing to reproduce itself wholly. As a means of maintaining the population on the European continent and compensating for this strong 'greying', immigration to Western Europe works out well.

It is not reasonable to assume that in the years to come Western Europe will generously open its borders to receive with open arms anyone who wishes to move to Europe. That would not only lead to uncontrolled growth of the population in Europe but also and above all have a disruptive effect on the emigration countries, from which the most enterprising members of the community would move out on too large a scale. In the years to come a very restrictive policy is to be expected in Western Europe, whereby only political and humanitarian reasons will be deciding factors.

West European countries can permit themselves less and less to follow a policy of their own with regard to immigration (Hulshof et al., 1992). The immigration flows would very quickly be aimed at the countries following the most liberal policy. Under the motto: 'Better late than never' the countries in Western Europe will come to realise that precisely in this field a co-ordinated policy is needed. And that co-ordinated policy will be determined by the policy of the countries that now follow the strictest admission policy rather than by the policy of the most hospitable countries.

Nevertheless, if for the coming decades we may expect a constant flow of immigrants — though one moving up and down in level — the question arises what will happen to this increasing number of immigrants in the countries of Western Europe. This chapter attempts to answer that question, with the emphasis on the way in which problems in the field of housing can be avoided or solved. This contribution is primarily based on Dutch experience and evidence but our prescriptive advice is meant for take up beyond the boundaries of Holland.

Experience teaches that immigrants in a certain country do not spread uniformly over the whole territory but concentrate strongly in the cities. The urban labour market probably offers immigrants the best chances of finding work. The unfortunate thing is that it is precisely cities that tend to be centres of housing shortage. That may create problems for the native population (Moors and Beets, 1991). Its members see the composition of the population around them changing greatly. The most active move away and their place is taken by all kinds of categories of foreigners whose language cannot be comprehended at first and whose customs are often not understood. In an extensive survey last year in the urban region of Rotterdam no less than 23 per cent of all respondents in the social rented sector (45 per cent in the pre-war multifamily rented stock) mentioned 'foreigners' as the principal cause of complaints about the social environment (Priemus et al., 1995). If the neighbourhoods and districts degenerate, the foreigners often get the blame. That natives have to wait for a dwelling or cannot find work is often laid at the door of the foreigners. Local authorities and social landlords often react to this situation with a spasmodic housing allocation policy. In the neighbourhoods with a high proportion of foreigners, in many cases no further dwellings are assigned to foreigners. These are redirected to districts with a relatively small proportion of foreigners. This type of policy is not often encountered in official policy documents, but nonetheless is seen to be applied in its implementation, with the tacit approval of politicians and administrators.

Should you spread foreigners out in such cases or not? (WRR, 1989). That is often the question asked. However, this question is not correct because it is preceded by another question: should local authorities, housing associations and others pay attention to differences in race and nationality when allocating dwellings? Yes, say some, because it is in the interests of natives and foreigners. No, say others, it is not a question of differences in ethnicity or nationality but of differences in housing culture and lifestyle. People prefer not to live next door to residents with a strongly differing housing culture. We then sometimes see a complicated type of housing policy that is implemented without the concept 'ethnicity' explicitly occurring in it. However if we look at the statistical relation between the variables 'ethnicity and housing culture', housing culture often proves to be an indirect way of being able to differentiate by ethnicity, and thus, in fact, to discriminate.

The Dutch Constitution (Article 1) states that one may not discriminate by sex, belief, race or nationality. In the constitutions of other West European countries we encounter similar passages. Nowhere is it said that the distribution of housing is excluded from this requirement. The Constitution also applies to the distribution of housing. Quite apart from the question whether such a policy is effective, considerations of principle lead to the conclusion that discrimination in the distribution of housing is altogether wrong. Insofar as there are tasks here for the government, the government should strictly supervise to ensure that landlords, intermediaries and sellers do not discriminate, directly or indirectly.

Is there then nothing at all to control? Must we let things slide on the housing market? Will this not lead in no time at all to ghettos of foreigners, living together highly concentrated in the most unattractive parts of the stock? And is that not precisely the result that we want to avoid? For foreigners and natives a number of points of departure apply that I should like to present:

- those seeking a dwelling, irrespective of whether they are foreigners or natives, should be given the best and most reliable information possible on the housing market. Where are dwellings becoming available? What is the rent or the price? What is the quality of those dwellings? What is the quality of the surroundings? What kind of people live in the neighbourhood? How long a wait has to be observed? To what extent do specific allocation rules apply?

- those seeking a dwelling, irrespective of whether they are foreigners or natives, should be able to make their wishes and preferences known. As much allowance as possible should be made for those wishes and preferences;

- those seeking a dwelling, irrespective of whether they are foreigners or natives, should at least have some choice. They will in principle have to be able to choose from several alternatives. On a tight housing market this choice will of necessity be very limited;

- those already resident there should have no voice in the question as to which newcomers are to live in the neighbourhood.

Voluntary clustering

Ghettos occur when a large majority of residents from one category (notably ethnicity) live together spatially in one neighbourhood or district and when that is not the result of a voluntary choice. If residents, given the limitations of income and supply, choose to live together kind by kind, that will have to be accepted. A spatial sorting of this kind, to which there are sometimes ideological objections, also has advantages. The residents can adapt facilities to their wishes. There is a basis for a mosque, a bathhouse and butchers and grocers geared to the specific wishes of the residents. Another advantage may be that in the homogeneous group fewer conflicts occur, because the same standards and values are shared. Newcomers can most easily be received in their own circle and familiarised with the new and strange society. One still encounters concentrations of Dutch people in Canada, Australia and New Zealand who supported one another at the time as immigrants, but who still keep in touch, speak Dutch and — the zenith of old cultural value — celebrate Saint Nicholas together every year. And yet these Dutch people are well integrated in the immigration country. However, they appreciate maintaining close contacts and adhering to a number of joint social and cultural traditions. This is perhaps not the ideal picture of the *melting pot* in which nothing more is to be found of the former origin, but more the picture of the *mosaic* in which the composite parts are still recognisable, but together form something cohesive and fine.

Members of each immigration category may perhaps not wish to be integrated into the receiving community to the same extent. Some categories perhaps want to go far in this, whereas other categories are more attached to the contacts in their own circle. Within each category there may also be differences in this between individuals, which may be, for instance, bound up with the generation to which they belong. In these processes no government control is required. However, the authorities, and above all local and regional authorities, should offer alternative possibilities, so that for foreigners too there is reasonable choice on the housing market.

Alternative possibilities

How do the authorities promote alternative possibilities for foreigners? We now enter a field in which an active, ambitious and well-meaning government can show itself at its best because the policy repertoire proves to be extensive.

First of all, we must establish that following a good and responsible housing policy benefits not only natives but also immigrants. Government must practise the craft of a good housing policy with verve. Three themes have long been central to that: availability, affordability and quality.

The government should simply ensure that there are enough dwellings, also (and precisely) in and round the cities; the dwellings should be affordable, measured by the financial capacity of the (prospective) occupants, and the quality of the dwellings (and their surroundings) should be sufficient. For keeping or making the stock affordable two elements are in general of strategic importance. First of all there should be a social rental sector that is of sufficient size in relation to the size of the target group. Furthermore, a form of individual subsidy, notably in the rental sector, proves to be of essential importance so as simultaneously to safeguard, for the lowest-paid, affordability, adequate quality and sufficient choice.

In brief, the central government and local/regional authorities should have mastered the ABC of housing policy. Unfortunately, much of that seems to be missing in practice in many European countries. Particularly in metropolitan areas, where policy-making bodies are mesmerised by the possibilities of modern businesses establishing themselves and the construction of prestigious infrastructural works, the housing shortages often prove to be the greatest. At the same time there is a very one-sided concentration on expensive new construction that can be sold only through filtering. In such situations the sticking points on the housing market are invariably concentrated at the bottom and the fact that a relatively large number of immigrants are encountered at the bottom end of the housing market may occasion no surprise. It is not the immigrant who is then the problem but the fact that insufficient account has been taken of immigrants in policy formulation in the first place.

Of great importance is the idea that, in any case, part of the new construction (for instance 30 per cent) is directly accessible for the low-paid (partly with the aid of individual rent subsidy). In this way a certain differentiation in the housing environment is brought about that reduces the chance of too extensive ghetto-formation. The other side of the coin is that considerable attention has to be paid to management of urban housing stock and the urban residential environment.

In a number of West European city districts the residents complain about lack of safety and vandalism. Objective figures on the location of petty and major crime show that these complaints are well-founded. Drug dealing, drug use, alcoholism and prostitution are often accompanying metropolitan phenomena. The latter probably cannot be driven out of the cities, but it is clear that they cannot be reconciled with the requirements that natives and immigrants have for a pleasant residential environment. Police and planners will therefore have to combat crime in the residential environment actively, or will have to tolerate such activities at certain spots where they cause the least nuisance. In the residential environment caretakers, district maintenance crews and watch patrols seem to be effective instruments for strengthening functional control and at the same time creating meaningful employment. For the quality of life in neighbourhoods and districts the local authority and police are primarily responsible, but social landlords can also make a major contribution.

Some districts were built at the time in great haste without any differentiation. They form large-scale islands of homogeneity and uniformity in a differentiated urban residential environment. This large-scale monotony proves to be not to the taste of residents in general. In a housing market leaving room for choice, efforts will often be made to avoid these areas. If there is room on the housing market, vacancy soon occurs here. Consequently, if there are general shortages, largely involuntary concentrations of residents with low incomes and few prospects are formed here.

Care must be taken to maintain a good and affordable urban housing stock of sufficient size. Supply and demand must also be considered at regional level. Within the constraint of a good and affordable housing stock of sufficient size a major effort is needed to increase the variation in the otherwise large scale monotonous residential districts. The following options may be envisaged:

- breaching the often one-sided residential function by strengthening job possibilities in the district and adding shops and amenities;

- if there is a demand for it, sale of a limited part of the stock of social rented dwellings. This reduces the average degree of turnover (which is often very high), strengthens the financial position of the landlord, who can perhaps use this to build affordable new housing elsewhere, increases the differentiation in the district and to some extent boosts home ownership (which is often very low in the cities), as a result of which suburbanization impulses are checked somewhat;

- the moment at which a dwelling becomes vacant through departure of the tenant can be utilised for improving the dwelling's level of facilities and quality thus, perhaps, raising the rent to or towards the market level. Such a policy increases the housing differentiation in the district and contributes to a gradual upgrading;

- (where necessary) increasing play areas and green spaces (sometimes by simultaneous demolition of the worst dwellings) and improvement of the quality and attractiveness of public spaces. Often a better parking bye-law makes a considerable contribution to improvement of the residential environment, as a result of which children can regain some of the ground that they have lost in past years to moving and stationary cars.

Along the lines indicated, differentiated residential districts come into being, each with their own qualities. These, in a well-functioning housing market, will not so easily lead to certain income categories living together in a large territory (income districts), neither at the top nor at the bottom of the housing market.

A policy better tailored to immigrants could be instituted by counselling and, above all, by encouraging actions that deal with the first reception and settling-in of newcomers. Incidentally, it is true here also that primary help in general need not come from the local authority or the social landlord. It comes first of all from fellow-countrymen who preceded the recent immigrants and who are in an outstanding position to show the newcomers the ropes. Volunteer organisations such as Vluchtelingwerk Nederland (Dutch Refugee Work) also have a vital role to play. Local authorities and social landlords should supply facilities. Newcomers should be enabled to learn the language of the host country: that costs money and manpower. The social landlords and community workers can take steps to familiarise immigrants with specifically native institutions, and also natives with specifically foreign institutions such as mosques and bathhouses. Such explorations provide good opportunities for establishing contacts with each other.

At the bottom end of the labour market there is more need for placement than at the top. Natives and foreigners who have problems entering the labour market will have to be helped to make a start, possibly via job pools or temporary employment agencies. Nor should any unnecessary obstacles be placed in the way of native and ethnic entrepreneurship.

The central government will have to create conditions that enable local authorities and social landlords to make their contribution to receiving, housing and settling in immigrants. The central government will have to take into account that, whatever the preferences of the State are, immigrants are particularly likely to move to cities. Allowance will have to be made for this in the distribution of resources among categories of local authorities. A sensitive aspect is that the State in general only can and will allow for legal immigrants. It is precisely illegal immigrants who can confront those concerned with great problems. First of all it should be established that some policies precisely encourage the influx of illegal immigrants. There will have to be a sustained effort to avoid such policies (e.g. general bans on prostitution, on the use of soft drugs, on the use of alcohol and the like), because this would lead to criminalization and illegalization of evidently ineradicable sectors of society. Furthermore, a major effort should be made (however difficult that is) to obtain a quantitative picture of illegal immigrants and their spatial distribution. With a view to both legal and illegal immigration, attention should be devoted to the stock of housing substitutes on the urban housing market: lodging-house keepers, boarding houses, houseboats, storerooms, summer-houses, empty industrial premises, subletting. Here the problems of the urban housing market often reach a nadir: sky-high housing costs, poor quality, vermin, fire hazards, unsafe and unhealthy housing situations. Classic tasks present themselves here for the Housing Inspection Service, which should intervene forthwith if health and safety are at risk. Above all immigrants (legal and illegal) disproportionately prove to be the victims of such abuses in the stock of housing substitutes. In The Netherlands we speak of `the basement of the housing market'. It is unnecessary to remark that first of all social landlords should create alternatives for these housing conditions in the informal circuit.

In a simple way positive impulses can also be given for an adequate and creative manner in which immigrants can be received and housed. In The Netherlands the Experimental Housing Steering Group is active. This organisation, supported by the Ministry of Housing, Physical Planning and Environment, encourages experiments in housing and evaluates the experiences with these experiments. It goes without saying that once a year the local authority and/or the social landlord that has made the most meaningful and creative contribution to receiving and housing immigrants should be given an award. On that occasion the experiences of local authorities with different approaches can be exchanged, so that they can learn directly from each other.

In every country we encounter among the immigrants a number of brilliant successes: the best footballers, athletes and other sportsmen and sportswomen are not infrequently recent immigrants. Sometimes we find recent immigrants among pop musicians, artists, university graduates and politicians. These special, successful immigrants can play an irreplaceable ambassadorial role in respect of the receiving country, and provide a particular incentive for the recent immigrants who are still far from achieving such success. In the often difficult process of immigrant absorption these high-fliers could be used more frequently than has commonly been the case up to now.

Conclusion

Many countries in Western Europe have had waves of immigration for centuries (King, 1993). In the distant past some countries were even not or hardly inhabited. Immigration is therefore in fact nothing special. To a certain extent we are all immigrants. If the time of immigration of our ancestors is somewhat further in the past, we no longer feel ourselves to be immigrants. Perhaps this is the most important point of departure for successful co-existence between natives and immigrants. In the beginning there are good reasons for following a specific policy, to facilitate naturalisation. In an initial situation it is acceptable that we make a distinction between natives and immigrants, so that the instruments can be better directed towards those who have recently entered the country. At a later stage instruments relating to, for instance, to the housing market and to labour policy should be aimed not so much at immigrants *per se*, but primarily at the bottom end of the housing and labour markets. There both natives and immigrants are encountered. The sooner the distinction between 'native' and 'immigrant' is eliminated in policy, the better. And the sooner the idea of 'us' and 'them' can be done away with (among both natives and immigrants), the better. There are problems as long as a distinction has to be made between 'us' and 'them'. As soon as we discover that we no longer need to make that distinction, we have found the solution to a multi-cultural Europe.

22 Housing Co-operative Ludwig-Frank, Mannheim

Claus Hachmann

The Ludwig-Frank Housing Co-operative provides an innovative example of how a dilapidated residential area, housing a multicultural population from 15 different countries, could be upgraded. The foundation of a new co-operative was seen as critical for the transformation of the district into an attractive area. Its lessons are applicable as a model for many parts of the world.

Born out of need

The two housing estates — in total 400 units — which comprise the Ludwig-Frank Housing Co-operative were built by the Municipal Housing Company immediately after World War II. According to the managers of the Municipal Housing Company these units should have been torn down and replaced by new dwellings. For this reason only key maintenance work had been carried out over the previous 15 to 20 years and, as a consequence, both estates were deteriorating to an increasing degree. From a distance first impressions were satisfactory, but, on closer examination enormous signs of decay became apparent, This made even building experts doubt that it would be worth trying to rehabilitate them, never mind carrying out a comprehensive modernisation scheme. The tenants themselves had tried, within their dwellings and on their balconies, to reduce the impression of dreariness — but with only limited success.

Increasingly the blocks became ghettos for foreigners, and for those in debt. In short they became 'social flashpoints', given the nickname of 'Little Chicago'. In the Neckarstadt estate — which, in 1949, had been renamed 'Dr Ludwig Frank' in memory of the SPD Member of Parliament who had been killed in 1914 — some 75 per cent of the 280 dwellings were occupied by foreigners. The housing office confirmed that even those in urgent need no longer wanted to move into these desolate buildings.

It is obvious that in such poor housing conditions no one worried about cleanliness anymore. Vandalism and alcohol and drug-related problems increased by the month. The intention to demolish was twice passed unanimously by the Board of Directors of the Municipal Housing Company. It was no wonder, under such conditions, that by 1989 around 100 dwellings were void and uninhabitable — often even the sanitary ware had been removed. Behaviour by the residents who remained took on more aggressive forms. Despite this many wanted to stay in these blocks because of the low rents and the familiar surroundings.

Help from Mannheim City Council

The tenants turned to the City Council. Walter Pahl, who, at the time was the leader of the SDP faction in the Council, addressed the issue. First of all he put forward the following motion: the dwellings were not to be demolished but rehabilitated and rented for at least a further number of years — in light of the big housing shortage for socially disadvantaged tenants. He won a majority for this motion.

The tenants had the idea of establishing their own co-operative and shaping their own destiny on the basis of self-help, taking over responsibility for managing the blocks of flats themselves. Walter Pahl helped them with this, because he was convinced that this was the best way to improve attitudes to the individual dwellings, to the blocks of flats and to their environment. At a series of meetings he made the residents aware of the co-operative ideals — including the rights and duties of members.

In 1990 the Co-operative was founded. The aims of the Co-operative were clearly established:

- to bring void dwellings into use by carrying out urgent maintenance work and by allocating them to disadvantaged families.

- to rehabilitate and maintain all other dwellings.

- to keep rents low, and to rent to low income groups with the proviso that they accept the principles of the Co-operative.

Now it was important to convince the City Council of the merits of the co-operative solution. The trust placed in Walter Pahl by the Council led to success. The blocks of flats and the land were transferred to the Co-operative on November 1 1990.

The Co-operative starts its work

Immediately after the blocks were taken over, the Co-operative agreed contracts with a number of builders and the renovation and rehabilitation work began. The windows were replaced first and were fitted with shutters. Roofs and electrical wiring were repaired or replaced. All dwellings received central heating. At the same time adjoining areas, cellars and stores were cleaned and rubbish removed. According to the Council more than 75 tons of rubbish were removed from two blocks of flats in the Neckerstadt estate and burnt. The 109 void dwellings were made habitable as quickly as possible — sanitary ware was installed immediately in void dwellings which were then allocated to families on the waiting list, with the most urgent cases being given priority. Most of the remaining dwellings were given new baths, and facilities for the disabled were provided as necessary.

The external shells were insulated. The concrete balconies were cleaned and then repaired and partly replaced as necessary. The strong colours used to decorate the blocks of flats gave the buildings a completely new look. In addition it was seen as important to involve the residents as much as possible, in keeping with the slogan of the Co-operative — 'working together creates peace'.

The letter boxes were incorporated into the front doors of the dwellings to counteract security problems. All door bells were renewed and intercom systems installed so that the front doors could remain closed.

All these improvements resulted in the residents improving their 'image' as well. Everywhere new curtains were visible, new furniture was acquired and flowers were to be seen in the windows and on the balconies. Shops were established in the middle of the estate in order to be accessible to tenants and also so that they would be close to the hub of events.

The City Council gave approximately 5 million DM to cover the most urgent repairs. Under the agreement between the Council and the Co-operative half of the housing to be allocated can be offered to existing members of the housing Co-operative, the remaining 50 per cent to be allocated to people nominated by the Council, although the Co-operative is entitled to choose from this list of nominations. This guarantees that the interests of the Co-operative will be respected.

Table 22.1 shows the breakdown of the housing stock in terms of number of rooms while Table 22.2 indicates how rents and running costs have changed.

Table 22.1
Structure of the rehabilitated dwelling units

Total	1 Room	2 Rooms	3 Rooms	4 Rooms
399	82	137	171	9

Table 22.2
Rent and additional running costs per month (DM)

	Basic Rent	Rent	Running Costs	Heating	Total
	(DM)	(DM/M^2)	(DM)	(DM)	(DM)
Before Rehabilitation (November 1990)	73.335	3.75	30.218	—	105.553
After Rehabilitation (November 1995)	132.934	6.62	52.663	22.080	207.686

However, circumstances were not basically improved simply by painting the outsides of the dwellings. Again and again the residents were invited to discussions. It required persistent work to reach the hearts and minds of the members of the Co-operative, and through this raise the commitment and outlook of the tenants. Shortly after the foundation of the Co-operative nearly 300 members were registered. This number climbed to nearly 700 by the end of 1995. In the same period the value of shares held rose from about 450,000 DM to 2,000,000 DM.

Social facilities and integration

Many of the Co-operative's members are Turkish families and in recognition of this the Mayor of Greater Ankara, Mr Marat Karayalcin, who is head of Kent Koop, the successful Turkish housing co-operative movement, came to Mannheim to talk to his fellow Turks in order to convince them of the co-operative ideas. His visit met with considerable success. A meeting place — a community centre — was created following a big children's festival, which prompted the residents to establish activities on an ongoing basis designed to meet their needs. There is a wide and varied programme of activities, a number of which are worth mentioning specifically — childminding, supervision of homework, silk painting, sowing classes, language courses, drum and theatre group, meetings of senior citizens, tenants meetings. In 1992 the Ludwig-Frank Co-operative won the World Habitat Award for its community centre. This award contributed to the popularity of this model project in the mass media.

In September 1994 the community centre was expanded for social and community work and a Kindergarten for 25 children was added. Not only did children come from the housing co-operative — they were also accepted from the wider neighbourhood in order to promote understanding and integration in the area.

A large open air children's playground encompassing some 300m^2 completes the facilities. Generous donations from the Lion's Club Rhein-Neckar and the German-American working group Mannheim-Ludwigshafen made it possible to create the Children's playground and the kindergarten.

Conclusion

The residents are grateful for the help they received from the Council and from charitable sources, but the Ludwig-Frank project in Mannheim highlights the fact that co-operation is the key to success. If Europe is to become a political union, the free movement of people living in the community will have to be a cornerstone of policy. Cultural and social exchanges between people of different nationalities will increase. The co-operative principal is a proven, world-wide way of practising peaceful co-existence and of regenerating a rundown urban housing estate, all on the basis of social integration.

Part Eight
Widening the remit

23 Ethnicity and language: issues for housing policy

Malcolm Fisk

Preamble

The cultural heterogeneity of the United Kingdom is to some extent acknowledged in legislative frameworks and guidelines that underpin policies and practices concerned with employment and public services. Prominent among these is the 1976 Race Relations Act which outlaws direct and indirect discrimination on the basis of race, colour, nationality and ethnic or national origin. Notable, however, is the paucity of legislation or guidelines which address other 'dimensions' of ethnicity such as religion and language.

These omissions are remarkable on account of the long-standing presence of groups of people in the United Kingdom for whom English is not their first language. These include some 550,000 speakers of Welsh and 80,000 and 50,000 speakers of Scots Gaelic and Irish respectively (Davies, 1993). In addition there are other languages belonging to more recently immigrant communities.

The attention given to the speakers of such 'smaller' languages is increasing. For Wales this, in part, follows a recognition of the difficulties encountered when attempts have been made to apply the Race Relations Act to deal with the rights of Welsh speakers, and the need to clarify their position in terms of ethnicity (Morris, 1995). For the United Kingdom as a whole it follows the effect of greater unity within Europe where ethnicity is being addressed in wider terms.

Hence, in the European Union there are moves to ensure that individual rights are recognised in terms of religion, racial origin and language. This reflects (a) a desire for peace, harmony and social integration; and (b) a belief that all people should be able to share in the opportunities for work, leisure and self-fulfilment that the European Union seeks to offer.

We may note that the European Union budget to help support smaller language groups and minority cultures increased from just 100,000 ECUs in 1983 to 4,000,000 ECUs in 1998. Such activity is re-enforced by the development of a Framework Convention for the Protection of National Minorities which affirms:

- the right to freedom of expression in minority languages;
- the right to use minority languages in dealing with administrative authorities;
- the right to official recognition of minority languages.

This Convention followed agreement on the 1992 European Charter for Regional or Minority Languages which sought to promote language rights and encourage the development of administrative structures to recognise and reflect these rights. Such rights are sometimes enshrined in legislation or bi-lateral agreements.

Examples include Catalan in Spain, Welsh in the United Kingdom and the agreement between Denmark and Germany which protects the rights of groups speaking their respective languages. At a municipal level there is recognition of Basque in parts of Spain and of Ladin, Friulan, Sard, German and French speaking communities in parts of Italy. The effectiveness of legislation to 'protect' smaller languages is, however, extremely variable and ethnic conflict in former communist countries is considered to have re-inforced the need for such recognition as a means of furthering the process of integration (Comisiwn y Cymunedau Ewropeaidd, 1995).

Policies concerned with the development of and access to housing can have a clear impact on the attainment of these goals. They are relevant in virtually all countries of the European Union, these being home to some 50 million (nearly one in seven) who do not speak the major or official language of the country in which they live.

This chapter examines the position in Wales and proposes parameters whereby the rights of language groups may be recognised. Such parameters should inform other agendas concerned with the way in which services are provided to meet the needs or demands of smaller language groups.

The position in Wales

Wales is a country within a country. It has been an integral part of the United Kingdom for more than four centuries. It has, however, distinctive characteristics that reflect its history, culture and ancient language. The Welsh language was spoken by most of the people of Wales during the last century. At its peak in 1911 it was spoken by nearly a million people. It is now confined to one in five of Wales' population (19 per cent). This represents half a million people, the language having a significant place in economic and social life over an extensive area (see Fig 23.1). In terms of smaller languages in the European Union, Welsh is one of the stronger. Other languages (of immigrant communities) also have a place in Wales' main towns and cities. In Cardiff speakers of other smaller languages (including Bengali, Somali, Punjabi, Arabic and Chinese) are estimated to number some 6,000.

In Cardiff, there are some 17,000 Welsh speakers. This number and the fact of its growth (in contrast to the decline in many places elsewhere) has led Aitchison and Carter to refer to such change as 'the quiet revolution' (1987). Being Wales' capital, the presence of the language is seen as appropriate to the City's status. It is legitimised by its usage in a growing number of national (Welsh) and local institutions and administrative bodies. As elsewhere in Wales, awareness of the language is enhanced through bilingual signs and the presence of the Welsh language media.

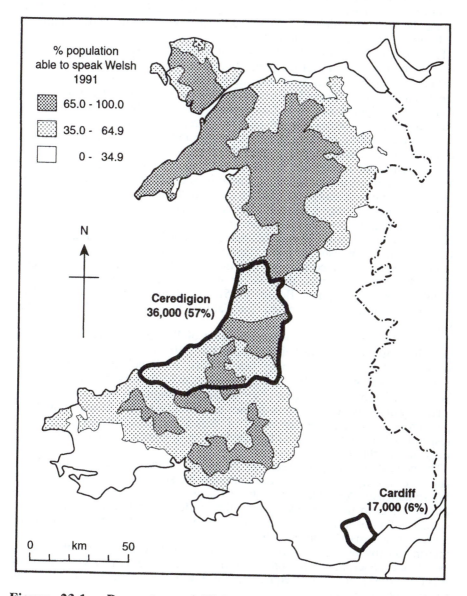

Figure 23.1   **Percentage of Welsh speakers in Wales, 1991**
Source: OPCS Census 1991

The position in urban Cardiff can be contrasted with that in rural Ceredigion where Welsh speakers number 36,000, 57 per cent of the total population. Ceredigion is an important part of the 'y Fro Gymraeg' or Welsh 'heartland' frequently described (see Davies, 1993; Aitchison and Carter, 1994), the latter being the area in which the Welsh language dominates in most 'domains' (education, commerce, worship, etc.).

The demography of Ceredigion is such that English is spoken by immigrants who represent a minority of the population. The Welsh language in Ceredigion has been under threat over several decades on account of both in-migration and the purchase (by 'outsiders') of second or holiday homes (see Coppock, 1977; Karn, 1977; Cyngor Dosbarth Ceredigion, 1994 and 1995). Such pressures have driven house prices upwards and have precluded many local people from entering the housing market. There are no sizeable in-migrant communities in Ceredigion who speak languages other than English.

Very significant, throughout Wales, is the long-term decline in the number of Welsh speakers. This decline is evidenced in successive Censuses since 1911 but, remarkably, appears to now have halted (Aitchison and Carter, 1994). This change in the language's fortune reflects the fact that more people in Wales consider it important to Welsh culture and have ensured that it has a growing place in social life, government, commerce and, notably, education. Increases in the numbers of Welsh speakers, therefore, are particularly evident among younger people educated through that medium, albeit that there are concerns about the extent to which they are or will be able to use the language in adulthood (Welsh Language Board, 1995). The attitudes and aspirations which underpin such changes are noted, for Cardiff, in research by Aitchison and Carter (1988).

Our knowledge of the number and location of Welsh speakers is reasonably good by virtue of questions being asked in the 1991 Census and specific survey work undertaken in the ensuing year (Office of Population Censuses and Surveys, 1994; Welsh Office, 1995). We can note, however, that apart from Welsh and English, there are no other *indigenous* languages in Wales.

The key dilemma relates to how frameworks of services can be configured that give proper recognition to the needs of Welsh speakers but which can also respond, where appropriate, to the needs of in-migrant communities speaking English and other languages?

The context has, in part, been set by virtue of the position of the Welsh language having been consolidated through legislation. Notable is the 1993 Welsh Language Act which established a Language Board part of whose role is to give effect to the principle that 'in the conduct of public business and the administration of justice in Wales, the English and Welsh languages should be treated on a basis of equality'. This is being achieved, in part, through the preparation (by public bodies) of language schemes which foster the use of Welsh and underpin service provision through that medium. As affirmed by Prentice (1993), however, 'equal validity is a matter of status' and does not necessarily reflect usage.

Not that the Act has been universally welcomed. There are fears among monoglot English speakers that bilingualism will become a more commonplace requirement giving access to jobs or promotion opportunities. Indeed, Prentice (1993) suggested that Welsh language rights will only be able to be effected through the concurrence of Wales' English speaking majority. That concurrence, however, cannot be taken for granted.

Such concerns are, to some extent, acknowledged by those seeking to promote the rights of speakers of smaller languages and are reflected in calls for a 'gradualist' approach to change (Williams, 1989; Law, 1993). They require, however, to be balanced against what might be regarded as a widespread failure to respond to the rights of smaller language groups to receive municipal and other services through the language of their choice. As affirmed by Williams (1992) 'the recognition of minority language rights places a new obligation on the modern state to provide the context within which such rights may be exercised'. For Cardiff and the other main urban centres, the question arises as to the extent to which such language rights should embrace other (non indigenous) language groups. This matter is not addressed by the Welsh Language Board in its guidelines for language schemes (1996).

Language has had only limited attention in the context of housing, despite the importance of housing policies and related planning mechanisms to the future of predominantly Welsh speaking communities. The pressures brought about by tourists and purchasers of second homes are, of course, commonplace to areas which are popular destinations for holidays or recreation. The benefits to local economies can be set against the disruption caused by holiday traffic, inflationary pressures on house prices and, for retirement destinations, the costs associated with supporting some additional older people. The situation in Wales therefore is similar, at least according to such parameters, to many other parts of the United Kingdom and some other countries of the European Union. Things are different, however, when account is taken of the additional factor of language — where the language of in-migrants (as opposed to transient holiday makers) is not the same as that of the majority of local people.

In Wales the housing measures taken to safeguard smaller languages fall into two groups. The first is concerned with the context in which housing is built or managed. It relates, therefore, to the institutions responsible for its development or management. The second is concerned with the ways in which housing development is controlled and embraces, therefore, planning frameworks pertaining to individual sites, the type and, sometimes, tenure of developments.

With regard to the context, the measures relate to institutions that are concerned with housing provision which includes an element of public subsidy. On the one hand are the municipal authorities many of which serve mainly Welsh-speaking communities; on the other are housing associations whose activities are increasingly focused on those people who are normally unable to afford to purchase their own home and have limited housing choices.

Several housing associations in Wales, while providing housing according to criteria of need that takes no account of language, operate predominantly through the medium of Welsh. Cymdeithas Tai Cantref (a housing association) which operates throughout Ceredigion affirmed, for instance, that 'promotion of the Welsh language ... [is] fundamental to the identity of the association' (Cymdeithas Tai Cantref, 1994) and is actively involved with small-scale housing developments in rural Welsh-speaking communities.

Some housing associations assist community stability through taking specific account of (among other things) local connection when assessing housing needs. This has been instrumental in helping reduce the extent to which Welsh language communities might have been dispersed. The dilemma, however, regarding ways in which housing associations should fulfil their responsibility to help maintain community stability while, at the same time, meeting objectively assessed housing needs underpins concerns about the 'weight' given to local connection.

Action in the context of planning for housing was facilitated by the introduction, in 1988, of a Government Circular (Welsh Office, 1988). It affirmed that, in relation to the strategic planning frameworks operating in Wales '... where the Welsh language is a component of the social fabric of a community it is clearly appropriate that the implications of this be taken into account in the formulation of land use policies'. The Welsh language, in other words, could be considered as a 'material consideration' in planning decisions.

This acknowledgement of the importance of the language is weakly reaffirmed in the Welsh Office's policy guidance (1992) and its draft replacement which states:

> Where a planning authority considers it appropriate to take account of the needs and interests of the Welsh language it should include in the reasoned justification of its development plan an explanation of how its policies reflect those matters. Decisions on individual cases where the needs and interests of the Welsh language may be a material consideration must be based on planning grounds and be reasonable.

Many authorities, utilising such guidance, are seeking to include formal policies in plans whereby such issues can begin to be addressed. Indeed, nearly three-quarters (73 per cent) of rural authorities in Wales cited the Welsh language as a factor which influenced the formulation of housing policies in their Local Plan (Littler et al., 1994). The extent to which such authorities will, by such measures, be successful in nurturing or helping to 'defend' Welsh-speaking communities remains to be seen.

A draft local plan (Cyngor Dosbarth Ceredigion, 1995) for Ceredigion affirmed the Welsh language as 'a component of the social fabric' of the area. This echoed the then Housing Strategy and Operational Plan (Cyngor Dosbarth Ceredigion, 1994) which stated that

> the Welsh language is an integral part of Ceredigion and its inhabitants. The decline of the language in successive years has been, and continues to be, a source of concern and the preservation and enhancement of the language are important issues within the District.

The draft plan sought to use the guidelines of the Welsh Office circular to incorporate a requirement that the occupation of new (or converted) homes in key communities be 'limited to persons and their dependants who originated from or who have lived for a period of five years before the date of occupancy either in Ceredigion or in an area no more than 25 miles from its boundary'. Forty six of Ceredigion's 51 communities were designated as 'key' according to the proportion of Welsh speakers recorded in the 1991 Census. The policy, if approved, would have been effected through the imposition of Section 106 obligations (following the 1991 Planning and Compensation Act).

Objections to this policy resulted in its omission from the deposit version of the local plan (Cyngor Dosbarth Ceredigion, 1998). A policy statement (W1) affirms, however, that 'proposals for development which can be demonstrated to be beneficial to the needs and interests of the Welsh language will be supported'. Such policies are anticipated as being carried forward into the Unitary Development Plan currently being prepared.

While it is premature to consider the overall effectiveness of these policies, it is possible to affirm that such housing and planning policy frameworks (albeit embryonic) have had some benefits as far as sustaining the Welsh language is concerned. This follows the simple existence of institutions and policies whose objectives are concerned with safeguarding the Welsh language and are underpinned by broader or more specific government legislation, subsidies to key organisations, or guidelines. More specifically the language issue has been an element which has helped determine the outcomes of at least a handful of planning applications and where the tenure of housing has been secured by legal agreements with housing associations (Tewdwr-Jones et al., 1998). The housing policy framework in Wales does, therefore, begin to address language issues and is responding, to some extent, to concerns about this aspect of Wales' cultural heritage (though the position of other language groups in Wales is neglected).

A proposed framework

The fact that some housing issues pertaining to language are beginning to be addressed in Wales signals a need to consider the parameters by which the importance of language groups might be determined and by which they might be 'officially recognised'. For some language groups, in other words, there is a 'right to language' that should be sustained by clear permissive and promotional legislation. Housing legislation and related policies can play their part in this.

The right to language among smaller language groups should be greater where they are indigenous, this acknowledging a 'heritage premium' — i.e. their historic contribution to the culture of the areas in which they are situated. To justify 'official status' would be to carry those rights (to services, educational, work and leisure opportunities, access to media, etc.) that are justified by virtue of the language group being sufficiently sizeable and distinct within the local municipal area or areas in which it is situated. The distinctiveness of such groups will, in part, reflect their geographical spread and the extent of their integration with speakers of other languages.

This is not to suggest that the needs of other language groups could or should be overlooked. In addition to responding to the rights of 'officially recognised' language groups there is the responsibility to assist other such groups where present in significant numbers.

In population terms a crude criterion for 'official' recognition is suggested as normally requiring a smaller language group to comprise 4000 or more people or at least 15 per cent of the population, such numbers or proportions being established through authoritative surveys/censuses and relating to people's first (spoken) or preferred language. No account is taken, in this 'basic' assessment, of the extent to which people may be bi- or multilingual.

Service needs, however, will vary significantly according to the urban or rural nature of municipalities and the concentration or dispersal of language groups. Housing and related planning policies considered appropriate to safeguard a smaller language group, where meeting the population but not the percentage criteria, would generally not be required where that group is widely dispersed. There would, however, be the need for municipal authorities to respond to 'language rights' in the context of other services such as education. Where the population *and* percentage criteria are met, however, specific policy responses would be apposite.

There is, in other words, a kind of hierarchy of services that is appropriate depending on the needs and the configuration of the language group in question. For Wales and the Welsh language this is suggestive of service 'zones' as invoked by Prentice (1993) and discussed further below.

For housing the focus would appropriately remain at the municipal level with policies requiring (under such a framework) to respond more specifically to the needs of language groups taking account of their characteristics in terms of their concentration or dispersal, wealth or poverty, and the extent to which their language is used in particular domains.

Conclusions

The issues relating to the ways in which service providers should respond to the needs of smaller language groups are extremely complex. This complexity arises from both the variety of languages that are encountered and the way in which their speakers are concentrated or dispersed, isolated or integrated with other language groups.

In this context, the proposed basis on which the 'official' status of a smaller language might be determined is, therefore, crude and will require refinement. It could, however, serve to stimulate consideration of the configuration of services in ways that reflect official recognition where appropriate (i.e. affirming language rights in certain municipal areas) or, for other languages, could be designed to assist (through e.g. language training) integration within larger language groups.

In Wales, application of the proposed criteria would mean that the Welsh language would have official status in up to 18 of the 22 municipal authorities. In recognition of the geography of the Welsh language this is suggestive of the need for a full range of municipal services (including the implementation of planning measures which acknowledge the Welsh language as a 'material' consideration) for housing and other policies in those areas where both population *and* percentage criteria are met. This includes up to 8 authorities comprising all areas within the former counties of Gwynedd, Dyfed and Powys, together with part of Clwyd. It represents, in effect, the 'primary' zone for Welsh language services.

Areas meeting just the population criterion, comprise the 'secondary' zone. Here, housing and related planning policies would not be specific in geographical terms, and would embrace up to 10 of the remaining authorities (the former Glamorgans and remaining parts of former Clwyd). The 4 authorities of former Gwent would then comprise the 'tertiary' zone with no requirement that municipal services therein should take account of the needs of Welsh speakers (see Figure 23.2). The populations of Zones 1 and 2

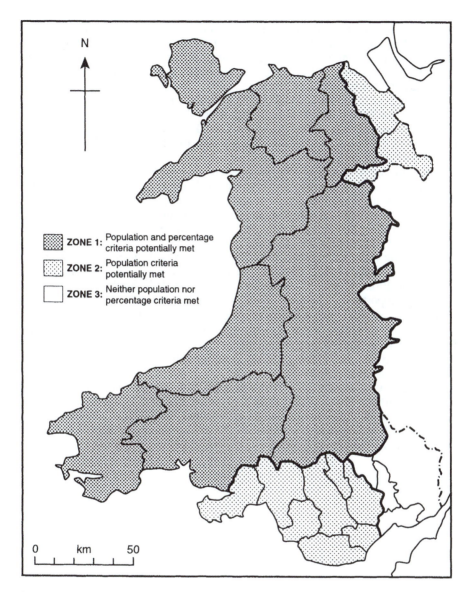

Figure 23.2   Proposed language zones in Wales

would, according to this configuration, be 856,000 (nearly 30 per cent of Wales' population) and 1,654,000 (57 per cent) respectively. Other smaller language groups in Wales are not affected on account of reaching neither the population or percentage thresholds.

The context is one, therefore, where housing policies concerned with the maintenance or nurturing of languages are appropriately considered as important in a substantial part of Wales. They respond to the pressure on the Welsh language that has resulted from the in-migration of monoglot English-speakers, the presence of whom has been manifest both in terms of reducing the strength of the Welsh language as the 'adhesive' of Welsh culture (Fisk, 1996) and, as noted earlier, in driving house prices upwards. The latter has been instrumental in reducing access for many local people to suitable housing in some areas.

To assert that such policies require further development is to acknowledge the importance of languages to the groups that speak them. Welsh, it is affirmed, is part of both the heritage of Wales and the rich diversity of smaller languages within the European Union.

To nurture the diversity of European languages requires the active promotion of institutions with legislative powers at a local level, pursuing objectives that include assessment of the needs of language groups, determination of their status, the provision of support where appropriate, and the promotion of services to reflect that status configured to accommodate social, economic and geographical considerations.

For housing this means that control must be exercised in relation to access to housing such that existing 'balances' between language groups are maintained and the position of smaller languages is safeguarded. Such provisions are especially important in Wales. They would and should not, however, be designed to *preclude* in-migration and the freedom of movement which is an entitlement to citizens of the United Kingdom and other countries of the European Union. Rather they should ensure that the *scale* of in-migration is not excessive and that the housing market is not unduly distorted by the extent of first or second home purchases.

Language, in this context, becomes and requires to be maintained as a 'material consideration' for housing and related planning policies in those areas where there are officially recognised language groups. To nurture such languages (through such policies) is to respond to the right to language and to appreciate the social and cultural significance of such languages to their speakers.

24 Ethnic minorities and leisure in the countryside: lessons from the American research

Simon Arlidge

The countryside

The British countryside is undergoing a period of major reconstruction greater than at any time in the last 130 years. This restructuring has come about, in the main, from the realisation that agricultural land has become surplus to national requirements and is available for a variety of other uses. There have been, and are, many actors and scenes involved in developing this awareness not the least of which has been the obvious and shambolic excesses of the Common Agricultural Policy (CAP), most clearly expressed through the food and wine surpluses of the late 1980s. One of the central policy directives in reducing this surplus, Set-aside, has become, arguably, the most potent symbol of this restructuring — that of taking land out of production and compensating farmers for its loss. Its potency lies in the fact that it begs the question 'what is to be done with the land?' and, in so doing opens the way for new initiatives.

Increased public awareness of, and involvement in, environmental issues generally over the last few decades has affected British governmental policies towards the countryside which are now directed less towards production targets and more towards eco-tourism and sustainable developments. These changing attitudes also mirror changing public perceptions of leisure, its role and significance in people's lives. Put plainly, the majority of us have more leisure time, more disposable income and far greater choice over how we choose to spend both our leisure and our income than at any other period this century. Public needs and aspirations have in turn become increasingly diverse and complex reflecting, some would say, the pluralities of a post-modern society (Crouch, 1990). Perhaps? But what is certain, though, is that because the countryside has suddenly become available for development, it has also become an arena for conflict — a conflict that reflects the competing interests of various groups and agencies ranging from The National Farmers Union to county conservation trusts. Within this arena minority groups are likely to be disadvantaged.

Ethnic minorities and the countryside

It has long been recognised that people from ethnic minorities are rarely seen in the British countryside (Countryside Commission, 1986; 1991; 1992), but little research has been undertaken on why this might be the case and almost none on whether it is colour related. In 1979 Stephen Kew, in a paper for the Social Science Research Council (SSRC), called for more research in the area of ethnic leisure, reflecting even then that 'there has been on the whole a conspicuous lack of analysis and research in this field' (Kew, 1979, p. 1). Unfortunately his call went unheeded and little research has been conducted since. Why minority leisure patterns, particularly outdoor leisure patterns, have been avoided in this country is unclear when it has been an ongoing area of research in various guises in the USA for over three decades. However, over the same period minorities have been widely studied in Britain in other areas such as health, ageing, education and employment (Blakemore and Boneham, 1994; Smaje, 1995) and there have been numerous studies on visitors and leisure in the countryside (including PhD theses such as Kassyk, 1986) but these have concentrated on variables such as age, sex, usage, distance travelled, ignoring cultural status.

The little research there has been on ethnic leisure and attitudes to the countryside has uncovered a paradox. On the one hand there appears to be the almost universally perceived dialectical relationship between the city and the country; the countryside embodying what the city lacks e.g. fresh air, a lack of rubbish, friendlier people (Harrison et al., 1986). On the other hand there has been considerable alienation and tension resulting from actual or perceived racism (Malik, 1992).

Sapna Malik questioned why black faces were rarely seen in the countryside and asked what could be done about it. Interviewing ethnic and non ethnic groups she found significant differences between the groups over the degree of satisfaction gained from the countryside, the quality of information available on it and the frequency of visits to it. In all three areas the non ethnic groups achieved far higher ratings than the ethnic groups. Malik also revealed that many of the ethnic respondents felt their colour alone was enough to bar them from visiting the countryside having previously been deterred by stares and explicit racism while others anticipated abuse and consequently had never visited. In contrast, the white respondents felt the deepest link through a sense of heritage.

Malik concluded that the countryside while supposedly available to all to enjoy was: 'in reality ... structurally, socially and racially selective' and 'without a change in attitude between black and white alike ... [would] remain an essentially white preserve accessible to an elite and self-selected few' (Malik, 1992, pp. 39-40). She recommended an increase in relevant information and an urgent need for more research and better funding; a call echoed two years later by the Council for the Protection of Rural England (CPRE, 1994).

Not directly related to leisure but nevertheless pertinent was an article by Julian Agyeman (1988) which explored ethnic involvement in environmental groups/issues. He found that there was a general lack of participation and blamed this on racism and its many manifestations. Environmental groups were seen as part of the establishment, in collusion with the decision makers and conferring notions of unsafe territories — the white landscape. He further argued that the very language of ecology/conservation was tainted by elitism which in turn was fermenting residual racism. Terms such as 'alien', 'introduced', and 'exotic' elevate the idea of the worthiness of native species over the introduced; the white over the coloured. If one accepts this notion and aligns it with the ideology which surrounds the Country Code — that of keeping quiet, appreciating landscapes, accepting restricted access and not straying from the path (technically, since 1993, a criminal offence) and the historical and contemporary record of power and ownership across the landscape (the hedge lines, the castles) — then it becomes powerfully persuasive and has ramifications for the way information is imparted on countryside issues whether on leisure related matters or in the planning process through Local Authority plans.

Almost certainly as a response to changing dynamics around the countryside referred to above, ethnicity and leisure patterns in the countryside is an expanding field of research in Britain. Research is currently being undertaken in several institutions with particular interests ranging from ethnic women and their attitudes to the countryside to ethnic groups in rural towns and villages. Given that research in Britain is expanding then it would seem judicious to study the experience gained from the American research, the methodologies employed and the problems encountered. There is no question here of judging particular results or seeking comparisons between the two countries — the different cultural and historical distinctions/emphases between the two countries make this largely untenable — but nevertheless it is useful to analyse methodological approaches if for no other reason than to aim for comparative and cumulative research rather than that which is disparate and decrescent.

American research

The debate on ethnic variations in outdoor leisure in the USA has been lively and various authors have claimed a multitude of conflicting results which have been compounded by a confusing array of methodologies resulting in no unified theoretical framework (O'Leary and Benjiman, 1982; Hutchison, 1988). The research findings from the USA, particularly from 1978, can be split between those who find differences between black and white leisure patterns (Jackson, 1973; Washburne, 1978; Washburne and Wall, 1979; Wendling, 1980; Antunes and Gaitz, 1975; Stamps and Stamps, 1985; Hutchison, 1987; Kaplan and Talbot, 1988)) and those who claim the differences are either inconclusive (Floyd et al., 1994) or have not led to any greater understanding (Allison, 1988).

Following from Washburne (1978) two conceptual approaches have been largely used to explain ethnic/racial variation. The first is the marginality thesis which suggests that differences are due to poverty and/or discrimination. Minorities are less likely to get access to services so that differences in participation patterns are related to socio-economic status and inequity in public resource allocations. The second is the ethnicity thesis which suggests that variations are due to subcultural patterns. Subcultural groups are presumed to have a distinct identity and integrity of their own which produces their own set of values, norms and expectations which in turn impact on leisure patterns. Much of the research has concentrated on these two theoretical approaches and consequently there has been a focus on social class indicators — the theory being that once these are controlled, differences in participation patterns should become clear (Allison, 1988).

Claims for difference are wide ranging with little consensus. Race has been found to be more important than class in determining leisure patterns and vice versa; blacks are less likely to go into wilderness areas, go hiking or camping. Blacks exhibit higher involvement in team sports and fitness activities. In terms of the marginality/ethnicity theses it seems that between black and white groups the data have come out in favour of the ethnicity — even after controlling socio-economic indicators both groups still tend to participate in different activities. However the marginality/ethnicity theses offer only a limited framework in interpreting perceived differences and for some authors it has reduced exploratory power (Stamps and Stamps, 1985). One area where the data appear to be more in agreement is in the relationship between age, ethnicity and leisure. In this instance it appears there are fewer differences in the leisure patterns of the elderly (Allison and Geiger, 1993; McGuire et al., 1987). Whether this is due to cultural assimilation is unclear.

Overall the American data appear dogged by a variety of ills. Much of it has been captured and constrained by the marginality/ethnicity theses, thus denying a variety of other theoretical explanations ranging from the effects of institutional structures and functions (Philipp, 1988) to the impact of inter-racial relations leisure activities (West, 1993). If anything stands out from the literature it is that it is theoretically difficult to explain ethnic leisure patterns and this, in turn, may explain why there is little in the way of methodological unity or cumulative results — one paper seems merely to confound another. With this in mind the USA literature and research has been problematic because of the following factors (in no particular order):

• *secondary data*: a reliance on secondary data not specially designed to test ethnicity and leisure issues;

• *black/white emphasis*: an over concentration on black/white leisure comparisons (Hutchison, 1988) which only comparatively recently has begun to change with groups such as Chinese and Hispanics now included. However, there appear to be very few comparative studies between ethnic groups — they are mostly compared to the majority white population — and, likewise little on comparative studies between white ethnic and coloured communities;

• *confusion over race/ethnicity*: questions over definitions of race and ethnicity have not been addressed. More often than not 'race' has been used to include or mean ethnicity. The corollary of this means that ethnic variations are subsumed within the homogenous whole i.e. 'race'. In Britain the concept and usage of 'race' is less widely developed or applied. 'Race', like ethnicity, is socially constructed and consequently can be extremely complicated. As an example some Asian groups define themselves as Black because this signifies colour discrimination (Blakemore and Boneham, 1994). Some organisations take this further. For the Black Environmental Action Group 'Black' is a generic term for anyone who defines themselves 'as belonging to or have a cultural background of Asian, African, Caribbean or other ethnic minority communities ...' (BEAG, 1994, p. 2). Conversely, there are those who reject such terms and refer only to their specific ethnic identity. In an applied situation — for example a face-to-face interview — it is perhaps best to leave the definition of cultural identity to those being sampled (as an example see Floyd et al., 1994).

- *cultural origin ignored*: the importance of cultural origin and length of residence and their possible links to distinctive variations have been largely ignored (Carr and Williams, 1993).

- *access and availability*: very few of the studies have incorporated accessibility factors within the public domain such as the respondents' access to public transport nodes, availability of transport routes and distance from leisure sites. All three criteria will have a strong influence on the choice of leisure activities.

- *'top-down' approach*: the research has been dominated by a 'top down' quantitative approach which conjures images of a dominant, usually white practitioner, hierarchical by breeding, traditional logical positivist by training, dissecting and ordering the comings and goings of the minority groups. The research has been overhung with a clinical coldness that is hard to fathom. It is extraordinary how little of the voices of those being studied are heard. I am not alone in this belief (Stanfield II, 1993) and there are those actively applying greater sensitivity (through contact and listening) and creativity in the research process (as an example, Facio, 1993).

While there is much that appears fundamentally flawed in the American research experience (and, of course, it is easy to judge with hindsight) there is one essential lesson that stands out: avoid using a top-down approach. Not only does it represent the majority-minority complex but often covertly implied within this top-down approach is the assumption that difference equates somehow to something being wrong; that deviance from the norm is a problem and that ultimately assimilation over integration is the hidden agenda.

Research is always cursed by the restraints of time and money and it is easy to see the attraction of using such methods — after all, secondary data is easier and cheaper to obtain and a top-down approach is essentially hands off. The increasingly fashionable 'bottom-up' or ethnographical approach now being promoted by some researchers (for a rural example see, Mason, 1990), that of becoming part of the group, ideally of the same ethnicity, allowing those being interviewed to be heard is, without a doubt, the most sensitive way and the method most likely to produce meaningful results. However, there are limitations. Not withstanding the limitations of time, money and the lack of ethnic scholars within the university system itself, the method is unsuited to multi-minority comparisons. A single researcher is unlikely to be able to afford the time to immerse him or herself in two or more cultural groups or to be able to lay claim to having a multi-ethnic background.

English experience

In Britain, over the last decade, various agencies and societies have called for groups disadvantaged by either age, class, mobility, ethnicity and/or language to be given the chance to gain a greater understanding of their rights in the countryside and the special enjoyment that it can impart — and thus for these disadvantaged groups to gain easier access to it (Countryside Commission, 1991; GMCRIP, 1992). The Countryside Commission — a quasi-government organisation primarily involved in recreation and access provision across the English countryside — has been instrumental in establishing links between disadvantaged groups and the countryside. Usually working alongside or supporting Local Authorities it has been involved in several long-term projects. One 3-year project undertaken by Birmingham City Council and the Countryside Commission attempted to increase inner city residents' awareness and understanding of nearby national parks. This was a successful project which also had an interesting, and unexpected result, in that it also increased the residents' pride and awareness of their own local surroundings (Birmingham City Council, 1993). What this might indicate is conjectural, but it does point to some of the problems associated with majority-minority research and, in particular, cross cultural research. While research seeking to identify and alleviate genuine disadvantage is essential, there is the cautionary note that perceptions of what constitutes 'disadvantage' are likely to be different according to a complex mixture of socio-economic status and cultural grouping. The assumption of need by the 'majority' or mass cultural group — whether it be because Asians are not frequently seen in the countryside or appear not to be interested in environmental issues — might not have been so clearly perceived or felt by the 'minority'. In the above case promoting the outside — the countryside — enhanced the inside local identity which in turns begs the question as to what extent an actual need existed in the first place?

Perhaps the lessons from this example are clear: consult with members of the community to clarify the scope of the research question. A simple case of looking before one leaps. While this may appear straightforward, it is not. As an example take the (genuine) case of the perceived problem being a lack of non-white involvement in environmental groups. Was the lack of participation due mainly to the recruitment practices of the organisations? Was it due to a lack of understanding of environmental issues, the alienating language of ecology/conservation or perhaps simply a lack of interest? The list goes on. One of the most common approaches adopted by social scientists in researching such questions is through the use of a questionnaire. The questions are carefully formulated, the interviews prepared, the sample taken, the results collated and the conclusion(s) drawn. In this instance the results clearly indicated that there was a lack of interest in joining voluntary organisations within certain Asian cultural groups. In reality this conclusion was somewhat off the mark. The problem lay in different connotations of voluntary. To the

researcher questions along the lines of 'Are you a member of any voluntary ...?';
'Would you be willing to join any ...?' appear harmless enough. Likewise to
the organisations themselves, who regularly call for and rely on volunteers.
However, in this case, voluntary was regarded by the Asian groups as a word
with negative connotations being associated with 'joining' the military. One
was called to 'volunteer' for military service and consequently one did not
volunteer for anything (Parmodh, 1995, personal communication). On the
other hand calls for service were clearly understood and, within the community
giving community service, was an accepted and established practice. If the
researchers had explored the subject matter with various members of the
communities involved then the random sample might have generated more
meaningful conclusions.

Conclusions

The purpose of this chapter has been to highlight some of the methodological
problems associated with the American research experience. The need for such
a review is in response to the growing emphasis in Britain on ethnic leisure
patterns and attitudes to the countryside. The essential lessons in undertaking
cross-cultural research that stand out from this review are:

1 ask first and listen. Ring local community groups, church groups, self help
   groups and arrange sessions. Listen to their advice and build the research
   characteristics around this.

2 let those being researched feel that they are part of the process and not being
   manipulated under a microscope.

3 follow up to clarify ones own conclusions. If necessary let the concerns,
   rejections and/or approvals of those being researched be stated clearly.
   There is little in this that is overly expensive or time consuming. There is,
   however, a great deal that is perilous. Allowing those being researched to be
   genuinely heard and incorporated in the conclusions — having their say
   ultimately in the quality of your analysis — is likely to require a great deal of
   clarity in the relationship (and clarity here implies a quickly developed trust)
   not withstanding the realities of the researcher's own ego.

Throughout this chapter I have asserted that the field of Rural Studies is about
to be expanded by a greater emphasis on ethnic minorities and their perceptions
of, and interactions with, rural Britain. I have claimed this is long overdue but
have pointed out the reasons why this situation is altering; as a response to the
dynamically changing countryside. I have also outlined problematic areas
within the American research experience and promoted a methodology which
attempts to address these problems. This method does not seek to immerse the
researcher within the specific culture(s) in a futile attempt to become part of that
cultural group. This is time consuming at best and delusion at worst. It seeks
the far simpler goal of allowing those being researched to be heard and
involved through a process of consultation, listening and returning for a

critique of one's findings. This is neither particularly expensive or time consuming and does not necessarily limit the researcher(s) to qualitative analysis and yet it offers a degree of mutual interaction that is likely to generate results that reflect the interests of the particular group(s) being studied.

25 Accommodating 'Travellers'

Liam Byrne

Introduction

The origins of the section of our community in Ireland known as Travellers are somewhat obscure. While their way of life compares with the Gypsies and Romany peoples of Europe, they are indigenous Irish people. We were taught that they were part of the upheaval of the famine and land problems of the nineteenth century. There are conflicting views on origins and culture and they will continue. Up to the early 1960s they wandered throughout the country mainly trading as tin smiths and beggars without much notice being taken of their lifestyles and living conditions.

Concerns regarding the living conditions of Travellers, then known generally as tinkers and itinerants, resulted in the setting up of a Commission in 1960 to examine all aspects of the lives of Travellers. It has been suggested in recent times that they had their own distinct ethnic culture. The 1960 Commission found that they did not constitute a single homogenous group, tribe or community within the nation nor did they constitute an ethnic group. This aspect is now the subject of some debate.

A special census taken of Travellers in 1960 recorded 1,198 families consisting of 6,591 persons. This indicated little change over a long period from census records in 1944, 1952 and 1956. The number recorded in the general population census of 1961 was 1,036 families with a total of 5,880 persons. The reason given at that time for the static nature of the numbers (despite a significantly higher birth rate than the general population) was that it was due to emigration.

There are many aspects to the problems that face Travellers in relation to education, social acceptance, health, employment, skills for living and all of them are inter linked with the aspect which I propose to deal with in this chapter, i.e. housing and settlement. Local authorities also assist and facilitate the provision of other social services to Travellers.

Housing conditions

The 1960 census showed the then appalling housing conditions of Travellers (Table 25.1). Policies evolved over a number of years as to the best way to approach the task of improving the living conditions of Travellers. Patterns emerged with three streams for housing Travellers, i.e. standard local authority housing, group housing schemes and provision of special halting

Table 25.1
Housing conditions of Travellers, 1960

Living in houses	56 Families
Living in motor trailers	60 Families
Living in horse drawn caravans or horse drawn caravans plus tents	738 Families
Living in tents only	335 Families
Others	9 Families
TOTAL	1,198 Families

sites Two of the categories in the 1960 census have virtually disappeared i.e. tents and horse drawn caravans. Another significant feature since 1960 has been a dramatic increase in the number of travelling families. In 1980 the number was 2,490 families (an increase of approximately 125 per cent over 1960). In 1990 the number had increased again to 3,542 families — an increase of almost 200 per cent in 30 years. In the interim period there was little or no emigration and there is evidence of a significant increase in the number of Traveller families returning from England and Northern Ireland.

Dramatic changes have taken place in this period in settlement and housing of Travellers. In the 1990 count the following was the position (Table 25.2):

Table 25.2
Housing conditions of Travellers, 1990

In standard housing	1,471 families
In group housing	223 families
In chalet sites	52 families
In trailers on sites	650 families
(Total fixed sites	2,396 families)
On roadside (mainly in trailers)	1,143 families
TOTAL	3,539 families

From this it can be seen that more than twice the number of families counted in 1960 were settled in 1990 and yet the task to be dealt with in 1990 was as large as the original task in 1960

The latest comprehensive study of Travellers, including all aspects of their living conditions and environment, was given to a Task Force in June 1993. The Task Force's report was submitted to the Minister for Equality and Law Reform in July 1995 (Task Force, 1995). The report made 341 recommendations under 11 major headings ranging from accommodation to sport and culture, from discrimination to health and co-ordination of services. Its main recommendations were:

1 An additional 3,100 units of accommodation for Travellers and phasing out of temporary accommodation

2 A national Traveller Accommodation Agency to oversee provision of accommodation

3 The cultural identity of the travelling community to be recognised with Traveller organisations supported and funded

4 Equal status legislation should ban discrimination

5 Travellers and settled people both being responsible for the bad relationship between the two. A strategy for reconciliation should be developed.

Support for fair treatment of travelling people to put them on a par with the privileges, opportunities, education, training and housing of the settled population is gradually increasing. However, there remains a substantial majority of the settled population who, while favouring settlement of the Travellers problems, oppose strenuously the provision of any type of special housing on halting sites in their home areas. An Irish Independent/IMS poll taken in early February 1995 confirms this view. It shows that 57 per cent of the population would reject a halting site within 1/4 mile of their houses while 38 per cent would accept one. The poll suggests that 73 per cent say the travelling lifestyle should be respected while 57 per cent express the view that seasonal migration by Travellers (the same thing as 'travelling lifestyle'!) is unreasonable, while 61 per cent said authorities should accommodate migrant lifestyle. In addition 64 per cent suggested special local authority housing separated from the settled community, 60 per cent would accept Local Authority housing within the settled community but 59 per cent suggested halting sites should be in areas removed from the settled community.

The implementation of the Task Force's recommendation on a strategy for reconciliation would help to relieve this Third World problem in our communities in the reasonably foreseeable future. The ability to handle the settlement task is within the competence of the local authorities but the political will of the people is slowing down and hampering the solution of the problem. This attitude results in every type of action, legal and otherwise, to frustrate local authority plans to settle the travelling families and has meant that time scales are ever lengthening despite the availability of capital to provide sites. This must change to facilitate a meaningful settlement programme.

While, as already stated, much has been done in settlement, a tough task remains to deal with the final 1/3 of the settlement task, even it if is accepted that part of the solution is to allow those currently living on the roadside to remain nomadic. The diversity of the type of accommodation i.e. houses, group houses and halting sites, if a full programme was implemented, would cater for the housing needs of the Travellers. The housing or siting of Travellers plays a pivotal role in dealing with the problems of travelling families in the other areas of health, employment, Social Services, family support, education and other areas of living skills. These services can be more regularly and easily delivered when the Travellers are static, either permanently or for reasonable periods of time.

Other services

Health and social services

The Local Authorities employ Social Workers who liaise with other agencies in the delivery of social and health and other community services. Over the past twenty years there have been significant improvements in the delivery of services and the Task Force made thirty three detailed recommendations in this area. The Eastern Health Board has been very flexible in its approach to serving Travellers especially problem Traveller areas involving children.

Education

This has been a major area in which the travelling community has trailed the general population. Over ten years ago, the vast majority of Travellers were illiterate. Special schools have been set up, special classes in local schools have been initiated. Much more is necessary. The Task Force report contained one hundred and sixteen recommendations in this field.

Training and employment

Training centres have been established in various parts of the country where Traveller support is strong. These need to be supplemented as the level of unemployment is very high among Travellers. In all of these areas, the churches and voluntary support groups have initiated and assisted to a very significant extent, and these support groups could help in the overall community relations aspect.

The Dublin area

In looking at the settlement problems specifically in the Dublin area one looks at 1960/61 when there were 85 families in County Dublin in the winter with only 46 in the Summer. This total jumped to 387 families in 1974, 573 in 1980 and 938 in 1993.

The 1993 figures for Dublin City and the three new Dublin Counties are as follows (Table 25.3):

Table 25.3
Housing conditions of Travellers, Dublin area, 1993

Housed in Standard Housing	193 Families
Housed in Group Housing	106 Families
Housed in Chalets	11 Families
Housed in trailers on sites	366 Families
Total settled	676 Families
Housed in trailers on roadside	262 Families
TOTAL:	938 Families

Much has been achieved in the Dublin area despite the inordinate and unprecedented growth in the number of travelling families locating in the area over the last twenty-five years. The number of families in the old County Dublin administrative area continues to rise. In 1992 seventy six new families arrived on the roadside in this area. In 1991 Dublin County Council adopted an enhanced programme to cater for the needs of the existing Travellers and normal growth patterns. The programme was primarily one of development of halting sites throughout the entire County with provision for a flow of families who were able and willing to progress to group housing or standard housing in due course.

In January 1994 Dublin County Council was abolished and replaced by three new Counties i.e. Dun Laoghaire-Rathdown, South Dublin and Fingal. These counties now surround the city of Dublin. The new Counties have largely followed through the programme initially adopted in 1991 but progress has been painfully slow. Efforts have been made to provide some large temporary sites as a solution pending the development of permanent sites and to help to change the climate against settlement which has been partly created by the large unsupervised, unauthorised sites.

The City Corporation had spearheaded the settlement of Travellers with the first site in the 1960s and a number of major sites around the city. It has a current programme complimentary to the other three counties and is in the course of redeveloping some of its halting and group housing schemes and also in the development of inner city sites for Travellers.

It is imperative that the programmes of the three new counties be implemented as quickly as possible and that all blockages placed in the way of progression be removed. Much of the development of sites has been achieved against a background of legal actions by local groups opposing development of halting sites. The Development Plan has been challenged, the provision of temporary sites to alleviate problems created by Traveller groups for residents has been legally opposed, and the disposal of land for sites by Charitable and Religious Institutes has been the subject of extreme local pressures. Opposition campaigns have been waged against almost every proposed site. The Travellers themselves, in their general lack of understanding of the fears of local people, have, mostly unwittingly, not helped either. Government financial support and insistence on proceeding with a programme of development of sites has been a positive feature. There is a determination on the part of the management of the three new counties to complete their programmes.

The drift of families to the Dublin area should be discouraged and some families indigenous to other counties should be encouraged to settle in their more traditional base. I am quite convinced that over the years Counties which have embarked on substantial programmes of settlement have attracted additional families from other Counties and have thereby increased their problems. Any national agency set up to oversee settlement should address this issue.

Conclusion

The task of settlement of Travellers is indeed one of 'accommodating difference'. Overall much has been achieved during the last 30 years, though I would be loathe to predict when the problem will be finally solved. It has built up over generations and will only be gradually solved over generations. Settlement will have to be gently forced. The real accomplishment of coexistence and integration will occur when the arrival of Travellers in an area is no longer a cause of fear in the receiving community.

26 The meaning of home for African-Caribbean-British people

Peter Somerville

The problem of ethnicity

There is a considerable literature on the subject of race and housing in Britain, but perhaps surprisingly very little of this has focused on the meaning of home, especially for African-Caribbeans. When the issue is touched upon, it is usually in the context of patterns of immigration to Britain. A good example of this is Watson (1977), where contributors such as Khan and Foner see the perceptions of home by ethnic minorities as produced by their experience of living 'between two cultures'. As Gilroy (1987) and others have pointed out, however, these perceptions are not necessarily transmitted to the next generation, and yet strong cultural differences from the majority white population persist. What appears to happen is that second and third generations of black people in Britain create and recreate their own culture partly as a means of adaptation to the 'host' culture and partly in order to preserve their links with their countries of origin. Further research is required, however, in order to establish the extent to which this is really the case. A focus on attitudes towards the home and home environment should be able to make a contribution to understanding the precise nature of any assimilation or resistance which may be taking place.

There is also a substantial and fast-growing literature on the subject of ethnicity and social or communal identity (Barth, 1969a; Dahya, 1974; Nash, 1988; Roosens, 1989; Liebkind, 1989; Sollors, 1989; O'Donnell, 1990; Modood, 1992; Anthias and Yuval-Davis, 1992; Eriksen, 1993), a little of which concerns specifically the position of Caribbean people in Britain (Pryce, 1979; Cross and Entzinger, 1988; Hiro, 1992, part 1). This literature, however, has not generally identified the experience and perception of home as an ethnic issue, except in relation to the question of 'roots'.

Roosens (1989) says that a claim to distinct ethnicity is made when a group interacts intensively with other groups and seeks to distinguish itself in terms of its cultural practices and artefacts, which are chosen selectively and may have little relationship to an original historical culture. Ethnic groups therefore do not exist in isolation, but only in relation to one another, and the distinctiveness of an ethnic group may be a product of mainly contemporary imagination and myth-making. This view of ethnicity in fact echoes that of earlier writers such as Barth (1969b), who saw ethnic groups as defined through their relationship to others, maintaining boundaries with those others which change through time.

This theme, of ethnicity being created and recreated in interaction between social groups, recurs frequently in the literature on ethnicity. For example, Greenhouse (1992), in a review of articles by J. Stone, M.H. Ross, L. Bobo and J.B. Childs, concludes that ethnicity and 'race' are seen as cultural, with conventionally assigned meanings which reflect very high stakes. Culture therefore creates ethnicity which in turn creates (ethnic) culture, in a perpetually self-reinforcing process, and the distinctiveness of an ethnic culture lies essentially in its created difference from other (ethnic) cultures. The stakes then relate to the configurations of power which lie behind the cultural formations and which make those formations specifically ethnic. This argument links in with analyses of contemporary racism which see the dominant racist ideology today as mainly a historical or pseudo-historical one grounded in the idea of culture (Blaut, 1992). Ethnicity and 'race' are therefore both viewed as modern illusions, but also as symbolic expressions of real historical tensions and conflicts between social groups.

Although ethnicity is bound up with culture, and expressed through culture, it is not the same as culture. This point is perhaps most clearly expressed by Eriksen (1993), who argues that ethnicity is essentially cultural difference which matters: 'only insofar as cultural differences are perceived as important, and are made socially relevant, do social relationships have an ethnic element' (Eriksen, 1993, p. 12). This argument raises a number of questions to which there is no easy answer, for example: why are certain cultural differences seen as important and not others? and: is it the members of the ethnic group themselves who have to perceive their cultural difference as important (the so-called 'emic' category of ethnic ascription) (Moerman, 1965), or do others have to see the difference as important, or both? Further studies of the dynamics of ethnicity are required before we can be sure of the answers to such questions.

Moving on to theories of race and housing, it is striking how often the same themes occur as in the discussion of ethnicity generally. Weberian theories, for example, self-consciously affirm the effects of culture as a social force, and link such effects to the power struggles between different social groups (Rex, 1986). Some writers have adapted Giddens' structuration theory and used it to explain the relations between institutional racism (structure) and strategies of resistance by minority groups (action) (Sarre et al., 1989). Others have focused in particular on the spatial expression of boundary making and remaking by ethnic majority and minority groups, in order to develop a theory of ethnic residential segregation (Smith, 1989). All such theories have made a contribution to our understanding of ethnicity, even though they have tended at times to over-simplify or ignore cultural differences, and consequently have under-emphasised the role of perceptions of the value of such differences in creating ethnicity.

Similarly, with theories relating to the meaning of home, notions which are common currency in the field of ethnic studies typically play a key role. In particular, concepts of privacy, identity and familiarity, which are arguably essential components of a theory of the social construction of home (Somerville, 1997), would appear to be equally relevant for a theory of ethnicity. Privacy, for example, means the control of boundaries, and, as we have seen, the control of boundaries is integral to the definition of an ethnic group. Identity is a matter of how we come to be 'at home' in the world, and in ethnic terms this is typically expressed in the language of myths of common origin and history (Eriksen, 1993). Finally, familiarity refers to our domestication of reality, such that potentially alien objects and people are made to seem 'homely' and almost as extensions of ourselves; in the context of ethnicity, this means 'metaphoric or fictive kinship' (Yelvington, 1991), or 'family' in a wider sense. Our idea of home is formed by the identity of our ascribed 'kith and kin' set within boundaries which are being continually renegotiated — and the ethnic group to which we belong is shaped in a similar way. Domesticity and ethnicity are indissolubly linked.

Additional relevant theories are those which link ethnicity with other social categories, such as class, gender and nationality. The overlap between ethnic and national identity has long been noted (Smith, 1991). Ethnic groups can turn themselves into nations by claiming dominion over a certain territory and as a result of political organisation and struggle over a long historical period. Like ethnicity, nationalism is invented (Gellner, 1983) or imagined (Anderson, 1991), and is perhaps essentially non-rational (Connor, 1993). Because of the features of inclusivity and exclusivity associated with nationalism, ethnicity becomes linked to issues of class (for example, with politically excluded ethnic groups being represented as part of an 'underclass') (Rex, 1986) and gender (for example, with nationalist and ethnic' strategies and ideologies being identified as inherently oppressive of women) (Walby, 1992; Foster-Carter, 1987). The ethnic group and the nation are typically seen as extensions of the traditional family, based on traditional gender roles, with women at the heart of the family, and hence of the nation, but excluded from real power over the nation's affairs (Yuval-Davis, 1993). In addition, there are hypotheses concerning the relation between ethnicity and modernity, which have been used in an attempt to explain the change in ethnicity from first-generation immigrants to the second generation. For example, Necef (1992) has argued that immigrants tend to express a nostalgia towards their cultural background and country of origin, while their children and grandchildren born and raised in the new country view their original culture in an increasingly distanced and detached way, sometimes leading to what is known as 'ethnic tourism'. Overall, therefore, there is good reason to be suspicious and critical of the language of ethnicity.

African-Caribbeans in Manchester

The author conducted a small-scale pilot survey of African-Caribbeans in Manchester, in order to explore in greater depth the perceptions and attitudes of African-Caribbean-British people to their homes, and to gather evidence which could be used to test some of the theories discussed in the last section. Respondents were asked about their sense of belonging to, or being part of, a particular group, and if so, what this group means to them. An attempt was made to identify any special characteristics of this group, or anything which makes people in this group in some sense different from other people. The possible origins of this sense of group identity were explored, and further questions sought to gain an understanding of how it is maintained and reproduced from day to day. The role of the home and home area was then considered in relation to this discussion, with questions directed in particular at ideas about neighbourhood and local community. One aim of this line of questioning was to discover if there is any link between a respondent's group affiliations and what makes them feel at home in a particular type of house or a particular area. It was hoped that it would prove possible to draw conclusions in particular about the relationship between group identity and sense of being at home in Britain relative to home in the Caribbean. These conclusions have implications for our understanding of immigration policy and help to throw some new light on the politics of identity and debates about Eurocentrism and multiculturalism.

The research findings can be grouped under a number of topic headings: attachment to current home, conception of ideal home, concept of neighbourliness, sense of group identity, relation between home and group identity, attitude to current home area, preferred sort of home area, home in Britain relative to home in the Caribbean, and attitude to the black community in Britain. Each of these topics is considered below.

Attachment to current home

Nearly all the respondents had a strong attachment to their homes. This was an attachment which had grown over the years, as they had become older. This process of becoming attached to home is well known, though this does not mean that it is well understood. According to the psychological theory of attachment, people construct mental representations of the world (Giuliani, 1991, p. 136), and then become attached to certain objects in the world insofar as they identify themselves with those objects and attempt to preserve this sense of identity in their everyday lives (Bretherton, 1985). Stage in the life cycle is thought to be particularly important in the development of attachment to home (Csikszentmihalyi and Rochberg-Halton, 1981), with a clear difference emerging between home-making and home-maintaining phases (Giuliani, 1991). Two respondents, however, differed strongly in their attachment to home despite being in similar stages of the life-cycle (both of them being parents of young children). This difference can be explained only by reference to differences in their constructions of their ethnic identity, with one accepting an identity of black English and therefore (though with some uncertainty and ambivalence) of permanent settlement in Britain, while the other was resistant to identities ascribed by others and was determined to see his black identity in a wider international context, and this meant possibly seeking a permanent home outside of Britain.

Conception of ideal home

All respondents had a conception of an ideal home as relatively large, well-built, having clearly marked boundaries, with a healthy environment, and in an area where they would feel comfortable. Differences of perception were mainly age-related, with elderly respondents not expecting, or even being prepared to tolerate, further changes in their housing circumstances. Tenure, however, also appeared to be important, with owner-occupiers tending to see themselves as having a greater capacity to achieve their ideal than tenants.

Concept of neighbourliness

Except for one respondent, who knew only a few of his neighbours, all the respondents knew all of their neighbours to say hello to. All had just one neighbour with whom they had a closer relationship, involving at least visiting each other. All five were also in agreement about what it takes to be a good neighbour, namely just being there in case of need, not interfering in people's affairs but knowing when there is a problem and being prepared to offer help as necessary.

Sense of group identity

There was considerable variation among the respondents concerning their sense of group identity. Affiliations volunteered by respondents included Caribbean, mixed black English, black West Indian, and citizen of the world. There were subtle differences lying behind these labels. One respondent was born and brought up in the Caribbean, and she retained strong family and cultural links with the Caribbean, so she classified herself as Caribbean. Her Caribbean identity was primarily a sense of her origins, which was periodically renewed through carnival and occasional special celebrations. In contrast, another had never been back to the Caribbean since she was a baby, so she did not feel Caribbean; instead she felt English, because England was the only country she had known. For her, group identity was defined predominantly not by her origins but by where she was brought up, namely a racially mixed area in England. She did not feel typically English, however, because she was black: hence the use of the word 'mixed', because 'black English' sounds almost a contradiction in terms.

The position of other respondents was quite different. They eschewed all nationalist, continentalist and culturalist labels, and recognised only a common — out of Africa — historical lineage. For them, however, this lineage was only one source of their current group identity. Their spiritual family included relatives and close friends, but they believed that it was capable of encompassing the whole world. Their group identity, therefore, used to be based upon their West Indian origins, but this had gradually faded over the years and had been replaced by an achieved identity based on a network of social relations in England.

For another respondent, the case was different again. He saw himself as primarily black, because of his experience of racism in Britain, but he also saw himself as West Indian, which he felt had different connotations in different parts of the world. In addition, he had chosen for himself a national identity, Jamaican, in order to distance himself from the British national identity which others sought to impose upon him. His group identity was therefore derived partly from his childhood experiences of racism, and partly from his recognition and acceptance of West Indian cultural difference and his belief in the importance of this difference.

Group identity therefore means very different things to different people, even when those people appear to be in objectively similar positions. Group identity can relate to origins, upbringing, the projects and experiences of adult life, or specific cultural practices.

The research findings raise a number of questions. Is Caribbean identity the same as West Indian identity, for example? One respondent took the view that it was not, because Caribbean people are not necessarily from Africa (he mentioned Arawaks, Caribs, and other groups), whereas the term 'West Indian' implied black. Other respondents also thought that being West Indian, at least in Britain, meant being black, but felt that West Indians had a characteristic culture as well. There was no general agreement, however, on the distinctiveness of this culture. One possibility arising from the research is that black British people are already reinventing Caribbean culture and calling it West Indian, in order to raise their self-esteem and give themselves a wider identity outside of the British context, which they see as restricting and oppressive.

Another interesting finding is the caution which all respondents exhibited towards the issue of national identity. Some rejected all nationalisms outright, and would not accept either national or ethnic categories as applying to themselves. Others accepted their Englishness, but not with any strong inner conviction. Only one described his (dual) national identity in a positive way (as Jamaican and British), and even he was careful to emphasise his West Indian identity over his Jamaican identity and pointed out that the national divisions which bedevil white European society do not have the same destructive and exclusionary effects in the Caribbean.

Relation between home and group identity

For all respondents the focus of the relationship between their home and their group identity was the area or neighbourhood in which they lived. For those whose relationship between home and group identity was fairly weak, the black identity imposed upon them by others still made it necessary for them to avoid white neighbourhoods. Those whose group identity was mixed felt more at home in a mixed neighbourhood. And those who felt that they had no permanent sense of home in Britain attributed this to the situation of being black in a white society.

Attitude to current home area

Respondents generally lived in racially mixed neighbourhoods, but attitudes varied mainly according to the characteristics of those living nearest to them. Some areas were seen as undesirable because of increasing numbers of anti-social and criminal residents. In all cases, however, it was the immediate neighbourhood which was the crucial issue (this might cover as few as half a dozen dwellings), not the wider area. This explained why certain respondents could be exceptionally happy within areas which in a wider sense were very run-down and highly stigmatised. In general, in spite of the problems in some neighbourhoods, respondents felt more comfortable in racially mixed areas.

Preferred sort of home area

All respondents thought it important to live in an area where they were not made to feel uncomfortable. Most of them recognised that in some, though not all, white-dominated neighbourhoods, it was not possible for black people to feel at ease and to live as they would wish. They therefore preferred to live in areas where there were plenty of black people around. One expressed the general opinion most clearly: his preferred home area would be one that is free of pollution, racism, snobbery, intolerance and interference from others. Moreover, his ideal home area would be one where black people were in the majority, because that would be the only way to ensure that he felt comfortable all the time.

Home in Britain relative to home in the Caribbean

Respondents differed considerably in their feelings about home in Britain relative to home in the Caribbean. Those who had come from the Caribbean originally and had put down roots in Britain (or at least in Manchester) tended to be more committed to their homes in Britain. They felt that they had a home in the Caribbean, because of the family they still had there, but the longer they stayed in Britain the weaker these family ties tended to become. For those of them who had reached pensionable age, the chances of a permanent return were very slim, so the quality of their home in Britain (or lack of it) assumed particular importance. For those a little way short of pensionable age, crucial decisions would soon have to be taken about whether to stay or to return, and the outcome of such decisions would depend mainly on two factors, namely the economic circumstances of the respondent and the nature of their family ties with the Caribbean.

Those respondents who had been born in Britain or had come over when they were very young children generally felt very differently. Like their parents, they spoke of the Caribbean as home, and a large proportion of them had been there for holidays and to visit relatives. For them, however, the Caribbean was a place of potential permanent return, although some recognised that this might never happen, largely for economic reasons (for example, in the case of single parents with insufficient wider family support). The reasons for this common view were perhaps best expressed by one respondent, who was a young married man with two children. Although he had lived all of his life in Britain, he did not feel at home in this country, he did not feel comfortable being a member of an ethnic minority. On the other hand, he had been to Jamaica only for short periods, and did not know it very well. He had no home in Jamaica, but he felt he could be more at home in Jamaica, because there he would not suffer racial discrimination. Freedom from racism was therefore the crucial issue rather than an attachment to Jamaica or the Caribbean as such.

Perhaps surprisingly, very few respondents identified such a thing as 'the black community' in Britain, that is a mixed community, encompassing churches, clubs and other institutions. Even these few did not feel that it defined their identity, and felt no strong commitment to any of its institutions. For other respondents, the term 'community' meant nothing, let alone 'black community'. All respondents referred back to the importance of family and friends rather than relying on essentially vague concepts of wider loyalties. One respondent, however, recognised that the idea of community could be made more meaningful by being identified with the performance of public service (he worked for a local charitable housing association).

Conclusions

What the research clearly shows is that the experience and perception of home cannot be understood in isolation from the issue of group identity, so this issue needs to receive more attention in research on the meaning of home. All respondents talked of home in a number of different senses, and each of these senses was related to a particular group identity (see Table 26.1).

Table 26.1
Meaning of home and group identity

Meaning of Home	Group Identity
Current dwelling	Household
Area of residence	Family and friends
Country of residence	Nation
Country of origin (or destination)	Shared ancestry
Continent of origin (or destination)	'Race'

First, home meant the house which they currently occupied. They differed in the degree of attachment which they felt towards home in this sense, but even the respondent who felt no such attachment agreed that home was where he and his wife and children lived. Next, home meant the area in which they resided: what made this area home for them was the co-residence in it of members of their family, especially parents (for younger respondents) and children (for older respondents), as well as friends of long standing. Thirdly, home signified country of residence, the country where they had a permanent home in the first two senses: generally, this meant England, and it was in this sense that the above-mentioned respondent did not have a home. Fourthly, home meant country of origin, such as Barbados or Jamaica, the country where they had been born and brought up, or where their parents had been born and brought up. This could also, in the case of some younger respondents, function as a country of destination. The key factor here was the historical lineage going back through generations. Finally, home referred to the part of the world, or the continent, from which their families had originated. This could in the simplest cases mean the Caribbean, or it could involve a more complex longer-term historical sense of their origins in Africa. This did not mean, however, that any of them actually saw Africa as their home: rather, they saw the exodus of their ancestors from Africa to the Caribbean as giving rise to a special sense of home for the descendants of those ancestors. Their sense of home was defined not by their relationship to a particular place, but by their common historical experience of being black or West Indian people coming to Britain via the Caribbean.

Returning to some of the theoretical approaches outlined earlier in this paper, a number of observations can be made. First of all, only one respondent accepted the validity of the term 'ethnic' or 'ethnicity', and his use of the term did in fact accord with that of Roosens (1989), that is he defined his group primarily in terms of cultural differences from other groups which he felt to be important. He was also well aware of the political stakes involved, centring on the issue of minority or majority status. Apart from him, however, very few respondents appeared to feel that cultural differences were important, and for them this was probably mainly because the culture provided them with links with what was left of their families in the Caribbean. The others were of course aware of being 'different', in the sense of being black or West Indian, but they did not attach any particular cultural importance to this. It would therefore be premature, to say the least, to classify West Indians in Britain as an ethnic group.

The interviews provide some evidence to support the claims of feminist writers such as Foster-Carter and Walby that an emphasis on ethnicity can be restrictive for black women, because of the unequal gender roles which are deemed to be culturally determined. They also suggest that the issue of nationality is a particularly difficult one for West Indians, because historically they have always comprised a multiplicity of nationalities, or potential nationalities. There is no Caribbean nation or homeland as such, so those West Indians wishing to lay claim to a distinctive ethnicity for their group do not have a defined territory in which such ethnicity can become a political reality.

The interviews reveal important differences among respondents on the issue of resistance to racism, with most of them preferring to ignore it as far as possible, or appearing simply to wish it away. This did not mean that they were not resisting racism, but they preferred to do it indirectly, for example through participating in the black community, through being members of non-racist organisations, or through forms of working class solidarity. Only one respondent was confronting racism directly, and even he saw resistance more in terms of establishing his own ethnic separateness rather than attempting actually to change white racism.

The sample of respondents (twenty) was too small to draw any firm conclusions about variations from one generation to another. Nevertheless, the findings unambiguously contradict those of Necef (1992). Whereas Necef found that first generation Turkish immigrants in Denmark were nostalgic about their origins, the research reported here found that first generation West Indian immigrants had no illusions on that score: on the contrary, the longer they lived in Britain, the more removed they felt from their origins, and the less inclined they were to go back. Similarly for second generation immigrants: Necef found that they were more detached in their attitude to their origins, but my research shows, if anything, a nostalgia for the celebrated 'island in the sun', where the evils of racial prejudice and discrimination are entirely absent. These findings could be explained either on the grounds that the respondents are untypical of first or second generation West Indians generally, or else that in some sense West Indians in Britain are in a radically different position from Turks in Denmark. Phenomenologically, it makes more sense that first generation immigrants would become more attached to their adopted country as time goes by, because this is the country in which they have decided to settle. In contrast, their children did not choose to live in this country, so the same motives which brought their parents here originally may now be leading them (the children) to set up home elsewhere. Their parents migrated to Britain primarily to improve their economic circumstances, and the children now feel the need to emigrate from Britain for much the same reason.

A final issue concerns the forward and backward orientations to home at different stages of the life-cycle which have been noted by phenomenologists (Giuliani, 1991, p. 137). It is now possible to see that this is not just a function of life-cycle stage, but also of a lived experience of an ascribed social status. The lived experience of majority status (equivalent to what has been described as 'comfortable' Britain) promotes home-making at the nuclear-family-building stage of the life cycle, whereas the lived experience of minority status causes home-making to be postponed, sometimes indefinitely. A member of an excluded minority never feels entirely at home because of the fact of her/his exclusion. She/he therefore has to make do with a less than satisfactory situation, or else create her/his own home elsewhere. This was the dilemma which, in different ways, confronted all the respondents.

In spite of the small-scale nature of this research, a number of implications can be drawn from it which are of wider sociological significance. For example, West Indians in Britain are clearly a highly fragmented group who are unlikely ever to exhibit a significant degree of collective action, at least on a residential basis. They are very far from seeing themselves as Europeans, but their position is not to be explained as simply a reaction to white European racism, although no doubt this has played a part. Rather, their exclusion from European society is partly self-determined as well as other-determined, as the product of a long cross-continental historical experience. The immigration policies of many European Union countries, including Britain, are therefore based on false assumptions with regard to this particular group: West Indians are not now, and never have been, clamouring to enter Britain in order to take advantage of its higher standard of living and generous welfare facilities. Rather, they came because they were invited to do so, and in many cases they have remained only because they have lost touch with their families back in the West Indies or because they have been too poor to afford the cost of return.

Part Nine
Pluralistic accommodation?

27 Putting it all together

Frederick Boal

> All good people agree
> And all good people say
> All nice people like Us, are We
> And Everyone else is They
>
> Rudyard Kipling 'We and They" (1926)

Where we came in

As noted in the Introduction, this volume has its roots in the 1995 Congress of the International Federation of Housing and Planning. At that time Belfast was enjoying the transformed atmosphere created by the declaration of cease-fires by local paramilitary terrorist groups. Although the IRA terminated their cease-fire later in the same year, it was subsequently reinstalled. Following this, in April 1998, an agreement was signed between the British and the Irish governments and many (though not all) of the Northern Ireland political parties. This (the 'Belfast' or 'Good Friday' Agreement) put in place a new set of structures that was intended to provide the basis for the 'accommodation' of what otherwise seemed to be irreconcilable differences. Of particular significance for our present discussion was the affirmation in the Agreement of 'the right to freely choose one's place of residence' and a declaration that 'an essential aspect of the reconciliation process is the promotion of a culture of tolerance at every level of society, including initiatives to facilitate and encourage integrated education and *mixed housing* [my emphasis] (Belfast Agreement, 1998, p.16 and p. 18). All this is to be achieved in an environment where ' ... equal opportunity in all social and economic activity, regardless of class, creed, disability, gender or ethnicity' is a fundamental human right (Belfast Agreement, 1998, p. 18).

Several recent reports highlight the imperatives now in place. For instance the Northern Ireland Department of the Environment (the land use planning authority for the Province) has recently issued a document entitled *Shaping our Future* (DOENI, 1998). This looks to the appropriate strategies for developing the region to 2025, declaring therein:

> ... in planning for a new future it is recognised that the divisions in Northern Ireland society are affected by public policies and that, in turn, these policies are affected by the divisions. Land designation, the location of employment,

and investment decisions on social, economic and physical infrastructure must respect the sensitivities of the divided nature of the community, while seeking ultimately to contribute to the healing of community divisions (DOENI, 1998, pp. 10-11).

More recently the Northern Ireland Housing Executive has issued a consultation paper — *Towards a Community Relations Strategy* (NIHE, 1999). In this the Executive makes a general policy statement that it 'will encourage and support the provision of integrated housing where there is evidence of community support'. This is really only a slightly more proactive restatement of the policy position found in the First Annual Report of the Executive, issued in 1971 (at the height of the violent conflict):

> We believe that people should have the maximum freedom of choice of where they wish to live. The Executive does not believe that forced integration is any more desirable than a policy of deliberate segregation. We can only hope that the provision of an attractive mixture of housing and a change of the social-political as well as the physical environment may ease the problem of polarisation by encouraging and enabling families who wish to live in integrated communities to do so (NIHE, 1971, p. 18).

From these recent Northern Ireland 'position' documents we can observe the emergence of three themes:

1. Integration or mixing is a desirable objective
2. Policies aimed at such an objective must be ones that create and sustain choice and a 'voluntaristic' environment
3. There must be an increased sensitivity to the 'accommodating differences' implications of policy implementation.

Let us now turn to briefly draw out a number of threads that are woven into the fabric of the contributions to this volume.

Themes

Segregation: good or bad?

There is undoubtedly a strong sense that, on balance, residential segregation is bad. Ceri Peach (Chapter 2) reviews the negative aspects of the residential separation of ethnic groups, but he also notes that such separation can be a significant contributor to the accommodation of differences. Richard Tomlins (Chapter 15) reports that a positive view of 'integration' is predominant with American writers on housing matters, but he goes on to observe that the positive attributes of clustering and the negative dimensions of 'assimilation' are rarely discussed in the contemporary literature on housing segregation. The two countervailing perspectives on segregation and mixing are also found in Eric Gallibour's description (Chapter 6) of the residential integration of immigrants in French Guyana, as providing, on the one hand, a mechanism for 'control' and on the other an aid to societal integration. Again, in Brendan Murtagh's references (Chapter 20) to Peter Marcuse's perspective on the role of walls in cities we find the same dichotomous interpretation — they contribute to control and management whilst simultaneously offering protection, insulation and an environment for community reproduction.

In their broadly based perspective on African America, James Upton and Rebeka Maples (Chapter 8) point to the debate that exists concerning integration versus separation as two opposing strategies for overcoming the same obstacle — 'national' (racial) oppression.

Different emphases on the desirability or otherwise of segregation are to be found in a number of the other contributions. Israeli strategy with regard to immigration is clearly integrationist (at 'reasonable cost') (Adam Buchman, Chapter 14), while there are concerns in Belfast that segregation limits housing choice (John McPeake, Chapter 19) and that it provides an environment conducive to political violence (Paul Doherty and Michael Poole, Chapter 17). In the Dutch case of the Bijlmer (Wicher Nieuwenhuis and Glenn Willemsen, Chapter 20) 100 different cultures 'live next to each other but not together. It [the Bijlmer] may rather be seen as a sort of island society — ethnic groups form little, autonomous islands without solid interrelations'. Finally we can note that Malcolm Fisk (Chapter 23) points to the desirability of a degree of segregation ('concentration') for the preservation of language communities. In the Welsh case he is concerned that spatial dilution by non-Welsh speakers will undermine the long-term viability of Welsh speaking communities.

Residential patterns and social provision

Whatever the view regarding the desirability or undesirability of segregation, a number of contributors to *Ethnicity and Housing* issue a strong plea for housing policy to be seen not in isolation but as one (vitally important) component of a much more extensive policy web. This perspective comes across particularly strongly with Richard Tomlins (Chapter 15) when he calls for a pluralistic housing policy that is part of a pluralistic social policy. Supporting this stance is the analysis provided by Wicher Nieuwenhuis and Glenn Willemsen (Chapter 20) when they write:

What on the surface seemed [in the Bijlmer] to be a housing and profitability problem, on closer examination appears to be part of an underlying social dynamic related to processes of international migration and a demand for diversity in society.

They then go on to point out the need not only for physical renewal of the built fabric, but for social renewal and the renewal of management approaches. Matters of educational provision, work availability and language and cultural integration should also be promoted as integral components of an overall strategy.

The broad contextualisation of housing policy with other social dimensions is brought out forcefully by Liam Byrne (Chapter 25) in his analysis of the situation of Travellers in Irish society. He claims that the housing or 'siting' of Travellers plays 'a pivotal role in dealing with the problems of travelling families in ... areas of health, employment, social services, family support, education and other areas of living skills'. He concludes that these services can be better delivered when the Travellers are static, either permanently or 'for reasonable periods of time'.

Making and keeping mixed neighbourhoods

Though, as noted above, there is room for debate regarding the positive and the negative aspects of residential segregation, there is nonetheless a strong, and, in the main justifiable current of opinion in favour of ethnically mixed neighbourhoods. Contributions to *Ethnicity and Housing* provide pointers as to how to retain those mixed neighbourhoods that do exist, how to promote mixing where it does not already exist and how to further encourage it where it does.

Retention of mixing is the focus of the Chicago analysis provided by Michael Maly and Philip Nyden (Chapter 10). They stress that the maintenance of diversity requires constant attention by community leaders. They underline the importance of perception — the need to place 'a positive spin on diversity', rather than on seeing diversity as an indicator of neighbourhood instability and decline. Just as we have earlier emphasised the need to see housing in a wide social context, so with the dynamics of preservation of mixed neighbourhoods. Maly and Nyden list a number of dimensions here — the need for economic development, for the provision of a full range of housing types and tenures, the requirement for community safety, the importance of quality school provision and the desirability of utilising local social networks for diversity maintenance purposes.

Promoting neighbourhood ethnic diversity inevitably will draw on those factors that contribute to the maintenance of such areas. However other policy initiatives seem, in the proactive situation, to be useful as well. For instance John Goering (Chapter 9) provides an incisive analysis of the United States Department of Housing and Urban Development's Section 8 programme. Here racial/ethnic segregation is reduced by widening the housing choices available to minority households — vouchers, counselling and help with housing search promote city-wide and, indeed, metropolitan area-wide residential mobility for low income families, and thereby for many minority households. Dispersal is encouraged by making the vouchers available for use in the less segregated residential locations. A parallel with this policy is found in the strategies pursued by the Israeli government (Churchman and Herbert, Chapter 13) where mortgage assistance and rent subsidy is made available to newly arrived immigrant households. This creates a geographically more dispersed (mixed) pattern than was the case earlier, when immigrants were directly provided with dwellings.

Mixing, both socio-economic and ethnic has also been successfully encouraged in Jwaneng, Botswana (González, Chapter 7) by a judicious mixing of housing types and by employing urban design sensitive to the cultural 'needs' of the diverse peoples occupying the town.

Racial mixing also receives encouragement in Abigail Goldberg's examination (Chapter 4) of Pageview / Vrededorp in South Africa. Despite the enforced segregation of apartheid, deeply preserved folk memories in Pageview

/Vrededorp deny and defy apartheid's segregation and provide optimistic indicators for reconstruction and reconciliation — many recall the earlier days when the area was racially mixed.

Despite the encouragements offered by some contributors to this volume, it is also clear that the maintenance and promotion of ethnic mixing in housing is not an easy task. Paul Doherty and Michael Poole (Chapter 17) sharply state that, in Belfast, 'a lengthy conflict free period must go by before there is any significant desegregation from the present [high] levels'. Thus segregation has a powerful momentum of its own, a point indirectly made by John McPeake (Chapter 19) where his research indicates that restricted search patterns — in part a product of existing segregation — in turn help to maintain segregation.

A final cautionary note can be added. This is there seems to be in many instances of ethnic mixing at neighbourhood level an asymmetry in the preferences of the groups concerned. We have some hints of this from the analyses in this book. For instance Ghazi Falah (Chapter 11) records that Jews in 'mixed' cities in Israel are more sensitive to the proportions of Arabs present than is the case the other way round. Likewise in Belfast, where Murtagh (Chapter 18) records what he calls an asymmetrical acceptance rule — Catholics being more open to mixing than Protestants, though he goes on to observe that this asymmetry is rooted, at least in part, in 'a genuine fear for the future of their territory and all that means for community survival'. Be that as it may, asymmetrical preferences create great potential for instability in mixed neighbourhoods. Thus, since it is impossible to simultaneously achieve the preferred levels for mixing held by (say) each of two groups, one group may be reluctant to enter a neighbourhood, while the other may decide that 'exit' is the only viable strategy.

Home

Members of ethnic groups, if they are to be properly 'accommodated', will need to feel comfortable with their dwellings and with their neighbourhoods — they will need to feel at home. Peter Somerville (Chapter 26) suggests that 'home' should be seen as existing at a number of different scales — the dwelling, the neighbourhood, the country of residence, the country of origin and the general part of the world from which the immigrants or their forebears came. If we concentrate on the dwelling and the neighbourhood, several policy pointers are to be found amongst the contributions to *Ethnicity and Housing*. The dwelling should be a source of privacy, identity and familiarity (Somerville, Chapter 26). It should be appropriate to the specific needs of the ethnic groups concerned — the right size, the right internal design (Tomlins, Chapter 15; Bowes, Dar and Sim, Chapter 16). Of course quality is also fundamental. Here Churchman and Herbert (Chapter 13) express a concern that in Israel 'roofs over heads' have been provided with admirable speed, but that quality has suffered in the process. The objective of quality improvement as a means of stabilising ethnically mixed housing is brought out in the Dutch case of the Bijlmer (Nieuwenhuis and Willemsen, Chapter 20) and in the radical improvements carried out at the Ludwig-Frank complex in Mannheim by the housing co-operative (Hachmann, Chapter 22).

The immediate context of the dwelling is also very much part of home. As noted above, there will be concerns amongst groups living in or considering moving into particular neighbourhoods as to the current ethnic composition of those neighbourhoods and their likely future state. Other dimensions are also important, however. Sergio-Albio González (Chapter 7) stresses those aspects of neighbourhood design in Jwaneng that facilitate Botswana's traditional cultural activities and social interactions, while Alison Bowes and her colleagues (Chapter 16) notes that Pakistani households in Glasgow seek residential contexts with attributes such as: proximity to other Pakistani families; good local schools and transport; access to Asian shops and to mosques — as well as the presence of 'good neighbours, no matter what ethnicity'. In Chapter 16 Richard Tomlins also refers to the quality of neighbourhoods when he observes that, even if members of ethnic communities choose to residentially concentrate, policies should be developed that provide financial resources aimed at ensuring that life chances in spatially differentiated areas are comparable to those in 'mainstream society'.

Ethnicity or income?

An analytic focus within the field of ethnic segregation has been on whether such segregation can be attributed to 'ethnic' or to 'economic' factors (or to both). Are members of an ethnic group residentially segregated because of cultural factors (voluntaristic or forced) or because of their economic position in society? The conclusions reached from such a debate will have very significant policy implications. John Muller (Chapter 5) lays considerable stress on the gap that exists in South Africa between the haves and the have-nots. If economic factors are key to the ethnic segregation process then reduction in socio-economic inequalities should reduce segregation. Again, if economic differences are generating, at least in part, ethnic segregation, then a possible approach is to provide a mixture of housing types in a wide range of neighbourhoods. Thus the Jwaneng plan (Chapter 7) mixes residential plots for households of different income levels, while Hugo Priemus (Chapter 21) argues for what he calls the 'redifferentiation' of housing stock in Dutch cities to reduce the 'largely involuntary concentration of low income residents' found in 'large scale islands of homogeneity' (many of these residents being immigrants). Priemus calls for a policy emphasis that will lead to the elimination of the distinction between 'native' and 'immigrant', though he also stresses that in the early stages of immigrant entry there will have to be an emphasis on cultural factors, as self-support networks among immigrant communities are assisted in the task of aiding immigrant adaptation. At the end of the day, however, Priemus wants to see the immigrant/native distinction disappear from Dutch society — 'as soon as we discover that we no longer need to make that distinction, we have found the solution to a multicultural Europe'.

National to local

Though much of the discussion in *Ethnicity and Housing* concentrates on individual cities and neighbourhoods, it is nonetheless necessary to take on board the role of national policy — for instance what kind of society is desired:

the polyethnicity of Guyanese society, the apartheid or democratic models of South Africa or the ethnonationalisms of Israel/Palestine or of Northern Ireland? These contexts fundamentally set the scene and place limits on action at lower levels (see Gallibour, Chapter 6; Upton and Maples, Chapter 10; Efrat, Chapter 12; Doherty and Poole, Chapter 17).

It is clearly desirable that there should be well defined state/national policy regarding ethnic groups. Otherwise ambiguity and uncertainty will create a diffused, ill-focused policy environment.

While national level policies provide frameworks for action, there is a strong current of opinion amongst the contributors to *Ethnicity and Housing* in support of a move from top-down initiatives to solutions generated at grassroots. For instance Richard Tomlins (Chapter 15) claims that solutions have tended to be paternalistic, while noting that there are alternatives on offer for 'grassroots activism within minority ethnic communities'. Wicher Nieuwenhuis and Glenn Willemsen (Chapter 20) critically observe the top-down organisation of management in the Bijlmer and state that 'we must create space for peoples and initiatives', while Claus Hachmann underlines the vital role played by residents in all decisions regarding the physical renovation of the dilapidated residential area taken over by the Ludwig-Frank Co-operative (Chapter 22).

Choice and empowerment

Though the contributors to this volume all are likely to have their own preferred outcomes to the process of accommodating differences, it is very evident that they strongly feel that 'choice' and 'empowerment' must lie at the base of policy development. Kader Asmal (Chapter 3) affirms that 'everyone should have the right to freely choose his or her place of residence anywhere in the national territory' while Churchman and Herbert's objective in the Israeli situation is to 'allow for diversity through the options of choice, and to create an orderly but flexible framework for change'. From a more research oriented position Ceri Peach (Chapter 2) underlines 'the need to know more about the dynamics of choice ... and the consequences of social engineering' while Richard Tomlins (Chapter 15) wishes to uphold the right of ethnic minorities 'to choose residential segregation' if that is clearly what they want.

We have noted above a number of calls for bottom-up policy development. This ties in with related appeals for 'empowerment'. Thus John Muller (Chapter 5), noting that many groups were disempowered in apartheid South Africa, says that 'it is essential in the empowerment of the deprived that the inequalities will be removed'. Richard Tomlins (Chapter 15) wishes to assert the primacy of empowerment, suggesting that at least some of the services targeted upon areas of minority ethnic residence should be controlled by the community receiving the service. Finally Wicher Nieuwenhuis and Glenn Willemsen (Chapter 20) claim that empowerment entails emphasising 'potential', 'possibilities' and 'opportunities', with the consequence that responsibility is put back where it belongs — in the hands of the people.

Research methods and professional approaches

There has already been a great deal of research on issues relating to housing and the accommodation of ethnic diversity. There is, inevitably, need for more. Moreover there are also issues to be considered that relate to how the research is to be done. Several contributions to *Ethnicity and Housing* express unease with respect to a number of matters — in particular the quantitative and top-down emphasis of much work. Thus Maly and Nyden (Chapter 10) decry the tendency for quantitative work to

> unintentionally de-emphasise the roles of local communities in determining their future. Reliance on national and metropolitan area statistics can misdirect policy making and future research projects towards national or regional organisations, ignoring the importance of community-level institutions.

Bowes, Dar and Sim (Chapter 16) note the quantitative nature of previous research and suggest that a more balanced and insightful approach would involve life history interviewing, which is sensitive to changing lives and which avoids stereotyping. Murtagh (Chapter 20) is pursuing a similar agenda when he argues that planners should 'embrace ethnographic techniques to understand complex dynamics at community level'. Simon Arlidge (Chapter 24) in his examination of rural recreational research and ethnicity criticises the top-down approach of much US work and concludes that researchers should ask first and listen, should let those being researched feel part of the process and should work to build trust in the researcher-researched relationship.

I think it would be true to say that these contributors are not calling for an end to quantitative, probably 'top-down' research, for such an approach is vital to establish context, comparison and temporal trends. Rather they are calling for a greater emphasis on the ethnographic, on the small scale and on the bottom-up as approaches complementary to more traditional research methodologies.

Just as a shift in research methods and approaches is called for, so too several authors issue appeals for changes in approaches to planning and to housing management where ethnic issues (including ethnic conflict) are to the fore. Thus John Muller (Chapter 5), writing out of the South African context, observes that the 'democratic imperative requires substantial departures from traditional planning practice, which is typically imposed from above and which projected itself as scientifically objective, apolitical, efficient and centralised'. Observing from another ethnic conflict environment (Belfast) Brendan Murtagh (Chapter 18) advocates an approach that requires the development of a different range of skills than those normally associated with planning and mainstream housing management. In particular he stresses the centrality of territoriality in land use planning conflicts and notes that 'the range of skills or specific techniques that students are taught at accredited planning and housing courses' does not involve consideration of how land use planners and housing professionals should respond to the exigencies of such territorial sensitivities.

This debate finds resonances in the categorisation of planners first introduced by Meron Benvenisti in 1983, and subsequently elaborated by Scott Bollens (1999). The first category in their scheme is the *professional/neutral planners* who employ functional-technical criteria in allocating resources and services, and who distance themselves from issues of ethnic identity, power inequalities and political exclusion. With this approach planning acts as an ethnically neutral, colour-blind mode of state intervention which is basically responsive to individual-level needs and differences.

The second type is the *equity planner,* who gives primacy to certain ethnic groups defined on the basis of their relative disadvantage. In this case the planner uses equity-based criteria in allocating urban services and spending. According to Bollens, 'an equity planner will be much more aware than a professional-technical planner of group-based inequalities and political imbalances ... and will recognise the need for remediation and affirmative action policies based on group identity' (Bollens, 1999, p. 25). The equity planner will seek the inclusion of the disempowered at the decision-making table.

The third planner model, the *resolver,* represents someone who seeks to transcend symptoms by emphasising solutions to the root causes of ethnic or ethnonational division. The resolver is the only one to attempt to deploy policies aimed at resolving conflict, rather than merely managing it. Empowerment for all ethnic groups involved is pursued.

Fourth and finally there is the *partisan planner,* who operates in the interests of particular ethnic groups' values and authority. Domination and control strategies are applied to land use planning and regulation in order to expand and entrench territorial claims or to enforce exclusionary control of access to resources and opportunities.

For the contributors to *Ethnicity and Housing* it seems evident that *partisan* planning would be quite unacceptable, that *neutral/professional* planning is inadequate and that a judicious mix of *equity* and *resolver* planning is the most effective strategy to adopt where ethnic differences have to be 'accommodated.

The call for ethnic sensitivity in planning and in housing management can be expanded to embrace a need for monitoring, policy evaluation and ethnic impact assessment. Directly addressing this issue, Richard Tomlins (Chapter 15) suggests that all government measures which are aimed at moderating structural inequality should be assessed for their impact upon minority ethnic communities. Brendan Murtagh (Chapter 18) reinforces this by underlining the desirability of ethnic audits and ethnic impact assessments to ensure that new developments are sensitive to ethnic spatial considerations and that they do not have wider negative effects on the stability of ethnically mixed communities and areas.

The end of the beginning?

Many lessons can be drawn from the preceding 26 chapters in *Ethnicity and Housing.* They should be read with this in mind. However I would still like to conclude by briefly stressing a number of points:

- Segregation is a subtle phenomenon. Our approach must be guided by our understanding of the extent to which the segregation is the result of 'negative' or 'positive' factors.

- Housing must be seen as one element of a multi-dimensional ethno-social fabric.

- Thought must be given as to the overall weight to be attributed to specific 'ethnic' factors or to more general 'economic' factors in the processes of societal inclusion and exclusion — and, indeed, to the interplay of the 'ethnic' with the 'economic'.

- Ethnically mixed neighbourhoods are, in many circumstances, considered desirable entities. Their maintenance and encouragement require a broadly based, sensitive approach.

- 'Bottom-up', grassroots initiatives are seen as having great significance.

- National level policies and societal attitudes with respect to ethnic difference need to be carefully thought out, need to be made explicit and need to be placed at the centre of the social and political policy agendas.

- Research, both to increase understanding of the processes of 'accommodating' ethnic differences and to provide well-founded policy guidelines, needs to become much more ethnographic and locality based as a complement to broad brush quantitative work.

- Housing and planning professionals need to openly take on board the ethnic dimensions of the societies within which they ply their trades.

- 'Choice' and 'empowerment' must lie at the heart of policy and action.

Much has been achieved in various parts of the world in terms of accommodating ethnic differences. However, as the daily news diet of ethnic and ethno-national conflict makes only too evident, much remains to be done.

Consolidated bibliography

Abelson, R. (1992), 'Advanced Building Sites', in Golani, Y., Eldor, S. and Garon, M. (eds.), *Planning and Housing in Israel in the Wake of Rapid Changes*, R and L Creative Communications: Tel Aviv, pp. 155-60.

Affandi-Joseph, E. et Gallibour, E. (1992), 'Pour une contribution des Sciences Sociales à la recherche sur le développement en Guyane', Communication à la Conférence Universitaire sur le développement des trois Guyane, 12-16 Octobre.

African National Congress (1994), *The Reconstruction and Development Programme*, Jumanyano Publications: Johannesburg.

Agyeman, J. (1988), 'Ethnic Minorities — an Environmental Issue?', *Ecos*, 9, (3), pp. 2-5.

Aitchison, J. and Carter, H. (1987), 'The Welsh Language in Cardiff: A Quiet Revolution', *Transactions of the Institute of British Geographers*, 12, pp. 482-92.

Aitchison, J. and Carter, H. (1988), *Yr Iaith Gymraeg yn Ardal Caerdydd: Arolwg o Blant Ysgol a'u Rhieni*, Uned Ymchwil Arolygon Gwledig, Coleg Prifysgol Cymru, Aberystwyth: Aberystwyth.

Aitchison, J. and Carter, H. (1994), *A Geography of the Welsh Language 1961-1991*, University of Wales Press: Cardiff.

Allison, M. (1988), 'Breaking Boundaries and Barriers', *Leisure Sciences*, 10, pp. 227-59.

Allison, M. and Geiger, C. (1993), 'Nature of Leisure Activities Among the Chinese-American Elderly', *Leisure Sciences*, 15, pp. 309-19.

Anderson, B. (1991) *Imagined Communities: Reflections on the Origins and Spread of Nationalism*, (2nd ed.), Verso: London.

Anderson, E. (1990), *Streetwise: Race, Class and Change in an Urban Community*, University of Chicago Press: Chicago.

Anthias, F. and Yuval-Davis, N. (1992), *Racialized Boundaries*, Routledge: London.

Antunes, G and Gaitz, C. (1975), 'Ethnicity and Participation', *Journal of Sociology*, 80, pp. 1192-211.

Arin, C. (1991), 'The Housing Market and Housing Polices for the Migrant Labour Population in West Berlin', in Huttman, E.D., Blauw, W. and Saltman, J. (eds.), *Urban Housing Segregation of Minorities in Western Europe and the United States*, Duke University Press: Durham, North Carolina, pp. 199-214.

Assocation of Metropolitan Authorities (1988), *A Strategy for Racial Equality in Housing: 3: Allocations*, A.M.A.: London.

Babbie, E. (1992), *The Practice of Social Research*, Wadsworth Publishing Company: Belmont.

Baker, J. (1990), *Arguing for Equality*, Verso: London.

Ballain, R. et Benguigui, F. (1995), *Loger de personnes défavorisées*, Ministère du Logement, Plan Construction et Architecture, La Documentation française: Paris.

Ballard, R. (1992), 'New Clothes for the Emperor?: the Conceptual Nakedness of the Race Relations Industry in Britain', *New Community*, 18, (3), pp. 481-92.

Bardon, J. (1982), *Belfast: an Illustrated History*, Blackstaff Press: Belfast.

Barrett, F. (1976), 'The Search Process in Residential Location', *Environment and Behaviour*, 8, (2), pp. 169-98.

Barth, F. (1969b), 'Introduction', in Barth, F. (ed.), *Ethnic Groups and Boundaries: The Social Organisation of Culture Difference*, Universitetsforlaget, Scandinavian University Press: Oslo, pp. 9-38.

Barth, F. (ed.) (1969a), *Ethnic Groups and Boundaries: The Social Organisation of Culture Difference*, Universitetsforlaget, Scandinavian University Press: Oslo.

Bassadien, S. 6/9/1995: Group workshop.

Bauman, J. (1987), *Public Housing, Race and Renewal: Urban Planning in Philadelphia, 1920–1974.*, Temple University Press: Philadelphia.

BEAG (1994), *Black Environmental Action Group: First Annual Report 1993/4:* London.

Beatty, S.E. and Smith, S.M. (1987), 'External Search Effort: an Investigation Across Several Product Categories', *Journal of Consumer Research*, 14, (June), pp. 83-95.

Behar, D. (1991) *Les territoires de l'exclusion: Synthèse des monographies produites par les agences d'urbanisme*, Fédération Nationale des Agents d'Urbanisme, Octobre.

Belfast Agreement (1998), *The Agreement: Agreement Reached in the Multiparty Negotiations*, Northern Ireland Office: Belfast.

Belfrage, S. (1988), *The Crack: A Belfast Year*, Grafton Books: London.

Bell, D. (1992), *Faces at the Bottom of the Well: The Permanence of Racism*, Basic Books: New York.

Benvenisti, M. (1983), *Jerusalem: Study of a Polarized Community*, West Bank Data Project: Jerusalem.

Berry, B. and Tischler, H.L. (1978), *Race and Ethnic Relations*, (Fourth Edition), Houghton Mifflin Company: Boston.

Best, A.C.G. (1970), 'Gaborone: Problems and Prospects of a New Capital', *The Geographical Review*, 60, pp. 1-14.

Beteille, A. (1993), *Development and Democracy*, Urban Foundation: Johannesburg.

Bhamjee, F. 21/9/95: Structured interview.

Bickford, A. and Massey, D. (1991), 'Segregation in the Second Ghetto: Racial and Ethnic Segregation in American Public Housing, 1977', *Social Forces*, 69, pp. 1011–36.

Bird, F. (1989), 'Conservation in Vrededorp', memorandum to the Transvaal Regional Committee of the National Monuments Council.

Birmingham City Council (1993), *The Birmingham National Parks Awareness Project 1987-1991*, Project Report, Birmingham City Council: Birmingham.

Blakemore, K. and Boneham, M. (1994), *Age, Race and Ethnicity: A Comparative Study*, Open University Press: Philadelphia.

Blanc, M. (1991), 'Urban Housing Segregation of North African "Immigrants" in France', in Huttman, E.D., Blauw, W. and Saltman, J. (eds.), *Urban Housing Segregation of Minorities in Western Europe and the United States*, Duke University Press: Durham, North Carolina, pp. 145-54.

Blaut, J.M. (1992), 'The Theory of Cultural Racism', *Antipode*, 24, (4), pp. 289-99.

Blauw, W. (1991), 'Housing Segregation for Different Population Groups in the Netherlands', in Huttman, E.D., Blauw, W. and Saltman, J. (eds.), *Urban Housing Segregation of Minorities in Western Europe and the United States*, Duke University Press: Durham, North Carolina, pp. 43-62.

Boal, F W (1969), 'Territoriality on the Shankill-Falls Divide, Belfast', *Irish Geography*, 6, pp. 30-50.

Boal, F W (1970) 'Social Space in The Belfast Urban Area', in Stephens, N. and Glasscock, R. (eds.), *Irish Geographical Studies*, Department of Geography, The Queen's University of Belfast: Belfast.

Boal, F. (1976), 'Ethnic Residential Segregation', in Herbert, D.T. and Johnston, R.J. (eds.), *Social Areas in Cities Vol 1*, John Wiley: Chichester, pp. 41-79.

Boal, F. (1981), 'Ethnic Residential Segregation, Ethnic Mixing and Resource Conflict: A study in Belfast, Northern Ireland', in Peach, C., Robinson, V. and Smith, S.J. (eds.) *Ethnic Segregation in Cities*, Croom Helm: London, pp. 235-51.

Boal, F.W. (1982), 'Segregating and Mixing: Space and Residence in Belfast', in Boal, F.W. and Douglas, J.N.H. (eds.), *Integration and Division: Geographical Perspectives on the Northern Ireland Problem*, Academic Press: London, pp. 249-80.

Boal, F.W. (1994), *Belfast: A City on Edge*, in Clout, H. (ed.), *Europe's Cities in the Late Twentieth Century*, Royal Dutch Geographical Society/Department of Human Geography, University of Amsterdam: Utrecht/Amsterdam, pp. 141-55.

Boal, F.W., Murray, R.C. and Poole, M.A. (1976), 'Belfast: The Urban Encapsulation of a National Conflict.', in Clark, S.E. and Obler, J.L. (eds.), *Urban Ethnic Conflict: A Comparative Perspective*, Institute for Research in Social Science, University of North Carolina at Chapel Hill: Chapel Hill, pp. 77-131.

Boddy, M. (1980), *The Building Societies*, Macmillan: London.

Body-Gendrot, S. (1993), 'Migration and the Racialization of the Postmodern City in France', in Cross, M. and Keith, M. (eds.), *Racism, the City and the State*, Routledge: London, pp. 77-92.

Bollens, S.A. (1999), *Urban Peace-building in Divided Societies: Belfast and Johannesburg*, Westview Press: Boulder.

Bossard, J.S.H. (1932), 'Residential Propinquity as an Element in Marriage Selection', *American Journal of Sociology*, 38, pp. 219-24.

Bowes, A., McCluskey, J., and Sim, D. (1989), *Ethnic Minority Housing Problems in Glasgow*, Glasgow City Council: Glasgow.

Boyle, K. and Hadden, T. (1994), *Northern Ireland: The Choice*, Penguin: London.

Bratt, R. (1994), 'The Role of HUD in Housing and Community Development Systems', Working Paper, National Academy of Public Administration: Washington, DC.

Breitman, G. (ed.) (1966), *Malcolm X Speaks*, Grove Press, Inc: Glencoe.

Bretherton, I. (1985), 'Attachment Theory: Retrospect and Prospect', in Bretherton, I. and Waters, E. (eds.), *Growing Points in Attachment Theory and Research*, Monographs of the Society for Research in Child Development 50 (1-2, Serial No. 209), p. 335.

Brett, C. (1986), *Housing a Divided Community*, Dublin: Gill and Macmillan.

Brimelow, P. (1995), *Alien Nation: Common Sense About America's Immigration Disaster*, Random House: New York.

Bristow, B. (1994), 'Sandton's First Twenty Five Years', *Proceedings: Symposium of the Planning History Study Group*.

Brown, C. (1984), *Black and White Britain: The Third PSI Survey*, Heinemann: London.

Brown, D. (1970) *Bury My Heart at Wounded Knee*, Henry Holt and Company: New York.

Buchanan, C. (1978), *Priorities in Conservation*, National Building Research Institute of the CSIR: Pretoria.

Carmon, N. and Czamanski, D. (1990), 'Israel', in van Vliet, W. (ed.), *International Handbook of Housing Policies and Practices*, Greenwood: New York, pp. 517-36.

Carr, D. and Williams, D. (1993), 'Understanding the Role of Ethnicity in Outdoor Recreation Experience', *Journal of Leisure Research*, 25, (1), pp. 22-38.

Carrim, N. (1990), *Fietas: A Social History of Pageview 1948-1988*. Save Pageview Association: Johannesburg.

Carruthers, J. (1994) *Sandton. The Making of a Town*, Celt Books: Rivonia.

Cashmore, E.E. (1984), *Dictionary of Race and Ethnic Relations*, Routledge and Kegan Paul: London.

Castles, S. (1995), 'How Nation-States Respond to Immigration and Ethnic Diversity', *New Community*, 21, (3), pp. 293-308.

Castles, S. and Miller, M.J. (1993), *The Age of Migration: International Population Movements in the Modern World*, Macmillan: Basingstoke.

Catton, W.R. and Smircich, R.J. (1964), 'A Comparison of Mathematical Models for the Effect of Residential Propinquity on Mate Selection', *American Sociological Review*, 29, pp. 522-9.

Chérubini, B. (1988), *Cayenne: Ville Créole et Polyethnique*, Karthala-Cenaddom: Paris.

Chism, N. van N. and Pruitt, A.S. (1995), 'Promoting Inclusiveness in College Teaching', in Wright, W.A. and Associates (eds.), *Teaching Improvement Practices: Successful Strategies For Higher Education*, Anker: Boston.

Churchman, A. and Mitrani, M. (1994), 'The Role of the Physical Environment in Culture Shock', Paper presented at IAPS 13: Manchester, England.

Churchman, A. (1991), *Housing for the Elderly and Meanings of Home*, Technion, Center for Urban and Regional Studies: Haifa.

Churchman, A. and Frenkel, A. (1992), *Guidelines for Residential Buildings for the Ultra-Orthodox Population*, Technion, Faculty of Architecture & Town Planning: Haifa.

Churchman, A. and Ginsberg, Y. (1991), 'Dimensions of Social Housing Policy: An Introduction', *Journal of Architectural and Planning Research*, 8, (4), pp. 271-5.

Clapham, D., Kintrea, K., and Munro, M. (1987), 'Tenure Choice: an Empirical Investigation', *Area*, 19, (1), pp. 11-18.

Clark, W.A.V. (1987), 'Theory and Practice in Housing Market Research' in Kemeny, J., Lundqvist, J.J. and Turner, B. (eds.), *Between State and Market*, Almquist and Wiksell: Stockholm, pp. 11-25.

Clark, W.A.V. and Morrison, P. (1995), 'Demographic Foundations of Political Empowerment in Multiminority Cities', *Demography*, 32, pp. 183-201.

Clark, W.A.V. and Smith, T.R. (1982), 'Housing Market Search Behaviour and Expected Utility Theory: 2. The Process of Search', *Environment and Planning A*, 14, pp. 717-37.

Comisiwn y Cymunedau Ewropeaidd (1995), *Ieithoedd Llai eu Defnydd yn yr Undeb Ewropeaidd: Addroddiad o'r Gweithgareddau 1989-1993*, Commission of the European Communities: Brussels.

Commission for Racial Equality (1988), *Homelessness and Discrimination: A Report of a Formal Investigation into the Borough of Tower Hamlets, London*, Commission for Racial Equality: London.

Commission for Racial Equality (1993), *Housing Associations and Racial Equality*, Commission for Racial Equality: London.

Commission for Racial Equality, (1988), *Homelessness and Discrimination*, Commission for Racial Equality: London.

Commission for Racial Equality, (1989), *Racial Discrimination in Liverpool City Council*, Commission for Racial Equality: London.

Community Relations Council (CRC) (1996) Belfast Interface Project, Internal Paper, Unpublished.

Compton, P.A. (1985), 'An Evaluation of the Changing Religious Composition of the Population of Northern Ireland', *The Economic and Social Review*, 16, (3), pp. 201-24.

Compton, P.A. (1990), 'Demographic Trends in the Belfast Region with Particular Reference to the Changing Distribution of Population', in Doherty, P. (ed.), *Geographical Perspectives on the Belfast Region*, The Geographical Society of Ireland: Newtownabbey, pp. 15-27.

Compton, P.A. (1993), 'Population Censuses in Northern Ireland: 1926-1991', in Dale, A. and Marsh, C. (eds.), *The 1991 Census Users' Guide*, HMSO: London, pp. 330-51.

Connor, W. (1993), 'Beyond Reason: The Nature of the Ethnonational Bond', *Ethnic and Racial Studies*, 16, (3), pp. 373-89.

Cooper, A.J. 1988 (original 1892), *A Voice From the South*, Oxford University Press: New York.

Coppock, J.T. (1977), 'Social Implications of Second Homes in Mid and North Wales', in Coppock J.T. (ed.), *Second Homes: Curse or Blessing?*, Pergamon: Oxford.

Cornell, S. and Hartmann, D. (1998), *Ethnicity and Race: Making Identities in a Changing World*, Pine Forge Press: Thousand Oaks, CA.

Cose, E. (1995), 'The Myth of Meritocracy', *Newsweek*, 3 April.

Costa, F.J. and Noble, A.G. (1986), 'Planning Arab Towns', *Geographical Review*, 76, pp. 160-72.

Costa-Lascoux, J. (1994), 'French Legislation Against Racism and Discrimination', *New Community*, 20, (3), pp. 371-9.

Countryside Commission (1986), *A Countryside for Everyone: CCP 265:* Cheltenham.

Countryside Commission (1991), *Visitors to the Countryside: CCP 341:* Cheltenham.

Countryside Commission (1992), *Enjoying the Countryside: CCP 371:* Cheltenham.

CPRE (Council for the Protection of Rural England) (1994), *Leisure Landscapes*, CPRE: London.

Crawley, R. and Lemos, G. (1993), *Training Needs Analysis of Existing and Emerging Black and Minority Ethnic Housing Associations in the Midlands*, BASE Trust/WMHTS: Leicester.

Cressey, P.F. (1938), 'Population Succession in Chicago', *American Journal of Sociology*, 44, pp. 56-9.

Cronin, F.J. (1982), 'Racial Differences in the Search for Housing', in Clark, W.A.V. (ed.), *Modelling Housing Market Search*, Croom Helm: London, pp. 81-105.

Crook, A.D.H. (1992), 'Private Rented Housing and the Impact of Deregulation', in Birchall, J. (ed.), *Housing Policy in the 1990s*, Routledge: London, pp. 91-112.

Cross, M. and Entzinger, H. (eds.), (1988), *Lost Illusions: Caribbean Minorities in Britain and the Netherlands*, Routledge: London.

Crouch, D. (1990), 'Culture in the Experience of Landscape', *Landscape Research*, 15, (1), pp. 11-19.

Csikszentmihalyi, M. and Rochberg-Halton, E. (1981), *The Meaning of Things: Domestic Symbols and the Self*, Cambridge University Press: Cambridge.

Cymdeithas Tai Cantref (1994), *Annual Report 93/94*, Cymdeithas Tai Cantref: Newcastle Emlyn.

Cyngor Dosbarth Ceredigion (1994), *Housing Strategy and Operational Plan 1994-97*, Cyngor Dosbarth Ceredigion: Aberystwyth.

Cyngor Dosbarth Ceredigion (1998), *Ceredigion Local Plan: Deposit Version*, Cyngor Dosbarth Ceredigion, Aberaeron.

Cyngor Dosbarth Ceredigion / Ceredigion District Council (1995), 'Cynllun Lleol Ceredigion / Ceredigion Local Plan, Drafft Ymgynghori / Consultation Draft', Cyngor Dosbarth Ceredigion: Aberaeron.

D.D.E.-Guyane (1990), *Les logements insalubres en Guyane*, Étude A.R.U.A.G., Septembre.

D.S.U. (1994), *Ville de Cayenne: Contrat de Ville*, Projet 1 Document interne.

Dahya, B. (1974), 'The Nature of Pakistani Ethnicity in Industrial Cities in Britain', in Cohen, A. (ed.), *Urban Ethnicity*, Tavistock: London, pp. 77-118.

Dalton, M. and Daghlian, S. (1989), *Race and Housing in Glasgow: The Role of Housing Associations*, CRE: London.

Darby, J. and Morris, G. (1974), *Intimidation in Housing*, Northern Ireland Community Relations Commission: Belfast.

Davies, J. (1993), *The Welsh Language*, University of Wales Press: Cardiff.

Davies, W.J. (1971), *Patterns of Non-White Population Distribution in Port Elizabeth with Special Reference to the Application of the Group Areas Act*, Series B, Special Publication 1, Institute for Planning Research, University of Port Elizabeth: Port Elizabeth.

de Beauvoir, S. (1989) (original 1953), *The Second Sex*, Vintage Books: New York.

De Ruddler, V. (1990), 'La cohabitation pluriethnique et ses enjeux', *Migrants-Formation*, 80, Mars.

De Ruddler, V. (1991), 'Integration et assimilation: des concepts aux conflits', *Les Cahiers de l'Habitat*, 15, Octobre.

Denton, N. (1994) 'Are African Americans Still Hypersegregated?' in Bullard, R., Grigsby, J.E. and Lee, C, (eds.), *Residential Apartheid: The American Legacy*, CAAS: University of California, Los Angeles.

Denton, N. and Massey, D. (1991), 'Patterns of Neighborhood Transition in a Multiethnic World: US Metropolitan Areas, 1970-1980', *Demography*. 28, (1), pp. 41-63.

DeSena, J. (1994), 'Women: The Gatekeepers of Urban Neighborhoods', *Journal of Urban Affairs*, 16, (3), pp. 271-84.

Despres, C. (1989), 'The Meaning of Home: Literature Review and Directions for Future Research and Theoretical Development', Paper presented at The International Housing Symposium: Gavle, Sweden.

Development Bank of Southern Africa (1994), *South Africa's Nine Provinces: A Human Development Profile*, Development Bank of Southern Africa: South Africa.

Dex, S., (ed.) (1991), *Life and Work History Analyses: Qualitative and Quantitative Developments*, (Sociological Review Monograph 37), Routledge: London.

DHSS (1992), *The Northern Ireland Census of Population 1991: Belfast Urban Area Report*, DHSS, Registrar General of Northern Ireland: Belfast.

Dix, G.B. (1965), 'Gaborone'. *Journal of the Town Planning Institute*, 51, pp. 290-5.

DOENI (1998), *Shaping Our Future: Towards a Strategy for the Development of the Region*, Department of the Environment for Northern Ireland: Belfast.

Doherty, P. (1989), 'Ethnic Segregation Levels in the Belfast Urban Area', *Area*, 21, (2), pp. 151-9.

Doherty, P. and Poole, M.A. (1995), *Ethnic Residential Segregation in Belfast.*, Centre for the Study of Conflict, The University of Ulster: Coleraine.

Domenach, H. et Picouet, M. (1988), *Dynamique de la population et migration en Guyane*, Collection, La Nature et l'Homme, O.R.S.T.R.O.M.: Cayenne.

Drier, P. and Atlas, J. (1995), 'US Housing Problems, Politics and Policies in the 1990s', *Housing Studies*, 10, pp. 245-69.

Drinberg, C. (1992), 'Central Problems Encountered In Neighborhood and Housing Planning', in Golani, Y., Eldor, S. and Garon, M. (eds.), *Planning and Housing in Israel in the Wake of Rapid Changes*, R and L Creative Communications: Tel Aviv, pp. 179-89.

Du Bois, W.E.B. (1965), *Souls of Black Folk*, in Franklin, J.H., *Three Negro Classics*, Avon Books: New York.

Du Bois, W.E.B. (1992a) (original 1897), 'The Conservation of Races', in Brotz, H. (ed.), *African-American Social and Political Thouqht 1850-1920*, Transaction Publishers: New Brunswick.

Du Bois, W.E.B. (1992b) (original 1909), 'The Evolution of the Race Problem', in Brotz, H. (ed.), *African-American Social and Political Thought 1850-1920*, Transaction Publishers: New Brunswick.

Duncan, O D and Lieberson, S. (1959), 'Ethnic Segregation and Assimilation' *American Journal of Sociology*, 64, pp. 364-74.

Duncan, O.D. and Duncan, B. (1955), 'A Methodological Analysis of Segregation Indices', *American Sociological Review*, 20, pp. 210-17.

Easterlin, R.A., Ward,D., Bernard, W.S. and Ueda, R. (1982), *Immigration*, The Belknap Press of Harvard University Press: Cambridge.

Economie et Humanisme (1993), *La ville test d'humanité, 326.*

Edsall, T. (1995), 'Masculinity on the Run', *The Washington Post* , (April 30), C1.

Efrat, E. (1988), *Geography and Politics in Israel Since 1967*, Frank Cass: London.

Efrat, E. and. Noble, A.G. (1988), 'Problems of Reunited Jerusalem', *Cities: The International Quarterly of Urban Policy*, 5, pp. 326-43.

Eriksen, T.H. (1993), *Ethnicity and Nationalism: Anthropological Perspectives*, Pluto Press: London.

Essien-Udom, E.U. (1962), *Black Nationalism: A Search for an Identity in America*, The University of Chicago Press: Chicago.

Essop, A. (1989), *Noorjehan and Other Stories*, Ravan Press: Johannesburg.

Evans, E.E. (1944), 'Belfast: the Site and the City', *Ulster Journal of Archaeology (3rd Series)*, 7, pp. 5-29.

EXTERN (1987), *Report of the Extern Working Party on Neighbourhood Disputes in Northern Ireland*, EXTERN: Belfast.

Eyles, J. (1988), *Research in Human Geography*, Blackwell: Oxford.

Facio, E. (1993), 'Ethnography as Personal Experience', in Stanfield II, J. and Rutleledge, M. (eds.), *Race and Ethnicity in Research Methods*, Sage Publications: Newbury Park.

Falah, G. (1996), 'Living Together Apart: Residential Segregation in Mixed Arab-Jewish Cities in Israel' *Urban Studies* , 33, (6), pp. 823-57.

Falah, G. (1997), 'Ethnic Perceptual Differences of Housing and Neighbourhood Quality in Mixed Arab-Jewish Cities in Israel', *Environment and Planning A*, 29, pp. 1663-74.

Falah, G. (1999), 'Welfare Geography of a Peripheralized National Minority: The Case of Israel's Arab Population', *Urban Geography* (forthcoming).

Feder, D. (1992), 'Multiculturalism Denigrates West's Great Achievements', *Columbus Dispatch*, 19 April.

Festinger, L., Schachter, S. and Back, K. (1959), *Social Pressure in Informal Groups : A Study of Human Factors in Housing*, Tavistock: London.

Fialkoff, C. (1993), 'Israel's Housing Policy in Flux: Review, Assessment and Prognosis', Paper presented at an International Symposium on Housing for a World in Need: Haifa.

Finkel, M. and Kennedy, S. (1992), 'Racial/Ethnic Differences in Utilization of Section 8 Existing Rental Vouchers and Certificates', *Housing Policy Debate*, 3, pp. 463-508.

Fisk, M.J. (1996), *Home Truths: Issues for Housing in Wales*, Gwasg Gomer: Llandysul.

Flournoy, C. and Rodriguez, G. (1985), 'Housing Divided: Officially Sanctioned Is Rule, Not Exception in East Texas', *Dallas Morning News*, February 12.

Floyd, F., McGuire, F., Shinew, K., and Noe, F. (1994), 'Race, Class and Leisure Activity Preference: Marginality and Ethnicity Revisited', *Journal of Leisure Research*, 26, (2), pp. 158-73.

Forbes, J., Lamont, D. and Robertson, I. (1979), *Intra-urban Migration in Greater Glasgow*, Scottish Development Department: Edinburgh.

Ford, H.L. (1975), 'A New Town in Botswana', *The Planner*, 61, pp. 145-9.

Ford, R.G. (1950), 'Population Succession in Chicago', *American Journal of Sociology*, 56, pp. 151-60.

Ford, R.G. and Smith, G.C. (1981), 'Spatial Aspects of Intraurban Migration Behaviour in a Mixed Housing Market', *Environment and Planning A*, 13, pp. 355-71.

Forrest, R. and Murie, A. (1988), *Selling the Welfare State: the Privatisation of Council Housing*, Routledge: London.

Foster-Carter, O. (1987), 'Ethnicity: The Fourth Burden of Black Women — Political Action', *Critical Social Policy*, 20, pp. 46-56.

Frank, R.H. (1989), 'Frames of Reference and the Quality of Life', *American Journal of Economics and Sociology*, 79, (2), pp. 80-5.

Franklin, J.H. (1965), *Three Negro Classics*, Avon Books: New York.

Frescura, F. and Radford, D. (1982), *The Physical Growth of Johannesburg*, South African Institute of Race Relations: Johannesburg.

Frey, W. (1991), 'Are Two Americas Emerging?', *Population Today*, 9, pp. 6-8.

Frey, W. (1995), 'Immigration and Internal Migration "Flight" from US Metropolitan Areas: Towards Demographic Balkanization', *Urban Studies*, 32, pp. 733-57.

Friedman, W. (1994), Personal conversation with Warren Friedman, Executive Director of the Chicago Alliance for Neighborhood Safety, November.

Friedmann, J. (1992), *Empowerment: the Politics of Alternative Development*, Blackwell; Oxford.

Frieling, D. (1993), 'Sociale Vernieuwing van de Bijlmermeer', Notities voor de bijeenkomst van 28 April.

Fryer, P. (1988), *Black People in the British Empire: An Introduction*, Pluto Press: London.

Gallibour, E. (1995), *L'accès à l'habitat: Le cas des immigrés haïtiens en Guyane française*, Rapport Intermédiare, Programme PIR-Villes/CNRS, Maison des Sciences de l'Homme d'Aquitaune, Laboratoire de Sociologie de la Santé, Université de Bordeaux II, Mars.

Gellner, E. (1983), *Nations and Nationalism*, Blackwell: Oxford.

Gilroy, P. (1987), *There Ain't No Black in the Union Jack*, Hutchinson: London.

Ginsberg, Y. (1993), 'Changes in Absorption and Housing Policies in Israel — Do they Make a Difference?', Paper presented at the International Workshop on Immigrant Absorption — The Interface Between Research and Policy Making: Haifa.

Giuliani, M.V. (1991), 'Towards an Analysis of Mental Representations of Attachment to the Home', *Journal of Architectural and Planning Research*, 8 (2), pp. 133-46.

Glasgow City Council (1994), *Special Needs and Community Care Strategy 1994*, Glasgow City Housing Department: Glasgow.

Glater, J. (1995), 'Racial Gap in Pay Gets a Degree Sharper, A Study Finds', *The Washington Post.*, November 2: D13.

Glazer, N. (1975), *Affirmative Discrimination: Ethnic Inequality and Public Policy*, Basic Books: New York.

GMCRIP (1992), *Greater Manchester Countryside Recreation Information Project: Project Officer's Report:* Manchester.

Goering, J. (1986), *Housing Desegregation and Federal Policy*, University of North Carolina: Chapel Hill.

Goering, J. (1993), 'Towards the Comparative Exploration of Public Housing Segregation in England and the United States', *Housing Studies*, 8, 256-73.

Goering, J. (1994), 'Anti-Discrimination Law on the Grounds of Race in the United States: Enforcement and Research Concerns', *New Community*, 20, pp. 393-414.

Goering, J., Kamely, A. and Richardson, T. (1994), *The Location and Racial Occupancy of Public Housing in the United States*, US Department of Housing and Urban Development: Washington, DC.

Goldberg, D.T. (1993), '"Polluting the Body Politic": Racist Discourse and Urban Location', in M. Cross and M. Keith (eds.), *Racism, the City and the State*, Routledge: London, pp. 45-60.

Goodwin, C. (1979), *The Oak Park Strategy: Community Control of Racial Change*, University of Chicago Press: Chicago.

Gordon, M.M. (1964), *Assimilation and American Life: The Role of Race, Religion and National Origins*, Oxford University Press: New York.

Gorgeon, C. (1985), 'L'immigration en Guyane', *Les Dossiers de L'Outre-Mer*, 81, 4ème trimestre, pp. 68-73.

Grafmeyer, Y. (1994), *Sociologie urbaine*, Nathan Université: Paris.

Grayson, L. and Young, K. (1994), *Quality of Life in Cities*, British Library: London.

Greed, C. (1994), 'The Real Place of Ethnography in Planning or is it Real Research?', *Planning Practice and Research*, 9, pp.19-26.

Greenhouse, C.J. (1992), 'Racial and Ethnic Conflict: a Commentary', *Studies in Law, Politics and Society*, 12, pp. 199-205.

Guinier, L. (1994), *The Tyranny of the Majority: Fundamental Fairness in Representative Democracy*, The Free Press: New York.

Hacker, A. (1992), *Two Nations: Black and White, Separate, Hostile, Unequal*, Ballantine Books: New York.

Hamilton, A., McCartney, C., Anderson, T. and Finn, A. (1990), *Violence and Communities*, Centre for the Study of Conflict, University of Ulster: Coleraine.

Harrison, C., Limb, M, and Burgess, J. (1986), 'Recreation 2000: Views of the Country from the City', *Landscape Research*, 11, (2), pp. 19-24.

Harrison, M. (1991), *Achievements and Options: Black and Minority Ethnic Housing Organisations in Action*, Armley Publications: Leeds.

Harrison, M. (1992), 'Black-Led Housing Organisations and the Housing Association Movement, *New Community* 18, (3), pp. 427-37.

Hartshorn, T.A. (1992), *Interpreting the City: An Urban Geography* (2nd Edition), John Wiley: New York.

Harvey, O.J. (1966), 'Ends, Means, and Adaptability' in Harvey, O.J. (ed.) *Experience, Structure and Adaptability*, Springer Publishing Company: New York, pp. 3-12.

Hasson, S. (1991), *Housing Preferences and Choice of Place of Residence of Immigrants from the Soviet Union*, Jerusalem Institute for the Study of Israel: Jerusalem.

Healey, P. (1989) *Planning for the 1990s*, Working Paper No.7, Department of Town and Country Planning, University of Newcastle.

Healey, P. (1992), 'Planning through Debate: The Communicative Turn in Planning Theory', *Town Planning Review*, 63, pp. 143-62.

Helson, H. (1964), *Adaptation-Level Theory*, Harper and Row Publishers: New York.

Hemple, D.J. (1970), *A Comparative Study of the House Buying Process in Two Connecticut Housing Markets*, Center for Real Estate and Urban Economic Studies, University of Connecticut, Storrs: Storrs.

Henderson, J. and Karn, V. (1987), *Race, Class and State Housing: Inequality and the Allocation of Public Housing in Britain*, Gower: Aldershot.

Hentoff, N. (1995), 'Segregation Forever?', *The Washington Post*, December 23, A17.

Hepburn, A.C. (1992), 'The Catholic Community of Belfast, 1850-1940', in Engman, M., Carter, F.W., Hepburn, A.C. et al. (eds.), *Ethnic Identity in Urban Europe* , Dartmouth: Aldershot, pp. 39-70.

Hepburn, A.C. (1994), 'Long Division and Ethnic Conflict: the Experience of Belfast', in Dunn, S. (ed.) *Managing Divided Cities*, Ryburn Publishing: Keele, pp. 88-104.

Herbert, G. (1978), 'The Theory of the Dynamic Dwelling', in Oxman, R., Meir-Brodnitz, M. and Amit, Y. (eds.) *Survey of Design and Development of Dynamic Systems*, Faculty of Architecture and Town Planning: Haifa.

Herbert, G., Churchman, A. and Dokow, R. (1984), *Performance Requirements for Spatial Elements within the Dwelling*, Technion, Faculty of Architecture and Town Planning: Haifa.

Herbert, G., Churchman, A. and Poreh, C. (1991), *A Method for Evaluating High Rise Residential Buildings Designed for Expansion*, Technion, Faculty of Architecture and Town Planning: Haifa.

Herbert, G., Keren, A. and Kalay, Y. (1978), *Some Performance Guidelines for the Design and Evaluation of Environmental Spaces in the Dwelling*, Technion, Faculty of Architecture and Town Planning: Haifa.

Herrnstein, R.J. and Murray, C. (1994), *The Bell Curve: Intelligence and Class Structure in American Life*, Free Press: New York.

Higham, J. (1968), *Strangers in the Land: Patterns of American Nativism 1860-1925*, Atheneum: New York.

Hiro, D. (1992), *Black British, White British: A History of Race Relations in Britain*, Paladin: London.

Hirsch, A. (1983), *Making the Second Ghetto: Race and Housing in Chicago, 1940–1960*, Cambridge University Press: New York.

Holscher, M. and Emmett, M. (1990), *Jo'burg City: Whose City?*, IDASA.

Huebner, J. (1994), 'The Panic in Wicker Park: What's Behind the Anti-Gentrification Backlash?', *The Chicago Reader*, 23, (47), August 26.

Hulshof, M., de Ridder, L. and Krooneman, P. (1992), *Asielzoekers in Nederland*, (Asylum Seekers in the Netherlands), University of Amsterdam: Amsterdam.

Hutchison, R. (1987), 'Ethnicity and Urban Recreation: Blacks, Whites and Hispanics in Chicago's Public Parks', *Journal of Leisure Research*, 19, (3), pp. 205-22.

Hutchison, R. (1988), 'A Critique of Race, Ethnicity and Social Class in Recent Leisure-recreation Research', *Journal of Leisure Research*, 20, (1), pp. 10-30.

Huttman, E.D. (1991), 'An Introduction', in Huttman, E.D., Blauw, W. and Saltman, J. (eds.), *Urban Housing Segregation of Minorities in Western Europe and the United States*, Duke University Press: Durham, North Carolina, pp. 21-42.

Huttman, E.D. and Jones, T. (1991), 'American Suburbs: Desegregation and Resegregation', in Huttman, E.D., Blauw, W. and Saltman, J. (eds.), *Urban Housing Segregation of Minorities in Western Europe and the United States*, Duke University Press: Durham, North Carolina, pp. 335-66.

IFHP (1995), *Accommodating Differences: IFHP International Congress Belfast: Registration Brochure and Call for Papers*, International Federation for Housing and Planning: The Hague.

Ignatieff, M. (1993), *Blood and Belonging: Journeys into the New Nationalism*, BBC Books: London.

Israel Central Bureau of Statistics (1991), *List of Localities, Their Population and Codes, 31 XII 1991*, Technical Publication Series No. 59: Jerusalem.

Israel Central Bureau of Statistics (1995), *List of Localities Their Population and Codes 31 XII 1994*, Technical Publications Series No. 67. Central Bureau of Statistics: Jerusalem.

Jackson, G. (1973), 'A Preliminary Bi-cultural Study of Value Orientations and Leisure Attitudes', *Journal of Leisure Research*, 5, pp. 10-24.

Jacobs, J. (1961), *The Death and Life of Great American Cities*, Vintage: New York.

James, W. (1993), 'Migration, Racism and Identity Formation: the Caribbean Experience in Britain' in James, W. and Harris, C. (eds.), *Inside Babylon: The Caribbean Diaspora in Britain*, Verso: London, pp. 231-87.

Jargowsky, P. (1994), 'Ghetto Poverty Among Blacks in the 1980s', *Journal of Policy Analysis and Management*, 13, pp. 288-310.

Johannesburg City Council (1967), *Vrededorp-Pageview: Rehabilitation and Renewal*, City Engineer's Department: Johannesburg.

Johnson, M.R.D. and Ward, R. (1985), *Five Year Review of Birmingham Inner City Partnership*, London/Birmingham: Department of the Environment/ Aston University Management Centre.

Jolivet, M-J., 'Les Créoles de Guyane', *Les Dossiers de l'Outre-Mer*, 85, 4ème trimestre, pp. 15-26.

Jones, E. (1956), 'The Distribution and Segregation of Roman Catholics in Belfast', *Sociological Review*, 4, (2), pp. 167-89.

Kaplan, R and Talbot, J. (1988), 'Ethnicity and Preference for Natural Settings: a Review of Recent Findings', *Landscape and Urban Planning*, 15, pp. 107-17.

Karn, V. (1977), *Retiring to the Seaside*, Routledge and Kegan Paul: London.

Kassyk, A. (1986), 'Leisure in the Countryside', Unpublished PhD thesis, University of Edinburgh.

Kazin, M. (1995), 'The Union in Us: Why Labor's Decline Hastens the Unraveling of America', *The Washington Post.*, September 3, C2.

Keane, M.C. (1990), 'Segregation Processes in Public Sector Housing', in Doherty, P. (ed.), *Geographical Perspectives on the Belfast Region*, The Geographical Society of Ireland: Newtownabbey, pp. 88-108.

Keating, D.W. (1994), *The Suburban Racial Dilemma: Housing and Neighborhoods*, Temple University Press: Philadelphia.

Keith, M. (1993), *Race, Riots and Policing: Lore and Disorder in a Multi-racist Society*, UCL Press: London.

Kennedy, R.J.R. (1943), 'Premarital Residential Propinquity and Ethnic Endogamy', *American Journal of Sociology*, 48, pp. 580-4.

Kennedy, R.J.R. (1944), 'Single or Triple Melting Pot?: Intermarriage Trends in New Haven, 1870-1940', *American Journal of Sociology*, 49, pp. 331-9.

Kennedy, R.J.R. (1952), 'Single or Triple Melting Pot?: Intermarriage in New Haven, 1870-1950' *American Journal of Sociology*, 58, pp. 56-9.

Kennedy, S.D. (1980), The Final Report of the Housing Allowance Demand Experiment, Abt Associates Inc.: Washington, DC.

Kew, S. (1979), *Ethnic Groups and Leisure*, Sports Council and Social Science Research Council: London.

King, Jr, M.L. (1967), *Where Do We Go From Here: Chaos or Community?*, Beacon Press: Boston.

King, R., (ed.) (1993), *Mass Migration in Europe: The Legacy and the Future*, Belhaven: London.

Klein, G. (1991), 'Planning for Transformation', *Town and Regional Planning*, 31.

Kuz, T.J. (1978), 'Quality of Life: an Objective and Subjective Variable Analysis', *Regional Studies*, 12, pp. 409-17.

La Lettre de l'IDEF (1993), *Réalités familiales, sanitaire et sociales dans les Départements d'Outre-mer*, Institut de l'Enfance et de la Famille, 80, Décembre.

Labov, W. (1972), *Language in the Inner City: Studies in Black English Vernacular*, Basil Blackwell: Oxford.

Lake, R.W. (1981), *The New Suburbanite: Race and Housing in the Suburbs*, Rutgers University Press, New Brunswick.

Law, P. (1993), Paper to 'Welsh in Local Government' Conference, Cardiff, 22 July.

Layton-Henry, Z. (1992), *The Politics of Immigration*, Blackwell: Oxford.

Lemann, N. (1991), *The Promised Land: The Great Black Migration and How it Changed America*, Alfred Knopf: New York.

Lemon, A. (ed.) (1991), *Homes Apart: South Africa's Segregated Cities*, David Philip: Cape Town.

Letchimy, S. (1992), *De l'habitat précaire à la ville: l'exemple Martiniquais,* l'Harmattan: Paris.

Letsholo, J.M.O. (1980), 'The New Towns of Botswana', in Botswana Society (eds.), *Symposium on Settlement in Botswana,* H.E.B., pp. 293-302.

Lewis, D.A. and Maxfield, M.G. (1980), 'Fear in the Neighborhoods', *Journal of Research in Crime and Delinquency,* 17, pp. 160-89.

Lewis, D.L. (1995), *W.E.B. Du Bois: A Reader,* Henry Holt and Company: New York.

Ley, D. (1974), *The Black Inner City as Frontier Outpost: Images and Behavior of a Philadelphia Neighborhood,* The Association of American Geographers: Washington DC.

Lieberson, S. (1963), *Ethnic Patterns in American Cities,* The Free Press of Glencoe: New York.

Lieberson, S. (1972), 'Stratification and Ethnic Groups', In Richmond, A.H. (ed.), *Readings in Race and Ethnic Relations,* Pergamon Press: Oxford, pp. 199-209.

Lieberson, S. (1980), *A Piece of the Pie: Blacks and White Immigrants since 1880,* University of California Press: Berkeley.

Liebkind, K. (ed.) (1989), *New Identities in Europe,* Gower: Aldershot.

Lindén, A-L. and Lindberg, G. (1991), 'Immigrant Housing Patterns in Sweden' in Huttman, E.D., Blauw, W. and Saltman, J. (eds.), *Urban Housing Segregation of Minorities in Western Europe and the United States,* Duke University Press: Durham, North Carolina, pp. 92-115.

Littler, S., Tewdwr-Jones M., Fisk, M. and Essex, S. (1994), 'Housing, Planning and the Development Process', Paper to Housing Studies Association Conference, University of Bristol, 8-9 September.

Loury, G.C. (1985), 'Blacks Must Fight the Enemy Within', *The Washinqton Post,* 15 August.

Loury, G.C. (1986), 'Beyond Civil Rights', in *The State of Black America,* National Urban League: Washington, DC.

Lower House of the States General (1994), *Policy on the Integration of Ethnic Minorities,* Ministry of the Interior: The Hague.

Machava, S. 27/9/1995: Structured interview.

Malik, S. (1992), 'Colours of the Countryside — a Whiter Shade of Pale', *Ecos,* 13, (4), pp. 33-40.

Mandela, N. (1994), *Long Walk to Freedom,* McDonald Purnell: Randburg.

Marcuse, P. (1994) 'Walls as Metaphor and Reality', in S. Dunn (ed.) *Managing Divided Cities,* Keele, Ryburn.

Marcuse, P. (1994), 'The Walled and Quartered Cities of the United States: Convergent Trends with European Cities?', Paper for ENHR Workshop, Housing-Social Integration and Exclusion.

Mason, K. (1990), 'Not Waving, But Bidding', in Burgess, R (ed.), *Studies in Qualitative Methodology,* Vol 2, JAI Press Inc: London.

Massad, J. (1996), 'Zionism's Internal Others: Israel and the Oriental Jews' *Journal of Palestine Studies,* 25, (4), pp.53-68.

Massey, D. and Denton, N. (1993), *American Apartheid: Segregation and the Making of the Underclass,* Harvard University Press: Cambridge.

Massey, D.S. and Denton, N.A. (1988), 'The Dimensions of Residential Segregation', *Social Forces,* 67, (2), pp. 281-315.

Massey, D.S. and Kanaiaupuni, S.M. (1993), 'Public Housing and the Concentration of Poverty', *Social Science Quarterly*, 74:1, pp. 109–22.
Matthew, Sir Robert H. (1964), *Belfast Regional Survey and Plan 1962*, HMSO: Belfast.
Mayer, S. and Jencks, C. (1995), 'War on Poverty: No Apologies Please', *The New York Times*, November 9, A19.
McCorry, J. (1991), Woodburn Interface Project, WIP, Belfast.
McGuire, F., O'Leary, J., Alexander, P. and Dottavio, F. (1987), 'A Comparison of Outdoor Recreation Preferences and Constraints of Black and White Elderly', *Activities, Adaptation and Aging*, 9, (4), pp. 95-104.
McLennan, G. (1995), *Pluralism*, Open University Press: Buckingham.
McPeake, J.W.R. (1995), 'Owner Occupier Search Behaviour in the Belfast Urban Area: An Investigation of Residential Search Behaviour in a Segregated Housing Market', Unpublished Ph.D Dissertation, University of Glasgow.
Michelson, W. (1977), *Environmental Choice, Human Behavior and Residential Satisfaction*, Oxford University Press: New York.
Mik, G. (1991), 'Housing Segregation and Policy in the Dutch Metropolitan Environment', in Huttman, E.D., Blauw, W. and Saltman, J. (eds.), *Urban Housing Segregation of Minorities in Western Europe and the United States*, Duke University Press: Durham, North Carolina, pp. 179-98.
Miles, R. and Muirhead, L. (1986), 'Racism in Scotland: a Matter for Further Investigation', in McCrone, D. (ed.), *Scottish Government Yearbook*, Paul Harris Publishing: Edinburgh.
Misra, A. (1995), 'Black and Ethnic Minority Housing Associations Strategy', Paper for the National Federation of Housing Associations Executive Committee.
Modood, T. (1990), 'Catching up with Jesse Jackson: Being Oppressed and Being Somebody', *New Community*, 17, (1), pp. 85-96.
Modood, T. (1992), *Not Easy Being British: Colour, Culture and Citizenship*, Runnymede Trust and Trentham Books: Stoke-on-Trent.
Moerman, M. (1965), 'Who are the Lue: Ethnic Identification in a Complex Civilisation', *American Anthropologist*, 67, pp. 1215-29.
Molefe, M. 6/9/1995: Group workshop.
Molotch, H. (1972), *Managed Integration: The Dilemmas of Doing Good in the City*, University of California Press: Berkeley.
Moore, E.G. (1966), 'Models of Migration and the Intra-urban Case', *Australia and New Zealand Journal of Sociology*, 2, pp. 16-37.
Moors, H. and Beets, G. (1991), 'Opvattingen over Buitenlanders Sterk Bepaald Door Politieke Kleur' (Opinions about foreigners strongly determined by political preference), *Demos*, 7, (7), pp. 55-6.
Morganthau, T. (1995), 'The View From the Far Right', *Newsweek*, 1 May.
Morris, D. (1995), 'Hiliaeth a'r Gymraeg', Barn, Rhif 394, Tachwedd.
Mouren-Lascaux, P. (1990), *La Guyane*, Karthala: Paris.
Mouton, J. (1989), *Introduction to the Philosophy of Social Science*, Human Sciences Research Council: Pretoria.
Moynihan, D.P. (1970), *Maximum Feasible Misunderstanding*, Free Press: New York.

Moynihan, D.P. (1971), 'Toward a National Urban Policy', in Lowenstein, L.K. (ed.), *Urban Studies: An Introductory Reader*, The Free Press, New York, pp. 127-45.

Mullard, Chr., Nimako, K. and Willemsen, G. (1989), *De Plurale Kubus. Een vertoog over emancipatiemodellen en minderhedenbeleid*, Den Haag.

Muller, J. (1992) 'From Survey to Strategy: Twentieth Century Development in Western Planning Methods' *Planning Perspectives*, 7.

Muller, J. (1994), 'Community Development and Decision-Making', *Urban Forum*, 5.

Murray, R. and Boal, F.W. (1979), 'The Social Ecology of Urban Violence' in Herbert, D.T. and Smith, D.M. (eds.), *Social Problems and the City*, Oxford University Press: Oxford, pp. 139-57.

Nakasa, N. (1975), *The World of Nat Nakasa*, Ravan Press: Johannesburg.

Nanton, P. (1989), 'The New Orthodoxy: Racial Categories and Equal Opportunity Policy', *New Community*, 15, (4), pp. 549-64.

Nash, M. (1988), *The Cauldron of Ethnicity in the Modern World*, University of Chicago Press: Chicago.

Necef, M.Ü. (1992), 'Modernitet og etnicitet', *Dansk Sociologi*, 3, (3), pp. 51-71.

Nel, A. (1962), 'Geographical Aspects of Apartheid in South Africa', *Tijdschrift voor Econ. en Soc. Geografie*, 53, pp. 197-209.

Newburger, H. (1995), 'Sources of Difference in Information Used by Black and White Housing Seekers: an Exploratory Analysis', *Urban Studies*, 32, (3), pp. 445-70.

NIHE (1971), *Northern Ireland Housing Executive First Annual Report*, Northern Ireland Housing Executive: Belfast.

NIHE (1987), *Coping with Conflict*, Northern Ireland Housing Executive: Belfast.

NIHE (1991), *Brick by Brick: A Short History of the Northern Ireland Housing Executive*, Northern Ireland Housing Executive: Belfast.

NIHE (1999), *Towards a Community Relations Strategy*, Northern Ireland Housing Executive: Belfast.

Nimako, K. and Willemsen, G. (1993), 'Multiculturalisme, verzuilde samenleving en verzorgingsstaat: naar een pluralistische democratie' in Pas, G. (ed.) *Achter de Coulissen, Gedachten over de Multiculturele Samenleving*, Wetenschappelijk Bureau Groenlinks: Amsterdam.

Nyden, P. (1988), *Perceptions of Neighborhood Change in South Evanston*, A Report to the City of Evanston Human Relations Commission.

Nyden, P. and Adams, J. (1996), *Saving Our Homes: The Lessons of Community Struggles to Preserve Affordable Housing in Chicago's Uptown*, A Report Completed by Researchers at Loyola University, Chicago in Collaboration with Organization of the Northeast.

Nyden, P. and Wiewel, W. (1992), 'Collaborative Research: Harnessing the Tensions Between Researcher and Practitioner', *The American Sociologist*, 23,(4), pp. 43-55.

Nyden, P., Adams, J. and Mason, M.A. (1992), *Our Hope for the Future: Youth, Family, and Diversity in the Edgewater and Uptown Communities*, Loyola University Chicago: Chicago.

O'Donnell, M. (1990), 'Culture and Identity in Multi-Ethnic Britain', *Social Studies Review*, 5, (3), pp. 86-90.

O'Hare, W. (1992), 'America's Minorities — The Demographics of Diversity', *Population Bulletin,* December, 47, (4).

O'Leary, J. and Benjamin, P. (1982), *Ethnic Variation in Leisure Behavior: the Indiana Case,* Indiana Department of Forestry and Natural Resources, Station Bulletin No. 349.

Oelsner, U. (1995), Address at the General Debate of the Preparatory Committee Habitat II: Nairobi, Kenya.

Office of Population Censuses and Surveys (1994), *1991 Census: Welsh Language, Topic Monitor,* Office of Population Censuses and Surveys: London.

Orfield, G., Eaton, S. and the Harvard Project on School Desegregation (1996), *Dismantling Desegregation: The Quiet Reversal of Brown v. Board of Education,* The New Press: New York.

Owen, D. (1993), *Ethnic Minorities in Great Britain: Housing and Family Characteristics 1991,* Census Statistical Paper No. 4, CRER, University Of Warwick: Coventry.

Owen, D. (1994), Spatial Variations in Ethnic Minority Group Populations in Great Britain, *Population Trends,* 78, pp. 23-33.

Pacione, M. (1982), 'The Use of Objective and Subjective Measures of Life Quality in Human Geography', *Progress in Human Geography,* 6, pp. 495-514.

Pacyga, D.A., Heinrich, C. and Smith, M.P. (1991), 'Southwest Catholic Cluster Project: Opportunities for Racial and Ethnic Cooperation', A Report Presented to the Neighborhood Tracking Research Project of the Policy Research Action Group.

Palm, R. (1976), 'The Role of Real Estate Agents as Information Mediators in Two American Cities', *Geografiska Annaler B,* 55, pp. 28-41.

Parmodh, S. (1995), Personal Communication. Chair: Black Environmental Action Group, Birmingham, England.

Pateman, C. (1970), *Participation and Democratic Theory,* Cambridge University Press: Cambridge.

Pather, T. 6/9/1995: Group workshop.

Pawley, M. (1968), 'The Time Machine', *Architectural Design,* July, pp. 399-402.

Peach, C. and Byron, M.(1993), 'Caribbean Tenants in Council Housing: Race, Class and Gender', *New Community,* 19, pp. 407-23.

Peach, C. (1974), 'Homogamy, Propinquity and Segregation: A Re-evaluation', *American Sociological Review,* 39, pp. 636-41.

Peach, C. (1980), 'Ethnic Segregation and Intermarriage', *Annals of the Association of American Geographers,* 70, pp. 371-81.

Peach, C. (1983), 'Ethnicity', in Pacione, M. (ed.), *Progress in Urban Geography,* Croom Helm: London, pp. 103-27.

Peach, C. (1996), 'Does Britain Have Ghettos?', *Transactions of the Institute of British Geographers,* 21, pp. 216-35.

Peach, C., Robinson, V., Maxted, J. and Chance, J. (1988), 'Immigration and Ethnicity', in Halsey, A.H. (ed.), *British Social Trends Since 1900,* Macmillan: London, pp. 561-615.

Pearlstein, S. (1995), 'Reshaped Economy Exacts Tough Toll: Competition, Efficiency Grown — As Does American's Income Disparity', *The Washington Post,* November 12, A1.

Peterson, G. and Williams, K. (1994), *Housing Mobility: What Has It Accomplished and What is its Promise?*, The Urban Institute: Washington, DC.

Petticrew, T.F. (1978), 'Three Issues in Ethncity: Boundaries, Deprivations and Perceptions', in Yinger, J.M. and Cutler, S.J. (eds.), *Major Social Issues*, Free Press; New York, pp. 25-49.

Philipp, S. (1988), 'Race, Institutions and Outdoor Leisure Participation', *Journal of Social and Behavioral Sciences*, 34, pp. 69-80.

Phillips, D. (1986), *What Price Equality?, A Report on the Allocation of GLC Housing in Tower Hamlets*, Greater London Housing and Research Policy Report, No 9.

Philpott, T.L. (1978), *The Slum and the Ghetto: Neighborhood Deterioration and Middle Class Reform, Chicago, 1880-1930*, Oxford University Press: New York.

Piven, F.F. and Cloward, R.A. (1977), *Poor People's Movements: Why They Succeed, How They Fail*, Vintage Books: New York.

Poole, M.A. (1995), 'The Spatial Distribution of Political Violence in Northern Ireland: an Update to 1993', in O'Day, A. (ed.), *Terrorism's Laboratory: the Case of Northern Ireland*, Dartmouth: Aldershot, pp. 27-45.

Poole, M.A. and Boal, F.W. (1973), 'Religious Residential Segregation in Belfast in Mid-1969: a Multi-level Analysis', in Clark, B.D. and Gleave, M.B. (eds.), *Social Patterns in Cities*, Institute of British Geographers: London, pp. 1-40.

Portes, A. and Zhou, M. (1994), 'Should Immigrants Assimilate?' *The Public Interest*, 116, pp. 18-33.

Prentice, R. (1993), *Change and Policy in Wales: Wales in the Era of Privatism*, Gomer Press: Llandysul.

Pressley, S.A. (1995), 'Housing Plans Break Dallas Pattern of Life', *The Washington Post*, December 27, A3.

Priemus, H., Wassenberg. F. and van Rosmalen, B. (1995), *Mozaïek Woningmarkt Stadsregio Rotterdam*, (Mosaic Housing Market Urban Region Rotterdam), deel 1. Hoofdrapport (vol. 1. Main report), Delft University Press: Delft.

Pritchard, R.M. (1976), *Housing and the Spatial Structure of the City*, Cambridge University Press: Cambridge.

Pryce, K. (1979), *Endless Pressure: A Study of West Indian Lifestyles in Bristol*, Bristol Classical Press: Bristol.

Pynoos, J. (1986), *Breaking the Rules: Bureaucracy and Reform in Public Housing*, Plenum Press: New York.

Radebe, P. 23/11/1993: Structured interview.

Ramnarain, B. 4/5/1995: Structured interview.

Ramsøy, N. (1966), 'Assortative Mating and the Structure of Cities'. *American Sociological Review*, 31, pp. 773-86.

Rex J. and Moore, R. (1967), *Race, Community and Conflict: A Study of Sparkbrook*, Oxford University Press: London.

Rex, J. (1981), 'Urban Segregation and Inner City Policy in Great Britain', in Peach, C., Robinson, V. and Smith, S.J. (eds.), *Ethnic Segregation in Cities*, Croom Helm: London, pp. 25-42.

Rex, J. (1986), *Race and Ethnicity*, Open University Press: Milton Keynes.

Rex, J. and Tomlinson, S. (1979), *Colonial Immigrants in a British City: A Class Analysis*, Routledge and Kegan Paul: London.

Rieder, J. (1985), *Canarsie: The Jews and Italians of Brooklyn Against Liberalism*, Harvard University Press: Cambridge.

Ripert, J. (1990), Commission sur l'Égalité Sociale et le Developpement Économique dans les D.O.M., *L'Égalité Sociale et le Developpement Économique dans les D.O.M.*, Rapport au Premier Ministre des D.O.M.-T.O.M., Porte-Parole du Gouvernement, La Documentation Française, Collection, Les Rapports Officiels: Paris.

Robinson, V. (1980), 'Asians and Council Housing', *Urban Studies*, 17, pp. 323-31.

Robinson, V. (1986), *Transients, Settlers and Refugees: Asians in Britain*, Clarendon Press: Oxford.

Rogers, A. (1995), 'Cinco de Mayo and 15 January: Contrasting Situations in a Mixed Ethnic Neighbourhood' in Rogers, A. and Vertovec, S. (eds.), *The Urban Context: Ethnicity, Social Networks and Situational Analysis*, Berg: Oxford, pp. 117-40.

Romann, M. and Weingrod, A. (1992), *Living Together Separately — Arabs and Jews in Contemporary Jerusalem*, Princeton University Press: Princeton.

Roncayolo, M. (1994), 'Préface', in Brun, J. et Rhein, C. (eds.), *La ségrégation dans la ville*, l'Harmattan: Paris.

Roosens, E.E. (1989), *Creating Ethnicity*, Sage: London.

Rosenbaum, J. (1993), 'Closing the Gap: Does Racial Integration Improve the Employment and Education of Low-Income Blacks?' in Joseph, L.B. (ed.), *Affordable Housing and Public Policy*, University of Illinois Press: Chicago.

Rosenbaum, J. (1994), 'Changing the Geography of Opportunity by Expanding Residential Choice: Lessons from the Gautreaux Program', Paper presented to the Fannie Mae Annual Housing Conference (May 4), Washington, DC.

Rosenbaum, J. and Popkin, S. (1990), *Economic and Social Impacts of Housing Integration*, A Report to the Charles Stewart Mott Foundation.

Sachs, B. (1973), *Mist of Memory*, Valentine Mitchell: London.

Saltman, J. (1990), *A Fragile Movement*, Greenwood Press: New York.

Sarre, P., Phillips, D. and Skellington, R. (1989), *Ethnic Minority Housing: Explanations and Policies*, Avebury: Aldershot.

Schermerhorn, R.A. (1978), *Comparative Ethnic Relations: A Framework for Theory and Research*, University of Chicago Press: Chicago.

Schönwälder, K. (1995), 'Research Notes: No Constitutionally Guaranteed Respect for Minorities in Germany', *New Community*, 21, (3), pp. 421-4.

Scott, J. (1984), 'The Public and Private Governance of Race Relations', *Sociological Focus*, 17, pp. 175-87.

Seedat, Y. 9/9/1995: Structured interview

Shamir, M. and Sullivan, J.L. (1985), 'Jews and Arabs in Israel: Everybody Hates Somebody, Sometime' *Journal of Conflict Resolution*, 29, pp. 283-305.

Shaw, A. (1988), *A Pakistani Community in Britain*, Basil Blackwell: Oxford.

Shook, L. (1982), *Cry, Cities*, Gabriel Books: Mankato, Minnesota.

Silk, J. (1971), *Search Behaviour: General Characteristics and Review of the Literature in Behavioural Sciences,* Department of Geography, University of Reading.

Simon, D. (1989), 'Crisis and Change in South Africa', *Transactions, Institute of British Geographers,* 14, pp. 189-205.

Singh, L. (1991), 'Current Issues of Concern for Black HA's', *Black Housing,* 7, (9/10), p. 8.

Singleton, D.A. (1995), Housing in Northern Ireland, *Ulster Architect.*

Sivanandan, A. (1985), 'RAT and the Degradation of Black Struggle', *Race and Class,* 26, (4), pp. 1-33.

Skogan, W. (1990), *Disorder and Decline: Crime and the Spiral of Decay in American Neighborhoods,* Free Press: New York.

Skogan, W. and Maxfield, M.G. (1981), *Coping with Crime: Individual and Neighborhood Reactions,* Sage: Beverly Hills.

Slim, H. and Thompson, P. (1993), *Listening — For a Change,* Panos Publications: London.

Smaje, C. (1995), *Health, Race and Ethnicity: Making Sense of the Evidence,* King's Fund Institute: London.

Smit, D. (1992), 'Slouching Towards Bethlehem to be Born: Reconstructing South Africa's Cities 1976-2000', unpublished paper, Planning History Symposium, University of the Witwatersrand: Johannesburg.

Smith, A.D. (1991), *National Identity,* Penguin Books: Harmondsworth.

Smith, D.J. and Chambers, G. (1991), *Inequality in Northern Ireland,* Clarendon Press: Oxford.

Smith, R. (1993), 'Creating Stable Racially Integrated Communities: A Review', *Journal of Urban Affairs,* 15, (2), pp. 115-40.

Smith, S.J. (1989), *The Politics of 'Race' and Residence: Citizenship, Segregation and White Supremacy in Britain,* Polity Press: Cambridge.

Smith, S.J. (1993), 'Bounding the Borders: Claiming Space and Making Space in Rural Scotland', *Transactions of the Institute of British Geographers,* 18, pp. 291-308.

Smith, S.J. (1993), 'Residential Segregation and the Politics of Racialization', in Cross, M. and Keith, M. (eds.), *Racism, the City and the State,* Routledge: London, pp. 128-43.

Smith, T.R. and Mertz, F. (1980), 'An Analysis of the Effects of Information Revision on the Outcome of Housing-market Search, with Special Reference to the Influence of Realty Agents', *Environment and Planning A,* 12, pp. 155-74.

Soja, E. and Hooper, B. (1993), 'The Spaces That Difference Makes: Some Notes on The Geographical Margins of the New Cultural Politics', in Keith, M. and Pile, S. (eds.), *Place and the Politics of Identity,* Routledge: London, pp. 183-205.

Sollors, W. (ed.) (1989), *The Invention of Ethnicity,* Oxford University Press: Oxford.

Somerville, P. (1997), 'The Social Construction of Home', *Journal of Architectural and Planning Research,* 14, (3), pp. 226-45.

Sommer, R. (1966), 'Man's Proximate Environment', *Journal of Social Issues,* 22, (4), pp. 59-69.

Sonnenfeld, J. (1966), 'Variable Values in Space and Landscape: An Inquiry into the Nature of Environmental Necessity', *Journal of Social Issues*, 22, (4), pp. 71-82.

Sonvadi, 30/11/1993: Structured interview

Sorenson, A., Taeuber, K. and Hollingsworth, L. (1975), 'Indexes of Residential Segregation for 109 Cities in the United States, 1940 to 1970', *Sociological Focus*, 8, pp. 125-42.

South Africa National Civic Organization (1944), *Making People-Driven Development Work,* South Africa National Civic Organization: Johannesburg.

Sowell, T. (1975), *Race and Economics*, David McKay Company: New York.

Speerpunt Vernieuwing Bijlmermeer (1995), *De Vernieuwing van de Bijlmermeer als Uitwerking van het Grote Stedenbeleid,* Amsterdam, October.

Spicer, E.H. (1982), *The American Indians*, The Belknap Press of Harvard University Press: Cambridge.

Stamps, S and Stamps, M. (1985), 'Race, Class and Leisure Activities of Urban Residents', *Journal of Leisure Research*, 17, (1), pp. 40-56.

Stanfield II, J. (1993), 'Methodological considerations', in Stanfield II, J. and Rutleledge, M. (eds.), *Race and Ethnicity in Research Methods*, Sage Publications: Newbury Park.

Steele, S. (1990), *The Content of our Character: A New Vision of Race in America,* St. Martin's Press: New York.

Stephanapoulos, G. and Edley, C. (1995), *Affirmative Action Review: Report to the President* (July), The White House: Washington, DC.

Stumpf, S.E. (1983), *Philosophy: History and Problems,* McGraw-Hill: New York.

Stuurgroep Vernieuwing Bijlmermeer (1992), *Werk Met Werk Maken,* Eindrapportage van de Stuurgroep Vernieuwing Bijlmermeer: Amsterdam.

Swyngedouw, M. (1995), 'The "Threatening Immigrant" in Flanders 1930-1980: Redrawing the Social Space', *New Community*, 21, (3), pp. 325-40.

Taeuber, K.E. and Taeuber, A. (1964), 'The Negro as an Immigrant Group', *American Journal of Sociology*, 69, pp. 374-82.

Taeuber, K.E. and Taeuber, A. (1965), *Negroes in Cities: Residential Segregation and Neighborhood Change,* Aldine: Chicago.

Taeuber, K. (1983), *Racial Residential Segregation, 28 Cities, 1970-1980,* Center for Demography and Ecology Working Paper 83-12. University of Wisconsin, Madison.

Tamarin, G. R. (1980), 'Three Decades of Ethnic Coexistence in Israel', *Plural Societies,* 11, (1), pp. 3-46.

Task Force (1995), *Report of the Task Force on the Travelling Community,* Stationary Office: Dublin.

Tatum, B. (1992), 'Talking about Race, Learning about Racism: The Application of Racial Identity Development Theory in the Classroom', *Harvard Educational Review*, 62, pp.1-24.

Taub, R., Taylor, G. and Dunham, J. (1984), *Paths of Neighborhood Change: Race and Crime in Urban America,* University of Chicago Press: Chicago.

Tewdwr-Jones, M., Gallent, N., Fisk, M., and Essex, S. (1998), 'Developing Corporate Approaches for the Provision of Affordable Housing in Wales', *Regional Studies*, 32, 1, pp. 85-91.

Tomlins, R. (1995) 'Towards a Pluralistic Ethnic Housing Policy', Paper read at the IFHP International Congress 1995, 'Accommodating Differences', Belfast.

Turner, M.A. and Mikelsons, M. (1992), 'Patterns of Racial Steering in Four Metropolitan Areas', *Journal of Housing Research*, 2, pp. 199-234.

Upton, J.N. (1994), 'A Culture of Violence', in Dunn, S. (ed.), *Managing Divided Cities*, Keele University Press: Keele, Staffordshire, pp. 191-213.

US National Advisory Commission on Civil Disorders (1968), *The Kerner Report*, Pantheon Books: New York.

van den Berghe, P.L. (1984), 'Race: Perspective Two', in Cashmore, E.E. (ed.), *Dictionary of Race and Ethnic Relations*, Routledge and Kegan Paul: London, pp. 216-18.

van Rensburg, S. 6/9/1995: Group workshop

Vander Zanden, J.W. (1983), *American Minority Relations*, Alfred A. Knopf: New York.

Various authors (1980), *Jwaneng Structure Plan, Final Report*, Department of Town and Regional Planning: Gabarone.

Vidal, A.C. (1980), *The Search Behaviour of Black Households in Pittsburgh in the Housing Demand Allowance Experiment*, Abt Associates Inc: Washington, DC.

Vidal, A.C. (1982), 'Racial Differences in Search Behaviour in an Urban Housing Market', Unpublished Ph.D Dissertation, Harvard University.

Viellard-Baron, H. (1991), 'Le ghetto, un lieu commun impropre et banal: Approches conceptuelles et représentations', *Les Annales de la Recherche Urbaine*, 49.

Walby, S. (1992), 'Woman and Nation', *International Journal of Comparative Sociology*, 33, pp. 81-100.

Waldorf, B.S. (1990), 'Housing Policy Impacts on Ethnic Segregation Patterns: Evidence from Dusseldorf, West Germany', *Urban Studies*, 27, pp. 637-52.

Washburne, R and Wall, P. (1979), *Black-White Ethnic Differences in Outdoor Recreation*, United States Department of Agriculture, Forest Service Research Paper No 249.

Washburne, R, (1978), 'Black Under Participation in Wildland Recreation', *Leisure Sciences*, 1, (2), pp. 175-89.

Watson, B.C. and Smith, W. (1987), 'Understanding the Current Debate over Public Policy', *Phylon*, 48, pp. 271-6.

Watson, J. (ed.), (1977), *Between Two Cultures: Migrants and Minorities in Britain*, Blackwell: Oxford.

Weber, M. (1971), Economie et société [1922], II, 4 'Les relations communitaires ethniques', Plon: Paris.

Welsh Language Board (1995), *An Outline Strategy for the Welsh Language*, Welsh Language Board: Cardiff.

Welsh Language Board (1996) *Welsh Language Schemes: Their Preparation and Approval in Accordance with the Welsh Language Act 1993*, Welsh Language Board: Cardiff.

Welsh Office (1988), *The Welsh Language — Development Plans and Development Control*, Circular 53/88, Welsh Office: Cardiff.

Welsh Office (1992), *Planning Policy Guidance 12 (Wales): Development Plans and Strategic Planning Guidance in Wales*, Welsh Office: Cardiff.

Welsh Office (1995), *1992 Welsh Social Survey: Report on the Welsh Language*, Welsh Office: Cardiff.

Wendling, R. (1980), *Black-White Differences in Outdoor Recreation Behavior: State of the Art Recommendations for Management and Research*, United States Department of the Interior, National Parks Service, Southeast Region.

West, P. (1993), 'The Tyranny of Metaphor: Interracial Relations, Minority Recreation, and the Wildland-Urban Interface', in Stanfield II, J. and Rutleledge, M. (eds.), *Race and Ethnicity in Research Methods*, Sage Publications: Newbury Park.

Western, J. (1981), *Outcast Cape Town*, George Allen and Unwin: London.

White, M. (1986), 'Segregation and Diversity: Measures in Population Distribution', *Population Index*, 88, pp. 1008-19.

Whiteford, A, Posel, D. and Kelatwang, T. (1995), *A Profile of Poverty, Inequality and Human Development*, Human Sciences Research Council: Pretoria.

Wiese, A. (1995), 'Neighborhood Diversity: Social Change, Ambiguity, and Fair Housing Since 1968', *Journal of Urban Affairs*, 17, (2), pp. 107-30.

Williams, C. (1989), 'New Domains of the Welsh Language: Education, Planning and the Law', in Day G. and Rees G. (eds.) *Contemporary Wales: An Annual Review of Economic and Social Research 3*, University of Wales Press: Cardiff, pp 41-75.

Williams, C. (1992), 'Assimilating Newcomers: An Insidious Threat or a Welcome Development?' in Dafis, L. (ed.), *Lesser Used Languages — Assimilating Newcomers*, Proceedings of the Conference held at Carmarthen, 1991.

Wilson, J.Q. and Kelling, G. (1982), 'Broken Windows', *Atlantic Monthly* (March), pp. 29-38.

Wilson, W.J. (1981), *The Declining Significance of Race*, University of Chicago Press: Chicago.

Wohlwill, J.F. (1974), 'Human Adaptation to Levels of Environmental Stimulation', *Human Ecology*, 2, (2), pp. 127-47.

Wolpert, J. (1966), 'Migration as an Adjustment to Environmental Stress', *Journal of Social Issues*, 22, (4), pp. 92-102.

Wood, E. (1957), *The Small Hard Core: The Housing of Problem Families in New York City, A Study and Recommendations*, Citizens' Housing and Planning Council: New York.

Wood, W. (1992), Conference Speech, *Black Housing*, 8, (9/10), p. 61.

WRR (Wetenschappelijke Raad voor het Regeringsbeleid) (1989), (Scientific Council for Public Policy), *Allochtonenbeleid*, (Immigrant Policy), Sdu: The Hague.

Yelvington, K. (1991), 'Ethnicity as Practice?: A Comment on Bentley', *Comparative Studies in Society and History*, 33, (1), pp. 158-68.

Yuval-Davis, N. (1993), 'Gender and Nation', *Ethnic and Racial Studies*, 16, (4), pp. 621-32.

Zonn, L.E. (1980), 'Information Flows in Black Residential Search Behavior', *The Professional Geographer*, 32, (1), pp. 43-50.

Index

Nationalism 7; ethnic nationalism 7; civic nationalism 7; race as nationality concept 73-82
Native Land Act 45
Native Urban Areas Act 38
Nativist tradition 75
Necef, M.U. 265, 271-2
Negro 80
Neighbourhood 99-100, 106, 226, 278, 268, 279, 280; diversity 108; in Jerusalem 133-5, 138; Catholic and Protestant 191; in Bijlmermeer 218
Neighbourhood Disputes Initiative 195
Neighbourliness 267
Neighbours 176, 193
Nel, A. 34
Netherlands 217; immigrants from Caribbean 218
New Amsterdam Housing Corporation 219-20
New Israeli Schekels (NIS) 127
New Jersey 200
New Lodge 195
Newburger, H. 200
NIBMYism 86
Nieuwenhuis, Wicher 277, 281
No-go areas 18
Non-Catholics 207-11
North Govanhill 175
Northern Ireland 17, 275, 276; ethnic split in 179-80; Troubles 182-3, 185, 198; unemployment in 192
Northern Ireland Housing Executive 202, 204, 276
Notting Hill Carnival 18
Nyden, Philip 278, 282
Oklahoma City 90
Old City, see Jerusalem
Orapa 61, 64
Orthodox groups 135
Owner occupation 170, 172-3, 203, 230, 267; residential search 198-214
Pageview/Vrededorp 35-42, 278; demolition 40-1
Pahl, Walter 234
Pakistanis 170-8; in Glasgow 170-8

Palestinians 117-8
Palm, R. 201
Party affiliation 128; Zionist 128-9; non-Zionist 128-9
Patlelo 68
Peace walls/lines 18, 190-7, 202
Peach Ceri 4, 276, 281
Perceptions 109
Peterson, G. 94
Petticrew, Thomas F. 4
Philadelphia 96
Phillips, Deborah 21-2, 164-5, 170, 172-3
Philpott, T.L. 13,
Planners, categorisation of 282-3
Planners, urban 60
Planning 49-50; capacitating participation 50; integrated 61-70; land for housing 159; practice 282
Planning methodologies 49-50
Plural ethnic spaces 53; pluri-ethnic grouping 60
Pluralism 8; legal 78
Policy co-ordination 226
Policy evaluation 283
Polyethnic spaces 53
Polyethnicity 54
Poole, Michael 279
Port Elizabeth 19
Portes, A 85
Post-Apartheid South Africa 43-50
Postmodernity 163
Poverty 22-3; areas 90
Powys 246
Prentice, R. 242, 246
Pretoria-Witwatersrand region 62
Priemus, Hugo 280
Property magazines 207
Protestants 179-89, 202, 279; demographics in Belfast 192
Public housing 20, 86, 88-9, 174-5; location of 91-2; in Israel 143-51; in Belfast 189, 203
Puerto Ricans 13
Punjabi 175
Quality of Life (QOL) 115
Race 5-6, 73-82
Race and housing 264

Race Relations Act (1965) 20;
(1976) 239
Racial 'other' 164
Racial fatigue 86
Racial harassment 177
Racial isolation 84
Racial transition 99
Racism 74, 264, 267, 269, 271
Racist backlash 169
Radebe, Petrus 38-9
Rainbow Nation 33, 42
Ramallah 138
Ramla 115
Ratchet effect, see segregation
Realtor's Code 20
Reconstruction and Development
Programme 32, 47-8
Regeneration of Unfit Dwellings
56, 59
Regression analysis 207-11
Rehabilitation 234
Religious residential segregation
202-4
Research 36, 96, 109, 118, 149-5,
282; quantitative and qualitative
methododologies 99, 170-1,
282; Dutch 165; semi-structured
schedule 171; life history
interviewing technique 178, 282;
regression methods 200, 205;
Belfast study hypotheses 204-5;
leisure 249-56; American 251-4;
ethnographic approach 253, 282
Residential search 198-214
Return migration 269
Rex, J. 21
Richardson, T. 90
Right to language 245-6
Robinson, V. 170, 174
Rogers Park 102, 105, 107
Roman Catholics 13, 179-89, 199,
202, 207-11, 279
Roosens, E.E. 263, 271
Rotterdam 226
Rural Studies 255
Russia 225
Sachs, Bernard 37
Sachs, Solly 38
San Francisco, marriage distance in
15

Sandton 46
Sarre, P. 22, 164-5, 170, 172-3
Schachter, S. 15
Schermerhorn, Richard A. 5
Schönwälder, K. 167
Schools 107-8, 194
Scotland 170
Scott, Joseph 78
Search and information 199, 201,
206-7; and racial differences
199-201; and effort 206; and
outcome 207; differences in
search behaviour 211; and
patterns 279
Seattle 90
Section 106 obligations 244
Section 8 Rental Assistance 87, 90,
93-4, 278; location of 91-2;
vouchers/certificates 93, 96
Segregation 8-9, 10-23, 34-42, 54,
55, 75, 86-93, 98-109, 137,
141-2, 164, 179-89, 190, 202-4,
217, 222, 227, 233, 276-7;
positive 14, 18, 227-8, 276-7;
negative 14, 18, 276-7; models
14; behavioural effects 14-18;
and language 14-15; and
friendship 15; and marriage 15-
16; and violence 16-17; and
hypersegregation 98-9; and
residence 164, 276; and ratchet
effect 183, 189; ethno-religious
191
Segregative tendencies 95
Selebe-Pikwe 61, 63
Separate cities, see Jerusalem
Separation 76
Sephardis 126-7
Services to travellers 260
Shankill (Road) 16-17
Shaping Our Future 275
Shaw, A. 17
Short Strand 191
Sim, D. 174-5, 282
Sivanandan, A.
Six Day War 138
Skellington, R. 22, 164-5, 170,
172-3
Slavery 75
Slovo, Joe 31

For Product Safety Concerns and Information please contact our EU
representative GPSR@taylorandfrancis.com Taylor & Francis Verlag GmbH,
Kaufingerstraße 24, 80331 München, Germany

Printed and bound by CPI Group (UK) Ltd, Croydon, CR0 4YY
08/06/2025
01897001-0002